English-Spanish
Spanish-English

Word to Word®
Bilingual Dictionary

with

Math, Science & Social Studies
Subject Vocabulary

Compiled and Translated by:
C. Sesma, M.A.

Bilingual Dictionaries, Inc.

Spanish Word to Word® with Subject Vocabulary
1st Edition © Copyright 2011

Published in the United States by:

Bilingual Dictionaries, Inc.
PO Box 1154
Murrieta, CA 92564
T: (951) 461-6893 • F: (951) 461-3092
www.BilingualDictionaries.com

ISBN13: 978-0-933146-72-3
ISBN: 0-933146-72-8
Printed in India

Table of Contents

Bilingual Dictionaries, Inc.

Bilingual Dictionaries, Inc. is committed to providing schools, libraries and educators with a great selection of bilingual materials for students. Along with bilingual dictionaries we also provide ESL materials, children's bilingual stories and children's bilingual picture dictionaries.

Sesma's Spanish Word to Word® with Subject Vocabulary Bilingual Dictionary was created specifically with students in mind to be used for reference and testing. This dictionary contains approximately 33,000 entries targeting common words used in the English language as well as subject specific vocabulary.

Subject Vocabulary

Bilingual Dictionaries, Inc. has compiled a list of approximately 11,000 math, science and social studies terms to accomodate student testing at the high school level. The terms are divided into sections according to subject: math, science or social studies.

In order to always deliver the best product possible for our students and teachers we would like to accept any feedback regarding improving our publications. Along with feedback we encourage teachers and students to submit any new words or lists of vocabulary that would further align our publications with student needs. We will do our best to include any new vocabulary or suggestions in the future editions of our Word to Word® with Subject Vocabulary series. Please submit all feedback or new vocabulary via email or visit us online for more information.

Email: support@bilingualdictionaries.com
Website: www.bilingualdictionaries.com

Word to Word®

Bilingual Dictionaries, Inc. has created a new series of over 30 languages, 100% Word to Word®, to provide ELL students with standardized bilingual dictionaries approved for state testing. Students with different language backgrounds can now use dictionaries from the same series, specifically designed to create an equal resource that strictly adheres to the guidelines set by districts and states.

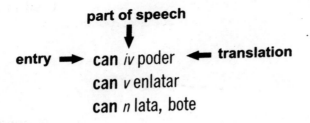

part of speech

entry ➡ can *iv* poder ⬅ **translation**

can *v* enlatar

can *n* lata, bote

entry: our selection of English vocabulary includes common words found in school usage and everyday conversation.

part of speech: part of speech is necessary to ensure the translation is appropriate. Entries can be spelled the same but have different translations and meanings depending on the part of speech.

translation: our translation is Word to Word® meaning no definitions or explanations. Purely the most simple common accurate translation.

List of Irregular Verbs

present - past - past participle

arise - arose - arisen
awake - awoke - awoken, awaked
be - was - been
bear - bore - borne
beat - beat - beaten
become - became - become
begin - began - begun
behold - beheld - beheld
bend - bent - bent
beseech - besought - besought
bet - bet - betted
bid - bade (bid) - bidden (bid)
bind - bound - bound
bite - bit - bitten
bleed - bled - bled
blow - blew - blown
break - broke - broken
breed - bred - bred
bring - brought - brought
build - built - built
burn - burnt - burnt *
burst - burst - burst
buy - bought - bought
cast - cast - cast
catch - caught - caught
choose - chose - chosen
cling - clung - clung
come - came - come
cost - cost - cost
creep - crept - crept
cut - cut - cut
deal - dealt - dealt
dig - dug - dug
do - did - done
draw - drew - drawn

dream - dreamt - dreamed
drink - drank - drunk
drive - drove - driven
dwell - dwelt - dwelt
eat - ate - eaten
fall - fell - fallen
feed - fed - fed
feel - felt - felt
fight - fought - fought
find - found - found
flee - fled - fled
fling - flung - flung
fly - flew - flown
forebear - forbore - forborne
forbid - forbade - forbidden
forecast - forecast - forecast
forget - forgot - forgotten
forgive - forgave - forgiven
forego - forewent - foregone
foresee - foresaw - foreseen
foretell - foretold - foretold
forget - forgot - forgotten
forsake - forsook - forsaken
freeze - froze - frozen
get - got - gotten
give - gave - given
go - went - gone
grind - ground - ground
grow - grew - grown
hang - hung * - hung *
have - had - had
hear - heard - heard
hide - hid - hidden
hit - hit - hit
hold - held - held
hurt - hurt - hurt
hit - hit - hit

hold - held - held	**set** - set - set
keep - kept - kept	**sew** - sewed - sewn
kneel - knelt * - knelt *	**shake** - shook - shaken
know - knew - known	**shear** - sheared - shorn
lay - laid - laid	**shed** - shed - shed
lead - led - led	**shine** - shone - shone
lean - leant * - leant *	**shoot** - shot - shot
leap - lept * - lept *	**show** - showed - shown
learn - learnt * - learnt *	**shrink** - shrank - shrunk
leave - left - left	**shut** - shut - shut
lend - lent - lent	**sing** - sang - sung
let - let - let	**sink** - sank - sunk
lie - lay - lain	**sit** - sat - sat
light - lit * - lit *	**slay** - slew - slain
lose - lost - lost	**sleep** - sleep - slept
make - made - made	**slide** - slid - slid
mean - meant - meant	**sling** - slung - slung
meet - met - met	**smell** - smelt * - smelt *
mistake - mistook - mistaken	**sow** - sowed - sown
must - had to - had to	**speak** - spoke - spoken
pay - paid - paid	**speed** - sped * - sped *
plead - pleaded - pled	**spell** - spelt * - spelt *
prove - proved - proven	**spend** - spent - spent
put - put - put	**spill** - spilt * - spilt *
quit - quit * - quit *	**spin** - spun - spun
read - read - read	**spit** - spat - spat
rid - rid - rid	**split** - split - split
ride - rode - ridden	**spread** - spread - spread
ring - rang - rung	**spring** - sprang - sprung
rise - rose - risen	**stand** - stood - stood
run - ran - run	**steal** - stole - stolen
saw - sawed - sawn	**stick** - stuck - stuck
say - said - said	**sting** - stung - stung
see - saw - seen	**stink** - stank - stunk
seek - sought - sought	**stride** - strode - stridden
sell - sold - sold	**strike** - struck - struck (stricken)
send - sent - sent	**strive** - strove - striven

swear - swore - sworn	wear - wore - worn
sweep - swept - swept	weave - wove * - woven *
swell - swelled - swollen *	wed - wed * - wed *
swim - swam - swum	weep - wept - wept
take - took - taken	win - won - won
teach - taught - taught	wind - wound - wound
tear - tore - torn	wring - wrung - wrung
tell - told - told	write - wrote - written
think - thought - thought	
throw - threw - thrown	
thrust - thrust - thrust	
tread - trod - trodden	**Those tenses with an * also have**
wake - woke - woken	**regular forms.**

English-Spanish

Bilingual Dictionaries, Inc.

Abbreviations

a-article
n-noun
e-exclamation
pro-pronoun
adj-adjective
adv-adverb
v-verb
iv-irregular verb
pre-preposition
c-conjunction

A

a *a* un, una
abandon *v* abandonar
abandonment *n* abandono
abbey *n* abadía
abbot *n* abad
abbreviate *v* abreviar
abbreviation *n* abreviatura
abdicate *v* abdicar
abdication *n* abdicación
abdomen *n* abdomen
abduct *v* secuestrar
abduction *n* secuestro
aberration *n* aberración
abhor *v* aborrecer
abide by *v* atenerse a
ability *n* habilidad, aptitud
ablaze *adj* ardiendo
able *adj* capaz
abnormal *adj* anormal
abnormality *n* anormalidad
aboard *adv* a bordo
abolish *v* abolir, suprimir
abort *v* abortar; cancelar
abortion *n* aborto
abound *v* abundar
about adv aproximadamente
about *pre* acerca de, sobre
above adv arriba, encima
above *pre* encima de
abreast *adv* de frente
abridge *v* abreviar
abroad *adv* en el extranjero
abrogate *v* revocar
abruptly *adv* de repente
absence *n* ausencia
absent *adj* ausente

absolute *adj* absoluto
absolution *n* absolución
absolve *v* absolver
absorb *v* absorber
absorbent *adj* absorvente
abstain *v* abstenerse
abstinence *n* abstinencia
abstract *adj* abstracto
absurd *adj* absurdo
abundance *n* abundancia
abundant *adj* abundante
abuse *v* abusar; maltratar
abuse *n* abuso; maltrato
abusive *adj* ofensivo
abysmal *adj* pésimo
abyss *n* abismo
academic *adj* académico
academy *n* academia
accelerate *v* acelerar
accelerator *n* acelerador
accent *n* acento
accept *v* aceptar
acceptable *adj* aceptable
acceptance *n* aceptación
access *n* acceso
accessible *adj* accesible
accident *n* accidente
accidental *adj* accidental
acclaim *v* aclamar
acclimatize *v* aclimatarse
accommodate *v* alojar; agradar
accompany *v* acompañar
accomplice *n* cómplice
accomplish *v* realizar, lograr
accomplishment *n* logro
accord *n* acuerdo
according to *pre* según
accordion *n* acordeón
account *n* cuenta; relato

account for v explicar
accountable adj responsable
accountant n contable
accumulate v acumular
accuracy n exactitud
accurate adj preciso, exacto
accusation n acusación
accuse v acusar
accustom v acostumbrar
ace n as
ache n dolor
achieve v lograr
achievement n logro
acid n ácido
acidity n acidez
acknowledge v reconocer
acorn n bellota
acoustic adj acústico
acquaint v informar
acquaintance n conocido
acquire v adquirir
acquisition n adquisición
acquit v absolver
acquittal n absolución
acre n acre
acrobat n acróbata
across pre a través
act v actuar
action n acción
activate v activar
activation n activación
active adj activo
activity n actividad
actor n actor
actress n actriz
actual adj verdadero
actually adv en realidad
acute adj agudo, grave
adamant adj firme

adapt v adaptar(se)
adaptable adj adaptable
adaptation n adaptación
adapter n adaptador
add v sumar, añadir
addicted adj adicto
addiction n adicción
addictive adj adictivo
addition n suma, adición
additional adj adicional
address n dirección
address v dirigirse a
addressee n destinatario
adequate adj adecuado
adhere v adherirse
adhesive adj adhesivo
adjacent adj junto a, adyacente
adjective n adjetivo
adjoin v lindar con
adjoining adj contiguo
adjourn v aplazar
adjust v ajustar
adjustable adj ajustable
adjustment n ajuste
administer v administrar
admirable adj admirable
admiral n almirante
admiration n admiración
admire v admirar
admirer n admirador
admissible adj admisible
admission n entrada; confesión
admit v admitir, confesar
admittance n entrada
admonish v reprender
admonition n amonestación
adolescence n adolescencia
adolescent n adolescente
adopt v adoptar

adoption *n* adopción
adoptive *adj* adoptivo
adorable *adj* adorable
adoration *n* adoración
adore *v* adorar
adorn *v* adornar
adrift *adv* a la deriva
adulation *n* adulación
adult *n* adulto
adulterate *v* adulterar
adultery *n* adulterio
advance *v* avanzar
advance *n* avance, progreso, adelanto
advantage *n* ventaja
Advent *n* Adviento
adventure *n* aventura
adverb *n* adverbio
adversary *n* adversario
adverse *adj* adverso
adversity *n* adversidad
advertise *v* anunciar
advertising *n* publicidad
advice *n* consejo
advisable *adj* aconsejable
advise *v* aconsejar
adviser *n* consejero
advocate *v* recomendar
aesthetic *adj* estético
afar *adv* lejos
affable *adj* afable
affair *n* asunto; aventura
affect *v* afectar
affection *n* afecto
affectionate *adj* cariñoso
affiliate *v* afiliarse
affiliation *n* afiliación
affinity *n* afinidad
affirm *v* afirmar
affirmative *adj* afirmativo

affix *v* pegar, fijar
afflict *v* afligir
affliction *n* afección, achaque
affluence *n* riqueza
affluent *adj* acomodado
afford *v* tener medios
affordable *adj* asequible
affront *v* ofender
affront *n* ofensa
afloat *adv* a flote
afraid *adj* temeroso
afresh *adv* de nuevo
after *pre* después
afternoon *n* tarde
afterwards *adv* después
again *adv* de nuevo
against *pre* contra
age *n* edad
agency *n* agencia
agenda *n* agenda
agent *n* agente
agglomerate *v* aglomerarse
aggravate *v* agravar, irritar
aggravation *n* agravamiento
aggregate *v* agregar
aggression *n* agresión
aggressive *adj* agresivo
aggressor *n* agresor
aghast *adj* horrorizado
agile *adj* ágil, ligero
agitator *n* agitador
agnostic *n* agnóstico
agonize *v* angustiarse
agonizing *adj* angustioso
agony *n* agonía
agree *v* acordar
agreeable *adj* agradable
agreement *n* acuerdo
agricultural *adj* agrario, agrícola**A**

A

agriculture *n* agricultura
ahead *pre* adelante
aid *n* ayuda
aid *v* ayudar
aide *n* ayudante
ailing *adj* débil
ailment *n* achaque, enfermedad
aim *v* apuntar
aimless *adj* a la deriva
air *n* aire
air *v* airear; ventilar
aircraft *n* vehículo aéreo, avión
airfare *n* billete de avión
airfield *n* campo de aviación
airline *n* línea aérea
airliner *n* avión de pasajeros
airmail *n* correo aéreo
airplane *n* avión
airplane *n* aeroplano, avión
airport *n* aeropuerto
airspace *n* espacio aéreo
airstrip *n* pista de aterrizaje
airtight *adj* hermético
aisle *n* pasillo
ajar *adj* entreabierto
akin *adj* similar
alarm *n* alarma
alarm clock *n* despertador
alarming *adj* alarmante
alcoholic *adj* alcohólico
alcoholism *n* alcoholismo
alert *n* alerta
alert *v* alertar
algebra *n* álgebra
alien *n* extranjero
alight *adv* en llamas
align *v* alinear
alignment *n* alineamiento
alike *adj* parecido, igual

alive *adj* vivo
all *adj* todos
allegation *n* acusación
allege *v* alegar
allegedly *adv* supuestamente
allegiance *n* lealtad, fidelidad
allegory *n* alegoría
allergic *adj* alérgico
allergy *n* alergia
alleviate *v* aliviar
alley *n* callejón
alliance *n* alianza
allied *adj* aliado
alligator *n* caimán
allocate *v* asignar
allot *v* asignar
allotment *n* ración, porción
allow *v* permitir
allowance *n* paga
allure *n* atractivo
alluring *adj* atractivo
allusion *n* alusión
ally *n* aliado
ally *v* aliarse
almanac *n* almanaque
almighty *adj* poderoso
almond *n* almendra
almost *adv* casi
alms *n* limosnas
alone *adj* solo
along *pre* por, a lo largo de
alongside *pre* al lado de
aloof *adj* distante
aloud *adv* en alta voz
alphabet *n* alfabeto
already *adv* ya
alright *adv* bien
also *adv* también
altar *n* altar

alter _v_ alterar
alteration _n_ alteración
altercation _n_ altercado
alternate _v_ alternar
alternate _adj_ alterno
alternative _n_ alternativa
although _c_ aunque
altitude _n_ altitud
altogether _adj_ en total, juntos
aluminum _n_ aluminio
always _adv_ siempre
amass _v_ amasar
amateur _adj_ aficionado
amaze _v_ asombrar
amazement _n_ asombro
amazing _adj_ asombroso
ambassador _n_ embajador
ambiguous _adj_ ambiguo
ambition _n_ ambición
ambitious _adj_ ambicioso
ambivalent _adj_ ambivalente
ambulance _n_ ambulancia
ambush _v_ emboscar
amenable _adj_ dócil
amend _v_ enmendar
amendment _n_ enmienda
amenities _n_ servicios
American _adj_ americano
amiable _adj_ amable
amicable _adj_ amistoso
amid _pre_ en medio de
ammunition _n_ municiones
amnesia _n_ amnesia
amnesty _n_ amnistía
among _pre_ entre
amoral _adj_ amoral
amortize _v_ amortizar
amount _n_ cantidad
amount to _v_ ascender

amphibious _adj_ anfibio
amphitheater _n_ anfiteatro
ample _adj_ amplio
amplifier _n_ amplificador
amplify _v_ amplificar
amputate _v_ amputar
amputation _n_ amputación
amuse _v_ divertir
amusement _n_ diversión
amusing _adj_ divertido
an _a_ un, una
analogy _n_ analogía
analysis _n_ análisis
analyze _v_ analizar
anarchist _n_ anarquista
anarchy _n_ anarquía
anatomy _n_ anatomía
ancestor _n_ antepasado
ancestry _n_ ascendencia, linaje
anchor _n_ ancla
anchovy _n_ anchoa
ancient _adj_ antiguo
and _c_ y
anecdote _n_ anécdota
anemia _n_ anemia
anemic _adj_ anémico
anesthesia _n_ anestesia
anew _adv_ de nuevo
angel _n_ ángel
angelic _adj_ angélico
anger _v_ enfadar
anger _n_ rabia, enojo
angina _n_ angina de pecho
angle _n_ ángulo
Anglican _adj_ anglicano
angry _adj_ enfadado
anguish _n_ angustia
animal _n_ animal
animate _v_ animar

animation *n* animación
animosity *n* animosidad
ankle *n* tobillo
annex *n* anexo
annihilate *v* aniquilar
annihilation *n* aniquilación
anniversary *n* aniversario
annotate *v* anotar
annotation *n* nota; anotación
announce *v* anunciar
announcement *n* anuncio
announcer *n* locutor
annoy *v* molestar, irritar
annoying *adj* fastidioso
annual *adj* anual
annul *v* anular
annulment *n* anulación
anoint *v* ungir
anonymity *n* anonimato
anonymous *adj* anónimo
another *adj* otro
answer *v* responder
answer *n* respuesta
ant *n* hormiga
antagonize *v* antagonizar
antecedent *n* anterior
antecedents *n* antecedentes
antelope *n* antílope
antenna *n* antena
anthem *n* himno
antibiotic *n* antibiótico
anticipate *v* esperar, prever
anticipation *n* expectativa
antidote *n* antídoto
antipathy *n* antipatía
antiquated *adj* anticuado
antiquity *n* antiguedad
anvil *n* yunque
anxiety *n* ansiedad

anxious *adj* ansioso
any *adj* cualquier
anybody *pro* cualquiera
anyhow *pro* de todos modos
anyone *pro* cualquiera
anything *pro* algo, nada
apart *adv* aparte
apartment *n* apartamento
apathy *n* apatía
ape *n* mono
aperitif *n* aperitivo
apex *n* cumbre, ápice
aphrodisiac *adj* afrodisiaco
apiece *adv* cada uno
apocalypse *n* apocalipsis
apologize *v* disculparse
apology *n* disculpa
apostle *n* apóstol
apostolic *adj* apostólico
apostrophe *n* apóstrofe
appall *v* horrorizar
appalling *adj* espantoso
apparel *n* ropa, ropaje
apparent *adj* aparente
apparently *adv* por lo visto
apparition *n* aparición
appeal *n* apelación; atracción
appeal *v* apelar; atraer
appealing *adj* atractivo
appear *v* aparecer; parecer
appearance *n* apariencia
appease *v* apaciguar
appendicitis *n* apendicitis
appendix *n* apéndice
appetite *n* apetito
appetizer *n* aperitivo
applaud *v* aplaudir
applause *n* aplauso
apple *n* manzana

appliance *n* aparato
applicable *adj* aplicable
applicant *n* solicitante
application *n* aplicación; solicitud
apply *v* aplicar; solicitar
apply for *v* solicitar
appoint *v* nombrar, designar
appointment *n* cita; nombramiento
appraisal *n* valoración
appraise *v* valorar
appreciate *v* apreciar; revalorizar
appreciation *n* aprecio; apreciación
apprehend *v* arrestar; entender
apprehensive *adj* aprensivo
apprentice *n* aprendiz
approach *v* acercarse
approach *n* enfoque
approachable *adj* accesible
approbation *n* aprobación
appropriate *adj* apropiado
approval *n* aprobación
approve *v* aprobar
approximate *adj* aproximado
apricot *n* albaricoque
April *n* abril
apron *n* delantal
aptitude *n* aptitud
aquarium *n* aquario
aquatic *adj* acuático
aqueduct *n* acueducto
Arabic *adj* árabe
arable *adj* arable
arbiter *n* árbitro
arbitrary *adj* arbitrario
arbitrate *v* arbitrar
arbitration *n* arbitraje
arc *n* arco
arch *n* arco
archaeology *n* arqueología

archaic *adj* arcaico
archbishop *n* arzobispo
architect *n* arquitecto
architecture *n* arquitectura
archive *n* archivo
arctic *adj* ártico
ardent *adj* ferviente
ardor *n* ardor
arduous *adj* arduo
area *n* área, región
arena *n* estadio, ruedo
argue *v* discutir
argument *n* argumento
arid *adj* árido
arise *iv* surgir
aristocracy *n* aristocracia
aristocrat *n* aristócrata
arithmetic *n* aritmética
ark *n* arca
arm *n* brazo
arm *v* armar
armaments *n* armamento
armchair *n* sillón
armor *n* armadura
armpit *n* sobaco
army *n* ejército
aromatic *adj* aromático
around *pro* alrededor
arouse *v* despertar; excitar
arrange *v* ordenar, organizar
arrangement *n* arreglo
array *n* conjunto
arrest *v* arrestar
arrest *n* arresto
arrival *n* llegada
arrive *v* llegar
arrogance *n* arrogancia
arrogant *adj* arrogante
arrow *n* flecha

arsenal *n* arsenal
arsenic *n* arsénico
arson *n* incendio
arsonist *n* pirómano
art *n* arte
artery *n* arteria
arthritis *n* artritis
artichoke *n* alcachofa
article *n* artículo
articulate *v* articular
articulation *n* articulación
artificial *adj* artificial
artillery *n* artillería
artisan *n* artesano
artist *n* artista
artistic *adj* artístico
artwork *n* ilustraciones
as *c* mientras
as *adv* como
ascend *v* ascender
ascendancy *n* ascendencia
ascertain *v* averiguar
ascetic *adj* ascético
ash *n* ceniza; fresno
ashamed *adj* avergonzado
ashore *adv* en tierra
ashtray *n* cenicero
aside *adv* a un lado
aside from *adv* además de
ask *v* preguntar; pedir
asleep *adj* dormido
asparagus *n* espárrago
aspect *n* aspecto
asphalt *n* asfalto
asphyxiate *v* asfixiar
asphyxiation *n* asfixia
aspiration *n* aspiración
aspire *v* aspirar
aspirin *n* aspirina

assail *v* asaltar
assailant *n* agresor
assassin *n* asesino
assassinate *v* asesinar
assassination *n* asesinato
assault *n* agresión
assault *v* asaltar
assemble *v* juntar; armar
assembly *n* asamblea, ensamblaje;
  montaje,
assent *v* aprobar
assert *v* afirmar
assertion *n* afirmación
assess *v* evaluar; valorar
assessment *n* evaluación
asset *n* ventaja
assets *n* fondos
assign *v* asignar
assignment *n* tarea; misión
assimilate *v* asimilar
assimilation *n* asimilación
assist *v* ayudar
assistance *n* ayuda
associate *v* asociar
association *n* asociación
assorted *adj* variado
assortment *n* surtido
assume *v* asumir, suponer
assumption *n* suposición
assurance *n* garantía
assure *v* asegurar
asterisk *n* asterisco
asteroid *n* asteroide
asthma *n* asma
asthmatic *adj* asmático
astonish *v* asombrar
astonishing *adj* asombroso
astound *v* pasmar
astounding *adj* pasmoso

astray *v* extraviarse
astrologer *n* astrólogo
astrology *n* astrología
astronaut *n* astronauta
astronomer *n* astrónomo
astronomic *adj* astronómico
astronomy *n* astronomía
astute *adj* astuto, sagaz
asunder *adv* en dos
asylum *n* asilo
at *pre* en
atheism *n* ateísmo
atheist *n* ateo
athlete *n* atleta
athletic *adj* atlético
atmosphere *n* atmósfera
atmospheric *adj* atmosférico
atom *n* átomo
atomic *adj* atómico
atone *v* expiar
atonement *n* expiación
atrocious *adj* atroz
atrocity *n* atrocidad
atrophy *v* atrofiarse
attach *v* unir, atar, pegar, añadir
attached *adj* adjunto, junto
attachment *n* apego, archivo
attack *n* ataque
attack *v* atacar
attacker *n* agresor
attain *v* alcanzar, conseguir
attainable *adj* asequible
attainment *n* logro
attempt *v* tratar de
attempt *n* intento
attend *v* acudir, asistir
attendance *n* asistencia
attendant *n* encargado
attention *n* atención

attentive *adj* atento
attenuate *v* atenuar
attenuating *adj* atenuante
attest *v* atestiguar
attic *n* ático, desván
attitude *n* actitud
attorney *n* abogado
attract *v* atraer
attraction *n* atracción, atractivo
attractive *adj* atractivo
attribute n atributo
attribute *v* atribuir
auction *n* subasta
auction *v* subastar
auctioneer *n* subastador
audacious *adj* audaz
audacity *n* audacidad
audible *adj* audible
audience *n* audiencia
audit *v* revisar
auditorium *n* auditorio
augment *v* aumentar
August *n* agosto
aunt *n* tía
auspicious *adj* favorable
austere *adj* austero
austerity *n* austeridad
authentic *adj* auténtico
authenticate *v* autentificar
authenticity *n* autenticidad
author *n* autor
authoritarian *adj* autoritario
authority *n* autoridad
authorization *n* autorización
authorize *v* autorizar
auto *n* coche, carro
autograph *n* autógrafo
automatic *adj* automático
automobile *n* automóvil

A
B

autonomous *adj* autónomo
autonomy *n* autonomía
autopsy *n* autopsia
autumn *n* otoño
auxiliary *adj* auxiliar
avail *v* aprovechar
availability *n* disponibilidad
available *adj* disponible
avalanche *n* avalancha
avarice *n* avaricia
avaricious *adj* avaricioso
avenge *v* vengar
avenue *n* avenida
average *n* promedio, media
averse *adj* reacio
aversion *n* aversión
avert *v* evitar
aviation *n* aviación
aviator *n* aviador
avid *adj* ávido
avoid *v* evitar
avoidable *adj* evitable
avoidance *n* evasión
avowed *adj* declarado
await *v* esperar
awake *iv* despertar
awake *adj* despierto
awakening *n* el despertar
award *v* otorgar
award *n* premio
aware *adj* consciente
awareness *n* conciencia
away *adv* lejos
awe *n* admiración
awesome *adj* formidable
awful *adj* horrible
awkward *adj* torpe; incómodo
awning *n* toldo
ax *n* hacha

axiom *n* axioma
axis *n* eje
axle *n* eje

babble *v* balbucear
baby *n* bebé
babysitter *n* niñera
bachelor *n* soltero, licenciado
back *n* espalda
back *adv* de vuelta
back *v* respaldar
back down *v* echarse a atrás
back up *v* apoyar
backbone *n* espina dorsal
backdoor *n* puerta trasera
backfire *v* fallar
background *n* fondo, antecedentes
backing *n* apoyo, respaldo
backlash *n* reacción fuerte
backlog *n* tarea atrasada
backpack *n* mochila
backup *n* respaldo
backward *adj* atrasado
backwards *adv* hacia atrás
backyard *n* patio trasero
bacon *n* tocino
bacteria *n* bacteria
bad *adj* malo
badge *n* placa, chapa
badly *adv* mal, gravemente
baffle *v* desconcertar
bag *n* bolsa, saco
baggage *n* equipaje

baggy *adj* uango, ancho
baguette *n* barra de pan
bail *n* fianza
bail out *v* pagar la fianza
bailiff *n* alguacil
bait *n* cebo
bake *v* cocer al horno
baker *n* panadero
bakery *n* panadería
balance *v* equilibrar
balance *n* equilibrio; saldo
balcony *n* balcón
bald *adj* calvo
bale *n* fardo
ball *n* pelota
balloon *n* globo
ballot *n* votación
ballroom *n* salón de baile
balm *n* bálsamo
balmy *adj* suave
bamboo *n* bambú
ban *n* prohibición
ban *v* prohibir
banality *n* banalidad
banana *n* plátano
band *n* banda; grupo
bandage *n* venda
bandage *v* vendar
bandit *n* bandido
bang *v* golpear
banish *v* desterrar
banishment *n* destierro
bank *n* banco; ribera
bankrupt *v* arruinar
bankrupt *adj* en quiebra
bankruptcy *n* quiebra, bancarrota
banner *n* estandarte
banquet *n* banquete
baptism *n* bautismo

baptize *v* bautizar
bar *n* barra, tableta
bar *v* prohibir
barbarian *n* bárbaro
barbaric *adj* brutal
barbarism *n* brutalidad
barbecue *n* barbacoa
barber *n* peluquero
bare *adj* desnudo, descubierto
barefoot *adj* descalzo
barely *adv* apenas
bargain *n* ganga
bargain *v* negociar
bargaining *n* negociación
barge *n* barcaza
bark *v* ladrar
bark *n* corteza; ladrido
barley *n* cebada
barmaid *n* mesera
barman *n* mesero
barn *n* granero
barometer *n* barómetro
barracks *n* cuartel
barrage *n* descarga
barrel *n* barril
barren *adj* estéril; árido
barricade *n* barricada
barrier *n* barrera
barring *pre* excepto
bartender *n* camarero
barter *v* intercambiar
base *n* base
base *v* basarse en
baseball *n* béisbol
baseless *adj* sin pruebas
basement *n* sótano
bashful *adj* tímido
basic *adj* básico, sencillo
basics *n* fundamentos

B

basin *n* lavabo, cuenca
basis *n* base
bask *v* tomar al sol
basket *n* cesta
basketball *n* baloncesto
bastard *n* bastardo
bat *n* murciélago; bate
batch *n* lote; grupo
bath *n* baño
bathe *v* bañarse
bathrobe *n* bata
bathroom *n* cuarto de baño
bathtub *n* bañera
baton *n* batuta
battalion *n* batallón
batter *v* maltratar
battery *n* batería, pila
battle *n* batalla
battle *v* luchar
battleship *n* acorazado
bay *n* bahía
bayonet *n* bayoneta
bazaar *n* bazar
be *iv* ser; estar
be born *v* nacer
beach *n* playa
beacon *n* faro
beak *n* pico
beam *n* rayo; viga
bean *n* judía, alubia
bear *n* oso
bear *iv* soportar, llevar
bearable *adj* llevadero
beard *n* barba
bearded *adj* barbudo
bearer *n* portador
beast *n* bestia
beat *iv* golpear; vencer
beat *n* latido; ritmo

beaten *adj* golpeado; vencido
beating *n* paliza
beautiful *adj* hermoso
beautify *v* embellecer
beauty *n* hermosura
beaver *n* castor
because *c* porque
because of *pre* por razón de
beckon *v* hacer señas
become *iv* llegar a ser
bed *n* cama, cauce
bedding *n* ropa de cama
bedroom *n* dormitorio
bedspread *n* colcha
bee *n* abeja
beef *n* carne
beef up *v* reforzar
beehive *n* colmena
beer *n* cerveza
beet *n* remolacha
beetle *n* escarabajo
before *adv* antes
before *pre* antes de
beforehand *adv* de antemano
befriend *v* hacerse amigo
beg *v* suplicar
beggar *n* mendigo
begin *iv* empezar
beginner *n* principiante
beginning *n* principio
beguile *v* engañar
behalf (on) *adv* en favor de
behave *v* comportarse
behavior *n* conducta
behead *v* decapitar
behind *pre* detrás de
behold *iv* contemplar
being *n* ser
belated *adj* atrasado

belch *v* eructar
belch *n* eruto
belfry *n* campanario
Belgian *adj* belga
Belgium *n* Bélgica
belief *n* creencia
believable *adj* verosímil
believe *v* creer
believer *n* creyente
belittle *v* menospreciar
bell *n* campana; timbre
bell pepper *n* pimiento
belligerent *adj* beligerante, agresivo
belly *n* barriga, panza
belly button *n* ombligo
belong *v* pertenecer
belongings *n* pertenencias
beloved *adj* querido
below *adv* abajo
below *pre* debajo de
belt *n* correa
bench *n* banco
bend n curva, recodo
bend *iv* doblar, torcer, curvar
bend down *v* agacharse
beneath *pre* debajo de
benediction *n* bendición
benefactor *n* bienhechor
beneficial *adj* beneficioso
beneficiary *n* beneficiario
benefit *n* beneficio
benefit *v* beneficiar
benevolence *n* benevolencia
benevolent *adj* benévolo
benign *adj* benigno
bequeath *v* legar
bereaved *adj* desconsolado
bereavement *n* duelo
beret *n* boina

berserk *adv* loco
berth *n* litera
beseech *iv* suplicar
beset *iv* acosar
beside *pre* al lado de
besides *pre* además
besiege *iv* asediar
best *adj* el mejor
best man *n* padrino de boda
bestial *adj* bestial
bestiality *n* bestialidad
bestow *v* otorgar
bet *iv* apostar
bet *n* apuesta
betray *v* traicionar; engañar
betrayal *n* traición; engaño
better *adj* mejor
between *pre* entre, en medio de
beverage *n* bebida
beware *v* tener cuidado
bewilder *v* desconcertar
bewitch *v* hechizar
beyond *adv* más allá
bias *n* prejuicio
Bible *n* Biblia
biblical *adj* bíblico
bibliography *n* bibliografía
bicycle *n* bicicleta
bid *n* oferta
bid *iv* hacer una oferta
big *adj* grande
bigamy *n* bigamia
bigot *adj* fanático
bigotry *n* fanatismo
bike *n* bicicleta
bile *n* bilis
bilingual *adj* bilingue
bill *n* cuenta, factura
billiards *n* billar

billion *n* billón

billionaire *n* billonario

bimonthly *adj* bimestral

bin *n* bote de basura

bind *iv* obligar; unir

binding *adj* obligatorio

binoculars *n* binoculares

biography *n* biografía

biological *adj* biológico

biology *n* biología

bird *n* pájaro, ave

birth *n* nacimiento

birthday *n* cumpleaños

biscuit *n* galleta

bishop *n* obispo

bison *n* bisonte

bit *n* trozo; un poco

bite *iv* morder; picar

bite *n* mordisco

bitter *adj* amargo

bitterly *adv* amargamente

bitterness *n* amargura

bizarre *adj* extravagante

black *adj* negro

blackberry *n* mora

blackboard *n* pizarra

blackmail *n* chantaje

blackmail *v* chantajear

blackness *n* oscuridad

blackout *n* apagón

blacksmith *n* herrero

bladder *n* vejiga

blade *n* cuchilla; hoja

blame *n* culpa

blame *v* culpar

blameless *adj* inocente

bland *adj* soso, insulso

blank *adj* en blanco

blanket *n* manta

blaspheme *v* blasfemar

blasphemy *n* blasfemia

blast *n* explosión

blaze *v* arder

bleach *v* blanquear, desteñir

bleach *n* lejía

bleak *adj* desolador

bleed *iv* sangrar

bleeding *n* hemorragia

blemish *n* mancha

blemish *v* manchar

blend *n* mezcla

blend *v* mezclar

blender *n* licuadora

bless *v* bendecir

blessed *adj* bendito

blessing *n* bendición

blind *v* cegar

blind *adj* ciego

blindfold *n* venda

blindfold *v* vendar los ojos

blindly *adv* a ciegas

blindness *n* ceguera

blink *n* parpadeo

blink *v* parpadear

bliss *n* felicidad

blissful *adj* feliz

blister *n* ampolla

blizzard *n* tormenta, ventisca

bloat *v* hincharse

bloated *adj* hinchado

block *n* bloque; tapón

block *v* bloquear, atascar; impedir

blockade *v* bloquear

blockade *n* bloqueo

blockage *n* obstrucción

blond *adj* rubio

blood *n* sangre

bloody *adj* sangriento

bloom v florecer
blossom v florecer
blot n borrón, mancha
blot v emborronar
blouse n blusa
blow n golpe
blow iv soplar; sonar
blow out iv apagar(se)
blow up iv estallar
blowout n reventón
bludgeon v aporrear
blue adj azul
blueprint n plano, plan
bluff v fanfarronear
blunder n error
blunt adj franco, sin punta
bluntness n franqueza
blur n borrón
blur v enturbiar, hacer borroso
blurred adj borroso
blush v sonrojarse
blush n rubor, sonrojo
boar n jabalí
board n tablero; tabla
board v embarcarse
boast v alardear
boat n barca
bodily adj corporal
body n cuerpo, grupo
bog n pantano
bog down v atascarse
boil v hervir
boil down to v reducirse a
boil over v rebosar
boiler n caldera
boisterous adj ruidoso
bold adj valiente; letra negra
boldness n valentía
bolster v reforzar, apoyar

bolt n pestillo; rayo
bolt v cerrar con pestillo
bomb n bomba
bomb v bombardear
bombing n bombardeo
bombshell n bomba
bond n fianza; unión
bondage n esclavitud
bone n hueso
bonfire n hoguera
bonus n bonificación
book n libro
bookcase n estantería
bookkeeper n contable
bookkeeping n contabilidad
booklet n folleto
bookseller n librero
bookstore n librería
boom n auge, estruendo
boom v crecer
boost v estimular
boost n estímulo
boot n bota
booth n cabina
booty n botín
booze n bebida
border n frontera; borde
border on v lindar con
borderline adj dudoso
bore v taladrar
bored adj aburrido
boredom n aburrimiento
boring adj aburrido
born adj nacido
borough n municipio
borrow v tomar prestado
bosom n seno, pecho
boss n jefe
boss around v dar órdenes

B

bossy *adj* mandón
botany *n* botánica
botch *v* estropear
both *adj* ambos
bother *v* molestar
bothersome *adj* preocupante
bottle *n* botella
bottle *v* embotellar
bottleneck *n* embotellamiento
bottom *n* fondo, pie, final
bottomless *adj* sin fondo
bough *n* rama
boulder *n* roca, canto rodado
boulevard *n* bulevar
bounce *v* rebotar, botar
bounce *n* rebote
bound *adj* obligado
bound for *adj* con destino a
boundary *n* frontera, borde, límite
boundless *adj* sin límites
bounty *n* recompensa
bourgeois *adj* burgués
bow *n* reverencia; proa
bow *v* inclinarse
bow out *v* ceder
bowels *n* entrañas
bowl *n* tazón, plato hondo
box *n* caja
box office *n* taquilla
boxer *n* boxeador
boxing *n* boxeo
boy *n* muchacho
boycott *v* boicotear
boyfriend *n* novio
boyhood *n* mocedad
bra *n* sostén
brace for *v* prepararse para
bracelet *n* pulsera
bracket *n* soporte

brag *v* jactarse
braid *n* trenza
brain *n* cerebro
brainwash *v* lavar el cerebro
brake *n* freno
brake *v* frenar
branch *n* rama
branch office *n* sucursal
branch out *v* extenderse
brand *n* marca
brand-new *adj* reciente
brandy *n* cognac
brat *adj* mocoso
brave *adj* valiente
bravely *adv* valerosamente
bravery *n* valentía
brawl *n* pelea
breach *n* infracción; brecha
bread *n* pan
breadth *n* anchura
break *n* fractura; descanso
break *iv* romper, descomponer
break away *v* separarse
break down *v* averiarse, romperse
break free *v* escaparse
break in *v* entrar
break off *v* romperse
break open *v* forzar
break out *v* estallar
break up *v* deshacer(se)
breakable *adj* frágil
breakdown *n* avería
breakfast *n* desayuno
breakthrough *n* avance
breast *n* pecho
breath *n* aliento, respiro
breathe *v* respirar
breathing *n* respiración
breathtaking *adj* imponente**

breed iv procrear, generar
breed n raza
breeze n brisa
brethren n hermanos
brevity n brevedad
brew v elaborar
brewery n cervecería
bribe v sobornar
bribe n soborno
bribery n soborno
brick n ladrillo
bricklayer n albañil
bridal adj nupcial
bride n novia
bridegroom n novio
bridesmaid n dama de honor
bridge n puente
bridle n freno
brief adj corto, breve
brief v informar
briefcase n cartera
briefing n informe
briefly adv brevemente
briefs n calzoncillos
brigade n brigada
bright adj brillante
brighten v alumbrar
brightness n brillo
brilliant adj brillante
brim n borde
bring iv traer
bring back v devolver
bring down v echar abajo
bring up v mencionar
brink n borde
brisk adj rapido
Britain n Gran Bretaña
British adj británico
brittle adj frágil

broad adj ancho
broadcast v transmitir
broadcast n emisión, trasmición
broadcaster n locutor
broaden v ampliar
broadly adv en general
broadminded adj liberal
brochure n folleto
broil v asar
broiler n asador
broke adj quebrado
broken adj roto
bronchitis n bronquítis
bronze n bronce
broom n escoba
broth n caldo
brothel n burdel
brother n hermano
brotherhood n hermandad
brother-in-law n cuñado
brotherly adj fraternal
brow n ceja, frente
brown adj marrón
browse v hojear; navegar
browser n navegador
bruise n moretón
bruise v magullar
brunch n almuerzo
brunette adj morena
brush n cepillo
brush v cepillar
brush aside v ignorar
brush up v repasar
brusque adj rudo
brutal adj brutal
brutality n brutalidad
brutalize v embrutecer
brute adj bruto
bubble n burbuja

B

bubble gum _n_ chicle
buck _n_ dólar
bucket _n_ balde, cubo
buckle _n_ hebilla
buckle up _v_ abrocharse
bud _n_ brote, capullo
buddy _n_ compañero
budge _v_ moverse; ceder
budget _n_ presupuesto
buffalo _n_ búfalo
bug _n_ bicho, microbio
bug _v_ molestar
build _iv_ edificar
builder _n_ constructor
building _n_ edificio
buildup _n_ acumulación
built-in _adj_ empotrado
bulb _n_ bombilla, bulbo
bulge _n_ bulto
bulk _n_ grueso, mayor parte
bulky _adj_ abultado, enorme
bull _n_ toro
bull fight _n_ corrida de toros
bull fighter _n_ torero
bulldoze _v_ derribar
bullet _n_ bala
bulletin _n_ boletín
bully _adj_ matón
bulwark _n_ baluarte
bum _n_ vagabundo
bump _n_ chinchón; bache
bump into _v_ tropezar con
bumper _n_ parachoques
bumpy _adj_ lleno de baches
bun _n_ bollo
bunch _n_ ramo; grupo
bundle _n_ fardo, haz, paquete, manojo
bundle _v_ envolver, atar
bunk bed _n_ litera

bunker _n_ refugio
buoy _n_ boya
burden _n_ carga
burden _v_ cargar
burdensome _adj_ pesado
bureau _n_ oficina
bureaucracy _n_ burocracia
bureaucrat _n_ burócrata
burger _n_ hamburguesa
burglar _n_ ladrón
burglarize _v_ robar
burglary _n_ robo
burial _n_ entierro
burly _adj_ fornido
burn _iv_ quemar, arder
burn _n_ quemadura
burp _v_ eructar
burp _n_ eructo
burrow _n_ madriguera
burst _iv_ reventar
burst into _v_ irrumpir
bury _v_ enterrar
bus _n_ autobús
bus _v_ llevar en autobús
bush _n_ arbusto
busily _adv_ afanosamente
business _n_ negocio
businessman _n_ negociante
bust _n_ busto
bustling _adj_ ajetreado
busy _adj_ ocupado
but _c_ pero
butcher _n_ carnicero
butchery _n_ carnicería
butler _n_ mayordomo
butt _n_ culata; colilla
butter _n_ mantequilla
butterfly _n_ mariposa
button _n_ botón

B
C

buttonhole *n* ojal
buy *iv* comprar
buy off *v* sobornar
buyer *n* comprador
buzz *n* zumbido
buzz *v* zumbar
buzzard *n* buitre
buzzer *n* timbre
by *pre* por, al lado de
bye *e* adiós
bypass *n* desviación
bypass *v* eludir; desviarse
by-product *n* derivado
bystander *n* espectador

C

cab *n* taxi
cabbage *n* berza, repollo
cabin *n* cabina
cabinet *n* armario; gabinete
cable *n* cable
cafeteria *n* cafetería
caffeine *n* cafeína
cage *n* jaula
cake *n* pastel
calamity *n* calamidad
calculate *v* calcular
calculation *n* cálculo
calculator *n* calculadora
calendar *n* calendario
calf *n* ternero
caliber *n* calibre
calibrate *v* calibrar
call *n* llamada; llamamiento

call *v* llamar; convocar
call off *v* cancelar
call on *v* visitar
call out *v* llamar a gritos
calling *n* vocación
callous *adj* cruel
calm *adj* calmado
calm *n* calma
calm down *v* calmar(se)
calorie *n* caloría
calumny *n* calumnia
camel *n* camello
camera *n* cámara
camouflage *v* camuflar
camouflage *n* camuflaje
camp *n* campamento, campo
camp *v* acampar
campaign *v* hacer campaña
campaign *n* campaña
campfire *n* fogata
can *iv* poder
can *v* enlatar
can *n* lata, bote
can opener *n* abrelatas
canal *n* canal
canary *n* canario
cancel *v* cancelar
cancellation *n* cancelación
cancer *n* cáncer
cancerous *adj* canceroso
candid *adj* franco
candidacy *n* candidatura
candidate *n* candidato
candle *n* vela, cirio
candlestick *n* candelero
candor *n* franqueza
candy *n* dulces
cane *n* caña; bastón
canister *n* bote

canned _adj_ enlatado
cannibal _n_ caníbal
cannon _n_ cañón
canoe _n_ canoa
canonize _v_ canonizar
cantaloupe _n_ melón
canteen _n_ cantina
canvas _n_ lienzo, lona
canvas _v_ solicitar
canyon _n_ cañon
cap _n_ gorra; tapadera
capability _n_ capacidad
capable _adj_ capaz
capacity _n_ capacidad
cape _n_ capa; cabo
capital _n_ capital
capital letter _n_ mayúscula
capitalism _n_ capitalismo
capitalize _v_ aprovecharse
capitulate _v_ capitular
capsize _v_ volcar
capsule _n_ cápsula
captain _n_ capitán
captivate _v_ cautivar
captive _n_ cautivo
captivity _n_ cautiverio
capture _v_ capturar
capture _n_ captura
car _n_ coche, auto
carat _n_ quilate
caravan _n_ caravana
carburetor _n_ carburador
carcass _n_ esqueleto
card _n_ tarjeta; naipe
cardboard _n_ cartón
cardiac _adj_ cardiaco
cardiac arrest _n_ paro cardiaco
cardiology _n_ cardiología
care _n_ cuidado

care _v_ cuidar
care about _v_ preocuparse
care for _v_ importar
career _n_ profesión, carrera
carefree _adj_ despreocupado
careful _adj_ cuidadoso
careless _adj_ descuidado
carelessness _n_ descuido
caress _n_ caricia
caress _v_ acariciar
caretaker _n_ encargado
cargo _n_ cargamento
caricature _n_ caricatura
caring _adj_ bondadoso
carnage _n_ matanza
carnal _adj_ carnal
carnation _n_ clavel
carol _n_ villancico
carpenter _n_ carpintero
carpentry _n_ carpintería
carpet _n_ alfombra
carriage _n_ vagón, carruaje
carrot _n_ zanahoria
carry _v_ llevar
carry on _v_ continuar
carry out _v_ llevar a cabo
cart _n_ carreta
cart _v_ acarrear
cartoon _n_ caricatura
cartridge _n_ cartucho
carve _v_ trinchar; tallar
cascade _n_ cascada
case _n_ caso; caja
cash _n_ dinero en efectivo
cashier _n_ cajero
casino _n_ casino
casket _n_ ataúd, cofre
casserole _n_ cazuela
cassock _n_ sotana

cast n molde, elenco
cast iv arrojar; fundir; moldear
castaway n náufrago
caste n casta
castle n castillo
casual adj casual, informal
casualty n víctima
cat n gato
cataclysm n cataclismo
catacomb n catacumba
catalog n catálogo
catalog v catalogar
cataract n catarata
catastrophe n catástrofe
catch iv coger, tomar
catch up v alcanzar
catching adj contagioso
catchword n eslogan
catechism n catecismo
category n categoría
cater to v satisfacer
caterpillar n oruga
cathedral n catedral
Catholic adj Católico
Catholicism n Catolicismo
cattle n ganado
cauliflower n coliflor
cause n causa, motivo
cause v causar
caution n cautela, precaución
cautious adj precavido
cavalry n caballería
cave n cueva
cave in v derrumbarse; ceder
cavern n caverna
cavity n cavidad, hoyo
cease v cesar
cease-fire n tregua
ceiling n techo

celebrate v celebrar, festejar
celebration n celebración
celebrity n celebridad
celery n apio
celestial adj celestial
celibacy n celibato
celibate adj célibe
cell phone n móvil, celular
cellar n bodega
cement n cemento
cement v cimentar
cemetery n cementerio
censorship n censura
censure v censurar
census n censo
cent n céntimo, centavo
centenary n centenario
center n centro
center v centrar
centimeter (cm) n centímetro (cm)
central adj central
centralize v centralizar
century n siglo
ceramic n cerámica
cereal n cereal
cerebral adj cerebral
ceremony n ceremonia
certain adj cierto, seguro
certainty n certeza
certificate n certificado
certify v certificar
chagrin n disgusto
chain n cadena
chain v encadenar
chainsaw n sierra eléctrica
chair n silla
chair v presidir
chairman n presidente
chalet n chalet, villa

chalice *n* cáliz
chalk *n* tiza
chalkboard *n* pizarra
challenge *v* desafiar
challenge *n* desafío
challenging *adj* estimulante
chamber *n* cámara, sala
champ *n* campeón
champion *n* campeón
champion *v* promover
chance *n* oportunidad; riesgo
chancellor *n* canciller
chandelier *n* araña (lámpara)
change *v* cambiar
change *n* cambio
channel *n* canal
chant *n* canto
chaos *n* caos
chaotic *adj* caótico
chapel *n* capilla
chaplain *n* capellán
chapter *n* capítulo
char *v* carbonizar
character *n* carácter
characteristic *adj* característico
charade *n* farsa
charbroil *adj* asar a la brasa
charcoal *n* carbón
charge *v* acusar; cobrar
charge *n* cargo; precio
charisma *n* carisma
charismatic *adj* carismático
charitable *adj* caritativo
charity *n* caridad
charm *v* encantar
charm *n* encanto
charming *adj* encantador
chart *n* gráfico; mapa
charter *n* estatutos; alquiler

charter *v* alquilar
chase *n* persecución
chase *v* perseguir
chase away *v* ahuyentar
chasm *n* sima, abismo
chaste *adj* casto
chastise *v* castigar
chastisement *n* castigo
chastity *n* castidad
chat *v* charlar
chauffeur *n* chófer
cheap *adj* barato
cheat *v* estafar, engañar
cheater *n* estafador
check *n* cheque; cuenta
check *v* comprobar, chequear
check in *v* registrar(se)
check up *n* examen
checkbook *n* chequera
cheek *n* mejilla
cheekbone *n* pómulo
cheeky *adj* descarado
cheer *v* vitorear
cheer up *v* animar
cheerful *adj* alegre
cheers *n* aclamaciones
cheese *n* queso
chef *n* jefe de cocina
chemical *adj* químico
chemist *n* farmacéutico
chemistry *n* química
cherish *v* apreciar
cherry *n* cereza
chess *n* ajedrez
chest *n* pecho; cofre
chestnut *n* castaña
chew *v* mascar
chick *n* pollito, jovencita
chicken *n* pollo

chicken out *v* acobardarse
chicken pox *n* viruela
chide *v* regañar
chief *n* jefe
chiefly *adv* principalmente
child *n* niño
childhood *n* niñez
childish *adj* pueril
childless *adj* sin hijos
children *n* niños
chill *n* resfriado
chill *v* enfriar
chill out *v* calmarse
chilly *adj* fresco, frío
chimney *n* chimenea
chimpanzee *n* chimpancé
chin *n* barbilla
chip *n* ficha; papa frita
chisel *n* cincel
chocolate *n* chocolate
choice *n* opción, elección
choir *n* coro
choke *v* ahogar(se)
cholera *n* cólera
cholesterol *n* colesterol
choose *iv* escoger, elegir
choosy *adj* exigente
chop *v* cortar
chop *n* chuleta
chopper *n* helicóptero
chord cuerda
chore *n* faena, tarea
chorus *n* coro
christen *v* bautizar
christening *n* bautizo
Christian *adj* cristiano
Christianity *n* Cristianismo
Christmas *n* Navidad
chronic *adj* crónico

chronicle *n* crónica
chronology *n* cronología
chubby *adj* regordete
chuckle *v* reirse entre dientes
chunk *n* trozo, pedazo
church *n* iglesia
chute *n* rampa
cider *n* sidra
cigar *n* cigarro
cigarette *n* cigarrillo
cinder *n* ceniza
cinema *n* cine
cinnamon *n* canela
circle *n* círculo
circle *v* rodear; volar
circuit *n* circuito
circular *adj* circular
circulate *v* circular
circulation *n* circulación
circumcise *v* circuncidar
circumcision *n* circuncisión
circumstance *n* circunstancia
circumstantial *adj* circunstancial
circus *n* circo
cistern *n* cisterna
citizen *n* ciudadano
citizenship *n* ciudadanía
city *n* ciudad
city hall *n* ayuntamiento
civic *adj* cívico
civil *adj* civil, cortés
civilization *n* civilización
civilize *v* civilizar
claim *v* reclamar, afirmar
claim *n* reclamación
clam *n* almeja
clamor *v* clamar
clamp *n* abrazadera
clamp down *v* suprimir

C

clan *n* clan, grupo
clandestine *adj* clandestino
clap *v* aplaudir
clarification *n* clarificación
clarify *v* clarificar, aclarar
clarinet *n* clarinete
clarity *n* claridad
clash *v* chocar
clash *n* choque
class *n* clase; categoría
classic *adj* clásico
classification clasificación
classify *v* clasificar
classmate *n* compañero
classroom *n* aula, salón de clases
classy *adj* elegante
clause *n* cláusula
claw *n* garra, zarpa
claw *v* arañar
clay *n* arcilla
clean *adj* limpio
clean *v* limpiar
cleaner *n* quitamanchas
cleanliness *n* limpieza
cleanse *v* limpiar
cleanser *n* crema de limpiar
clear *adj* claro, despejado
clear *v* despejar; absolver
clearance *n* rebaja; espacio
clear-cut *adj* definido
clearly *adv* claramente
clearness *n* claridad
cleft *n* grieta
clemency *n* clemencia
clench *v* apretar
clergy *n* clero
clergyman *n* cura, ministro
clerical *adj* clerical
clerk *n* dependiente

clever *adj* listo
click *v* chasquear
client *n* cliente
clientele *n* clientela
cliff *n* acantilado
climate *n* clima
climatic *adj* climático
climax *n* apogeo
climb *v* escalar, subir
climbing *n* ascenso
clinch *v* afianzar, rematar
cling *iv* agarrarse
clinic *n* clínica
clip *v* recortar; cortar
clipping *n* recorte; fragmento
cloak *n* capa, manto
clock *n* reloj
clog *v* atascar
cloister *n* claustro
clone n clón
clone *v* clonar
cloning *n* clonar, clonación
close *v* cerrar
close *adj* cercano
close to *pre* cerca de
closed *adj* cerrado
closely *adv* de cerca
closet *n* armario
closure *n* cierre, clausura, fin
clot *n* coágulo
cloth *n* tela, trapo
clothe *v* vestir
clothes *n* ropa
clothing *n* ropa
cloud *n* nube
cloudless *adj* sin nubes
cloudy *adj* nubloso
clown *n* payaso
club *n* club, porra

club *v* apporrear, golpear
clue *n* pista
clumsiness *n* torpeza
clumsy *adj* torpe
cluster *n* agrupación, grupo, racimo
cluster *v* agrupar
clutch *n* embrague
coach *v* entrenar, preparar
coach *n* entrenador
coaching *n* entrenamiento
coagulate *v* coagular
coagulation *n* coagulación
coal *n* carbón
coalition *n* coalición
coarse *adj* áspero, grueso, tosco; grosero
coast *n* costa, litoral
coastal *adj* costero
coastline *n* costa
coat *n* chaqueta; mano
coax *v* persuadir
cob *n* mazorca
cobblestone *n* adoquín
cobweb *n* telaraña
cocaine *n* cocaína
cock *n* gallo
cockpit *n* cabina
cockroach *n* cucaracha
cocktail *n* cóctel
cocky *adj* arrogante
cocoa *n* cacao
coconut *n* coco
cod *n* bacalao
code *n* código; clave
codify *v* codificar
coefficient *n* coeficiente
coerce *v* coaccionar
coercion *n* coacción
coexist *v* coexistir

coffee *n* café
coffin *n* ataúd
cohabit *v* cohabitar
coherent *adj* coherente
cohesion *n* cohesión
coin *n* moneda
coincide *v* coincidir
coincidence *n* coincidencia
coincidental *adj* casual
cold *adj* frío
coldness *n* frialdad
colic *n* cólico
collaborate *v* colaborar
collaboration *n* colaboración
collaborator *n* colaborador
collapse *v* hundirse
collapse *n* desplome
collar *n* collar, cuello
collarbone *n* clavícula
collateral *adj* colateral
colleague *n* colega
collect *v* colectar, juntar, recoger
collection *n* colección, acumulación
collector *n* coleccionista
college *n* colegio
collide *v* chocar
collision *n* choque, colisión
cologne *n* colonia
colon *n* colon; dos puntos
colonel *n* coronel
colonial *adj* colonial
colonization *n* colonización
colonize *v* colonizar
colony *n* colonia
color *n* color
color *v* teñir; colorear
colorful *adj* colorido
colossal *adj* colosal
colt *n* potro

C

column *n* columna
coma *n* coma
comb *n* peine
comb *v* peinar
combat *n* combate
combat *v* combatir
combatant *n* combatiente
combination *n* combinación
combine *v* combinar
combustible *n* combustible
combustion *n* combustión
come *iv* venir
come about *v* acontecer
come across *v* topar con
come apart *v* deshacerse
come back *v* volver
come down *v* bajar; caer
come forward *v* presentarse
come from *v* ser de, venir de
come in *v* entrar
come out *v* salir; descubrirse
come over *v* venir
come up *v* surgir; subir
comeback *n* vuelta
comedian *n* comediante
comedy *n* comedia
comet *n* cometa
comfort *n* bienestar
comfortable *adj* cómodo
comforter *n* colcha
comical *adj* cómico
coming *n* llegada
coming *adj* próximo
comma *n* coma
command *v* mandar
commander *n* comandante
commandment *n* mandamiento
commemorate *v* conmemorar
commence *v* comenzar

commend *v* elogiar
commendation *n* elogio
comment *v* comentar
comment *n* comentario
commerce *n* comercio
commercial *adj* comercial
commission *n* comisión, tarea
commit *v* cometer; comprometer
commitment *n* compromiso
committed *adj* dedicado
committee *n* comité
common *adj* común
commotion *n* alboroto
communicate *v* comunicar
communication *n* comunicación
communion *n* comunión
communism *n* comunismo
communist *adj* comunista
community *n* comunidad
commute *v* conmutar; viajar
compact *adj* compacto
compact *v* comprimir
companion *n* compañero
companionship *n* compañía
company *n* compañía
comparable *adj* comparable
comparative *adj* comparativo
compare *v* comparar(se)
comparison *n* comparación
compartment *n* compartimento
compass *n* brújula, compás
compassion *n* compasión
compassionate *adj* compasivo
compatibility *n* compatibilidad
compatible *adj* compatible
compatriot *n* paisano
compel *v* forzar, obligar
compelling *adj* contundente
compendium *n* compendio

compensate *v* compensar
compensation *n* compensación
compete *v* competir
competence *n* competencia
competent *adj* competente
competition *n* concurso
competitive *adj* competitivo
competitor *n* competidor
compile *v* compilar
complain *v* quejarse
complaint *n* queja
complement *n* complemento
complete *adj* completo
complete *v* completar
completely *adv* completamente
completion *n* terminación
complex *adj* complejo
complexion *n* tez
complexity *n* complejidad
compliance *n* cumplimiento
compliant *adj* obediente
complicate *v* complicar
complication *n* complicación
complicity *n* complicidad
compliment *n* elogio, piropo
complimentary *adj* gratis, elogioso
comply *v* cumplir con
component *n* componente
compose *v* componer, calmarse
composed *adj* compuesto, calmado
composer *n* compositor
composite compuesto
composition *n* composición
compost *n* abono
composure *n* compostura
compound *n* recinto; compuesto
compound *v* agravar
comprehend *v* comprender
comprehensive *adj* completo

compress *v* comprimir
compression *n* compresión
comprise *v* consistir en
compromise *n* compromiso, arreglo
compromise *v* transigir
compulsion *n* compulsión
compulsive *adj* compulsivo
compulsory *adj* obligatorio
compute *v* calcular
computer *n* computadora
comrade *n* camarada
con man *n* estafador
conceal *v* ocultar
concede *v* conceder
conceited *adj* presumido
conceive *v* concebir
concentrate *v* concentrar
concentration *n* concentración
concentric *adj* concéntrico
concept *n* concepto
conception *n* concepción
concern *v* concernir, preocupar
concern *n* preocupación
concerning *pre* acerca de, sobre
concert *n* concierto
concession *n* concesión
conciliate *v* conciliar
conciliatory *adj* conciliatorio
concise *adj* conciso
conclude *v* concluir, terminar
conclusion *n* conclusión, final
conclusive *adj* concluyente
concoct *v* mezclar; urdir
concoction *n* brebaje
concrete *n* hormigón, cemento
concrete *adj* concreto, sucinto
concur *v* coincidir
concurrent *adj* simultáneo
concussion *n* golpe cerebral

C

condemn v condenar
condemnation n condenación
condensation n condensación
condense v condensar
condescend v condescender
condiment n condimento
condition n condición
conditional adj condicional
conditioner n suavizante
condo n condominio
condolences n pésame
condone v justificar
conducive adj conducente
conduct n conducta
conduct v comportarse, dirigir, conducir
conductor n chófer, director, conductor
cone n cono
confer v otorgar; deliberar
conference n conferencia
confess v confesar(se)
confession n confesión
confessional n confesionario
confessor n confesor
confidant n confidente
confide v confiar
confidence n confianza
confident adj confiado
confidential adj confidencial
confine v limitarse; recluir
confinement n prisión
confirm v confirmar
confirmation n confirmación
confiscate v confiscar
confiscation n confiscación
conflict n conflicto
conflict v chocar
conflicting adj opuesto

conform v conformarse
conformist adj conformista
conformity n conformidad
confound v confundir
confront v enfrentarse
confrontation n confrontación
confuse v confundir
confusing adj confuso
confusion n confusión
congenial adj agradable
congested adj congestionado
congestion n congestión
congratulate v felicitar
congratulations n felicitaciones
congregate v congregar
congregation n congregación
congress n congreso
conjugal adj conyugal
conjugate v conjugar
conjunction n conjunción
conjure up v evocar
connect v conectar
connection n conexión
connive v ser cómplice
connote v connotar
conquer v conquistar
conqueror n conquistador
conquest n conquista
conscience n conciencia
conscious adj consciente
consciousness n conciencia
conscript n recluta
consecrate v consagrar
consecration n consagración
consecutive adj consecutivo
consensus n consenso
consent v consentir
consent n consentimiento
consequence n consecuencia**

consequent *adj* consistente
conservation *n* conservación
conservative *adj* conservador
conserve *v* conservar
conserve *n* mermelada
consider *v* considerar
considerable *adj* considerable
considerate *adj* considerado
consideration *n* consideración
consignment *n* envío
consist *v* consistir
consistency *n* coherencia, consistencia
consistent *adj* coherente; constante
consolation *n* consuelo
console *v* consolar
consolidate *v* consolidar
consonant *n* consonante
conspicuous *adj* visible
conspiracy *n* conspiración
conspirator *n* conspirador
conspire *v* conspirar
constancy *n* constancia
constant *adj* constante
constellation *n* constelación
consternation *n* consternación
constipate *v* estreñir
constipated *adj* estreñido
constipation *n* estreñimiento
constitute *v* constituir
constitution *n* constitución
constrain *v* restringir, limitar
constraint *n* restricción, límite
construct *v* construir
construction *n* construcción
constructive *adj* constructivo
consul *n* cónsul
consulate *n* consulado
consult *v* consultar

consultation *n* consulta
consume *v* consumir
consumer *n* consumidor
consumption *n* consumo
contact *v* contactar
contact *n* contacto
contagious *adj* contagioso
contain *v* contener
container *n* contenedor, recipiente
contaminate *v* contaminar
contamination *n* contaminación
contemplate *v* contemplar
contemporary *adj* contemporáneo
contempt *n* desprecio
contend *v* competir
contender *n* contendiente
content *adj* contento
content *v* contentar
contentious *adj* polémico
contents *n* contenido
contest *n* concurso; lucha
contestant *n* concursante
context *n* contexto
continent *n* continente
continental *adj* continental
contingency *n* contingencia
contingent *adj* contingente
continuation *n* continuación
continue *v* continuar
continuity *n* continuidad
continuous *adj* continuo
contour *n* contorno
contraband *n* contrabando
contract *v* contraer(se), reducir
contract *n* contrato
contraction *n* contracción, reducción
contradict *v* contradecir
contradiction *n* contradicción
contrary *adj* contrario

C

C

contrast v contrastar
contrast n contraste
contribute v contribuir, aportar
contribution n aportación
contributor n colaborador; donante
contrition n contrición
control n control
control v controlar
controversial adj polémico
controversy n controversia
convalescent adj convaleciente
convene v convocar
convenience n conveniencia
convenient adj conveniente
convent n convento
convention n convención
conventional adj convencional
converge v convergir
conversation n conversación
converse v conversar
conversely adv por el contrario
conversion n conversión
convert v convertir
convert n converso
convey v transmitir; transportar
convict v declarar culpable
conviction n convicción; condena
convince v convencer
convincing adj convincente
convoluted adj enrevesado
convoy n convoy
convulse v retorcerse
convulsion n convulsión
cook v cocinar
cook n cocinero
cookie n galleta
cooking n cocina
cool adj fresco; sereno
cool v enfriar

cool down v calmar; enfriar
cooling adj refrescante
coolness n frialdad; frío
cooperate v cooperar
cooperation n cooperación
cooperative adj servicial
coordinate v coordinar
coordinate n coordenada
coordination n coordinación
coordinator n coordinador
cop n policía
cope v arreglárselas
copier n copiadora
copper n cobre
copy v copiar
copy n copia
copyright n derechos de autor
cord n cuerda; cable
cordial adj cordial
cordless adj inalámbrico
cordon n cordón
cordon off v acordonar
core n núcleo, centro, esencia
cork n corcho
corn n maíz
corner n esquina; rincón
cornerstone n piedra angular
cornet n corneta
corollary n consecuencia
coronary adj coronario
coronation n coronación
corporal adj corporal
corporal n cabo
corporation n corporación
corpse n cadáver
corpulent adj corpulento
corpuscle n corpúsculo
correct v corregir
correct adj correcto

C

correction *n* corrección
correlate *v* correlacionar
correspond *v* corresponder
correspondent *n* corresponsal
corresponding *adj* correspondiente
corridor *n* pasillo
corroborate *v* corroborar
corrode *v* corroer
corrupt *v* corromper
corrupt *adj* corrupto; corrompido
corruption *n* corrupción
cosmetic *n* cosmético
cosmic *adj* cósmico
cosmonaut *n* cosmonauta
cost *iv* costar
cost *n* costo, coste
costly *adj* costoso, caro
costume *n* traje
cottage *n* casita
cotton *n* algodón
couch *n* sofá
cough *n* tos
cough *v* toser
council *n* consejo
counsel *v* aconsejar
counsel *n* abogado; consejo
counselor *n* consejero
count *v* contar
count *n* cuenta, conde
countdown *n* cuenta atrás
countenance *n* semblante
counter *n* mostrador
counter *v* responder
counteract *v* contrarrestar
counterfeit *v* falsificar
counterfeit *adj* falso
counterpart *n* homólogo
countess *n* condesa
countless *adj* innumerables

country *n* país; campo
countryman *n* compatriota
countryside *n* campo
county *n* condado
coup *n* golpe
couple *n* pareja; par
coupon *n* cupón
courage *n* valentía
courageous *adj* valiente
courier *n* mensajero
course *n* curso; plato
court *n* corte, tribunal; cancha
court *v* cortejar
courteous *adj* cortés
courtesy *n* cortesía
courthouse *n* juzgado
courtship *n* noviazgo
courtyard *n* patio
cousin *n* primo
cove *n* cala
covenant *n* pacto
cover *n* cubierta; funda
cover *v* cubrir(se); cobijar
cover up *v* encubrir
coverage *n* cobertura
covert *adj* secreto
cover-up *n* encubrimiento
covet *v* desear
cow *n* vaca
coward *n* cobarde
cowardice *n* cobardía
cowardly *adv* cobardemente
cowboy *n* vaquero
cozy *adj* cómodo
crab *n* cangrejo
crack *n* grieta, raja
crack *v* rajarse; descifrar
cradle *n* cuna
craft *n* oficio; arte

craftsman _n_ artesano
cram _v_ meter a la fuerza
cramp _n_ calambre, retorcijón
cramped _adj_ apretado
crane _n_ grúa
crank _n_ manivela
cranky _adj_ malhumorado
crap _n_ porquería
crappy _adj_ de mala calidad
crash _n_ choque; desplome
crash _v_ estrellarse; hundirse
crass _adj_ grosero
crater _n_ cráter
crave _v_ ansiar
craving _n_ ansia
crawl _v_ arrastrarse
crayon _n_ tiza
craziness _n_ locura
crazy _adj_ loco
creak _v_ rechinar, crujir
creak _n_ chirrido
cream _n_ crema
creamy _adj_ cremoso
crease _n_ pliegue, arruga
crease _v_ arrugar
create _v_ crear
creation _n_ creación
creative _adj_ creativo
creativity _n_ creatividad
creator _n_ creador
creature _n_ criatura
credibility _n_ credibilidad
credible _adj_ creíble
credit _n_ crédito
creditor _n_ acreedor
creed _n_ credo
creek _n_ arroyo
creep _v_ moverse lento
creepy _adj_ horroroso

cremate _v_ incinerar
crematorium _n_ crematorio
crest _n_ cresta, cima
crevice _n_ grieta
crew _n_ tripulación
crib _n_ cuna
cricket _n_ grillo
crime _n_ crimen
criminal _adj_ criminal
cripple _adj_ inválido, lisiado
cripple _v_ paralizar
crisis _n_ crisis
crisp _adj_ fresco
crispy _adj_ crujiente
criss-cross _v_ atravesar
criterion _n_ criterio
critical _adj_ crítico, crucial
criticism _n_ crítica
criticize _v_ criticar
critique _n_ crítica
crockery _n_ loza, platos
crocodile _n_ cocodrilo
crony _n_ amigo
crook _n_ ladrón
crooked _adj_ torcido, malo
crop _n_ cosecha, cultiva
cross _n_ cruz
cross _adj_ enfadado
cross _v_ cruzar, atravesar
cross out _v_ tachar
crossfire _n_ fuego cruzado
crossing _n_ travesía
crossroads _n_ cruce
crosswalk _n_ paso de peatones
crossword _n_ crucigrama
crouch _v_ agacharse
crow _n_ cuervo
crow _v_ cacarear
crowbar _n_ palanca

C

crowd *n* muchedumbre
crowd *v* aglomerarse
crowded *adj* abarrotado
crown *n* corona
crown *v* coronar
crowning *n* coronación
crucial *adj* crucial, decisivo
crucifix *n* crucifijo
crucifixion *n* crucifixión
crucify *v* crucificar
crude *adj* grosero; crudo
cruel *adj* cruel
cruelty *n* crueldad
cruise *v* viajar en crucero
crumb *n* miga
crumble *v* desmoronarse
crunchy *adj* crujiente
crusade *n* cruzada
crusader *n* cruzado
crush *v* aplastar
crushing *adj* aplastante
crust *n* corteza; costra
crusty *adj* crujiente
crutch *n* muleta
cry *n* grito, llanto
cry *v* llorar
cry out *v* gritar
crying *n* lloro
crystal *n* cristal
cub *n* cachorro
cube *n* cubo
cubic *adj* cúbico
cubicle *n* cubículo
cucumber *n* pepino
cuddle *v* abrazar
cuff *n* puño; dobladillo
cuisine *n* cocina
culminate *v* culminar
culpability *n* culpabilidad

culprit *n* culpable
cult *n* secta
cultivate *v* cultivar
cultivation *n* cultivo
cultural *adj* cultural
culture *n* cultura
cumbersome *adj* enrevesado
cunning *adj* astuto
cup *n* taza
cupboard *n* alacena
curable *adj* curable
curator *n* director
curb *v* frenar; limitar
curb *n* bordillo, freno
curdle *v* cuajarse, cortarse
cure *v* curar
cure *n* cura
curfew *n* toque de queda
curiosity *n* curiosidad
curious *adj* curioso
curl *v* rizar
curl *n* rizo
curly *adj* rizado
currency *n* moneda
current *adj* corriente, actual
currently *adv* actualmente
curse *v* maldecir
curtail *v* restringir, acortar
curtain *n* cortina, telón
curve *n* curva
curve *v* curvarse
cushion *n* cojín
cushion *v* amortiguar
cuss *v* maldecir
custard *n* natillas
custodian *n* guardián
custody *n* custodia
custom *n* costumbre
customary *adj* habitual

customer *n* cliente
custom-made *adj* a medida
customs *n* aduana
cut *n* cortada
cut *iv* cortar
cut back *v* reducir
cut down *v* cortar, talar
cut off *v* aislar
cut out *v* recortar
cute *adj* gracioso, lindo
cutlery *n* cubiertos
cutter *n* alicates
cyanide *n* cianuro
cycle *n* ciclo
cyclist *n* ciclista
cyclone *n* ciclón
cylinder *n* cilindro
cynic *adj* cínico
cynicism *n* cinismo
cypress *n* ciprés
cyst *n* quiste
czar *n* zar

D

dad *n* papá, padre
dagger *n* puñal, daga
daily *adv* diariamente
dairy farm *n* lechería
daisy *n* margarita
dam *n* presa, dique, represa, embalse
damage *n* daño
damage *v* dañar
damaging *adj* perjudicial
damn *v* condenar

damnation *n* condenación
damp *adj* húmedo
dampen *v* mojar; desanimar
dance *n* baile
dance *v* bailar
dancing *n* baile
dandruff *n* caspa
danger *n* peligro
dangerous *adj* peligroso
dangle *v* colgar
dare *v* atreverse
dare *n* atrevimiento
daring *adj* atrevido
dark *adj* oscuro
darken *v* oscurecer
darkness *n* oscuridad
darling *adj* querido
darn *v* zurcir
dart *n* dardo
dash *v* correr; frustrar
dashing *adj* deslumbrante
data *n* datos
database *n* base de datos
date *n* fecha; dátil
date *v* fechar; salir con
daughter *n* hija
daughter-in-law *n* nuera
daunt *v* desalentar
daunting *adj* desalentador
dawn *n* amanecer, alba
day *n* día, jornada
daydream *v* soñar despierto
daze *v* aturdir
dazed *adj* aturdido
dazzle *v* deslumbrar
dazzling *adj* deslumbrante
deacon *n* diácono
dead *adj* muerto
dead end *n* sin salida**

deaden *v* amortiguar
deadline *n* fecha tope
deadlock *adj* estancado
deadly *adj* mortal
deaf *adj* sordo
deafen *v* ensordecer
deafening *adj* ensordecedor
deafness *n* sordera
deal *iv* tratar (de, con)
deal *n* pacto, acuerdo
dealer *n* comerciante
dealings *n* tratos
dean *n* decano
dear *adj* querido
dearly *adv* caramente
death *n* muerte
death toll *n* número de víctimas
death trap *n* trampa mortal
deathbed *n* lecho de muerte
debase *v* rebajar(se)
debatable *adj* discutible
debate *v* debatir
debate *n* debate
debit *n* débito
debrief *v* interrogar
debris *n* escombros
debt *n* deuda
debtor *n* deudor
debunk *v* refutar
debut *n* estreno
decade *n* década
decadence *n* decadencia
decaf *adj* descafeinado
decapitate *v* decapitar
decay *v* pudrirse
decay *n* descomposición
deceased *adj* difunto
deceit *n* engaño, mentira
deceitful *adj* engañoso

deceive *v* engañar
December *n* diciembre
decency *n* decencia
decent *adj* decente
deception *n* engaño
deceptive *adj* engañoso
decide *v* decidir
deciding *adj* decisivo
decimal *adj* decimal
decimate *v* diezmar
decipher *v* descifrar
decision *n* decisión
decisive *adj* decisivo
deck *n* cubierta
declaration *n* declaración
declare *v* declarar
declension *n* declinación
decline *v* rehusar
decline *n* descenso
decompose *v* descomponerse
décor *n* decoración
decorate *v* decorar
decorative *adj* decorativo
decorum *n* decoro
decrease *v* disminuir
decrease *n* disminución
decree *n* decreto
decree *v* decretar
decrepit *adj* decrépito
dedicate *v* dedicar
dedication *n* dedicación
deduce *v* deducir
deduct *v* descontar
deductible *adj* deducible
deduction *n* deducción
deed *n* acción, hecho
deem *v* juzgar, estimar
deep *adj* profundo
deepen *v* profundizar

D

deer *n* ciervo
deface *v* desfigurar
defame *v* difamar
defeat *v* derrotar
defeat *n* derrota
defect *n* defecto
defect *v* desertar
defection *n* defección
defective *adj* defectuoso
defend *v* defender
defendant *n* acusado
defender *n* defensor
defense *n* defensa
defenseless *adj* indefenso
defer *v* aplazar, diferir
defiance *n* desafío
defiant *adj* desafiante
deficiency *n* falta, carencia
deficient *adj* deficiente
deficit *n* déficit
defile *v* manchar
define *v* definir
definite *adj* definitivo
definition *n* definición
definitive *adj* definitivo
deflate *v* desinflar
deform *v* deformar
deformity *n* deformidad
defraud *v* defraudar
defray *v* sufragar
defrost *v* descongelar
deft *adj* diestro
defuse *v* desactivar
defy *v* desafiar
degenerate *v* degenerar
degenerate *adj* degenerado
degeneration *n* degeneracion
degradation *n* degradacion
degrade *v* degradar

degrading *adj* degradante
degree *n* grado, título
dehydrate *v* deshidratar
deign *v* dignarse
deity *n* deidad
dejected *adj* desanimado
delay *v* aplazar
delay *n* retraso, demora
delegate *v* delegar
delegate *n* delegado
delegation *n* delegación
delete *v* eliminar, borrar, tachar
deliberate *v* deliberar
deliberate *adj* intencionado
delicacy *n* delicadeza
delicate *adj* delicado
delicious *adj* delicioso
delight *n* placer
delight *v* agradar
delightful *adj* agradable
delinquency *n* delincuencia
delinquent *adj* delincuente
deliver *v* entregar, dar
delivery *n* entrega; parto
delude *v* engañar
deluge *n* diluvio
delusion *n* engaño
deluxe *adj* lujoso
demand *v* exigir
demand *n* reclamación
demanding *adj* exigente
demean *v* rebajarse
demeaning *adj* degradante
demeanor *n* conducta
demented *adj* demente
demise *n* fin, final
democracy *n* democracia
democratic *adj* democrático
demolish *v* derribar

demolition *n* demolición
demon *n* demonio
demonstrate *v* demostrar
demonstrative *adj* demonstrativo
demoralize *v* desmoralizar
demote *v* degradar
den *n* guarida; estudio
denial *n* negación
denigrate *v* denigrar
Denmark *n* Dinamarca
denominator *n* denominador
denote *v* denotar
denounce *v* denunciar
dense *adj* denso; espeso
density *n* densidad
dent *v* abollar
dent *n* abolladura
dental *adj* dental
dentist *n* dentista
dentures *n* dentadura postiza
deny *v* negar
deodorant *n* desodorante
depart *v* salir, marchar
department *n* departamento
departure *n* salida
depend *v* depender
dependable *adj* confiable
dependence *n* dependencia
dependent *adj* dependiente
depict *v* describir
deplete *v* agotar
deplorable *adj* deplorable
deplore *v* deplorar
deploy *v* desplegar
deployment *n* despliegue
deport *v* deportar
deportation *n* deportatión
depose *v* deponer
deposit *n* depósito

depot *n* almacén, cochera
deprave *adj* depravado
depravity *n* depravación
depreciate *v* depreciarse
depreciation *n* depreciación
depress *v* deprimir
depressing *adj* deprimente
depression *n* depresión
deprivation *n* privación
deprive *v* privar
deprived *adj* necesitado
depth *n* profundidad
derail *v* descarrilar
derailment *n* descarrilamiento
deranged *adj* transtornado
derelict *adj* abandonado
deride *v* mofarse de
derivative *adj* derivado
derive *v* derivar(se); obtener
derogatory *adj* despectivo
descend *v* descender
descendant *n* descendiente
descent *n* descenso, descendencia,
  bajada
describe *v* describir
description *n* descripción
descriptive *adj* descriptivo
desecrate *v* desecrar
desegregate *v* desegregar
desert *n* desierto
desert *v* desertar; dejar
deserted *adj* abandonado
deserter *n* desertor
deserve *v* merecer
deserving *adj* merecedor
design *n* diseño, designio
designate *v* designar
desirable *adj* deseable
desire *n* deseo

desire *v* desear
desist *v* desistir
desk *n* escritorio, recepción
desolate *adj* desolado
desolation *n* desolación
despair *n* desesperación
desperate *adj* desesperado
despicable *adj* despreciable
despise *v* despreciar
despite *c* a pesar de
despondent *adj* desanimado
despot *n* déspota
despotic *adj* despótico
dessert *n* postre
destination *n* destino
destiny *n* destino
destitute *adj* desamparado
destroy *v* destruir
destroyer *n* destructor
destruction *n* destrucción
destructive *adj* destructivo
detach *v* separar
detachable *adj* separable
detail *n* detalle
detail *v* enumerar
detain *v* detener
detect *v* detectar
detective *n* detective
detector *n* detector, indicador
detention *n* detención
deter *v* disuadir
detergent *n* detergente
deteriorate *v* deteriorar
deterioration *n* deterioro
determination *n* determinación
determine *v* determinar
deterrence *n* disuasión
detest *v* odiar
detestable *adj* detestable

detonate *v* detonar
detonation *n* detonación
detonator *n* detonador
detour *n* desviación
detriment *n* detrimento
detrimental *adj* perjudicial
devaluation *n* devaluación
devalue *v* devaluar
devastate *v* desvastar
devastating *adj* desvastador
devastation *n* devastación
develop *v* desarrollar
development *n* desarrollo
deviation *n* desviación
device *n* aparato
devil *n* demonio
devious *adj* engañoso
devise *v* idear
devoid *adj* vacío
devote *v* dedicarse
devotion *n* devoción
devour *v* devorar
devout *adj* devoto
dew *n* rocío
diabetes *n* diabetes
diabetic *adj* diabético
diabolical *adj* diabólico
diagnose *v* diagnosticar
diagnosis *n* diagnóstico
diagonal *adj* diagonal
diagram *n* diagrama
dial *n* esfera
dial *v* marcar
dial tone *n* tono de marcar
dialect *n* dialecto
dialogue *n* diálogo
diameter *n* diámetro
diamond *n* diamante
diaper *n* pañal

diarrhea *n* diarrea
diary *n* diario
dice *n* dados
dictate *v* dictar
dictator *n* dictador
dictatorial *adj* dictatorial
dictatorship *n* dictadura
dictionary *n* diccionario
die *v* morir
die out *v* desaparecer
diet *n* dieta
differ *v* discrepar
difference *n* diferencia
different *adj* diferente
difficult *adj* difícil
difficulty *n* dificultad
diffuse *v* difundir(se)
dig *iv* cavar
digest *v* digerir
digestion *n* digestión
digestive *adj* digestivo
digit *n* dígito
dignify *v* dignarse
dignitary *n* dignatario
dignity *n* dignidad
digress *v* divagar
dilapidated *adj* desmoronado
dilemma *n* dilema
diligence *n* diligencia
diligent *adj* diligente
dilute *v* diluir
dim *adj* oscuro, tenue
dim *v* atenuar
dime *n* diez centavos
dimension *n* dimensión
diminish *v* disminuir
dine *v* cenar, comer
diner *n* restaurante
dining room *n* comedor

dinner *n* comida, cena
dinosaur *n* dinosaurio
diocese *n* diócesis
diphthong *n* diptongo
diploma *n* diploma
diplomacy *n* diplomacía
diplomat *n* diplomático
diplomatic *adj* diplomático
dire *adj* desesperado
direct *adj* directo
direct *v* dirigir
direction *n* dirección
director *n* director
directory *n* directorio
dirt *n* suciedad
dirty *adj* sucio
disability *n* incapacidad
disabled *adj* incapacitado
disadvantage *n* desventaja
disagree *v* discrepar
disagreeable *adj* desagradable
disagreement *n* desacuerdo
disappear *v* desaparecer
disappearance *n* desaparición
disappoint *v* decepcionar
disappointing *adj* decepcionante
disappointment *n* decepción
disapproval *n* desaprobación
disapprove *v* desaprobar
disarm *v* desarmar
disarmament *n* desarme
disaster *n* desastre
disastrous *adj* desastroso
disband *v* disolver
disbelief *n* incredulidad
disburse *v* desembolsar
discard *v* descartar, tirar
discern *v* discernir
discharge *v* dar de alta; supurar

discharge *n* descarga; emisión
disciple *n* discípulo
discipline *n* disciplina
disclaim *v* negar
disclose *v* revelar
discomfort *n* incomodidad
disconnect *v* desconectar
discontent *adj* descontento
discontinue *v* descontinuar
discord *n* discordia
discordant *adj* discordante
discount *n* descuento
discount *v* descontar
discourage *v* desanimar
discouragement *n* desaliento
discouraging *adj* desalentador
discourtesy *n* descortesía
discover *v* descubrir
discovery *n* descubrimiento
discredit *v* desacreditar
discreet *adj* discreto
discrepancy *n* discrepancia
discretion *n* discreción
discriminate *v* discriminar
discrimination *n* discriminación
discuss *v* discutir
discussion *n* discusión
disdain *n* menosprecio
disease *n* enfermedad
disembark *v* desembarcar
disenchanted *adj* desencantado
disentangle *v* desenredar
disfigure *v* desfigurar
disgrace *n* deshonor
disgrace *v* deshonrar
disgraceful *adj* vergonzoso
disgruntled *adj* descontento
disguise *v* disfrazar(se)
disguise *n* disfraz

disgust *n* asco, repugnancia
disgusting *adj* repugnante
dish *n* plato
dishearten *v* desalentar
dishonest *adj* deshonesto
dishonesty *n* deshonestidad
dishonor *n* deshonra
dishonorable *adj* deshonroso
dishwasher *n* lavaplatos
disillusion *n* desilusión
disinfect *v* desinfectar
disinfectant *v* desinfectante
disinherit *v* desheredar
disintegrate *v* desintegrar
disintegration *n* desintegración
disinterested *adj* desinteresado
disk *n* disco
dislike *v* tener aversión, disgustar
dislike *n* aversión, antipatía
dislocate *v* dislocar
dislodge *v* desplazar
disloyal *adj* desleal
disloyalty *n* deslealtad
dismal *adj* espantoso
dismantle *v* desarmar
dismay *n* consternación
dismay *v* consternar
dismiss *v* despedir; rechazar
dismissal *n* despido
dismount *v* desmontar
disobedience *n* desobediencia
disobedient *adj* desobediente
disobey *v* desobedecer
disorder *n* desorden
disorganized *adj* desorganizado
disoriented *adj* desorientado
disown *v* repudiar
disparity *n* disparidad
dispatch *v* enviar

dispel v disipar
dispensation n dispensa
dispense v dispensar, dar
dispersal n dispersión
disperse v dispersar(se)
displace v desplazar
display n muestra
display v exponer, mostrar
displease v desagradar
displeasing adj desagradable
displeasure n desagrado
disposable adj desechable
disposal n eliminación
dispose v deshacerse
disprove v refutar
dispute n disputa
dispute v discutir
disqualify v descalificar
disregard v ignorar, desatender
disrepair n deterioro
disrespect n falta de respeto
disrespectful adj irrespetuoso
disrupt v interrumpir, trastornar
disruption n trastorno
dissatisfied adj insatisfecho
disseminate v propagar
dissent n disidencia, disentimiento
dissent v disentir
dissident adj disidente
dissimilar adj distinto
dissipate v disipar, esfumarse
dissolute adj disoluto
dissolution n disolución
dissolve v disolver(se)
dissonant adj disonante
dissuade v disuadir
distance n distancia
distant adj distante
distaste n desagrado

distasteful adj desagradable
distill v destilar
distinct adj distinto, claro
distinction n distinción
distinctive adj distintivo
distinguish v distinguir
distort v distorsionar
distortion n distorsión
distract v distraer
distraction n distracción
distraught adj angustiado
distress n angustia
distress v afligir, angustiar
distressing adj angustioso
distribute v distribuir
distribution n distribución
district n distrito
distrust n desconfianza
distrust v desconfiar
distrustful adj desconfiado
disturb v perturbar, molestar
disturbance n disturbio
disturbing adj perturbador
disunity n desunión
disuse n desuso
ditch n zanja
dive v zambullirse
diver n buzo
diverse adj diverso
diversify v diversificar
diversion n desvío
diversity n diversidad
divert v desviar
divide v dividir
dividend n dividendo
divine adj divino
diving n buceo
divinity n divinidad
divisible adj divisible

D

division *n* división
divorce *n* divorcio
divorce *v* divorciar
divorcee *n* divorciado
divulge *v* divulgar
dizziness *n* mareo
dizzy *adj* mareado
do *iv* hacer
docile *adj* dócil
docility *n* docilidad
dock *n* muelle, dique
dock *v* atracar, amarrar, poner (un barco) en dique
doctor *n* doctor, médico
doctrine *n* doctrina
document *n* documento
documentary *n* documental
documentation *n* documentación
dodge *v* esquivar
dog *n* perro
dogmatic *adj* dogmático
dole out *v* repartir
doll *n* muñeca
dollar *n* dólar
dolphin *n* delfín
dome *n* cúpula
domestic *adj* doméstico, nacional
domesticate *v* domesticar
dominate *v* dominar
domination *n* dominación
domineering *adj* dominante
dominion *n* dominio, poder
donate *v* donar
donation *n* donativo
donkey *n* asno
donor *n* donante
doom *n* destino, suerte
doomed *adj* condenado
door *n* puerta

doorbell *n* timbre
doorstep *n* peldaño
doorway *n* entrada
dope *n* droga
dope *v* drogarse
dormitory *n* dormitorio
dosage *n* dosis
dossier *n* expediente
dot *n* punto
double *adj* doble
double *v* doblar, duplicar
double-check *v* asegurarse
double-cross *v* traicionar
doubt *n* duda
doubt *v* dudar
doubtful *adj* dudoso
dough *n* masa
dove *n* paloma
down *adv* abajo
down payment *n* pago inicial, entrada
downcast *adj* deprimido
downfall *n* caída
downhill *adv* cuesta abajo
downpour *n* aguacero
downsize *v* reducir
downstairs *adv* abajo
down-to-earth *adj* práctico
downtown *n* centro
downtrodden *adj* pordiosero
downturn *n* bajón
dowry *n* dote
doze *n* cabezada
doze *v* dormitar
dozen *n* docena
draft *n* corriente; borrador
draft *v* reclutar
draftsman *n* dibujante
drag *v* arrastrar

D

dragon *n* dragón
drain *v* escurrir, drenar
drainage *n* drenaje, desague
dramatic *adj* dramático
dramatize *v* dramatizar
drape *n* cortina
drastic *adj* drástico
draw *n* empate
draw *iv* dibujar; atraer
drawback *n* inconveniente
drawer *n* cajón
drawing *n* dibujo
dread *v* tener horror
dreaded *adj* temible
dreadful *adj* horroroso
dream *iv* soñar
dream *n* sueño
dress *n* vestido
dress *v* vestirse
dresser *n* tocador
dressing *n* vendaje
dried *adj* seco
drift *v* ir a la deriva
drift apart *v* distanciarse
drifter *n* vagamundo
drill *v* taladrar; practicar
drill *n* broca; instrucción
drink *iv* beber
drink *n* bebida
drinkable *adj* potable
drinker *n* bebedor
drip *v* gotear
drip *n* gota
drive *n* vuelta; energía
drive *iv* conducir, manejar
drive at *v* insinuar
drive away *v* marcharse
driver *n* conductor
driveway *n* entrada

drizzle *v* lloviznar
drizzle *n* llovizna
drop *n* gota; descenso
drop *v* dejar caer, caer
drop in *v* visitar
drop off *v* dejar, entregar
drop out *v* abandonar
drought *n* sequía
drown *v* ahogar(se)
drowsy *adj* soñoliento
drug *n* droga
drug *v* drogar(se)
drugstore *n* farmacia
drum *n* tambor; barril
drunk *adj* borracho
drunkenness *n* borrachera
dry *v* secar
dry *adj* seco
dry-clean *v* limpiar en seco
dryer *n* secadora
dual *adj* doble
dubious *adj* dudoso
duchess *n* duquesa
duck *n* pato
duck *v* agacharse, evitar
duct *n* conducto
due *adj* debido
duel *n* duelo
dues *n* cuota
duke *n* duque
dull *adj* aburrido; sordo
duly *adv* debídamente
dumb *adj* mudo; estúpido
dummy *n* copia
dummy *adj* falso, idiota
dump *v* tirar, arrojar
dump *n* basurero
dung *n* estiércol
dungeon *n* calabozo

D
E

dupe *v* engañar
duplicate *v* duplicar
duplication *n* duplicado
durable *adj* duradero
duration *n* duración
during *pre* durante
dusk *n* anochecer
dust *n* polvo
dusty *adj* polvoriento
Dutch *adj* holandés
duty *n* deber
dwarf *n* enano
dwell *iv* habitar
dwelling *n* alojamiento
dwindle *v* disminuir
dye *v* teñir
dye *n* tinte
dying *adj* moribundo
dynamic *adj* dinámico
dynamite *n* dinamita
dynasty *n* dinastía

E

each *adj* cada
each other *adj* cada uno
eager *adj* deseoso
eagerness *n* entusiasmo
eagle *n* águila
ear *n* oído, oreja; espiga
earache *n* dolor de oídos
eardrum *n* tímpano
early *adv* temprano
earmark *v* destinar
earn *v* ganar

earnestly *adv* en serio
earnings *n* salario
earphones *n* auriculares
earring *n* pendiente
earth *n* tierra
earthquake *n* terremoto
earwax *n* cera del oído
ease *v* aliviar; facilitar
ease *n* facilidad
easily *adv* fácilmente
east *n* este
eastbound *adj* hacia el este
Easter *n* Pascua
eastern *adj* oriental
easterner *n* del oriente
eastward *adv* hacia el este
easy *adj* fácil
eat *iv* comer
eat away *v* corroer
eavesdrop *v* escuchar
ebb *v* bajar, disminuir
eccentric *adj* escéntrico
echo *n* eco
eclipse *n* eclipse
ecology *n* ecología
economical *adj* económico
economize *v* ahorrar
economy *n* economía
ecstasy *n* éxtasis
ecstatic *adj* extático
edge *n* borde
edgy *adj* nervioso, tenso
edible *adj* comestible
edifice *n* edificio
edit *v* editar; cambiar
edition *n* edición
educate *v* educar
educational *adj* educativo
eerie *adj* misterioso

E

effect *n* efecto
effective *adj* vigente
effectiveness *n* eficacia
efficiency *n* eficiencia
efficient *adj* eficaz, eficiente
effigy *n* efigie
effort *n* esfuerzo
effusive *adj* efusivo
egg *n* huevo
egg white *n* clara
egoism *n* egoísmo
egoist *n* egoísta
eight *adj* ocho
eighteen *adj* dieciocho
eighth *adj* octavo
eighty *adj* ochenta
either *adj* cada uno (de dos)
either *adv* tampoco
eject *v* expulsar
elapse *v* transcurrir
elastic *adj* elástico
elated *adj* eufórico
elbow *n* codo
elder *n* mayor
elderly *adj* de edad
elect *v* elegir
election *n* elección
electric *adj* eléctrico
electrician *n* electricista
electricity *n* electricidad
electrify *v* electrificar
electrocute *v* electrocutar
electronic *adj* electrónico
elegance *n* elegancia
elegant *adj* elegante
element *n* elemento
elementary *adj* elemental
elephant *n* elefante
elevate *v* elevar

elevation *n* altura, elevación
elevator *n* ascensor
eleven *adj* once
eleventh *adj* undécimo
eligible *adj* elegible
eliminate *v* eliminar
elm *n* olmo
eloquence *n* elocuencia
else *adv* otro
elsewhere *adv* en otra parte
elude *v* eludir
elusive *adj* evasivo
emaciated *adj* demacrado
emanate *v* emanar
emancipate *v* emancipar
embalm *v* embalsamar
embark *v* embarcar
embarrass *v* avergonzar
embassy *n* embajada
embellish *v* embellecer
embers *n* ascua
embezzle *v* malversar
embitter *v* amargar
emblem *n* emblema
embody *v* personificar
emboss *v* grabar
embrace *v* abrazar; abarcar
embrace *n* abrazo
embroider *v* bordar
embroidery *n* bordado
embroil *v* meterse en líos
emerald *n* esmeralda
emerge *v* emergir, brotar
emergency *n* emergencia
emigrant *n* emigrante
emigrate *v* emigrar
emission *n* emisión
emit *v* emitir
emotion *n* emoción

E

emotional *adj* emocional
emperor *n* emperador
emphasis *n* énfasis
emphasize *v* hacer énfasis
empire *n* imperio
employ *v* emplear
employee *n* empleado
employer *n* patrón
employment *n* empleo
empress *n* emperatriz
emptiness *n* vacío
empty *adj* vacío
empty *v* vaciar
enable *v* permitir
enchant *v* encantar
enchanting *adj* encantador
encircle *v* cercar, rodear, circular
enclave *n* enclave
enclose *v* adjuntar; rodear, encerrar
enclosure *n* recinto
encompass *v* abarcar; rodear
encounter *v* encontrarse
encounter *n* encuentro
encourage *v* animar
encroach *v* usurpar
encyclopedia *n* enciclopedia
end *n* fin
end *v* terminar
end up *v* acabar en
endanger *v* poner en peligro
endeavor *v* esforzarse
endeavor *n* esfuerzo
ending *n* final
endless *adj* sin fin
endorse *v* endorsar; apoyar
endorsement *n* apoyo, respaldo
endure *v* aguantar
enemy *n* enemigo
energetic *adj* enérgetico

energy *n* energía
enforce *v* hacer cumplir, imponer
engage *v* dedicarse a
engaged *adj* comprometido
engagement *n* compromiso; batalla
engine *n* motor
engineer *n* ingeniero
England *n* Inglaterra
English *adj* inglés
engrave *v* grabar
engraving *n* grabado
engrossed *adj* absorto
engulf *v* envolver, devorar
enhance *v* realzar
enjoy *v* gozar
enjoyable *adj* agradable
enjoyment *n* gozo
enlarge *v* ampliar
enlargement *n* aumento
enlighten *v* iluminar
enlist *v* alistarse, reclutar
enormous *adj* enorme
enough *adv* bastante
enrage *v* enfurecer
enrich *v* enriquecer
enroll *v* inscribir(se)
enrollment *n* inscripción
ensure *v* asegurar
entail *v* llevar consigo
entangle *v* enredarse
enter *v* entrar
enterprise *n* empresa
entertain *v* entretener
entertaining *adj* divertido
entertainment *n* diversión
enthrall *v* cautivar
enthralling *adj* cautivador
enthuse *v* entusiasmar
enthusiasm *n* entusiasmo

entice *v* atraer
enticement *n* incentivo
enticing *adj* tentador
entire *adj* entero
entirely *adv* totalmente
entrance *n* entrada
entreat *v* suplicar
entree *n* plato
entrenched *adj* arraigado, atrincherado
entrepreneur *n* empresario
entrust *v* confiar
entry *n* entrada
enumerate *v* enumerar
envelop *v* envolver, cubrir
envelope *n* sobre
envious *adj* envidioso
environment *n* ambiente
envisage *v* imaginar
envoy *n* enviado
envy *n* envidia
envy *v* envidiar
epidemic *n* epidemia
epilepsy *n* epilepsia
episode *n* episodio
epistle *n* carta
epitaph *n* epitafio
epitomize *v* resumir
epoch *n* época
equal *adj* igual
equality *n* igualdad
equate *v* equiparar
equation *n* ecuación
equator *n* ecuador
equilibrium *n* equilibrio
equip *v* equipar
equipment *n* equipo
equivalent *adj* equivalente
era *n* época

eradicate *v* erradicar
erase *v* borrar
eraser *n* goma de borrar
erect *v* erigir, levantar
erect *adj* erguido, derecho, erecto
err *v* equivocarse
errand *n* mandado
erroneous *adj* erróneo
error *n* error
erupt *v* estallar, brotar
eruption *n* erupción, brote
escalate *v* intensificar
escalator *n* escalera eléctrica
escapade *n* aventura
escape *v* escaparse
escort *n* acompañar
esophagus *n* esófago
especially *adv* especialmente
espionage *n* espionaje
essay *n* ensayo; artículo
essence *n* esencia
essential *adj* esencial
establish *v* establecer
estate *n* finca, hacienda
esteem *v* estimar, apreciar
estimate *v* calcular
estimation *n* estima
estranged *adj* separado
estuary *n* estuario
eternity *n* eternidad
ethical *adj* ético
ethics *n* ética
etiquette *n* etiqueta
euphoria *n* euforia
Europe *n* Europa
European *adj* europeo
evacuate *v* evacuar
evade *v* evadir
evaluate *v* evaluar

E

E

evaporate *v* evaporar
evasion *n* evasión
evasive *adj* evasivo
eve *n* víspera
even *adj* llano, igualado
even if *c* aún si
even more *c* aún más
evening *n* tarde, noche
event *n* evento, acontecimiento
eventuality *n* eventualidad
eventually *adv* tarde o temprano, finalmente
ever *adv* alguna vez
everlasting *adj* perenne
every *adj* cada
everybody *pro* cada uno
everyday *adj* cotidiano
everyone *pro* cada uno
everything *pro* cualquier cosa
evict *v* desahuciar
evidence *n* evidencia
evil *n* mal
evil *adj* malo
evoke *v* evocar
evolution *n* evolución
evolve *v* evolucionar
exact *adj* exacto
exaggerate *v* exagerar
exalt *v* exaltar
examination *n* exámen
examine *v* examinar
example *n* ejemplo
exasperate *v* irritar
excavate *v* excavar
exceed *v* exceder
exceedingly *adv* sumamente
excel *v* sobresalir
excellence *n* excelencia
excellent *adj* excelente

except *pre* excepto
exception *n* excepción
exceptional *adj* excepcional
excerpt *n* extracto
excess *n* exceso
excessive *adj* excesivo
exchange *v* cambiar, intercambio
excite *v* entusiasmar
excitement *n* emoción
exciting *adj* emocionante
exclaim *v* exclamar
exclude *v* excluir
excruciating *adj* doloroso
excursion *n* excursión
excuse *v* excusar
excuse *n* excusa
execute *v* ejecutar
executive *n* ejecutivo
exemplary *adj* ejemplar
exemplify *v* ejemplificar
exempt *adj* exento
exemption *n* exención
exercise *n* ejercicio
exercise *v* hacer ejercicios
exert *v* esforzarse; ejercer
exertion *n* esfuerzo; ejercicio
exhaust *v* agotar, cansar
exhausting *adj* agotador
exhaustion *n* agotamiento
exhibit n exhibición
exhibit *v* exhibir, exponer
exhibition *n* exposición
exhilarating *adj* estimulante
exhort *v* exhortar
exile *v* desterrar
exile *n* destierro
exist *v* existir
existence *n* existencia
exit *n* salida**

exodus n éxodo
exonerate v exculpar
exorbitant adj exorbitante
exorcist n exorcista
exotic adj exótico
expand v ampliar, extender
expansion n expansión, ampliación
expect v esperar; suponer
expectancy n esperanza
expectation n expectativa
expediency n conveniencia
expedient adj conveniente
expedition n expedición
expel v expulsar
expenditure n gastos
expense n gasto
expensive adj caro
experience n experiencia
experiment n experimento
expert adj experto
expiate v expiar
expiation n expiación
expiration n caducidad, expiración
expire v caducar
explain v explicar
explicit adj explícito
explode v estallar
exploit v explotar
exploit n hazaña
exploitation n explotación
explore v explorar
explorer n explorador
explosion n explosión
explosive adj explosivo
export n exportación
export v exportar
expose v exponer
exposed adj expuesto
express adj expreso, rápido

expression n expresión
expressly adv expresamente
expropriate v expropiar
expulsion n expulsión
exquisite adj exquisito
extend v extender(se)
extension n prórroga, extensión
extent n medida, alcance
extenuating adj atenuante
exterior adj exterior, externo
exterminate v exterminar
external adj externo
extinct adj extinguido
extinguish v extinguir(se), apagar
extort v extorsionar
extortion n extorsión
extra adv de más
extract v sacar, extraer
extradite v extraditar
extradition n extradición
extraneous adj ajeno
extravagance n derroche
extravagant adj extravagante
extreme adj extremo
extremist adj extremista
extremities n extremidades
extricate v liberar
extroverted adj extrovertido
exude v rebosar
exult v alegrarse
eye n ojo
eyebrow n cejas
eye-catching adj llamativo
eyeglasses n gafas
eyelash n pestaña
eyelid n párpado
eyesight n vista
eyewitness n testigo ocular

E

F

fable *n* fábula
fabric *n* tela, tejido
fabricate *v* fabricar
fabulous *adj* fabuloso
face *n* cara
face up to *v* afrontar
facet *n* faceta; lado
facilitate *v* facilitar
facing *pre* frente a
fact *n* hecho
factor *n* factor
factory *n* fábrica
factual *adj* real
faculty *n* facultad
fad *n* novedad, moda
fade *v* desteñirse
faded *adj* descolorido
fail *v* fracasar
failure *n* fracaso
faint *v* desmayarse
faint *n* desmayo
faint *adj* vago, débil
fair *n* feria
fair *adj* justo; rubio, blanco
fairness *n* imparcialidad
fairy *n* hada
faith *n* fe; confianza
faithful *adj* fiel
fake *v* falsificar
fake *adj* falso
fall *n* caída; bajón
fall *iv* caer, descender
fall back *v* recurrir a
fall behind *v* retrasarse
fall down *v* caerse
fall through *v* fracasar

fallacy *n* error
fallout *n* consecuencia
falsehood *n* falsedad
falsify *v* falsificar
falter *v* fallar
fame *n* fama
familiar *adj* familiar
family *n* familia
famine *n* hambre
famous *adj* famoso
fan *n* ventilador; hincha
fanatic *adj* fanático
fancy *adj* lujoso
fang *n* colmillo
fantastic *adj* fantástico
fantasy *n* fantasía
far *adv* lejos
faraway *adj* lejano
farce *n* farsa
fare *n* precio del billete
farewell *n* despedida
farm *n* granja
farmer *n* agricultor, granjero
farming *n* cultivo
farmyard *n* corral
farther *adv* más lejos
fascinate *v* fascinar
fashion *n* moda
fashionable *adj* de moda
fast *adj* rápido
fasten *v* sujetar
fat *n* grasa, grueso, gordo
fat *adj* gordo
fatal *adj* fatal
fate *n* destino
fateful *adj* fatídico
father *n* padre
fatherhood *n* paternidad
father-in-law *n* suegro

fatherly *adj* paternal
fathom out *v* comprender
fatigue *n* fatiga
fatten *v* engordar
fatty *adj* grasoso
faucet *n* grifo, llave
fault *n* culpa, defecto
faulty *adj* defectuoso
favor *n* favor
favorable *adj* favorable
favorite *adj* favorito
fear *v* temer
fear *n* miedo
fearful *adj* miedoso, temeroso
feasible *adj* factible, viable
feast *n* fiesta
feat *n* proeza, hazaña
feather *n* pluma
feature *n* característica, rasgo
February *n* febrero
fed up *adj* harto
federal *adj* federal
fee *n* pago, cuota
feeble *adj* débil
feed *iv* alimentar
feedback *n* reacción, comentarios
feel *iv* sentir; pensar
feeling *n* sensación
feelings *n* sentimientos
feet *n* pies
feign *v* fingir
fellow *n* compañero
fellowship *n* compañerismo
felon *n* criminal
felony *n* crimen, delito
female *n* hembra, mujer
feminine *adj* femenino
fence *n* valla, cerca
fencing *n* esgrima

fend *v* valerse uno mismo
fend off *v* evitar, defend
fender *n* parachoque
ferment *v* fermentar
ferment *n* fermento
ferocious *adj* feroz
ferocity *n* ferocidad
ferry *n* barco
fertile *adj* fértil
fertility *n* fertilidad
fertilize *v* fertilizar
fervent *adj* ferviente
fester *v* enconarse
festive *adj* festivo
festivity *n* festividad
fetid *adj* fétido
fetus *n* feto
feud *n* enemistad
fever *n* fiebre
feverish *adj* con fiebre
few *adj* pocos
fewer *adj* menos
fiancé *n* novio
fiber *n* fibra
fickle *adj* voluble
fiction *n* ficción
fictitious *adj* ficticio
fiddle *n* violín
fidelity *n* fidelidad
field *n* campo
fierce *adj* feroz
fiery *adj* ardiente
fifteen *adj* quince
fifth *adj* quinto
fifty *adj* cincuenta
fifty-fifty *adv* a medias
fig *n* higo
fight *iv* luchar
fight *n* lucha

F

fighter n combatiente
figure n figura
figure out v resolver
file v archivar; limar
file n archivo; lima
fill v llenar
filling n relleno
film n película
filter n filtro
filter v filtrar
filth n suciedad
filthy adj sucio
fin n aleta
final adj final
finalize v finalizar
finance v financiar
financial adj financiero
find iv encontrar
find out v descubrir
fine fino
fine n multa
fine v multar
fine adv bien
fine adj elegante; bueno
fine print n letra pequeña
finger n dedo
fingernail n uña
fingerprint n huella dactilar
fingertip n punta del dedo
finish v terminar
Finland n Finlandia
Finnish adj finlandés
fire v disparar; despedir
fire n fuego
firearm n arma de fuego
firecracker n cohete
firefighter n bombero
fireman n bombero
fireplace n chimenea

firewood n leña
fireworks n fuegos artificiales
firm adj firme
firm n empresa, firme
firmness n firmeza
first adj primero
fish n pescado, pez
fisherman n pescador
fishy adj sospechoso
fist n puño
fit n ataque
fit v ajustar(se)
fitness n salud
fitting adj apropiado
five adj cinco
fix v arreglar
fjord n fiordo
flag n bandera
flagpole n asta de bandera
flamboyant adj extravagante
flame n llama
flammable adj inflamable
flank n flanquear
flare n llamarada
flare-up v encenderse
flash n destello
flashlight n linterna
flashy adj ostentoso
flat n apartamento, plano, piso
flat adj llano, chato
flatten v allanar
flatter v halagar
flattery n piropo
flaunt v alardear
flavor n gusto, sabor
flaw n defecto, fallo
flawless adj impecable
flea n pulga
flee iv huir

F

fleece *n* desplumar
fleet *n* flota
fleeting *adj* fugaz
flesh *n* carne
flex *v* tensar
flexible *adj* flexible
flicker *v* parpadear
flier *n* folleto; aviador
flight *n* vuelo, huida
flimsy *adj* débil
flip *v* dar la vuelta a
flirt *v* coquetear, flirtear
float *v* flotar
flock *n* rebaño
flog *v* azotar
flood *v* inundar
floodgate *n* compuerta
flooding *n* inundación
floodlight *n* foco
floor *n* suelo
flop *n* fracaso
floss *n* hilo dental
flour *n* harina
flourish *v* florecer
flow *v* circular
flow *n* flujo
flower *n* flor
flowerpot *n* tiesto
flu *n* gripe
fluctuate *v* fluctuar
fluently *adv* con fluidez
fluid *n* líquido, fluído
flunk *v* suspender
flush *v* tirar de
flute *n* flauta
flutter *v* aletear
fly *iv* volar
fly *n* mosca
foam *n* espuma

focus *n* foco
focus on *v* concentrarse
foe *n* enemigo
fog *n* niebla
foggy *adj* brumoso, nubloso
foil *v* frustrar
fold *v* doblar
folder *n* carpeta
folks *n* familiares
folksy *adj* popular
follow *v* seguir
follower *n* seguidor
folly *n* locura
fond *adj* aficionado; cariñoso
fondle *v* tocar, acariciar
fondness *n* cariño
food *n* comida
foodstuff *n* comestibles
fool *v* engañar
fool *adj* tonto
foolproof *adj* infalible
foot *n* pie
football *n* fútbol
footnote *n* nota
footprint *n* huella
footstep *n* paso
footwear *n* calzado
for *pre* para
forbid *iv* prohibir
force *n* fuerza
force *v* forzar
forceful *adj* enérgico
forcibly *adv* a la fuerza
forecast *iv* pronosticar
forefront *n* vanguardia
foreground *n* primer plano
forehead *n* frente
foreign *adj* extranjero; ajeno
foreigner *n* extranjero

foreman *n* capataz
foremost *adj* principal
foresee *iv* prever
foreshadow *v* presagiar
foresight *n* previsión
forest *n* bosque
foretaste *n* anticipo
foretell *v* pronosticar
forever *adv* para siempre
forewarn *v* avisar
foreword *n* prólogo
forfeit *v* renunciar
forge *v* falsificar
forgery *n* falsificación
forget *v* olvidar
forgivable *adj* perdonable
forgive *v* perdonar
forgiveness *n* perdón
fork *n* tenedor
form *n* forma
formal *adj* formal
formality *n* trámite
formalize *v* formalizar
formally *adv* oficialmente, formalmente
format *n* formato
formation *n* formación
former *adj* anterior, primero
formerly *adv* antes
formidable *adj* formidable
formula *n* fórmula
forsake *iv* abandonar
fort *n* fuerte
forthcoming *adj* próximo
forthright *adj* franco, directo
fortify *v* fortificar
fortitude *n* fortaleza
fortress *n* fortaleza
fortunate *adj* afortunado

fortune *n* fortuna
forty *adj* cuarenta
forward *adv* adelante
fossil *n* fósil
foster *v* fomentar; acoger
foul *adj* asqueroso
foundation *n* fundación,base
founder *n* fundador
foundry *n* fundición
fountain *n* fuente
four *adj* cuatro
fourteen *adj* catorce
fourth *adj* cuarto
fox *n* zorro
foxy *adj* atractiva
fraction *n* fracción
fracture *n* fractura
fragile *adj* frágil
fragment *n* fragmento, trozo
fragrance *n* fragancia
fragrant *adj* oloroso
frail *adj* frágil, débil
frailty *n* fragilidad
frame *n* marco; montura
frame *v* enmarcar
framework *n* estructura; marco
France *n* Francia
franchise *n* franquicia
frank *adj* franco
frankly *adv* francamente
frankness *n* franqueza
frantic *adj* fuera de sí
fraternal *adj* fraternal
fraternity *n* fraternidad
fraud *n* fraude
fraudulent *adj* fraudulento
freckle *n* peca
freckled *adj* pecoso
free *v* liberar

free *adj* libre; gratis
freedom *n* libertad
freeway *n* autopista
freeze *iv* congelar
freezer *n* congelador
freezing n congelación
freezing *adj* helado
freight *n* carga
French *adj* francés
frenetic *adj* frenético
frenzied *adj* frenético
frenzy *n* frenesí
frequency *n* frecuencia
frequent *adj* frecuente
frequent *v* frecuentar
fresh *adj* fresco, nuevo
freshen *v* refrescar
freshness *n* frescura
friar *n* fraile
friction *n* fricción, roce
Friday *n* viernes
fried *adj* frito, freído
friend *n* amigo
friendship *n* amistad
fries *n* papas fritas
frigate *n* fragata
fright *n* susto
frighten *v* asustar
frightening *adj* aterrador
frigid *adj* frígido
fringe *n* margen, flequillo
frivolous *adj* frívolo
frog *n* rana
from *pre* de, desde
front *n* frente, portada, fachada
front *adj* delantero
frontage *n* fachada
frontier *n* frontera
frost *n* helada, escarcha

frostbite *n* congelación
frostbitten *adj* congelado
frosty *adj* glacial
frown *v* fruncir el ceño
frozen *adj* helado, congelado
frugal *adj* frugal
frugality *n* frugalidad
fruit *n* fruta, fruto
fruitful *adj* provechoso
fruity *adj* afrutado
frustrate *v* frustrar
frustration *n* frustración
fry *v* freír
frying pan *n* sartén
fuel *n* combustible
fuel *v* mantener
fugitive *n* fugitivo
fulfill *v* realizar
fulfillment *n* satisfacción
full *adj* lleno
fully *adv* completamente
fumes *n* gases
fumigate *v* fumigar
fun *n* diversión
function *n* función
fund *n* fondo, reserva
fund *v* financiar
fundamental *adj* fundamental
funds *n* fondos
funeral *n* funeral
fungus *n* hongo
funny *adj* gracioso
fur *n* piel, pelaje
furious *adj* furioso
furiously *adv* furiosamente
furnace *n* horno
furnish *v* amueblar; proveer
furnishings *n* muebles
furniture *n* muebles

F

furor *n* furor
furrow *n* surco
furry *adj* peludo
further *adv* más lejos
furthermore *adv* además
fury *n* furia
fuse *n* fusible
fuss *n* conmoción
fussy *adj* exigente
futile *adj* inútil
futility *n* inutilidad
future *n* futuro
fuzzy *adj* borroso

F
G

G

gadget *n* aparato
gag *n* mordaza
gag *v* amordazar
gage *v* medir
gain *v* ganar
gain *n* ganancia
gal *n* moza
galaxy *n* galacia
gale *n* vendaval
gall bladder *n* vesícula biliar
gallant *adj* galante
gallery *n* galería
gallon *n* galón
gallop *v* galopar
gallows *n* horca
galvanize *v* galvanizar
gamble *v* arriesgar
game *n* juego
gang *n* pandilla

gangrene *n* gangrena
gangster *n* gangster
gap *n* hueco; intervalo
garage *n* garaje
garbage *n* basura
garden *n* jardín
gardener *n* jardinero
gargle *v* hacer gárgaras
garland *n* guirnalda
garlic *n* ajo
garment *n* vestido
garnish *v* adornar
garnish *n* adorno, aderezo
garrison *n* guarnición
garrulous *adj* charlatán
garter *n* liga
gas *n* gas
gash *n* corte profundo
gasoline *n* gasolina
gasp *v* jadear
gastric *adj* gástrico
gate *n* puerta
gather *v* recoger
gathering *n* reunión
gauge *v* medir, calibrar
gauze *n* gasa, venda
gaze *v* mirar fijamente
gear *n* marcha; equipo
geese *n* gansos
gem *n* piedra preciosa
gender *n* género
gene *n* gen
general *n* general
generalize *v* generalizar
generate *v* generar
generation *n* generación
generator *n* generador
generic *adj* genérico
generosity *n* generosidad

G

genetic *adj* genético
genial *adj* simpático
genius *n* genio
genocide *n* genocidio
genteel *adj* elegante
gentle *adj* suave, tierno
gentleman *n* caballero
gentleness *n* suavidad
genuflect *v* arrodillarse
genuine *adj* auténtico
geography *n* geografía
geology *n* geología
geometry *n* geometría
germ *n* microbio, germen
German *adj* alemán
Germany *n* Alemania
gerund *n* gerundio
gestation *n* gestación
gesticulate *v* hacer gestos
gesture *n* gesto, muestra
get *iv* obtener
get along *v* llevarse bien
get away *v* escaparse
get back *v* volver
get by *v* manejarse
get down *v* bajarse
get down to *v* ponerse a
get in *v* entrar
get off *v* apearse
get out *v* salir
get over *v* recobrarse
get together *v* reunirse
get up *v* levantarse
getaway n fuga
geyser *n* géiser
ghastly *adj* espantoso
ghost *n* fantasma
giant *n* gigante
gift *n* regalo

gifted *adj* dotado
gigantic *adj* enorme
giggle *v* reírse tontamente
gimmick *n* truco
ginger *n* jenjibre
gingerly *adv* con cuidado
giraffe *n* girafa
girl *n* chica
girlfriend *n* amiga
give *iv* dar
give away *v* regalar
give back *v* devolver
give in *v* ceder
give out *v* distribuir
give up *v* rendirse
glacier *n* glaciar
glad *adj* contento
gladiator *n* gladiador
glamorous *adj* atractivo
glance *v* ojear
glance *n* ojeada
gland *n* glándula
glare *n* brillo
glass *n* vaso; vidrio
glasses *n* gafas
glassware *n* cristalería
gleam *n* resplandor
gleam *v* brillar
glide *v* planear
glimmer *n* luz tenue; rayo
glimpse *n* vistazo
glimpse *v* vislumbrar
glitter *v* relucir
globe *n* globo
globule *n* glóbulo
gloom *n* obscuridad
gloomy *adj* obscuro; triste
glorify *v* glorificar
glorious *adj* glorioso

glory *n* gloria
gloss *n* brillo
glossary *n* glosario
glossy *adj* brilloso
glove *n* guante
glow *v* brillar
glucose *n* glucosa
glue *n* goma de pegar
glue *v* pegar
glut *n* abundancia
glutton *n* glotón
gnaw *v* roer
go *iv* ir
go ahead *v* seguir adelante
go away *v* marcharse
go back *v* volver
go down *v* bajar
go in *v* entrar
go on *v* continuar
go out *v* salir
go over *v* examinar
go through *v* atravesar
go under *v* hundirse
go up *v* subir
goad *v* aguijonear
goal *n* objectivo, meta; gol
goalkeeper *n* portero
goat *n* cabra
gobble *v* engullir, devorar
go-between n mediador
God *n* Dios
goddess *n* diosa
godless *adj* ateo
godsend n bendición
goggles *n* gafas, espejuelos de protección
gold *n* oro
golden *adj* dorado
good *adj* bueno

good-looking *adj* guapo
goodness *n* bondad
goods *n* mercancía
goodwill *n* buena voluntad
goof *v* meter la pata
goose *n* ganso
gore v cornear
gorge *n* barranco
gorgeous *adj* muy bueno
gorilla *n* gorila
gory *adj* sangriento
gosh e caramba
gospel *n* evangelio
gossip *v* cotillear
gossip *n* chisme
gout *n* gota
govern *v* gobernar
government *n* gobierno
governor *n* gobernador
gown *n* bata; toga
grab *v* coger, agarrar
grace *n* gracia
graceful *adj* elegante
gracious *adj* amable
grade *n* nota
gradual *adj* gradual
graduate *v* graduarse
graduation *n* graduación
graft *v* injertar
graft *n* injerto; soborno
grain *n* grano
gram *n* gramo
grammar *n* gramática
grand *adj* grandioso
grandchild *n* nieto
granddad *n* abuelito
grandfather *n* abuelo
grandmother *n* abuela
grandparents *n* abuelos

grandson *n* nieto

grandstand *n* tribuna

granite *n* granito

granny *n* abuelita

grant *v* conceder, otorgar

grant *n* beca; subvención

grape *n* uva

grapefruit *n* toronja

grapevine *n* vid

graphic *adj* gráfico, descriptivo

grasp *n* comprensión

grasp *v* agarrar; entender

grass *n* hierba, césped

grassroots *adj* popular

grate *v* rallar

grateful *adj* agradecido

gratify *v* gratificar

gratifying *adj* grato

gratitude *n* gratitud

gratuity *n* propina

grave *adj* grave, serio

grave *n* sepultura

gravel *n* grava

gravely *adv* gravemente

gravestone *n* lápida

graveyard *n* cementerio

gravitate *v* gravitar

gravity *n* gravedad

gravy *n* salsa

gray *adj* gris

grayish *adj* canoso

graze *v* pacer; rozar

graze *n* rasguño; roce

grease *v* engrasar

grease *n* grasa

greasy *adj* grasoso

great *adj* magnífico

greatest adj el mayor, mejor, más
  importante

greatness *n* grandeza

Greece *n* Grecia

greed *n* avaricia

greedy *adj* avaro

Greek *adj* griego

green *adj* verde

green bean *n* vaina, ejote

greenhouse *n* invernadero

Greenland *n* Groenlandia

greet *v* saludar

greetings *n* saludos

gregarious *adj* social

grenade *n* granada

greyhound *n* galgo

gridlock n atasco

grief *n* pena

grievance *n* queja

grieve *v* sufrir por

grill *v* asar; interrogar

grill *n* parrilla

grim *adj* sombrío

grimace *n* mueca

grime *n* mugre, suciedad

grind *iv* moler; rechinar

grip *v* agarrar

grip *n* asa

gripe *n* queja

grisly *adj* horrible

groan *v* gemir, gruñir

groan *n* quejido

groceries *n* comestibles

groin *n* ingle

groom *n* novio

groom v arreglarse

groove *n* ranura

gross *adj* grosero; bruto

grossly *adv* sumamente

grotesque *adj* grotesco

grotto *n* gruta

G

grouch *v* refunfuñar
grouchy *adj* quejón, gruñón
ground *n* suelo, tierra; motivo
ground floor *n* planta baja
groundless *adj* sin fundamento
groundwork *n* preparación
group *n* grupo
grow *iv* crecer
grow up *v* criarse
growl *v* gruñir; rugir
grown-up *n* adulto
growth *n* crecimiento
grudge *n* rencor
grudgingly *adv* de mala gana
grueling *adj* duro, agotador
gruesome *adj* horrible
grumble *v* refunfuñar
grumpy *adj* gruñón
guarantee *v* garantizar
guarantee *n* garantía
guarantor *n* garante
guard *n* guarda
guard *v* vigilar
guardian *n* guardián
guerrilla *n* guerrillero
guess *v* adivinar
guess *n* conjetura
guest *n* invitado
guidance *n* orientación
guide *v* guiar
guide *n* guía
guidebook *n* manual
guidelines *n* normas
guild *n* gremio
guile *n* astucia, fraude
guillotine *n* guillotina
guilt *n* culpa
guilty *adj* culpable
guise *n* apariencia

guitar *n* guitarra
gulf *n* golfo
gull *n* gaviota
gullible *adj* crédulo
gulp *v* tragar
gulp *n* trago
gulp down *v* engullir
gum *n* encía; goma
gun *n* pistola
gun down *v* matar a tiros
gunfire *n* disparos
gunman *n* pistolero
gunpowder *n* pólvora
gunshot *n* tiro
gust *n* ráfaga de viento
gusto *n* ilusión, gusto
gusty *adj* ventoso
gut *n* intestino, tripa
guts *n* agallas, valor
gutter *n* canalón, cuneta
guy *n* tipo, gente
guzzle *v* tragar
gymnasium *n* gimnasio
gynecology *n* ginecología
gypsy *n* gitano
gyrate *v* girar

habit *n* costumbre, hábito
habitable *adj* habitable
habitual *adj* habitual
hack *v* dar tajos; piratear
haggle *v* regatear
hail *n* granizo

hail *v* granizar; aclamar
hair *n* pelo
hairbrush *n* cepillo de pelo
haircut *n* corte de pelo
hairdo *n* peinado
hairdresser *n* peluquera
hairpiece *n* peluca
hairy *adj* peludo
half *n* mitad
half *adj* medio
hall *n* pasillo, sala
hallucinate *v* halucinar
hallway *n* pasillo
halt *v* parar, detenerse
halve *v* partir por la mitad
ham *n* jamón
hamburger *n* hamburguesa
hamlet *n* aldea
hammer *n* martillo
hammer *v* martillar
hammock *n* hamaca
hamper n cesta
hamper v poner trabas
hand *n* mano
hand down *v* transmitir
hand in *v* entregar
hand out *v* repartir
hand over *v* entregar
handbag *n* bolso
handbook *n* manual
handcuff *v* esposar
handcuffs *n* esposas
handful *n* puñado
handgun *n* pistola
handicap *n* desventaja
handkerchief *n* pañuelo
handle *v* manejar
handle *n* asa
handmade *adj* hecho a mano

handout *n* limosna
handrail *n* barandilla
handshake *n* apretón de manos
handsome *adj* guapo
handwriting *n* escritura
handy *adj* práctico
hang *iv* ahorcar
hang around *v* quedarse
hang on *v* esperar
hang up *v* colgar
hanger *n* percha
hang-up *n* complejo
happen *v* suceder
happening *n* suceso
happiness *n* felicidad
happy *adj* feliz
harass *v* acosar
harassment *n* acoso
harbor *n* puerto
harbor *v* proteger, albergar
hard *adj* duro
harden *v* endurecer
hardly *adv* apenas
hardness *n* dureza
hardship *n* privación
hardware *n* ferretería
hardwood *n* leña
hardy *adj* fuerte
hare *n* liebre
harm *v* dañar
harm *n* daño
harmful *adj* dañino
harmless *adj* inofensivo
harmonize *v* armonizar
harmony *n* armonía
harp *n* arpa
harpoon *n* arpón
harrowing *adj* horrendo
harsh *adj* severo

H

H

harshly *adv* con dureza
harshness *n* dureza
harvest *n* cosecha
harvest *v* cosechar
hassle *v* molestar
hassle *n* lata
haste *n* prisa
hasten *v* apresurar(se)
hastily *adv* apresudaramente
hasty *adj* apresurado
hat *n* sombrero
hatch *v* tramar
hatchet *n* hacha
hate *v* odiar
hateful *adj* odioso
hatred *n* odio
haughty *adj* altanero
haul *v* transportar
haunt *v* perseguir
have *iv* tener
have to *v* tener que
haven *n* refugio
havoc *n* estragos
hawk *n* halcón
hay *n* heno
haystack *n* pajar
hazard *n* peligro
hazardous *adj* peligroso
haze *n* neblina
hazelnut *n* avellana
hazy *adj* brumoso
he *pro* él
head *n* cabeza
head for *v* dirigirse a
headache *n* dolor de cabeza
heading *n* encabezamiento
head-on *adv* de frente
headphones *n* auriculares
headquarters *n* sede central

headway *n* progreso
heal *v* curar
healer *n* curandero
health *n* salud
healthy *adj* sano
heap *n* montón
heap *v* amontonar
hear *iv* oir
hearing *n* oído
hearsay *n* rumor
hearse *n* coche fúnebre
heart *n* corazón
heartbeat *n* latido
heartburn *n* acidez
hearten *v* animar
heartfelt *adj* sincero
hearth *n* chimenea
heartless *adj* despiadado
hearty *adj* sano, bueno
heat *v* calentar
heat *n* calor
heat wave *n* ola de calor
heater *n* calentador
heathen *n* pagano
heating *n* calefacción
heatstroke *n* insolación
heaven *n* cielo
heavenly *adj* celestial
heaviness *n* pesadez
heavy *adj* pesado
heckle *v* abuchear
hectic *adj* agitado
heed *v* hacer caso
heel *n* talón, tacón
hefty adj sustancial
height *n* altura
heighten *v* elevar
heinous *adj* horrible
heir *n* heredero

heiress *n* heredera
heist *n* robo violento
helicopter *n* helicóptero
hell *n* infierno
hello *e* hola
helm *n* timón
helmet *n* casco
help *v* ayudar
help *n* ayuda
helper *n* ayudante
helpful *adj* útil
helpless *adj* impotente
hem *n* dobladillo
hemisphere *n* hemisferio
hemorrhage *n* hemorragia
hen *n* gallina
hence *adv* por lo tanto
henchman *n* sicario
her *adj* su, de ella
herald *v* anunciar
herald *n* heraldo, anuncio
herb *n* hierba
here *adv* aquí
hereafter *adv* en el futuro
hereby *adv* por la presente
hereditary *adj* hereditario
heresy *n* herejía
heretic *adj* herético
heritage *n* patrimonio
hermetic *adj* hermético
hermit *n* ermitaño
hernia *n* hernia
hero *n* héroe
heroic *adj* heróico
heroin *n* heroína
heroism *n* heroísmo
hers *pro* suya, de ella
herself *pro* ella misma
hesitant *adj* vacilante

hesitate *v* vacilar
hesitation *n* vacilación
heyday *n* apogeo
hiccup *n* hipo
hidden *adj* oculto
hide *iv* esconder
hideaway *n* escondite
hideous *adj* horrendo
hierarchy *n* jerarquía
high *adj* alto
highlight *n* punto culminante
highlight *v* resaltar
highly *adv* altamente
Highness *n* Alteza
highway *n* carretera
hijack *v* secuestrar
hijacker *n* secuestrador
hijacking *n* secuestro
hike *v* caminar; aumentar
hike *n* caminata; subida
hilarious *adj* divertido
hill *n* colina
hillside *n* ladera
hilltop *n* cima
hilly *adj* montañoso
hilt *n* puño
himself *pro* el mismo
hinder *v* obstaculizar
hindrance *n* impedimento
hindsight *n* retrospectiva
hinge *v* depender
hinge *n* bisagra
hint *n* pista
hint *v* dar a entender
hip *n* cadera
hire *v* alquilar
his *adj* su
his *pro* suyo, de él
Hispanic *adj* hispano

H

hiss *v* silbar
historian *n* historiador
historic adj histórico
history *n* historia
hit *n* golpe, éxito
hit *iv* golpear
hit back *v* responder
hitch *n* problema
hitch up *v* enganchar
hitchhike *n* autostop
hitherto *adv* hasta ahora
hive *n* colmena
hoard *v* acumular
hoarse *adj* ronco
hoax *n* engaño
hobby *n* pasatiempo
hoe n azada
hog *n* cerdo
hoist *v* levantar, alzar
hoist *n* montacargas
hold *iv* sostener, tener
hold back *v* guardar
hold on to *v* afferrarse
hold out *v* aguantar
hold up *v* atracar
holdup *n* atraco
hole *n* agujero
holiday *n* día de fiesta
holiness *n* santidad
Holland *n* Holanda
hollow *adj* hueco, vacío
holocaust *n* holocausto
holy *adj* santo
homage *n* homenaje
home *n* casa
homeland *n* patria
homeless *adj* sin hogar
homely *adj* acogedor
homemade *adj* casero

homesick *adj* nostálgico
hometown *n* ciudad natal
homework *n* tareas
homicide *n* homicidio
homily *n* sermón
honest *adj* honesto
honesty *n* honestidad
honey *n* miel
honeymoon *n* luna de miel
honk *v* pitar, tocar
honor *n* honor
hood *n* capucha
hoodlum *n* malvado
hoof *n* pezuña
hook *n* gancho; anzuelo
hook *v* enganchar
hooligan *n* gamberro
hoop n aro
hop *v* saltar, brincar
hope *n* esperanza
hope *v* esperar
hopeful *adj* optimista
hopefully *adv* con tiempo
hopeless *adj* sin remedio, inútil
horizon *n* horizonte
horizontal *adj* horizontal
hormone *n* hormona
horn *n* cuerno
horrendous *adj* horrendo
horrible *adj* horrible
horrific adj horroroso
horrify *v* horrorizar
horror *n* horror
horror *adj* de miedo
horse *n* caballo
horseshoe n herradura
hose *n* manguera
hospital *n* hospital
hospitality *n* hospitalidad

hospitalize v hospitalizar
host n huésped, anfitrión
hostage n rehén
hostess n anfitriona
hostile adj hostil, enemigo
hostility n hostilidad
hot adj caliente
hotel n hotel
hound n perro de caza
hound v acosar
hour n hora
hourly adv cada hora
house n casa
household n hogar, familia
household adj familiar
housekeeper n sirvienta
housewife n ama de casa
housework n faenas de casa
hover v flotar en el aire
how adv cómo
however c sin embargo
howl v aullar
howl n aullido
hub n centro
huddle v acurrucarse
hug v abrazar
hug n abrazo
huge adj grande, enorme
hull n casco
hum v tararear
human adj humano
human being n ser humano
humane adj humano
humanitarian adj humanitario
humanities n humanidades
humankind n humanidad
humble adj humilde
humbly adv humíldemente
humid adj húmedo

humidity n humedad
humiliate v humillar
humility n humildad
humor n humor
humorous adj gracioso
hump n joroba
hunch n presentimiento
hunchback n joroba
hunched adj jorobado
hundred adj cien
hundredth adj centésimo
hunger n hambre
hungry adj hambriento
hunt v cazar
hunter n cazador
hunting n caza
hurdle n obstáculo
hurl v arrojar, lanzar
hurricane n huracán
hurriedly adv apresuradamente
hurry v apresurarse
hurry up v dase prisa
hurt iv herir, doler
hurt adj herido
hurtful adj hiriente
husband n marido
hush n silencio
hush up v encubrir
husky adj ronco
hustle n ajetreo, bullicio
hut n cabaña
hydraulic adj hidráulico
hydrogen n hidrógeno
hyena n hiena
hygiene n higiene
hymn n himno
hyphen n guión
hypnosis n hipnosis
hypnotize v hipnotizar

H

I

hypocrisy *n* hipocresía
hypocrite *adj* hipócrita
hysteria *n* histeria
hysterical *adj* histérico

I *pro* yo
ice *n* hielo
ice cream *n* helado
ice cube *n* cubo de hielo
ice skate *v* patinar
iceberg *n* iceberg
icebox *n* congelador
ice-cold *adj* helado
icon *n* icono
icy *adj* helado
idea *n* idea
ideal *adj* ideal
identical *adj* idéntico
identify *v* identificar
identity *n* identidad
ideology *n* ideología
idiom *n* modismo
idiot *n* idiota
idiotic *adj* idiota
idle *adj* ocioso
idol *n* ídolo
idolatry *n* idolatría
if *c* si
ignite *v* encender
ignorance *n* ignorancia
ignorant *adj* ignorante
ignore *v* ignorar
ill *adj* enfermo

illegal *adj* ilegal
illegible *adj* ilegible
illegitimate *adj* ilegítimo
illicit *adj* ilícito
illiterate *adj* analfabeto
illness *n* enfermedad
illogical *adj* ilógico
illuminate *v* iluminar
illusion *n* ilusión
illustrate *v* ilustrar
illustration *n* ilustración
illustrious *adj* ilustre
image *n* imagen
imagination *n* imaginación
imagine *v* imaginarse
imbalance *n* desequilibrio
imitate *v* imitar
imitation *n* imitación
immaculate *adj* inmaculado
immature *adj* inmaduro
immaturity *n* inmadurez
immediately *adv* inmediatamente
immense *adj* inmenso
immensity *n* inmensidad
immerse *v* sumergir
immersion *n* inmersión
immigrant *n* inmigrante
immigrate *v* inmigrar
immigration *n* inmigración
imminent *adj* inminente
immobile *adj* inmóvil
immobilize *v* inmobilizar
immoral *adj* inmoral
immorality *n* inmoralidad
immortal *adj* inmortal
immortality *n* inmortalidad
immune *adj* inmune
immunity *n* inmunidad
immunize *v* inmunizar

immutable *adj* inmutable
impact *n* impacto
impact *v* impactar
impair *v* perdudicar
impartial *adj* imparcial
impatience *n* impaciencia
impatient *adj* impaciente
impeccable *adj* impecable
impediment *n* obstáculo
impending *adj* inminente
imperfection *n* imperfección
imperial *adj* imperial
imperialism *n* imperialismo
impersonal *adj* impersonal
impertinence *n* impertinencia
impertinent *adj* impertinente
impetuous *adj* impetuoso
implacable *adj* implacable
implant *v* implantar
implement *v* implementar
implicate *v* implicar
implication *n* implicación
implicit *adj* implícito
implore *v* implorar
imply *v* implicar
impolite *adj* mal educado
import *v* importar
importance *n* importancia
importation *n* importación
impose *v* imponer
imposing *adj* imponente
imposition *n* imposición
impossibility *n* imposibilidad
impossible *adj* imposible
impotent *adj* impotente
impound *v* embargar
impoverished *adj* empobrecido
impractical *adj* impráctico
imprecise *adj* impreciso

impress *v* impresionar
impressive *adj* impresionante
imprison *v* encarcelar
improbable *adj* improbable
impromptu *adv* improvisado
improper *adj* incorrecto, impropio
improve *v* mejorar
improvement *n* mejora
improvise *v* improvisar
impulse *n* impulso
impulsive *adj* impulsivo
impunity *n* impunidad
impure *adj* impuro
in *pre* en
in depth *adv* a fondo
inability *n* incapacidad
inaccessible *adj* inacesible
inaccurate *adj* incorrecto
inadequate *adj* insuficiente
inadmissible *adj* inadmisible
inappropriate *adj* inapropiado
inasmuch as *c* ya que
inaugurate *v* inaugurar
inauguration *n* inaguración
incalculable *adj* incalculable
incapable *adj* incapaz
incapacitate *v* incapacitar
incarcerate *v* encarcelar
incense *n* incienso
incentive *n* incentivo
inception *n* principio
incessant *adj* incesante
inch *n* pulgada
incident *n* incidente
incidentally *adv* a propósito
incision *n* incisión
incite *v* provocar
incitement *n* provocación
inclination *n* inclinación

incline v inclinar
include v incluir
inclusive adv incluído
incoherent adj incoherente
income n ingresos
incoming adj entrante
incompatible adj incompatible
incompetence n incompetencia
incompetent adj incompetente
incomplete adj incompleto
inconsistent adj incongruente
incontinence n incontinencia
inconvenient adj inconveniente
incorporate v incorporar
incorrect adj incorrecto
incorrigible adj incorregible
increase v aumentar
increase n aumento
increasing adj creciente
incredible adj increíble
increment n incremento
incriminate v incriminar
incur v incurrir
incurable adj incurable
indecency n indecencia
indecision n indecisión
indecisive adj indeciso
indeed adv ciertamente
indefinite adj indefinido
indemnify v indemnizar
indemnity n indemnización
independence n independencia
independent adj independiente
index n índice
indicate v indicar
indication n indicación, indicio
indict v acusar
indifference n indiferencia
indifferent adj indiferente

indigent adj indigente
indigestion n indigestión
indirect adj indirecto
indiscreet adj indiscreto
indiscretion n indiscreción
indispensable adj indispensable
indisposed adj indispuesto
indisputable adj indiscutible
indivisible adj indivisible
indoctrinate v adoctrinar
indoor adv dentro
induce v provocar
indulge v satisfacer
indulgent adj indulgente
industrious adj trabajador
industry n industria
ineffective adj ineficaz
inefficient adj ineficiente
inept adj inepto
inequality n desigualdad
inevitable adj inevitable
inexcusable adj inexcusable
inexpensive adj económico, barato
inexperienced adj inexperto
inexplicable adj inexplicable
infallible adj infalible
infamous adj infame
infancy n infancia
infant n bebé
infantry n infantería
infect v infectar
infection n infección
infectious adj contagioso
infer v inferir, deducir
inferior adj inferior
infertile adj estéril
infested adj plagado
infidelity n infidelidad
infiltrate v infiltrar

infiltration *n* infiltración
infinite *adj* infinito
infirmary *n* enfermería
inflammation *n* inflamación
inflate *v* inflar, hinchar
inflation *n* inflación
inflexible *adj* inflexible
inflict *v* infligir
influence *n* influencia
influential *adj* influyente
influenza *n* gripe
influx *n* afluencia
inform *v* informar
informal *adj* informal
informality *n* informalidad
informant *n* confidente
information *n* información
informer *n* chivato
infraction *n* infracción
infrequent *adj* infrecuente
infringe *v* infringir, vulnerar
infringement *n* vulneración
infuriate *v* enloquecer
infusion *n* infusión
ingenuity *n* ingeniosidad
ingest *v* ingerir
ingot *n* lingote
ingrained *adj* arraigado
ingratiate *v* engraciarse
ingratitude *n* ingratitud
ingredient *n* ingrediente
inhabit *v* habitar
inhabitable *adj* inhabitable
inhabitant *n* habitante
inhale *v* inhalar
inherit *v* heredar
inheritance *n* herencia
inhibit *v* impedir
inhuman *adj* inhumano

initial *adj* inicial
initially *adv* al principio
initials *n* iniciales
initiate *v* empezar
initiative *n* iniciativa
inject *v* inyectar
injection *n* inyección
injure *v* herir
injurious *adj* dañoso
injury *n* herida
injustice *n* injusticia
ink *n* tinta
inkling *n* sospecha
inlaid *adj* incrustado
inland *adv* adentro
inland *adj* interior
in-laws *n* suegros
inmate *n* recluso
inn *n* posada, mesón
innate *adj* innato
inner *adj* interior
innocence *n* inocencia
innocent *adj* inocente
innovation *n* novedad
innuendo *n* indirecta
innumerable *adj* innumerable
input *n* aportación, entrada
inquest *n* investigación
inquire *v* preguntar.
inquiry *n* indagación, pregunat,
  investigación
inquisition *n* inquisición
insane *adj* loco
insanity *n* locura
insatiable *adj* insaciable
inscription *n* inscripción
insect *n* insecto
insecurity *n* inseguridad
insensitive *adj* insensible

inseparable *adj* inseparable
insert *v* introducir, insertar
insertion *n* inserción
inside *adj* interior
inside *pre* dentro de
inside out *adv* al revés
insignificant *adj* insignificante
insincere *adj* falso
insincerity *n* insinceridad
insinuate *v* insinuar
insinuation *n* insinuación
insipid *adj* insípido
insist *v* insistir
insistence *n* insistencia
insolent *adj* descarado
insoluble *adj* insoluble
insomnia *n* insomnio
inspect *v* inspeccionar
inspection *n* inspeción
inspector *n* inspector
inspiration *n* inspiración
inspire *v* inspirar
instability *n* inestabilidad
install *v* instalar
installation *n* instalación
installment *n* plazo
instance *n* ejemplo
instant *n* instante
instantly *adv* al momento
instead *adv* en lugar de
instigate *v* instigar
instill *v* inculcar
instinct *n* instinto
institute *v* establecer
institution *n* institución
instruct *v* instruír
instructor *n* instructor
insufficient *adj* insuficiente
insulate *v* aislar

insulation *n* aislamiento
insult *v* insultar
insult *n* insulto
insurance *n* seguro
insure *v* asegurar
insurgency *n* insurgencia
insurrection *n* insurrección
intact *adj* intacto
intake *n* ingestión
integrate *v* integrar
integration *n* integración
integrity *n* integridad
intelligent *adj* inteligente
intend *v* tener intención
intense *adj* intenso
intensify *v* intensificar
intensity *n* intensidad
intensive *adj* intensivo
intention *n* intención
intercede *v* interceder
intercept *v* interceptar
intercession *n* intercesión
interchange *v* intercambiar
interchange *n* intersección
interest *n* interés
interested *adj* interesado
interesting *adj* interesante
interfere *v* interferir
interference *n* interferencia
interior *adj* interior
interlude *n* intervalo
intermediary *n* intermediario
intern *v* internar
interpret *v* interpretar
interpretation *n* interpretación
interpreter *n* intérprete
interrogate *v* interrogar
interrupt *v* interrumpir
interruption *n* interrupción

intersect *v* cruzarse
intertwine *v* entrelazar
interval *n* intervalo
intervene *v* intervenir
intervention *n* intervención
interview *n* entrevista
intestine *n* intestino
intimacy *n* intimidad
intimate *adj* íntimo
intimidate *v* meter miedo
intolerable *adj* intolerable
intolerance *n* intolerancia
intoxicated *adj* embriagado
intravenous *adj* intravenoso
intrepid *adj* intrépido
intricate *adj* intrincado
intrigue *n* intriga
intriguing *adj* intrigante
intrinsic *adj* intrínsico
introduce *v* introducir
introduction *n* introducción
introvert *adj* introvertido
intrude *v* entrometerse
intruder *n* intruso
intrusion *n* intromisión
intuition *n* intuición
inundate *v* inundar
invade *v* invadir
invader *n* invasor
invalid *n* inválido
invalidate *v* invalidar
invaluable *adj* inestimable
invasion *n* invasión
invent *v* inventar
invention *n* invención
inventory *n* inventario
invest *v* invertir
investigate *v* investigar
investigation *n* investigación

investment *n* inversión
investor *n* inversor
invincible *adj* invencible
invisible *adj* invisible
invitation *n* invitación
invite *v* invitar
invoice *n* factura
invoke *v* invocar
involve *v* implicar, participar
involved *adj* complicado, implicado
involvement *n* participación
inward *adj* interior
inwards *adv* hacia dentro
iodine *n* yodo
irate *adj* enojado
Ireland *n* Irlanda
Irish *adj* irlandés
iron *n* hierro
iron *v* planchar
ironic *adj* irónico
irony *n* ironía
irrational *adj* irracional
irrefutable *adj* irrefutable
irregular *adj* irregular
irrelevant *adj* irrelevante
irreparable *adj* irreparable
irresistible *adj* irresistible
irrespective *adj* independiente de
irreversible *adj* irreversible
irrevocable *adj* irrevocable
irrigate *v* regar
irrigation *n* regadío
irritate *v* irritar
irritating *adj* fastidioso
Islamic *adj* islámico
island *n* isla
isle *n* isla
isolate *v* aislar
isolation *n* aislamiento

I

issue *n* cuestión
Italian *adj* italiano
italics *adj* cursiva
Italy *n* Italia
itch *v* picar
itchiness *n* picazón
item *n* artículo
itemize *v* detallar
itinerary *n* intinerario
ivory *n* marfil

J

jackal *n* chacal
jacket *n* chaqueta
jackpot *n* premio gordo
jaguar *n* jaguar
jail *n* cárcel
jail *v* encarcelar
jailer *n* carcelero
jam *n* mermelada; atasco
janitor *n* conserje
January *n* enero
Japan *n* Japón
Japanese *adj* japonés
jar *n* tarro, jarro, jarra
jasmine *n* jazmín
jaw *n* mandíbula
jealous *adj* celoso
jealousy *n* celos, envidia
jeans *n* vaqueros
jeopardize *v* poner en peligro
jerk *v* tirar
jerk *n* sacudida; tirón
jersey *n* suéter

Jew *n* judío
jewel *n* joya
jeweler *n* joyero
jewelry store *n* joyería
Jewish *adj* judío
jigsaw *n* rompecabezas
job *n* trabajo
jobless *adj* desempleado
join *v* juntar, unirse
joint *n* articulación, unión
jointly *adv* juntos
joke *n* chiste
joke *v* bromear
jokingly *adv* en broma
jolly *adj* alegre
jolt *v* sacudir
jolt *n* sacudida
journal *n* revista; diario
journalist *n* corresponsal
journey *n* camino
jovial *adj* jovial
joy *n* alegría
joyful *adj* alegre
joyfully *adv* alegremente
jubilant *adj* jubiloso
Judaism *n* Judaísmo
judge *n* juez
judgment *n* juicio
judicious *adj* juicioso
jug *n* jarra
juggler *n* malabarista
juice *n* jugo
juicy *adj* jugoso
July *n* julio
jump *v* saltar
jump *n* salto
jumpy *adj* nervioso
junction *n* cruce, unión
June *n* junio

jungle *n* selva, jungla
junior *adj* más joven
junk *n* trastos
jury *n* jurado
just *adj* justo
justice *n* justicia
justify *v* justificar
justly *adv* con razón
juvenile *n* menor
juvenile *adj* juvenil

kangaroo *n* canguro
karate *n* karate
keep *iv* guardar
keep on *v* continuar
keep up *v* seguir
keg *n* barril
kennel *n* perrera
kettle *n* tetera, hervidor
key *n* llave; clave
key ring *n* llavero
keyboard *n* teclado
kick *v* dar una patada
kickback *n* soborno
kickoff *n* saque
kid *n* chiquillo; cabrito
kidnap *v* secuestrar
kidnapper *n* secuestrador
kidnapping *n* secuestro
kidney *n* riñón
kidney bean *n* frijol rojo
kill *v* matar
killer *n* asesino

killing *n* asesinato
kilogram *n* kilogramo
kilometer *n* kilómetro
kilowatt *n* kilovatio
kind *adj* amable
kindle *v* avivar
kindly *adv* amablemente
kindness *n* amabilidad
king *n* rey
kingdom *n* reino
kinship *n* parentesco
kiosk *n* quiosco
kiss *v* besar
kiss *n* beso
kitchen *n* cocina
kite *n* cometa
kitten *n* gatito
knee *n* rodilla
kneecap *n* rótula
kneel *iv* arrodillarse
knife *n* cuchillo
knight *n* caballero
knit *v* tejer
knob *n* tirador
knock *n* golpe
knock *v* golpear, llamar
knot *n* nudo
know *iv* conocer
know-how *n* conocimientos
knowingly *adv* a sabiendas
knowledge *n* conocimiento

J
K

L

lab *n* laboratorio
label *n* etiqueta
labor *n* trabajo, mano de obra, obreros
laborer *n* trabajador
labyrinth *n* laberinto
lace *n* encaje
lack *v* carecer
lack *n* falta, carencia
lad *n* muchacho
ladder *n* escalera
laden *adj* cargado
lady *n* señora
ladylike *adj* femenino
lag v rezagarse
lagoon *n* laguna
lake *n* lago
lamb *n* cordero
lame *adj* cojo; pobre
lament *v* lamentarse
lament *n* lamento
laminate v laminar
lamp *n* lámpara
lamppost *n* farol
lampshade *n* pantalla
lance n lanza
land *n* tierra
land *v* aterrizar
landfill *n* vertedero, relleno sanitario
landing *n* aterrizaje
landlady *n* dueña
landlocked *adj* encerrado
landlord *n* dueño
landscape *n* paisaje
lane *n* carril; callejón
language *n* lengua

languid adj lánguido
languish *v* languidecer
lantern *n* linterna, farol
lap *n* regazo; vuelta
lapse *n* desliz; intervalo
lapse *v* transcurrir
larceny *n* latrocinio
lard *n* manteca
large *adj* grande
largely adv en gran parte
larynx *n* laringe
laser *n* láser
lash *n* pestaña; azote
lash *v* azotar
lash out *v* arremeter
last *v* durar
last *adj* último
last name *n* apellido
last night *adv* anoche
lasting *adj* duradero
lastly *adv* por último
latch *n* pestillo
late *adv* tarde
late adj difunto; tardío
lately *adv* últimamente
latent adj latente
later *adv* más tarde
later *adj* posterior
lateral *adj* lateral
latest *adj* el último
lather *n* espuma
latitude *n* latitud
latter *adj* último
laudable adj loable
laugh *v* reírse
laugh *n* risa
laughable *adj* ridículo, risible
laughing stock *n* hazmerreir
laughter *n* risa

launch *n* lanzamiento
launch *v* lanzar; botar
launder v lavar, blanquear
laundry *n* lavandería
lavatory *n* baño
lavish *adj* expléndido
lavish *v* prodigar, derrochar
law *n* ley
law-abiding *adj* respetuoso
lawful *adj* legítimo, lícito
lawmaker *n* legislador
lawn *n* césped
lawsuit *n* pleito
lawyer *n* abogado
lax *adj* negligente
laxative *adj* laxante
lay *adj* laico, lego
lay *iv* poner; dejar
lay off *v* despedir
layer *n* capa, estrato
layman *n* laico, lego
layout *n* plano, diseño
laziness *n* pereza
lazy *adj* perezoso
lead *iv* guiar, conducir
lead *n* pista; plomo
leaded *adj* con plomo
leader *n* jefe, líder
leadership *n* liderazgo
leading *adj* principal
leaf *n* hoja
leaflet *n* folleto, hojuela
league *n* liga
leak *v* gotear, salirse
leak *n* gotera, escape
leakage *n* escape, fuga
lean *adj* flaco, magro
lean *iv* inclinarse
lean back *v* reclinarse

lean on *v* apoyarse
leaning *n* inclinación
leap *iv* saltar
leap *n* salto
leap year *n* año bisiesto
learn *iv* aprender
learned *adj* aprendido, erudito, sabido
learner *n* estudiante
learning *n* aprendizaje
lease *v* arrendar
lease *n* arriendo
leash *n* correa
least *adj* el menor, el menos
leather *n* cuero, piel
leave *iv* dejar; salir
leave out *v* omitir
leaven n levadura
lectern *n* atril
lecture *n* conferencia
ledger *n* libro de cuentas
leech *n* sanguijuela
leeway n libertad
leftover adj sobrante
leftovers *n* sobras
leg *n* pierna
legacy *n* legado
legal *adj* legal
legality *n* legalidad
legalize *v* legalizar
legend *n* leyenda
legendary adj legendario
legible *adj* legible
legion *n* legión
legislate *v* legislar
legislation *n* legislación
legislature *n* legislatura
legitimate *adj* legítimo
legitimate v legitimar
leisure *n* ocio

L

lemon *n* limón
lemonade *n* limonada
lend *iv* prestar
lender n prestamista
length *n* longitud
lengthen *v* alargar
lengthy *adj* largo
leniency *n* compasión
lenient *adj* indulgente
lens *n* lente
Lent *n* cuaresma
lentil *n* lenteja
leopard *n* leopardo
leper *n* leproso
leprosy *n* lepra
less *adj* menos
lessee *n* inquilino
lessen *v* disminuir
lesser *adj* menor
lesson *n* lección
lessor *n* arrendador
lest *c* para que no
let *iv* permitir
let down *v* decepcionar
let go *v* soltar
let in *v* dejar entrar
let out *v* dejar salir
letdown n decepción
lethal *adj* mortal
lethargy n letargo
letter *n* carta; letra
lettuce *n* lechuga
leukemia *n* leucemia
level *v* nivelar, allanar
level *n* nivel, altura
level with *v* sincerarse
level-headed adj sensato
lever *n* palanca, resorte
leverage *n* influencia

levy *v* recaudar
lewd *adj* obsceno
liability *n* obligación
liable *adj* responsable
liaison *n* enlace, contacto
liar *n* mentiroso
libel *n* calumnia, difamación
liberate *v* liberar
liberation *n* liberación
liberty *n* libertad
librarian *n* bibliotecario
library *n* biblioteca
lice *n* piojos
license *n* licencia
license *v* autorizar
lick *v* lamer
lid *n* tapa, tapadera
lid n párpado
lie *iv* acostarse
lie *v* mentir
lie *n* mentira
lieu *n* lugar
lieutenant *n* teniente
life *n* vida
lifeguard *n* socorrista
lifeless *adj* sin vida
lifespan n período de la vida
lifestyle *n* estilo de vida
lifetime *adj* de por vida
lift *v* levantar, alzar
lift off *v* despegar
lift off *n* despegue
ligament *n* ligamento
light *iv* encender
light *adj* ligero
light *n* luz
lighten *v* aclarar, brillar
lighter *n* encendedor, mechero
lighthouse *n* faro

L

lighting *n* iluminación
lightly *adv* ligeramente
lightning *n* rayo
lightweight *n* peso ligero
likable *adj* simpático
like *pre* como
like *v* gustar
likelihood *n* probabilidad
likely *adv* probablemente
liken v comparar
likeness *n* parecido
likewise *adv* del mismo modo,
  también, igualmente
liking *n* gusto, simpatía
limb *n* miembro; rama
lime *n* cal; lima
limestone *n* piedra caliza
limit *n* límite; colmo
limit *v* límitar
limitation *n* limitación
limp *v* cojear
limp *n* cojera
linchpin *n* cimiento, base
line *n* línea
line up *v* hacer cola
lined adj reglado
linen *n* ropa blanca, lino
linger *v* perdurar
lingerie *n* lencería
lingering *adj* persistente
lining *n* forro
link *v* unir, conectar
link *n* eslabón, enlace
lion *n* león
lioness *n* leona
lip *n* labio
lipstick n barra de labios
liqueur *n* licor
liquid *n* líquido

liquidate *v* liquidar
liquidation *n* liquidación
liquor *n* licor
list *v* enumerar
list *n* lista
listen *v* escuchar
listener *n* oyente
litany *n* letanía
liter *n* litro
liter *n* litro
literal *adj* literal
literally *adv* literalmente
literate *adj* culto
literature *n* literatura
litigate *v* litigar
litigation *n* litigio
litter *n* basura
litter v ensuciar
little *adj* poco
little bit *n* poquito
little by little *adv* poco a poco
liturgy *n* liturgia
live *adj* vivo; en directo
live *v* vivir
live off *v* vivir de gorra
live up *v* gozar
livelihood *n* sustento
lively *adj* animado
liver *n* hígado
livestock *n* ganado
livid *adj* furioso
living room *n* sala de estar
lizard *n* lagarto
load *v* cargar
load *n* carga, peso
loaded *adj* cargado, borracho
loaf *n* barra de pan
loan *v* prestar
loan *n* préstamo

L

89

loathe v odiar
loathing n odio
loathsome adj odioso
lobby n vestíbulo
lobby v presionar
lobster n langosta
local adj local, de aquí
localize v localizar
locate v situar; localizar
located adj situado
location n lugar
lock v cerrar con llave
lock n cerradura, candado
lock up v encarcelar
locker room n vestuario
locksmith n cerrajero
locust n langosta
lodge v alojarse
lodging n alojamiento
lofty adj elevado, noble
log n tronco; diario
log v anotar
log in v entrar
log off v salir
logic n lógica
logical adj lógico
loin n lomo
loiter v vagar
loneliness n soledad
lonely adv solo
loner n solitario
lonesome adj triste, solo
long adj largo
long for v anhelar
longing n anhelo
longitude n longitud
long-standing adj antiguo
long-term adj duradero
look n mirada, aspecto

look v mirar; parecer
look after v cuidar
look at v mirar
look down v despreciar
look for v buscar
look forward v desear
look into v investigar
look out v tener cuidado
look over v repasar
look through v hojear
looking glass n espejo
looks n aspecto
loom n telar
loom v surgir; amenazar
loop n lazo
loophole n resquicio
loose v soltar
loose adj suelto, ancho
loosen v aflojar
loot v saquear
loot n botín
lopsided adj ladeado
lord n señor
lordship n señoría
lose iv perder
loser n fracasado
loss n pérdida
lost adj perdido
lot adv mucho
lotion n loción
lots adj muchos
lottery n lotería
loud adj alto, fuerte
loudly adv fuertemente
loudspeaker n altavoz
lounge n salón, sala de estar
louse n piojo
lousy adj asqueroso
lovable adj adorable

love *v* amar, encantar
love *n* amor
lovely *adj* encantador
lover *n* amante
loving *adj* cariñoso
low *adj* bajo, corto
lower *adj* más bajo
low-key *adj* callado
lowly *adj* humilde
loyal *adj* leal
loyalty *n* lealtad, devoción, fidelidad
lubricate *v* engrasar
lubrication *n* engrase
lucid *adj* lúcido
luck *n* suerte
lucky *adj* afortunado
lucrative *adj* lucrativo
ludicrous *adj* ridículo
luggage *n* equipaje
lukewarm *adj* tibio
lull *n* tregua
lumber *n* madera
luminous *adj* luminoso
lump *n* bulto, hinchazón
lump sum *n* pago único
lump together *v* poner juntos
lumpy adj lleno de bultos
lunacy *n* locura
lunatic *adj* loco
lunch *n* almuerzo
lung *n* pulmón
lure *v* atraer
lure n cebo, atractivo
lurid *adj* llamativo
lurk *v* acechar
luscious adj sensual
lush *adj* exhuberante
lust *v* codiciar
lust *n* lujuria

lustful *adj* lujurioso
luxurious *adj* lujoso
luxury *n* lujo
lynch *v* linchar
lynx *n* lince
lyrics *n* letra de canción

machine *n* máquina
machine gun *n* ametralladora
machinery n maquinaria
mad *adj* enfadado
madam *n* señora
madden *v* volver loco
maddening adj exasperante
made-up adj inventado, falso
madhouse n manicomio
madly *adv* locamente
madman *n* loco
madness *n* locura
magazine *n* revista
magic *n* magia
magical *adj* mágico
magician *n* mago
magistrate *n* magistrado
magnet *n* imán
magnetic *adj* magnético
magnetism *n* magnetismo
magnificent *adj* magnífico
magnify *v* aumentar
magnitude *n* magnitud, inmensidad
maid *n* criada
maiden *n* doncella
mail *v* echar a correos

L
M

mail _n_ correo
mailbox _n_ buzón
mailman _n_ cartero
maim _v_ mutilar
main _adj_ principal
mainland _n_ tierra firme
mainly _adv_ principalmente
mainstream adj corriente
maintain _v_ mantener
maintenance _n_ mantenimiento
majestic _adj_ majestuoso
majesty _n_ majestad
major _n_ comandante
major _adj_ principal; grande
major in _v_ especializarse
majority _n_ mayoría
make _n_ marca
make _iv_ hacer, obligar
make up _v_ maquillarse
make up for _v_ compensar por
maker _n_ fabricante
makeshift adj improvisado
makeup _n_ maquillaje
malaria _n_ malaria
male _n_ macho, varón
male adj masculino
malevolent _adj_ malévolo
malfunction _v_ mal funcionamiento
malfunction _n_ fallo
malice _n_ malicia
malicious adj malicioso
malign _v_ calumniar
malignancy _n_ maldad
malignant _adj_ maligno
mall _n_ centro comercial
malnourished adj malnutrido
malnutrition _n_ desnutrición
malpractice _n_ negligencia
maltreatment n maltrato

mammal _n_ mamífero
mammoth _n_ mamut
man _n_ hombre
man v tripular; manejar
manage _v_ apañarse; dirigir
manageable _adj_ manejable
management _n_ dirección
manager _n_ director
mandate _n_ misión; mandato
mandatory _adj_ obligatorio
maneuver _n_ maniobra
maneuver v maniobrar
manger _n_ pesebre
mangle _v_ destrozar
manhandle _v_ maltratar
manhood n edad adulta
manhunt _n_ búsqueda
maniac _adj_ maniático
manifest _v_ manifestar
manifold adj múltiple
manipulate _v_ manipular
mankind _n_ humanidad
manliness _n_ virilidad
manly _adj_ varonil
manner _n_ manera, forma
mannerism _n_ peculiaredad
manners _n_ modales
manor n finca, señorío
manpower _n_ mano de obra
mansion _n_ mansión
manslaughter _n_ homicidio
manual _n_ handbook
manual _adj_ manual
manufacture _v_ fabricar
manure _n_ estiércol
manuscript _n_ manuscrito
many _adj_ muchos
map _n_ mapa, plano
map v delinear, dibujar

M

marathon n maratón
marble n mármol
march v marchar, desfilar
march n marcha, desfile
March n marzo
mare n yegua
margin n márgen
marginal adj marginal
marinate v marinar
marine adj marino, marítimo
marital adj conyugal, marital
mark n marca, huella
mark v marcar
mark down v rebajar
mark up v aumentar
marker n marcador
market n mercado
marksman n tirador
marmalade n mermelada
maroon adj rojo oscuro
marriage n matrimonio
married adj casado
marrow n médula, meollo, tuétano
marry v casar(se)
Mars n Marte
marshal n mariscal; jefe
martial adj marcial, militar
martyr n mártir
martyr v martirizar
martyrdom n martirio
marvel n maravilla
marvel v maravillarse
marvelous adj maravilloso
Marxist adj marxista
masculine adj masculino
mash v machacar, moler
mask n máscara
mask v encubrir
masochism n masoquismo

mason n albañi; masón
masquerade n farsa
masquerade v disfrazarse
mass n masa; cantidad
mass v juntarse
massacre n masacre
massage n masaje
massage v dar masajes
masseur n masajista
masseuse n masajista
massive adj masivo
mast n mástil
master n amo, dueño
master v dominar
masterful adj magistral
mastermind n cerebro
mastermind v dirigir
masterpiece n obra maestra
mastery n maestría
mat n estera
match n cerilla; partido
match v igualar; hacer juego
mate n compañero(a), pareja; colega
mate adj sin brillo
material n material; tejido
materialism n materialismo
maternal adj maternal
maternity n maternidad
math n matemáticas
matriculate v matricular
matrimony n matrimonio
matter n asunto; problema
matter v importar
mattress n colchón
mature adj maduro
mature v madurar
maturity n madurez
maul v magullar
maxim n máxima

M

M

maximize v maximizar
maximum *adj* máximo
May *n* mayo
may *iv* poder
may-be *adv* quizá, tal vez
mayhem *n* caos
mayor *n* alcalde
maze *n* laberinto
meadow *n* pradera, prado
meager *adj* escaso; flaco
meal *n* comida
mean *iv* significar, pretender
mean *adj* tacaño, cruel
mean n promedio
meander v serpentear, vagar
meaning *n* significado
meaningful *adj* significativo
meaningless *adj* sin sentido
meanness *n* tacañería
means *n* medios
meantime *adv* mientras tanto
meanwhile *adv* mientras tanto
measles *n* sarampión
measure *v* medir
measure n medida
measure up v estar a la altura
measurement *n* medida
meat *n* carne; meollo
meatball *n* albóndiga
mechanic *n* mecánico
mechanism *n* mecanismo
mechanize *v* mecanizar
medal *n* medalla
medallion *n* medallón
meddle *v* entrometerse
mediate *v* mediar
mediation n mediación
mediator *n* intermediario
medication *n* medicación

medicinal *adj* medicinal
medicine *n* medicina
medieval *adj* medieval
mediocre *adj* mediocre
mediocrity *n* mediocridad
meditate *v* meditar
meditation *n* meditación
medium *adj* mediano, medio
meek *adj* manso, dócil
meekness *n* mansedumbre
meet *iv* reunir(se)
meeting *n* reunión
melancholic adj melancólico
melancholy *n* melancolía
melee n pelea, barullo
mellow *adj* suave, blando
mellow *v* sosegar, madurar
melodic *adj* melódico
melody *n* melodía
melon *n* melón
melt *v* fundir, derritir(se)
member *n* miembro
membership *n* membrecía
membrane *n* membrana
memento *n* recuerdo
memo *n* nota
memoirs *n* memorias
memorable *adj* memorable
memorize *v* memorizar
memory *n* memoria; recuerdo
men *n* hombres
menace *n* amenaza
menacing adj amenazador
mend *v* reparar
meningitis *n* meningitis
menopause *n* menopausia
menstruation *n* menstruación
mental *adj* mental
mentality *n* mentalidad

mentally *adv* mentalmente
mention *v* mencionar
mention *n* mención
menu *n* menú
mercenary n mercenario
merchandise *n* mercancía
merchant *n* comerciante
merciful *adj* compasivo
merciless *adj* despiadado
Mercury *n* Mercurio
mercy *n* compasión
mere adj mero, simple
merely *adv* simplemente
merge *v* unir, fundirse
merger *n* unión; fusión
merit *n* mérito
merit *v* merecer
mermaid *n* sirena
merry *adj* alegre
mesh *n* malla, trama
mesh v enredarse
mesmerize *v* hechizar
mess *n* desorden
mess around *v* perder el tiempo
mess up *v* desordenar
message *n* mensaje
messenger *n* mensajero
Messiah *n* Mesías
messy *adj* sucio; revuelto
metal *n* metal
metallic *adj* metálico
metaphor *n* metáfora
meteor *n* meteoro
meteoric adj meteórico
meter *n* metro; contador
method *n* método
methodical *adj* metódico
meticulous *adj* cuidadoso
metric *adj* métrico

metropolis *n* metrópolis
Mexican *adj* mexicano
mice *n* ratones
microbe *n* microbio
microphone *n* micrófono
microscope *n* microscopio
microscopic adj microscópico
microwave *n* microondas
midair *n* en el aire
midday *n* mediodía
middle *n* centro; medio
middleman *n* intermediario
midget *n* enano
midget adj diminutivo
midnight *n* medianoche
midst pre en medio de
midsummer *n* pleno verano
midwife *n* comadrona
mighty *adj* poderoso
migraine *n* jaqueca
migrant *n* emigrante
migrate *v* emigrar
mild *adj* suave, apacible
mildew *n* moho
mile *n* milla
mileage *n* millaje
milestone *n* hito
milieu n entorno
militant *adj* militante
milk *n* leche
milky *adj* lechoso
mill *n* molino
millennium *n* milenio
million *n* millón
millionaire *adj* millonario
mime *v* mímica
mimic v imitar
mince *v* picar; ser franco
mincemeat *n* carne picada

M

mind *v* importar; cuidar
mind *n* mente, intención
mind-boggling *adj* increíble
mindful *adj* consciente
mindless *adj* inconsciente
mine *n* mina
mine *v* minar
mine *pro* mío
minefield *n* campo minado
miner *n* minero
mineral *n* mineral
mingle *v* mezclar(se)
miniature *n* miniatura
minimal *adj* mínimo
minimize *v* minimizar
minimum *n* mínimo
miniskirt *n* minifalda
minister *n* ministro, sacerdote
minister *v* atender
ministry *n* ministerio
minor *adj* menor
minority *n* minoría
mint *n* menta
mint *v* acuñar
minus *adj* menos
minute *n* minuto
miracle *n* milagro
miraculous *adj* milagroso
mirage *n* espejismo
mirror *n* espejo
mirror *v* reflejar
misbehave *v* portarse mal
miscalculate *v* calcular mal
miscarriage *n* aborto
miscarry *v* fracasar
mischief *n* travesura
mischievous *adj* travieso
misconduct *n* mala conducta
misconstrue *v* interpretar mal

misdemeanor *n* delito
miser *n* avaro
miserable *adj* miserable
misery *n* miseria
misfit *n* inadaptado
misfortune *n* desgracia
misgivings *n* dudas
misguided *adj* equivocado
mishap n percance
misinterpret *v* interpretar mal
misjudge *v* juzgar mal
mislead *v* engañar
misleading *adj* engañoso
mismanage *v* administrar mal
misplace *v* extraviar
misprint *n* errata
miss *v* extrañar
miss *n* señorita
missile *n* projectil
missing *adj* perdido
mission *n* misión
missionary *n* misionero
mist *n* neblina
mistake *iv* equivocarse
mistake *n* error
mistaken *adj* equivocado
mister *n* señor
mistreat *v* maltratar
mistreatment *n* maltrato
mistress *n* amante
mistrust *n* desconfianza
mistrust *v* desconfiar
misty *adj* brumoso
misunderstand *v* entender mal
misuse *n* mal uso
mitigate *v* mitigar
mix *v* mezclar
mixed-up *adj* confuso
mixer *n* mezcladora

M

mixture _n_ mezcla

mix-up _n_ confusión

moan _v_ gemir

moan _n_ gemido

mob _v_ acosar, asediar

mob _n_ gentío, turba

mobile _adj_ móvil

mobilize _v_ mobilizar

mobster _n_ gángster

mock _v_ burlarse, imitar

mock adj simulado

mockery _n_ burla

mode _n_ modo

model _n_ modelo

model v modelar

moderate _adj_ moderado

moderate v moderar(se)

moderation _n_ moderación

modern _adj_ moderno

modernize _v_ modernizar

modest _adj_ modesto, ligero

modesty _n_ modestia, pudor

modify _v_ modificar

module _n_ módulo

moisten _v_ humedecer, mojar

moisture _n_ humedad

molar _n_ muela

mold _v_ moldear

mold _n_ molde, moho

moldy _adj_ mohoso

moldy _adj_ mohoso

mole _n_ lunar; topo; espía

molecule _n_ molécula

molest _v_ molestar, acosar

mollify v calmar

molten adj derritido

mom _n_ mamá

moment _n_ momento

momentarily _adv_ en un rato

momentary adj momentáneo

momentous _adj_ importante

monarch _n_ monarca

monarchy _n_ monarquía

monastery _n_ monasterio

monastic _adj_ monástico

Monday _n_ lunes

money _n_ dinero

money order _n_ giro

monitor _v_ supervisar, controlar

monk _n_ monje

monkey _n_ mono

monogamy _n_ monogamia

monologue _n_ monólogo

monopolize _v_ monopolizar

monopoly _n_ monopolio

monotonous _adj_ monótono

monotony _n_ monotonía

monster _n_ monstruo

monstrous _adj_ monstruoso

month _n_ mes

monthly _adv_ mensualmente

monthly adj mensual

monument _n_ monumento

monumental _adj_ monumental

mood _n_ humor

moody _adj_ triste

moon _n_ luna

moor _v_ amarrar

mop _v_ limpiar, fregar

moral _adj_ moral

moral _n_ moraleja

morality _n_ moralidad

moralize v moralizar

morbid adj morboso

more _adj_ más

moreover _adv_ además

morning _n_ mañana

moron _adj_ imbécil

morphine n morfina

morsel n bocado, porción

mortal adj mortal

mortality n mortalidad

mortar n cemento

mortgage n hipoteca

mortification n mortificación

mortify v mortificar

mortuary n funeraria

mosaic n mosaico

mosque n mezquita

mosquito n mosquito

moss n musgo

most adj mayor parte

mostly adv principalmente

motel n motel

moth n polilla

mother n madre

motherhood n maternidad

mother-in-law n suegra

motion n movimiento

motionless adj inmóvil

motivate v motivar

motive n motivo

motor n motor

motorcycle n motocicleta

motto n lema

mount n monte

mount v montar

mountain n montaña

mountainous adj montañoso

mourn v llorar la muerte

mourning n luto, duelo

mouse n ratón

mouth n boca

mouthpiece n boquilla

movable adj movible

move n jugada

move v mover

move back v retroceder

move forward v avanzar

move out v mudarse

move over v dejar sitio

move up v ascender

movement n movimiento

movie n película

moving adj conmovedor

mow v cortar, segar

much adv mucho

mucus n mucosidad

mud n barro, lodo

muddle n enturbiar

muddy adj embarrado

muffle v amortiguar

muffler n silenciador

mug v atracar, asaltar

mugger n atracador

mugging n atraco

mule n mula

multiple adj múltiple

multiplication n multiplicación

multiply v multiplicar

multitude n multitud

mumble v refunfuñar

mummy n momia

mumps n paperas

munch v mascar

munitions n armamento

murder n asesinato

murder v asesinar

murderer n asesino

murky adj turbio

murmur v murmurar

murmur n murmullo

muscle n músculo

museum n museo

mushroom n hongo, seta

mushy adj pastoso

music *n* música
musician *n* músico
Muslim *adj* musulmán
must *iv* tener que
mustache *n* bigote
mustard *n* mostaza
muster *v* reunir, juntar
mutate *v* transformarse
mute *adj* mudo
mute v atenuar
mutilate *v* mutilar
mutiny *n* motín
mutter v murmullar
mutually *adv* mutuamente
muzzle *v* amordazar
muzzle *n* hocico; bozal
my *adj* mi
myopia n miopía
myopic *adj* miope
myself *pro* yo mismo
mysterious *adj* misterioso
mystery *n* misterio
mystic *adj* místico
mystify *v* dejar perplejo
myth *n* mito

N

nag *v* dar la lata
nagging *adj* continuo
nail *n* uña; clavo
nail down v clavar
naive *adj* ingenuo
naked *adj* desnudo
name *n* nombre

namely *adv* a saber
nanny *n* niñera
nap *n* siesta
napkin *n* servilleta
narcotic *n* narcótico
narrate *v* narrar
narration n narración
narrow *adj* estrecho
narrowly *adv* por poco
nasty *adj* asqueroso
nation *n* nación
national *adj* nacional
nationality *n* nacionalidad
nationalize *v* nacionalizar
native *adj* nativo
natural *adj* natural
naturally *adv* naturalmente
nature *n* naturaleza
naughty *adj* travieso
nausea *n* náusea
nave *n* nave
navel *n* ombligo
navigate *v* navegar
navigation *n* navegación
navy *n* armada
navy blue *adj* azul marino
near *pre* cerca de
nearby *adj* cercano
nearly *adv* casi
nearsighted *adj* miope
neat *adj* ordenado, limpio
neatly *adv* esmeradamente
necessary *adj* necesario
necessitate *v* necesitar
necessity *n* necesidad
neck *n* cuello
necklace *n* collar
necktie *n* corbata
need *v* necesitar

M
N

need *n* necesidad
needle *n* aguja
needle v pinchar
needless *adj* innecesario
needy *adj* necesitado
negative *adj* negativo
neglect *v* descuidar
neglect *n* descuido
negligence *n* negligencia
negligent *adj* negligente
negotiate *v* negociar
negotiation *n* negociación
neighbor *n* vecino
neighborhood *n* barrio, vecindario
neighboring adj vecino
neither *adj* ninguno
neither *adv* tampoco
nephew *n* sobrino
nerve *n* nervio
nervous *adj* nervioso
nervousness n nerviosismo
nest *n* nido
net *n* red
net v atrapar
Netherlands *n* Países Bajos
network *n* red, cadena
neurotic *adj* neurótico
neuter v capar
neuter adj neutro
neutral *adj* neutral
neutralize *v* neutralizar
never *adv* nunca
nevertheless *adv* sin embargo
new *adj* nuevo
newborn *n* recién nacido
newcomer *n* recién llegado
newly *adv* recientemente
newlywed *adj* recién casados
news *n* noticias

newscast *n* noticiero
newsletter *n* boletín
newspaper *n* periódico
newsstand *n* quiosco
next *adj* próximo
next door *adj* de al lado
nibble *v* picar, morder
nibble n mordisco
nice *adj* simpático
nicely *adv* amablemente
nickel *n* níquel
nickname *n* apodo, mote
nicotine *n* nicotina
niece *n* sobrina
night *n* noche
nightfall *n* anochecer
nightgown *n* bata de dormir
nightingale *n* ruiseñor
nightly adj cada noche
nightmare *n* pesadilla
nil n nada
nine *adj* nueve
nineteen *adj* diecinueve
ninety *adj* noventa
ninth *adj* noveno
nip *n* pellizco
nip *v* pellizcar
nipple *n* pezón
nitpicking *adj* quisquilloso
nitrogen *n* nitrógeno
no one *pro* ninguno
nobility *n* nobleza
noble *adj* noble
nobleman *n* hidalgo
nobody *pro* nadie
nocturnal *adj* nocturno
nod *v* saludar; asentir
noise *n* ruido
noisily *adv* ruidosamente

N

noisy *adj* ruidoso
nomad adj nómada
nominate *v* nombrar
nomination n nombramiento
nominee n candidato
none *pre* ninguno
nonetheless *c* no obstante
nonsense *n* disparate
nonsmoker *n* no fumador
nonstop *adv* sin parar
noodles n fideos
noon *n* mediodía
noose *n* lazo, soga
nor *c* ni
norm *n* norma
normal *adj* normal
normalize *v* normalizar
normally *adv* normalmente
north *n* norte
northeast *n* noroeste
northern *adj* del norte
northerner *adj* norteño
Norway *n* Noruega
Norwegian *adj* noruego
nose *n* nariz; hocico
nosedive *v* caer en picado
nostalgia *n* nostalgia
nostril *n* orificio nasal
nosy *adj* curioso
not *adv* no
notable *adj* notable
notably *adv* notablemente
notary *n* notario
notation n anotación
note *n* nota, anotación
note *v* notar
note down v anotar
notebook *n* cuaderno
noteworthy *adj* notable, digno

nothing *n* nada
notice *v* observar; notar
notice *n* aviso; letrero
noticeable *adj* obvio
notification *n* notificación
notify *v* notificar
notion *n* noción, idea
notorious *adj* notorio
notwithstanding pre a pesar de
noun *n* nombre
nourish *v* alimentar, nutrir
nourishing adj nutritivo
nourishment *n* alimento
novel *n* novela
novelist *n* novelista
novelty *n* novedad
November *n* noviembre
novice *n* novicio, novato
now *adv* ahora
nowadays *adv* hoy en día
nowhere *adv* en ningún lugar
noxious *adj* nocivo
nozzle *n* boquilla
nuance *n* matiz
nuclear *adj* nuclear
nude *adj* desnudo
nudism *n* nudismo
nudist *n* nudista
nudity *n* desnudez
nuisance *n* molestia
null *adj* nulo
nullify *v* anular
numb *adj* entumecido
number *n* número
numbness *n* entumecimiento
numerous *adj* numeroso
nun *n* monja
nurse *n* enfermera
nurse *v* cuidar

N

nursery *n* guardería; vivero
nurture *v* criar, nutrir
nut *n* nuez; tuerca
nutrient adj nutriente
nutrition *n* nutrición
nutritious *adj* nutritivo
nutshell *n* cáscara de nuez
nutty *adj* tocado, chalado
nylon n nilón

oak *n* roble
oar *n* remo
oasis *n* oasis
oath *n* juramento
oatmeal *n* avena
obedience *n* obediencia
obedient *adj* obediente
obese *adj* obeso, gordo
obey *v* obedecer
object *v* oponerse
object *n* objeto
objection *n* objeción
objective *n* objetivo
obligate *v* obligar
obligation *n* obligación
obligatory *adj* obligatorio
oblige *v* obligar
obliged *adj* agradecido
oblique *adj* oblicuo
obliterate *v* borrar, destruir
oblivion *n* olvido
oblivious *adj* inconsciente
oblong *adj* rectangular

obnoxious *adj* detestable
obscene *adj* obsceno
obscenity *n* obscenidad
obscure *adj* obscuro
obscurity *n* obscuridad
observation *n* observación
observatory *n* observatorio
observe *v* observar, notar
observer n observador
obsess *v* obsesionar
obsession *n* obsesión
obsolete *adj* en desuso
obstacle *n* obstáculo
obstinacy *n* terquedad
obstinate *adj* terco
obstruct *v* obstruir
obstruction *n* obstrucción
obtain *v* obtener
obvious *adj* evidente
obviously *adv* evidentemente
occasion *n* ocasión
occasionally *adv* a veces
occult *adj* oculto
occupant *n* ocupante
occupation *n* ocupación
occupy *v* ocupar
occur *v* ocurrir
occurrence *n* suceso
ocean *n* océano
October *n* octubre
octopus *n* pulpo
odd *adj* raro, extraño
oddity *n* rareza
odds *n* probabilidades
odious *adj* odioso
odometer *n* odómetro
odor *n* olor, hedor
odyssey *n* odisea
of *pre* de

off *adv* lejos
offend *v* ofender
offense *n* ofensa
offensive *adj* ofensivo
offer *v* ofrecer
offer *n* oferta
offering *n* ofrenda
office *n* oficina
officer *n* agente
official *adj* oficial
officiate *v* oficiar
offset *v* compensar
offspring *n* descendencia
off-the-record *adj* confidencial
often *adv* a menudo
oil *n* aceite, petróleo
oily adj grasiento
ointment *n* unguento
okay *adv* bien
okay v aprobar
old *adj* viejo, antiguo
old age *n* vejez
old-fashioned *adj* anticuado
olive *n* aceituna
Olympics *n* olimpiada
omelet *n* tortilla
omen *n* presagio
ominous *adj* amenazador
omission *n* omisión
omit *v* omitir
on *pre* en, encima, sobre
once *adv* una vez
once *c* una vez que
oncoming adj venidero
one *adj* uno
oneself *pre* uno mismo
ongoing *adj* continuo
onion *n* cebolla
onlooker *n* espectador

only *adv* solamente
onset *n* comienzo
onslaught *n* embestida
onwards *adv* hacia adelante
opaque *adj* opaco, obscuro
open *v* abrir
open *adj* abierto
open up *v* abrirse
opener n abridor
opening *n* vacante
open-minded *adj* imparcial
openness *n* franqueza
opera *n* ópera
operate *v* operar, actuar
operation *n* operación
opinion *n* opinión
opinionated *adj* testarudo
opium *n* opio
opponent *n* adversario
opportune *adj* oportuno
opportunity *n* oportunidad
oppose *v* oponerse
opposite *adj* opuesto
opposite *adv* en frente
opposite *n* contrario
opposition *n* oposición
oppress *v* oprimir
oppression *n* opresión
oppressive adj agobiante
opt for *v* optar por
optical *adj* óptico
optician *n* optometrista
optimism *n* optimismo
optimistic *adj* optimista
option *n* opción
optional *adj* opcional
opulence *n* opulencia
or *c* o
oracle *n* oráculo

O

orally *adv* oralmente
orange *n* naranja
orbit *n* órbita
orchard *n* huerto
orchestra *n* orquesta
ordain *v* ordenar
ordeal *n* tormento
order *n* orden
ordinarily *adv* ordinariamente
ordinary *adj* corriente
ordination *n* ordenación
ore *n* mineral
organ *n* órgano
organism *n* organismo
organist *n* organista
organization *n* organización
organize *v* organizar
orient *n* oriente
oriental *adj* oriental
orientation *n* orientación
oriented *adj* orientado
origin *n* origen
original *adj* original
originally *adv* al principio
originate *v* originar(se)
ornament *n* adorno
ornamental *adj* decorativo
orphan *n* huérfano
orphanage *n* orfanatorio
orthodox *adj* ortodoxo
ostentatious *adj* ostentoso
ostrich *n* avestruz
other *adj* otro
otherwise *adv* de lo contrario
otter *n* nutria
ought to *iv* deber
ounce *n* onza
our *adj* nuestro
ours *pro* nuestro

ourselves *pro* nosotros mismos
oust *v* desalojar
out *adv* afuera, fuera
outbreak *n* estallido; comienzo
outburst *n* arrebato
outcast *adj* abandonado
outcome *n* resultado
outcry *n* protesta
outdated *adj* anticuado
outdo *v* superar
outdoor *adj* al aire libre, exterior
outdoors *adv* fuera
outer *adj* exterior
outfit *n* conjunto
outgoing *adj* extrovertido
outgrow *v* dejar atrás
outing *n* excursión
outlast *v* durar más que
outlaw *v* prohibir
outlet *n* salida; enchufe
outline *n* perfil; esquema
outline *v* resumir, esbozar
outlive *v* sobrevivir
outlook *n* perspectiva
outmoded *adj* anticuado
outnumber *v* superar a
outpatient *n* paciente
outperform *v* superar
outpouring *n* manifestación
output *n* producción
outrage *n* indignación
outraged adj indignado
outrageous *adj* atroz
outright *adj* rotundo, claro
outrun *v* adelantar
outset *n* principio
outshine *v* eclipsar
outside *adv* afuera
outside adj exterior

O

outsider *n* forastero
outskirts *n* alrededores
outspoken *adj* muy franco
outstanding *adj* destacado
outstretched *adj* extendido
outward *adj* externo
outweigh *v* sobrepesar
oval *adj* ovalado
ovary *n* ovario
ovation *n* ovación
oven *n* horno
over *pre* sobre
overall *adv* en general
overall adj general
overbearing *adj* abrumador
overboard *adv* por la borda
overcast *adj* nublado
overcharge *v* cobrar de más
overcoat *n* abrigo
overcome *v* superar
overcrowded *adj* superpoblado
overdo *v* exagerar
overdone *adj* demasiado hecho
overdose *n* sobredosis
overdue *adj* retrasado
overestimate *v* sobreestimar
overflow *v* desbordarse
overhaul *v* revisar
overlap *v* coincidir, duplicar
overload *v* sobrecargar
overlook *v* pasar por alto
overnight *adv* por la noche
overpower *v* dominar
overrate *v* sobreestimar
override *v* invalidar
overrule *v* anular
overrun *v* invadir
overseas *adv* en el extranjero
oversee *v* supervisar

overshadow *v* eclipsar
oversight *n* descuido
overstate *v* exagerar
overstep *v* pasarse de la raya
overtake *v* adelantar
overthrow *v* derrocar
overthrow *n* derrocamiento
overtime *adv* horas extras
overturn *v* volcar
overview *n* vista general
overweight *adj* obeso
overwhelm *v* abrumar
owe *v* deber
owing to *adv* debido a
owl *n* buho
own *v* poseer
own *adj* propio
owner *n* dueño
ownership *n* posesión
ox *n* buey
oxen *n* bueyes
oxygen *n* oxígeno
oyster *n* ostra

O
P

P

pace *v* dar pasos
pace *n* paso
pacify *v* pacificar
pack *v* empaquetar
package *n* paquete
package v empaquetar
packed adj abarrotado
pact *n* pacto
pad *v* rellenar

padding *n* relleno
paddle *v* chapotear
padlock *n* candado
pagan *adj* pagano
page *n* página; paje
pail *n* balde, cubo
pain *n* dolor
painful *adj* doloroso
painkiller *n* calmante
painless *adj* sin dolor
painstaking adj esmerado
paint *v* pintar
paint *n* pintura
paintbrush *n* brocha
painter *n* pintor
painting *n* pintura; cuadro
pair *n* par
pajamas *n* pijamas
pal *n* compañero
palace *n* palacio
palatable adj aceptable
palate *n* paladar
pale *adj* pálido
paleness *n* palidez
palm *n* palma; palmera
palpable *adj* palpable
paltry *adj* miserable
pamper *v* mimar
pamphlet *n* folleto
pan *n* cazuela
pancreas *n* páncreas
pander *v* complacer
pang *n* punzada
panic *n* pánico
panorama *n* panorama
pant *v* jadear
panther *n* pantera
pantry *n* despensa
pants *n* pantalones

pantyhose *n* media
papacy *n* papado
paper *n* papel
paper v empapelar
paperclip *n* sujetapapeles
paperwork *n* papeleo
parable *n* parábola
parachute *n* paracaídas
parade *n* desfile
parade v desfilar
paradise *n* paraíso
paradox *n* paradoja
paragraph *n* párrafo
parakeet *n* periquito, loro
parallel *n* paralelo
paralysis *n* parálisis
paralyze *v* paralizar
parameters *n* límites
paramount *adj* primordial
paranoid *adj* paranoico
parasite *n* parásito
paratrooper *n* paracaidista
parcel *n* paquete
parcel post *n* correos
parched *adj* seco
parchment *n* pergamino
pardon *v* perdonar
pardon *n* perdón
pare v cortar
pare down v reducir
parenthesis *n* paréntesis
parents *n* padres
parish *n* parroquia
parishioner *n* parroquiano
parity *n* paridad
park *v* aparcar
park *n* parque
parking *n* aparcamiento
parliament *n* parlamento

P

parlor n salón
parochial adj parroquial
parrot n perico, loro
parsley n peregil
parsnip n remolacha
part v separarse
part n parte
partial adj parcial
partially adv parcialmente
participate v participar
participation n participación
participle n participio
particle n partícula
particular adj particular
particularly adv sobre todo
parting n separación
partisan n partidario
partition n partición, tabique
partly adv en parte
partner n socio
partnership n sociedad
partridge n perdiz
party n grupo; fiesta
party v irse de juerga
pass n puerto; pase
pass v pasar; aprobar
pass around v repartir
pass away v fallecer
pass out v desmayarse
passage n travesía, pasillo
passenger n pasajero
passer-by n transeúnte
passion n pasión
passionate adj apasionado
passive adj pasivo
passport n pasaporte
password n contraseña
past adj pasado
paste v pegar

paste n engrudo
pasteurize v pausterizar
pastime n pasatiempo
pastor n párroco
pastoral adj pastoral
pastry n pastel
pasture n pasto
pat n palmada, caricia
pat v acariciar
patch v remendar, reparar
patch n remiendo, parche
patchy adj desigual
patent n patente
patent adj claro, evidente
paternity n paternidad
path n camino
pathetic adj patético
pathway v camino
patience n paciencia
patient adj paciente
patio n patio
patriarch n patriarca
patrimony n patrimonio
patriot n patriota
patriotic adj patriótico
patrol n patrulla
patrol v patrullar
patron n patrono; patrón
patronage n patrocinio
patronize v patrocinar
pattern n patrón, modelo
pause n pausa
pause v hacer una pausa
pavement n acera, calzada, pavimento
pavilion n caseta
paw n pata, garra
pawn v empeñar
pawn n peón

P

pawnbroker *n* prestamista
pay *n* paga, sueldo
pay *iv* pagar
pay back *v* devolver
pay off *v* saldar, liquidar
pay slip *n* recibo
payable *adj* pagadero
paycheck *n* sueldo
payee *n* portador
payment *n* pago
payroll *n* nómina
pea *n* guisante
peace *n* paz
peaceful *adj* pacífico
peach *n* melocotón
peacock *n* pavo real
peak *n* cumbre, cima
peal n tañido, repique
peanut *n* cacahuete
pear *n* pera
pearl *n* perla
peasant *n* campesino
pebble *n* guijarro
peck *v* picotear
peck *n* picotazo
peculiar *adj* peculiar
pedagogy *n* pedagogía
pedal *n* pedal
pedantic *adj* pedante
peddle v vender, traficar
pedestrian *n* peatón
peek v ojeada
peel *v* pelar; despegar
peel *n* cáscara
peep *v* mirar a escondidas
peer *n* compañero
pelican *n* pelícano
pellet *n* perdigón, bolita
pen *n* pluma

penalize *v* penalizar
penalty *n* multa; penalti
penance *n* penitencia
penchant *n* predilección
pencil *n* lápiz
pendant *n* pendiente
pending *adj* pendiente
pendulum *n* péndulo
penetrate *v* penetrar
penguin *n* pinguino
penicillin *n* penicilina
penicillin v penicilina
peninsula *n* península
penitent *n* penitente
penniless *adj* indigente
penny *n* penique
pension *n* pensión
pensioner v pensionista
pentagon *n* pentágono
penthouse v ático
pent-up *adj* reprimido
people *n* gente
pep v animar
pepper *n* pimienta
per *pre* por
perceive *v* percibir
percent *adv* por ciento
percentage *n* porcentage
perception *n* percepción
perch v percha
perennial *adj* perenne
perfect *adj* perfecto
perfection *n* perfección
perforate *v* perforar
perforation *n* perforación
perform *v* realizar; actuar
performance *n* actuación; resultado
perfume *n* perfume
perfunctory adj superficial

P

perhaps *adv* quizás
peril *n* peligro
perilous *adj* peligroso
perimeter *n* perímetro
period *n* periodo
periodic v periódico
periphery n periferia
perish *v* perecer
perishable *adj* perecedero
perjury *n* perjurio
perks n ventajas
permanent *adj* permanente
permeate *v* penetrar
permission *n* permiso
permit *v* permitir
permit n pemiso, licencia
pernicious *adj* pernicioso
perpetrate *v* perpetrar
perpetual adj perpetuo
perplex v dejar perplejo
persecute *v* perseguir
persecution n persecución
persevere *v* perseverar
persist *v* persistir
persistence *n* persistencia
persistent *adj* persistente
person *n* persona
personal *adj* personal
personality *n* personalidad
personify *v* personificar
personnel *n* personal
perspective *n* perspectiva
perspiration *n* sudor
perspire *v* sudar
persuade *v* persuadir
persuasion *n* persuasión
persuasive *adj* persuasivo
pertain *v* pertenecer
pertinent *adj* pertinente

perturb *v* perturbar
perverse *adj* perverso
perversion n distorsión
pervert *v* pervertir
pervert *adj* pervertido
pessimism *n* pesimismo
pessimistic *adj* pesimista
pest *n* molestia, de plagas
pester *v* molestar, dar la lata
pesticide *n* pesticida
pet *n* animal doméstico
petal *n* pétalo
petite *adj* pequeño
petition *n* petición
petrified *adj* petrificado
petroleum *n* petróleo
pettiness *n* mezquindad
petty *adj* mezquino, pequeño
pew *n* banco de iglesia
phantom *n* fantasma
pharmacist *n* farmacéutico
pharmacy *n* farmacia
phase *n* fase
pheasant *n* faisán
phenomenon *n* fenómeno
philosopher *n* filósofo
philosophy *n* filosofía
phobia *n* fobia
phone *n* teléfono
phone *v* telefonear
phony *adj* falso, fingido
phosphorus *n* fósforo
photo *n* fotografía
photocopy *n* fotocopia
photograph *v* fotografía
photographer *n* fotógrafo
photography *n* fotografía
phrase *n* frase
physically *adj* físicamente

P

physician n médico
physics n física
pianist n pianista
piano n piano
pick v escoger, elegir; recoger
pick up v recoger
pickpocket n ratero
pickup n furgoneta
picture n cuadro, dibujo, foto
picture v imaginar(se)
picturesque adj pintoresco
pie n tarta, pastel
piece n pieza
piecemeal adv por partes
pier n muelle
pierce v perforar
piercing n perforación
piety n piedad, devoción
pig n cerdo
pigeon n paloma
piggy bank n hucha
pile v acumular
pile n montón
pile up v amontonarse
pilfer v robar, saquear
pilgrim n peregrino
pilgrimage n peregrinación
pill n pastilla
pillage v saquear
pillar n columna
pillow n almohada
pillowcase n funda
pilot n piloto
pimple n grano, espinilla
pin n alfiler
pincers n tenazas
pinch v pellizcar
pinch n pellizco, pizca
pine n pino

pineapple n piña
pink adj rosado
pinpoint v precisar
pint n pinta
pioneer n pionero
pious adj piadoso
pipe n tubo, caño
pipeline n oleoducto
piracy n piratería
pirate n pirata
pistol n pistola
pit n hoyo; fosa
pitch-black adj muy negro
pitchfork n horca
pitfall n escollo; riesgo
pitiful adj lastimoso
pity n compasión
pity v sentir lástima
placard n letrero, pancarta
placate v apaciguar
place n lugar, sitio
place v colocar
placement n colocación
placid adj apacible
plague n plaga
plain n llanura
plain adj claro, simple; liso
plainly adv claramente
plaintiff n demandante
plan v hacer planes
plan n plan, plano
plane n avión
planet n planeta
plank n tabla de madera
plant v plantar, sembrar
plant n planta
plaque n placa
plaster n yeso
plaster v enyesar

P

plastic n plástico
plate n plato
plateau n meseta
platform n plataforma
platinum n platino
platoon n pelotón
plausible adj verosímil
play v jugar; tocar
play n juego; obra
player n jugador
playful adj juguetón
playground n lugar de recreo
plea n súplica, apelación
plead v suplicar, defender
pleasant adj agradable
please v agradar
pleasing adj agradable
pleasure n placer
pleat n pliegue
pleated adj doblado
pledge v prometer
pledge n promesa
plentiful adj abundante
plenty n mucho
pliable adj flexible
pliers n alicates
plot v tramar
plot n trama, parcela
plow v arar
ploy n estratagema
pluck v coger
plug v enchufar; tapar
plug n enchufe; tapón
plum n ciruela
plumber n fontanero
plumbing n fontanería
plummet v caer en picado
plump adj rechoncho
plunder v saquear

plunge v lanzarse; hundir
plunge n caida, salto
plural n plural
plus adv más
plush adj lujoso
plutonium n plutonio
pneumonia n neumonía, pulmonía
pocket n bolsillo
pocket v embolsarse
poem n poema
poet n poeta
poetry n poesía
poignant adj conmovedor
point n punto; cuestión
point v señalar
pointed adj afilado; mordaz
pointless adj sin sentido
poise n elegancia
poison v envenenar
poison n veneno
poisoning n envenenamiento
poisonous adj venenoso
Poland n Polonia
polar adj polar
pole n poste; polo
police n policía (la)
policeman n policía (el)
policy n póliza, política
Polish adj polaco
polish n betún, brillo
polish v pulir, sacar brillo
polite adj cortés
politeness n cortesía
politician n político
politics n política
poll n encuesta, votación
poll v encuestar
pollen n polen
pollute v ensuciar

P

pollution *n* polución, contaminación
polygamist *adj* polígamo
polygamy *n* poligamia
pomegranate *n* granada
pomposity *n* pomposidad
pond *n* estanque
ponder *v* ponderar
pontiff *n* pontífice
pool *n* piscina; billar
pool *v* juntar
poor *n* pobre
poorly *adv* mal, pobremente
popcorn *n* palomitas
Pope *n* Papa
poppy *n* amapola
popular *adj* popular
popularize *v* popularizar
populate *v* poblar
population *n* población
porcelain *n* porcelana
porch *n* pórtico
porcupine *n* puercoespín
pore *n* poro
pork *n* carne de cerdo
porous *adj* poroso
port *n* puerto
portable *adj* portátil
portent *n* augurio
porter *n* maletero, mozo
portion *n* porción
portrait *n* retrato
portray *v* describir
portrayal n actuación
Portugal *n* Portugal
Portuguese *adj* portugués
pose *v* posar; plantear
posh *adj* elegante
position *n* posición
positive *adj* positivo

possess *v* poseer
possession *n* posesión
possessive adj posesivo
possibility *n* posibilidad
possible *adj* posible
post *n* puesto; poste
post office *n* correos
postage *n* sello
postcard *n* tarjeta postal
poster *n* cartel, póster
posterity *n* posteridad
posthumous adj póstumo
postman *n* cartero
postmark *n* matasellos
postpone *v* aplazar
postponement *n* aplazamiento
posture n postura
pot *n* olla; tiesto
potato *n* patata
potent *adj* potente
potential *adj* potencial
pothole *n* bache
poultry *n* aves de corral
pound *v* golpear
pound *n* libra
pour *v* echar, verter
poverty *n* pobreza
powder *n* polvo
power *n* poder
powerful *adj* poderoso
powerless *adj* impotente
practical *adj* práctico
practice *v* ejercicio
practice *v* practicar
practicing *adj* practicante
pragmatist *adj* pragmático
prairie *n* pradera
praise *v* alabar
praise *n* alabanza

P

praiseworthy *adj* loable
prank *n* travesura
prawn *n* gamba
pray *v* rezar
prayer *n* oración
preach *v* predicar
preacher *n* predicador
preaching *n* predicación
preamble *n* preámbulo
precarious *adj* precario, débil
precaution *n* precaución
precede *v* preceder
precedent *n* precedente
preceding *adj* anterior
precept *n* mandato
precious *adj* precioso
precipice *n* precipicio
precipitate *v* precipitar(se)
precise *adj* preciso, exacto
precision *n* precisión
preclude v descartar
precocious *adj* precoz
precursor *n* precursor
predecessor *n* antecesor
predicament *n* apuro
predict *v* predecir, pronosticar
prediction *n* predicción
predilection *n* predilección
predisposed *adj* predispuesto
predominate *v* predominar
preempt *v* adelantarse
pre-emptive adj preventivo
prefabricate *v* prefabricar
preface *n* prefacio
prefer *v* preferir
preference *n* preferencia
prefix *n* prefijo
pregnancy *n* embarazo
pregnant *adj* embarazada

prehistoric *adj* prehistórico
prejudice *n* prejuicio
prejudicial adj perjudiciar
preliminary *adj* preliminar
prelude *n* preludio
premature *adj* prematuro
premeditate *v* premeditar
premeditation *n* premeditación
premier *adj* estreno
premise *n* premisa
premises *n* local
premonition *n* premonición
preoccupation *n* preocupación
preoccupy *v* preocuparse
preparation *n* preparación
prepare *v* preparar
preposition *n* preposición
prerequisite *n* prerequisito
prerogative *n* prerrogativa
presage n presagio
prescribe *v* recetar
prescription *n* prescripción
presence *n* presencia
present *adj* presente
present *v* presentar
presentation *n* presentación
preserve *v* preservar
preset v programar
preside *v* presidir
presidency *n* presidencia
president *n* presidente
press *n* prensa, imprenta
press *v* insistir; apretar
pressing *adj* apremiante
pressure *v* presionar
pressure *n* presión
prestige *n* prestigio
presume *v* suponer
presumption *n* presunción

P

113

presuppose v presuponer
presupposition n suposición
pretend v pretender
pretense n excusa; farsa
pretension n pretensión
pretentious adj pretencioso
pretext n pretesto
pretty adj lindo, bonito
prevail v prevalecer
prevalent adj extendido
prevent v impedir, prevenir
prevention n prevención
preventive adj preventivo
preview n preestreno
previous adj anterior, previo
previously adv antes, previamente
prey n presa
price n precio
pricey adj caro
prick v pinchar, picar
prickle n pincho
pride n orgullo
priest n sacerdote
priestess n sacerdotisa
priesthood n sacerdocio
primacy n primacía
primarily adv ante todo, principalmente
prime adj primordial
primitive adj primitivo
prince n príncipe
princess n princesa
principal adj principal
principle n principio
print v imprimir
print n huella
printer n impresor
printing n imprenta
prior adj previo, anterior

priority n prioridad
prism n prisma
prison n prisión
prisoner n prisionero
privacy n intimidad
private adj privado
privation n privación
privilege n privilegio
prize n premio
probability n probabilidad
probable adj probable
probe v investigar
probe n investigación
probing n investigación
problem n problema
problematic adj problemático
procedure n procedimiento
proceed v continuar
proceedings n proceso
proceeds n ganancias
process v tramitar, procesar
process n proceso
procession n desfile
proclaim v proclamar
proclamation n proclamación
procrastinate v demorar
procreate v procrear
procure v conseguir
prod v empujar, forzar
prodigious adj prodigioso
prodigy n prodigio
produce v producir
produce n vegetales
producer n productor
product n producto
production n producción
productive adj productivo
profane adj profano
profess v profesar

profession n profesión
professional adj profesional
professor n profesor
proficiency n competencia
proficient adj competente
profile n perfil
profit v aprovechar
profit n beneficio
profitable adj rentable
profound adj profundo
prognosis n pronóstico
program n programa
programmer n programador
progress v avanzar
progress n progreso
progressive adj progresista
prohibit v prohibir
prohibition n prohibición
project v proyectar
project n proyecto
projectile n proyectil
projection n proyección
proliferate v proliferar
prologue n prólogo
prolong v prolongar
promenade n paseo
prominent adj prominente
promiscuous adj promiscuo
promise n promesa
promising adj prometedor
promote v fomentar
promotion n ascenso
prompt adj puntual, rápido
prone adj propenso
pronoun n pronombre
pronounce v pronunciar
proof n prueba
propaganda n propaganda
propagate v propagar

propel v propulsar
propensity n propensión
proper adj apropiado
properly adv correctamente
property n propiedad
prophecy n profecía
prophet n profeta
proportion n proporción
proposal n propuesta
propose v proponer
proposition n proposición
prose n prosa
prosecute v procesar
prosecutor n fiscal
prospect n probabilidad
prosper v prosperar
prosperity n prosperidad
prosperous adj próspero
prostate n próstata
prostrate adj prostrado
protect v proteger
protection n protección
protein n proteína
protest v protestar
protest n protesta
protocol n protocolo
prototype n prototipo
protract v prolongar
protracted adj prolongado
protrude v sobresalir
proud adj orgulloso
proudly adv orgullosamente
prove v probar
proven adj probado
proverb n proverbio
provide v proveer
providence n providencia
providing that c siempre que
province n provincia

P

provision n suministro
provisional adj provisional
provocation n provocación
provoke v provocar
prow n proa
prowl v merodear
proximity n proximidad
proxy n poder
prudence n prudencia
prudent adj prudente
prudish adj puritano
prune v podar
prune n ciruela seca
prurient adj lascivo
pry v entrometerse
pseudonym n seudónimo
psychiatrist n psiquiatra
psychiatry n psiquiatría
psychic adj psíquico
psychology n psicología
psychopath n psicópata
psychosis n psicosis
puberty n pubertad
public adj público
publication n publicación
publicity n publicidad
publicly adv públicamente
publish v publicar
publisher n editor
pudding n pudín
puerile adj infantil
puff n soplo, bocanada
puffed adj hinchado
pull v tirar, arrastrar, halar
pull ahead v adelantar
pull down v derribar; bajar
pull out v sacar
pulley n polea
pulp n pulpa

pulpit n púlpito
pulsate v latir, pulsar
pulse n pulso
pulverize v pulverizar
pump v bombear
pump n bomba
pumpkin n calabaza
punch v golpear, agujerear
punch n puñetazo, golpe
punctual adj puntual
punctuation n puntuación
puncture n pinchazo
punish v castigar
punishable adj castigable
punishment n castigo
puny adj insignificante
pupil n alumno
puppet n títere
puppy n cachorro
purchase v comprar
purchase n compra
purchaser n comprador
pure adj puro, limpio
puree n puré
purgatory n purgatorio
purge n purga
purge v purgar
purification n purificación
purify v purificar
purity n pureza
purple adj morado
purpose n fin, propósito
purposely adv adrede
purse n bolso
pursue v perseguir; buscar
pursuit n búsqueda; logro
pus n pus
push v empujar
pushy adj insistente

P

put *iv* poner
put aside *v* separar
put away *v* guardar
put off *v* aplazar
put out *v* apagar
put up *v* levantar
put up with *v* aguantar
putrefy v pudrir(se)
putrid *adj* pútrido
puzzle *n* rompecabezas
puzzle *v* desconcertar
puzzled adj perplejo
puzzling *adj* desconcertante
pyramid *n* pirámide
python *n* serpiente pitón

Q

quagmire *n* atolladero
quail *n* codorniz
quake *v* terremoto
qualify *v* calificar
quality *n* calidad
qualm *n* reparo, escrúpulo
quandary *n* dilema
quantity *n* cantidad
quarantine *n* cuarentena
quarrel *v* reñir, pelear
quarrel *n* riña, pelea
quarrelsome *adj* peleón
quarry *n* cantera
quarter *n* cuarto; barrio
quarterly *adj* trimestral
quarters *n* alojamiento
quash *v* aplastar; anular

queen *n* reina
queer *adj* raro
quell *v* sofocar
quench *v* saciar, sofocar
quest *n* búsqueda
question *v* preguntar
question *n* pregunta
questionable *adj* dudoso
questionnaire *n* cuestionario
queue *n* cola
quick *adj* rápido
quicken *v* apresurar
quickly *adv* rápidamente
quicksand *n* arena movediza
quiet *adj* quieto, callado
quietness *n* silencio, quietud
quilt *n* colcha
quince n membrillo
quirk n rareza
quit *iv* dejar, abandonar
quite *adv* bastante
quiver *v* estremecerse
quiz *v* interrogar
quotation *n* cita
quote *v* citar
quotient *n* cociente

P
Q
R

R

rabbi *n* rabino
rabbit *n* conejo
rabies *n* rabia
raccoon *n* racún
race *v* competir
race *n* carrera; raza

racism *n* racismo
racist *adj* racista
racket *n* raqueta; estafa
racketeering *n* extorsión
radar *n* radar
radiation *n* radiación
radiator *n* radiador
radical *adj* radical
radio *n* radio
radish *n* rábano
radius *n* radio
raffle *n* sorteo, rifa
raft *n* balsa
rag *n* trapo
rage *n* rabia
ragged *adj* harapiento
raid *n* asalto; redada
raid *v* asaltar, atacar
raider *n* asaltante
rail *n* carril; baranda
railroad *n* ferrocarril
rain *n* lluvia
rain *v* llover
rainbow *n* arco iris
raincoat *n* impermeable
rainfall *n* lluvia
rainstorm n chaparrón
rainy *adj* lluvioso
raise *n* aumento
raise *v* aumentar; levantar
raisin *n* pasa
rake *n* rastrillo
rally *n* mitin, reunión
ram *n* carnero
ram *v* embestir
ramble v divagar
rambling adj confuso
ramification *n* ramificación
ramp *n* rampa

rampage *v* arrasar
rampant *adj* extendido
ranch *n* rancho
rancor *n* rencor
randomly *adv* al azar
range *n* alcance, rango; sierra
rank *n* rango; tropa
rank *v* clasificar
ransack *v* desvalijar
ransom *v* rescatar
ransom *n* rescate
rape *v* violar
rape *n* violación
rapid *adj* rápido
rapist *n* violador
rapport *n* relacción
rare *adj* poco común, raro
rarely *adv* raramente
rascal *n* pícaro, pillo
rash *v* precipitarse
rash *n* prisa
rash adj precipitado
rasp v raspar
raspberry *n* mora
rat *n* rata
rate *n* tarifa; ritmo, tipo
rather *adv* más bien
ratification *n* ratificación
ratify *v* ratificar
ratio *n* proporción
ration *v* racionar
ration *n* ración
rational *adj* racional
rationalize *v* justificar
rattle *v* traquetear
ravage *v* arrasar
ravage *n* estragos
raven *n* cuervo
ravine *n* barranco

raw *adj* crudo
ray *n* rayo
raze *v* arrasar
razor *n* navaja (máquinilla) de afeitar
reach *v* alcanzar
reach *n* alcance
react *v* reaccionar
reaction *n* reacción
reactivate v reactivar
read *iv* leer
reader *n* lector
readiness *n* preparación
reading *n* lectura
readjust v reajustar
ready *adj* preparado
real *adj* real, genuino
realism *n* realismo
realistic adj realista
reality *n* realidad
realize *v* darse cuenta
really *adv* de verdad
realm *n* reino
realty *n* inmobiliaria
reap *v* cosechar
reappear *v* reaparecer
rear *v* criar
rear *n* retaguardia
rear *adj* trasero, último
rearrange v reordenar
reason *v* razonar
reason *n* razón
reasonable *adj* razonable
reasonableness n racionabilidad
reasoning *n* razonamiento
reassure *v* tranquilizar
rebate *n* reembolso, rebaja
rebel *v* rebelarse
rebel *n* rebelde
rebellion *n* rebelión

rebirth *n* renacimiento
rebound *v* rebotar
rebound n rebote
rebuff *v* rechazar, desairar
rebuff *n* desaire, rechazo
rebuild *v* reconstruir
rebuke *v* reprender
rebuke n reprimenda
rebut *v* rebatir
recalcitrant adj obstinado
recall *v* recordar, revocar
recant *v* desdecirse
recap *v* resumir
recapture *v* reconquistar
recede *v* retroceder, retirarse
receipt *n* recibo
receive *v* recibir
recent *adj* reciente
recently adv recientemente
receptacle n receptáculo
reception *n* recepción
receptionist *n* recepcionista
receptive *adj* acogedor
recess *n* descanso, hueco
recession *n* recesión
recharge *v* recargar
recipe *n* receta
reciprocal *adj* recíproco
recital *n* recital
recite *v* recitar
reckless *adj* imprudente
reckon *v* estimar, creer
reckon on *v* contar con
reclaim *v* reclamar
recline *v* reclinar
recluse *n* solitario
recognition *n* reconocimiento
recognize *v* reconocer
recollect *v* recordar

R

recollection *n* recuerdo
recommend *v* recomendar
recompense *v* recompensar
recompense *n* recompensa
reconcile *v* reconciliar
reconsider *v* reconsiderar
reconstruct *v* reconstruir
record *v* grabar; registrar
record *n* disco; récord
recorder *n* grabadora
recording *n* grabación
recount *n* recuento
recount *v* relatar
recoup *v* recuperar
recourse *v* recurrir
recourse *n* recurso
recover *v* recobrar, recuperar
recovery *n* recuperación
recreate *v* recrear
recreation *n* recreación
recruit *v* reclutar
recruit *n* recluta
recruitment *n* reclutamiento
rectangle *n* rectángulo
rectangular *adj* rectangular
rectify *v* rectificar
rector *n* rector
rectum *n* recto
recuperate *v* reponerse
recur *v* repetirse
recurrence *n* repetición
recycle *v* reciclar
recycling n reciclaje
red *adj* rojo
red tape *n* papeleo
redden *v* enrojecer(se)
redeem *v* redimir
redemption *n* redención
redhead adj pelirojo

red-hot *adj* candente
redo *v* rehacer
redouble *v* redoblar
redress *v* reparar
reduce *v* reducir
redundant *adj* superfluo
reed *n* junco, caña, carrizo
reef *n* arrecife
reel *n* carrete; rollo
reelect *v* reelegir
reenactment *n* recreación
reentry *n* vuelta
refer to *v* referirse a
referee *n* árbitro
reference *n* referencia
referendum *n* referendum
refill *v* rellenar
refinance *v* refinanciar
refine *v* refinar
refinery *n* refinería
reflect *v* reflejar, reflexionar
reflection *n* reflejo, reflexión
reflexive *adj* reflexivo
reform *v* reformar
reform *n* reforma
refrain *v* abstenerse
refresh *v* refrescar
refreshing *adj* refrescante
refreshment *n* refresco
refrigerate *v* refrigerar
refuel *v* repostar
refuge *n* refugio
refugee *n* refugiado
refund *v* devolver
refund *n* reembolso
refurbish *v* restaurar
refusal *n* negativa
refuse *v* rehusar
refuse *n* basura

R

refute *v* refutar
regain *v* recobrar
regal *adj* regio
regard *v* considerar
regarding *pre* con respecto a
regardless *adv* sin reparar en
regards *n* saludos
regeneration *n* regeneración
regent *n* regente
regime *n* régimen
regiment *n* regimiento
region *n* región
regional *adj* regional
register *v* registro; registar(se)
registration *n* matrícula
regret *v* lamentar
regret *n* pena, pesar
regrettable *adj* lamentable
regularity *n* regularidad
regularly *adv* regularmente
regulate *v* regular
regulation *n* regla, reglamento, regulación
rehabilitate *v* rehabilitar
rehearsal *n* ensayo
rehearse *v* ensayar
reign *v* reinar
reign *n* reinado
reimburse *v* reembolsar
reimbursement *n* reembolso
rein *v* frenar, controlar
rein *n* rienda
reindeer *n* reno
reinforce *y* reforzar
reinforcement *n* refuerzo
reinstate *v* readmitir
reiterate *v* reiterar
reject *v* desechar, rechazar
rejection *n* rechazo

rejoice *v* regocijarse
rejoin *v* juntarse
rejuvenate *v* rejuvenecer
rekindle *v* reavivar
relapse *n* recaída
relapse *v* reincidir
relate *v* referirse
related *adj* relacionado
relation *n* relación
relationship *n* relación
relative *adj* relativo
relative *n* pariente
relax *v* descansar
relax *n* descanso
relaxation *n* relajación
relaxed *adj* relajado
relaxing *adj* relajante
relay *v* transmitir
release *n* liberación
release *v* soltar
relegate *v* relegar
relent *v* ceder
relentless *adj* implacable
relevant *adj* pertinente, relevante
reliability *n* fiabilidad
reliable *adj* seguro, confiable
reliance *n* confianza
relic *n* reliquia
relief *n* alivio
relieve *v* aliviar, relevar
religion *n* religión
religious *adj* religioso
relinquish *v* abandonar
relish *v* saborear
relive *v* revivir
relocate *v* mudarse
relocation *n* translado
reluctance *n* desgana
reluctant *adj* reacio

R

reluctantly *adv* de mala gana
rely on *v* contar con
remain *v* quedarse, permanecer
remainder *n* resto, remanente
remaining *adj* restante
remains *n* restos, sobras
remake *v* rehacer
remark *v* comentar, observar
remark *n* comentario
remarkable *adj* notable
remarry *v* casarse de nuevo
remedy *v* remediar
remedy *n* remedio
remember *v* acordarse
remembrance *n* recuerdo
remind *v* recordar
reminder *n* recordatorio
remiss *adj* negligente
remission *n* remisión, perdón
remit *v* remitir, perdonar
remittance *n* envío
remnant *n* resto
remodel *v* remodelar
remorse *n* remordimiento
remorseful *adj* arrepentido
remote *adj* remoto, lejano
removal *n* eliminación
remove *v* eliminar, quitar
remunerate *v* recompensar
renew *v* renovar
renewal *n* renovación
renounce *v* renunciar
renovate *v* renovar
renovation *n* renovación
renowned *adj* famoso
rent *v* rentar
rent *n* renta
renunciation *n* renuncia
reopening *n* reapertura

reorganize *v* reorganizar
repair *v* reparar
reparation *n* reparación
repatriate *v* repatriar
repay *v* devolver, pagar
repayment *n* reembolso
repeal *v* revocar
repeal *n* revocación
repeat *v* repetir
repeat n repetición
repel *v* rechazar
repellent adj repelente
repent *v* arrepentirse
repentance *n* arrepentimiento
repetition *n* repetición
replace *v* reemplazar
replacement *n* reemplazo, sustitución
replay *n* repetición
replenish *v* reponer
replete *adj* repleto
replica *n* réplica
replicate *v* replicar, reproducir
reply *v* contestar
reply *n* respuesta
report *v* reportar
report *n* reporte
reportedly *adv* según dicen
reporter *n* periodista
repose *v* descansar
repose *n* reposo
represent *v* representar
representation n representación
repress *v* reprimir
repression *n* represión
reprieve *n* indulto, alivio
reprimand *n* reprimenda
reprint *v* reimprimir
reprint *n* reimpresión

reprisal *n* represalia
reproach *v* reprochar(se)
reproach *n* reproche
reproduce *v* reproducir
reproduction *n* reproducción
reptile *n* reptil
republic *n* república
repudiate *v* repudiar, rechazar
repugnant *adj* repugnante
repulse *v* rechazar
repulse *n* rechazo
repulsion n repulsión
repulsive *adj* repulsivo
reputation *n* reputación
repute n reputación
reputedly *adv* según dicen
request *v* solicitar
request *n* petición
require *v* requerir
required adj requerido
requirement *n* requisito
requisite n requisito
re-rout v desviar
rescind v rescindir
rescue *v* rescatar
rescue *n* rescate
research *v* investigar
research *n* investigación
resemblance *n* parecido
resemble *v* parecerse
resent *v* resentirse
resentment *n* resentimiento
reservation *n* reservación
reserve *v* reservar
reservoir *n* pantano
reset v reajustar
reside *v* residir
residence *n* residencia
residue *n* residuo

resign *v* dimitir, resignar(se)
resignation *n* renuncia, dimisión
resilient *adj* resistente
resist *v* resistir
resistance *n* resistencia
resistant adj resistente
resolute *adj* resuelto
resolution *n* resolución
resolve *v* resolver
resort *v* recurrir
resound v resonar
resounding *adj* sonoro
resource *n* recurso
respect *v* respetar
respect *n* respeto
respectful *adj* respetuoso
respective *adj* respectivo
respiration *n* respiración
respite *n* respiro
respond *v* responder
response *n* respuesta, reacción
responsibility *n* responsabilidad
responsible *adj* responsable
responsive *adj* sensible, atento
rest *v* descansar
rest *n* descanso, reposo
rest room *n* aseos
restaurant *n* restaurante
restful *adj* descansado
restitution *n* restitución
restive adj intranquilo
restless *adj* inquieto
restoration *n* restauración
restore *v* restaurar
restrain *v* contener
restraint *n* moderación
restrict *v* restringir
result v resultar
result *n* resultado

R

resume _v_ reanudar
resumption _n_ reanudación
resurface _v_ reaparecer
resurrection _n_ resurrección
resuscitate _v_ resucitar
retain _v_ retener, conservar
retaliate _v_ retaliar
retaliation _n_ represalia
retarded _adj_ retrasado
retention _n_ retención
retire _v_ jubilarse; retirar(se)
retirement _n_ jubilación, retiro
retouch v retocar
retract _v_ retractarse
retreat _v_ retirarse
retreat _n_ retiro, retirada
retrieval _n_ recuperación
retrieve _v_ recobrar
retroactive _adj_ retroactivo
retrograde adj retrógado
return _v_ volver
return _n_ regreso
reunion _n_ encuentro
revamp v renovar
reveal _v_ revelar
revealing _adj_ revelador
revel _v_ gozar
revelation _n_ revelación
revenge _v_ vengarse
revenge _n_ venganza
revenue _n_ ingresos
reverberate v resonar
revere v venerar
reverence _n_ reverencia
reversal _n_ cambio
reverse _n_ reverso, contrario
reversible _adj_ reversible
revert _v_ volver a
review _v_ repasar, revisar

review _n_ revista; crítica
revise _v_ revisar, cambiar
revision _n_ revisión
revive _v_ revivir
revoke _v_ revocar
revolt _v_ sublevarse
revolt _n_ sublevación
revolting _adj_ desagradable
revolution n revolución
revolve _v_ dar vueltas, girar, revolver
revolver _v_ revólver
revue _n_ revista
revulsion _n_ repugnancia
reward _v_ recompensar
reward _n_ recompensa
rewarding _adj_ agradable
rheumatism _n_ reumatismo
rhinoceros _n_ reinoceronte
rhyme _n_ rima
rhythm _n_ ritmo
rib _n_ costilla
ribbon _n_ cinta
rice _n_ arroz
rich _adj_ rico
rid of _iv_ deshacerse
riddle _n_ acertijo
ride _iv_ viajar; montar
ridge _n_ cresta, cadena
ridicule _v_ burlarse
ridicule _n_ burla
ridiculous _adj_ ridículo
rife adj plagado
rifle _n_ fusil
rift _n_ grieta
right _adv_ bien
right _adj_ correcto; derecho
right _n_ derecho
righteous adj honrado
rightful adj legítimo

R

rigid *adj* rígido
rigor *n* rigor
rigorous adj riguroso
rim *n* borde, llanta
ring *iv* sonar
ring *n* anillo; timbrazo
ringleader *n* cabecilla
rinse *v* enjuagar
riot *v* amotinarse
riot *n* disturbio, motín
rip *v* rasgar
rip apart *v* destrozar
rip off *v* timar, engañar
ripe *adj* maduro
ripen *v* madurar
ripple *n* onda
rise *iv* levantarse, subir, ascender
risk *v* arriesgar
risk *n* riesgo
risky *adj* arriesgado
rite *n* rito
rival *n* rival
rivalry *n* rivalidad
river *n* río
rivet *v* remachar
riveting *adj* fascinante
roach n cucaracha
road *n* carretera
roam *v* vagar
roar *v* rugir
roar *n* rugido
roast *v* asar
roast *n* carne asada
rob *v* robar
robber *n* ladrón
robbery *n* robo
robe *n* albornoz, bata
robe n bata, toga
robust *adj* robusto

rock *n* roca, peñasco
rocket *n* cohete
rocky *adj* rocoso
rod *n* vara, caña
rodent *n* roedor
roll n rollo, rodillo
roll *v* enrollar, rodar
rolling adj ondulado, rodante
romance *n* romance
romantic adj romántico
roof *n* tejado, techo
room *n* cuarto; lugar
roomy *adj* amplio
rooster *n* gallo
root *n* raíz
root v arraigar
rope *n* cuerda
rosary *n* rosario
rose *n* rosa
rosy *adj* prometedor
rot *v* pudrirse
rot *n* podredumbre
rotate *v* girar, rotar
rotation *n* rotación
rotten *adj* podrido
rough adj áspero, tosco; aproximado
round v redondear
round *adj* redondo
roundup *n* redada
rouse *v* excitar
rousing *adj* caluroso
rout v derrotar
route *n* ruta, camino
routine *n* rutina
row *v* remar
row *n* remo; fila; bronca
rowdy *adj* ruidoso
royal *adj* real
royalty *n* realeza

R

rub v frotar
rubber n goma
rubbish n basura
rubble n escombros
ruby n rubí
rudder n timón
rude adj rudo, tosco
rudeness n descortesía
rudimentary adj rudimentario
rug n alfombra
ruin v arruinar
ruin n ruina
rule v gobernar, regir
rule n norma, regla
ruler n regla, gobernante
rum n ron
rumble v retumbar
rumble n sonido sordo
rumor n rumor
run iv correr
run away v huir
run into v tropezar con
run out v agotarse
run over v atropellar
run up v acumular
runner n corredor
runway n pista de aterrizaje
rupture n ruptura
rupture v romperse
rural adj rural
ruse n artimaña
rush n prisa
rush v apresurar, precipitarse
Russia n Rusia
Russian adj ruso
rust v oxidarse
rust n herrumbre
rustic adj rústico
rust-proof adj inoxidable

rusty adj oxidado
ruthless adj despiadado
rye n centeno

S

sabotage v sabotear
sabotage n sabotaje
sack v saquear; despedir
sack n saco; saqueo
sacrament n sacramento
sacred adj sagrado
sacrifice n sacrificio
sacrilege n sacrilegio
sad adj triste
sadden v entristecer
saddle n silla de montar
sadist n sadista
sadness n tristeza
safe adj seguro
safeguard n protección
safety n seguridad
sail v navegar
sail n vela
sailboat n velero
sailor n marinero
saint n santo
salad n ensalada
salary n salario
sale n venta
sale slip n recibo
salesman n vendedor
saliva n saliva
salmon n salmón
saloon n bar, salón

R
S

salt *n* sal
salty *adj* salado
salvage *v* recuperar
salvation *n* salvación
same *adj* mismo, igual
sample *n* muestra
sanctify *v* santificar
sanction *v* sancionar, aprobar
sanction *n* sanción, multa
sanctity *n* santidad
sanctuary *n* santuario
sand *n* arena
sandal *n* sandalia
sandpaper *n* papel de lijar
sandwich *n* bocadillo
sane *adj* cuerdo
sanity *n* sensatez
sap *n* savia
sap *v* desecar
sapphire *n* safiro
sarcasm *n* sarcasmo
sarcastic *adj* sarcástico
sardine *n* sardina
satanic *adj* satánico
satellite *n* satélite
satire *n* sátira
satisfaction *n* satisfacción
satisfactory *adj* satisfactorio
satisfy *v* satisfacer
saturate *v* saturar
Saturday *n* sábado
sauce *n* salsa
saucepan *n* cacerola
saucer *n* platillo
sausage *n* salchicha
savage *adj* feroz
savagery *n* salvajismo
save *v* ahorrar; salvar
savings *n* ahorros

savior *n* salvador
savor *v* saborear
saw *iv* serrar
saw *n* sierra
say *iv* decir
saying *n* dicho, proverbio
scaffolding *n* andamio
scald *v* escaldar
scale *v* trepar
scale *n* escala, balanza; escama
scalp *n* cabellera
scam *n* timo
scan *v* otear
scandal *n* escándalo
scandalize *v* escandalizar
scapegoat *n* chivo expiatorio
scar *n* cicatriz
scarce *adj* escaso
scarcely *adv* apenas
scarcity *n* escasez
scare *v* asustar
scare *n* susto
scare away *v* ahuyentar
scarf *n* bufanda
scary *adj* de miedo
scatter *v* desparramar
scavenger n limpiador, carroñero
scenario *n* situación
scene *n* escena; bastidor
scenery *n* escenario
scenic *adj* pintoresco
scent *n* perfume; pista
schedule *v* programar
schedule *n* horario; programa
scheme *n* plan; intriga
schism *n* cisma
scholar *n* erudito
scholarship *n* beca
school *n* escuela

S

science *n* ciencia
scientific *adj* científico
scientist *n* científico
scissors *n* tijeras
scoff *v* mofarse
scold *v* regañar
scolding *n* regaño
scooter *n* moto
scope *n* ámbito
scorch *v* quemar
score *n* resultado, puntaje
score *v* marcar
scorn *v* despreciar
scornful *n* despreciativo
scorpion *n* escorpión
scoundrel *n* canalla
scour *v* fregar; rastrear
scourge *n* tormento
scout *n* explorador
scramble *v* darse prisa
scrambled *adj* revueltos
scrap *n* chatarra
scrap *v* descartar
scrape *v* raspar; rozar
scratch *v* rascarse, rayar
scratch *n* rasguño
scream *v* chillar
scream *n* chillido
screech *v* chirriar
screen *n* pantalla; mampara
screen *v* proyectar; bloquear
screw *v* atornillar, arruinar
screw *n* tornillo
screwdriver *n* atornillador
scribble *v* hacer garabatos
script *n* guión
scroll *n* manuscrito
scrub *v* restregar
scruples *n* escrúpulos

scrupulous *adj* escrupuloso
scrutiny *n* escrutinio
scuffle *n* refriega
sculptor *n* escultor
sculpture *n* escultura
sea *n* mar
seafood *n* pescado
seagull *n* gaviota
seal *v* sellar
seal *n* foca; sello
seal off *v* acordonar, aislar
seam *n* costura
seamless *adj* sin junturas
seamstress *n* modista
search *v* buscar
search *n* búsqueda
seashore *n* orilla del mar
seasick *adj* mareado
seaside *adj* costero
season *n* estación
seasonal *adj* temporal
seasoning *n* condimento
seat *n* asiento
seated *adj* sentado
secede *v* separarse
secluded *adj* retirado
seclusion *n* aislamiento
second *n* segundo
secondary *adj* secundario
secrecy *n* secreto
secret *n* secreto
secretary *n* secretario
secretly *adv* en secreto
sect *n* secta
section *n* sección, parte
sector *n* sector
secure *v* asegurar
secure *adj* seguro
security *n* seguridad

S

sedate v calmar
sedation n sedación
seduce v seducir
seduction n seducción
see iv ver
seed n semilla
seedless adj sin pepitas
seedy adj de mala fama
seek iv buscar
seem v parecer
see-through adj transparente
segment n segmento
segregate v segregar
segregation n segregación
seize v agarrar; incautar
seizure n ataque
seldom adv raramente
select v seleccionar
selection n selección
self-conscious adj tímido
self-esteem n autoestima
self-evident adj obvio
self-interest n interés propio
selfish adj egoísta
selfishness n egoísmo
self-respect n amor propio
sell iv vender
seller n vendedor
sellout n liquidación
semblance n apariencia
semester n semestre
seminary n seminario
senate n senado
senator n senador
send iv enviar
sender n remitente
senile adj senil
senior adj de mayor edad
seniority n antiguedad

sensation n sensación
sense v sentir, notar
sense n sentido; sensatez
senseless adj sin sentido
sensible adj sensato
sensitive adj sensible
sensual adj sensual
sentence v sentenciar
sentence n sentencia; frase, oración
sentiment n sentimiento
sentimental adj sentimental
sentry n centinela
separate v separar
separate adj separado
separation n separación
September n septiembre
sequel n continuación
sequence n secuencia
serenade n serenata
serene adj sereno
serenity n serenidad
sergeant n sargento
series n serie
serious adj serio; grave
seriousness n seriedad; gravedad
sermon n sermón
serpent n serpiente
serum n suero
servant n siervo, sirviente
serve v servir; atender
service n servicio; saque
service v revisar
session n sesión
set n juego, conjunto
set iv poner
set about v ponerse a
set off v partir; causar
set out v partir, marchar
set up v establecer

S

setback n contratiempo
setting n marco
settle v resolver; calmar
settle down v establecerse
settle for v conformarse
settlement n acuerdo; colonia
settler n colono
setup n trampa, situación; instalación
seven adj siete
seventeen adj diecisiete
seventh adj séptimo
seventy adj setenta
sever v cortar, romper
several adj varios
severance n ruptura
severe adj severo; grave
severity n gravedad
sew v coser
sewage n aguas sucias
sewer n alcantarilla
sewing n costura
sex n sexo
sexuality n sexualidad
shabby adj raído, gastado
shack n chabola
shackle n grillos, cadenas
shade n matiz; sombra
shadow n sombra
shady adj sombreado
shake iv sacudir
shaken adj conmovido
shaky adj inestable
shallow adj poco profundo; superficial
sham n farsa
shambles n caos
shame v avergonzar
shame n verguenza
shameful adj vergonzoso
shameless adj sinverguenza

shape v dar forma, formar
shape n forma
share v compartir
share n porción; acción
shareholder n accionista
shark n tiburón
sharp adj afilado, definido
sharpen v afilar; sacar punta
sharpener n sacapuntas
shatter v hacer añicos
shattering adj demoledor
shave v afeitarse
she pro ella
shear iv esquilar
shed iv derramar
sheep n oveja
sheets n sábanas
shelf n estante
shell n cáscara, capa, concha
shellfish n mariscos
shelter v albegar, proteger
shelter n albergue, refugio
shelves n estanterías
shepherd n pastor
sherry n jerez
shield v proteger
shield n escudo
shift n cambio; turno
shift v mover, cambiar
shine iv resplandecer
shiny adj brillante
ship n barco
shipment n envío
shipwreck n naufragio
shipyard n astillero
shirk v eludir
shirt n camisa
shiver v tiritar
shiver n escalofrío

S

shock *v* dar un susto
shock *n* susto; descarga
shocking *adj* espantoso
shoddy *adj* de pacotilla
shoe *n* zapato
shoe polish *n* betún
shoe store *n* zapatería
shoelace *n* cordón
shoot *iv* disparar; rodar
shoot down *v* derribar
shop *v* ir de compras
shop *n* tienda
shoplifting *n* robo
shopping *n* compras
shore *n* orilla, costa
short *adj* corto; bajo
shortage *n* escasez
shortcoming *n* defecto
shortcut *n* atajo
shorten *v* acortar
shorthand *n* taquigrafía
short-lived *adj* efímero
shortly *adv* enseguida
shorts *n* pantalón corto
shortsighted *adj* miope
shot *n* disparo; inyección
shotgun *n* escopeta
shoulder *n* hombro
shout *v* gritar
shout *n* grito
shouting *n* griterío
shove *v* empujar
shove *n* empujón
shovel *n* pala
show *iv* mostrar
show off *v* presumir
show up *v* aparecer
showdown *n* enfrentamiento
shower *n* ducha

shrapnel *n* metralla
shred *v* desmenuzar
shred *n* triza, trozo
shrewd *adj* astuto
shriek *v* chillar
shriek *n* alarido, chillido
shrimp *n* camarón
shrine *n* santuario
shrink *iv* encogerse
shroud *n* sudario
shrouded *adj* envuelto
shrub *n* arbusto
shrug *v* encoger (hombros)
shudder *n* escalofrío
shudder *v* estremecerse
shuffle *v* barajar
shun *v* esquivar
shut *iv* cerrar
shut off *v* cortar
shut up *v* callarse
shuttle *v* conectar
shy *adj* tímido
shyness *n* timidez
sick *adj* enfermo
sicken *v* enfermarse
sickening *adj* repugnante
sickle *n* hoz
sickness *n* enfermedad
side *n* lado
sideburns *n* patillas
sidestep *v* evadir
sidewalk *n* acera
sideways *adv* de lado
siege *n* cerco, sitio
siege *v* sitiar
sift *v* cribar
sigh *n* suspiro
sigh *v* suspirar
sight *n* vista

S

sightseeing *n* visita de lugares
sign *v* firmar
sign *n* señal; letrero
signal *n* señal
signature *n* firma
significance *n* importancia
significant *adj* significativo
signify *v* significar
silence *n* silencio
silence *v* acallar
silent *adj* callado
silhouette *n* silueta
silk *n* seda
silly *adj* estúpido
silver *n* plata
silver plated *adj* plateado
silversmith *n* platero
silverware *n* cubiertos
similar *adj* semejante
similarity *n* semejanza
simmer *v* hervir despacio
simple *adj* simple
simplicity *n* simplicidad
simplify *v* simplificar
simply *adv* simplemente
simulate *v* simular
simultaneous *adj* simultáneo
sin *v* pecar
sin *n* pecado
since *c* ya que
since *pre* desde
since then *adv* desde entonces
sincere *adj* sincero
sincerity *n* sinceridad
sinful *adj* pecaminoso
sing *iv* cantar
singer *n* cantante
single *n* soltero
single *adj* solo, único, sencillo

singlehanded *adj* sin ayuda
single-minded *adj* firme
singular *adj* singular
sinister *adj* siniestro
sink *iv* hundir
sink in *v* penetrar
sinking *n* hundimiento
sinner *n* pecador
sip *v* sorber
sip *n* sorbito
sir *n* señor
siren *n* sirena
sirloin *n* solomillo
sissy *adj* afeminado
sister *n* hermana
sister-in-law *n* cuñada
sit *iv* sentarse
site *n* sitio, lugar
sitting *n* sesión
situated *adj* situado
situation *n* situación
six *adj* seis
sixteen *adj* dieciséis
sixth *adj* sexto
sixty *adj* sesenta
sizable *adj* considerable
size *n* tamaño, talla
size up *v* evaluar, medir
skate *v* patinar
skate *n* patín
skeleton *n* esqueleto
skeptic *adj* escéptico
skeptic *adj* escéptico
sketch *v* esbozar, dibujar
sketch *n* bosquejo, dibujo
sketchy *adj* incompleto
ski *v* esquiar
skill *n* destreza
skillful *adj* diestro

S

skim *v* desnatar

skin *v* despellejar

skin *n* piel

skinny *adj* flaco

skip *v* saltarse

skip *n* salto, brinco

skirmish *n* escaramuza

skirt *n* falda

skull *n* cráneo

sky *n* firmamento

skylight *n* claraboya

skyscraper *n* rascacielos

slab *n* losa

slack *adj* flojo

slacken *v* aflojar

slacks *n* pantalones

slam *v* cerrar con golpe

slander *n* calumnia

slanted *adj* parcial, inclinado

slap *n* bofetada

slap *v* dar un cachete

slash *n* corte, raja

slash *v* acuchillar, cortar

slate *n* pizarra

slaughter *v* matar

slaughter *n* matanza

slave *n* esclavo

slavery *n* esclavitud

slay *iv* matar

sleazy *adj* de mala fama

sleep *iv* dormir

sleep *n* sueño

sleeve *n* manga

sleeveless *adj* sin mangas

sleigh *n* trineo

slender *adj* esbelto; remoto

slice *v* cortar

slice *n* tajada, rodaja

slide *iv* deslizarse

slightly *adv* un poco, ligeramente

slim *adj* delgado; remoto

slip *v* resbalar

slip *n* resbalón, desliz

slipper *n* zapatilla

slippery *adj* resbaladizo

slit *iv* rajar

slob *adj* sucio, dejado

slogan *n* lema

slope *v* inclinar

slope *n* ladera, cuesta, pendiente

sloppy *adj* descuidado

slot *n* ranura, hueco

slow *adj* lento

slow down *v* ir despacio

slow motion *n* cámara lenta

slowly *adv* despacio

sluggish *adj* lento

slum *n* arrabal

slump *v* desplomarse

slump *n* desplome, bajón

slur *v* pronunciar mal

sly *adj* astuto

smack *n* bofetada

smack *v* abofetar

small *adj* pequeño

small print *n* letra pequeña

smallpox *n* viruela

smart *adj* listo, vivo

smash *v* chocar, estrellarse

smear *n* borrón, mancha

smear *v* difamar; untar

smell *iv* oler

smelly *adj* maloliente

smile *v* sonreír

smile *n* sonrisa

smith *n* herrero

smoke *v* fumar

smoked *adj* ahumado

S

smoker _n_ fumador
smoking gun _n_ prueba
smooth _v_ allanar, suavizar
smooth _adj_ suave, liso
smoothly _adv_ suavemente
smoothness _n_ suavidad
smother _v_ sofocar
smuggler _n_ contrabandista
snail _n_ caracol
snake _n_ serpiente
snapshot _n_ foto instantánea
snare _v_ engañar
snare _n_ trampa
snatch _v_ agarrar
sneak _v_ entrar a escondidas
sneeze _v_ estornudar
sneeze _n_ estornudo
sniff _v_ olfatear
sniper _n_ francotirador
snitch _v_ delatar
snooze _v_ dormitar
snore _v_ roncar
snore _n_ ronquido
snow _v_ nevar
snow _n_ nieve
snowfall _n_ nevada
snowflake _n_ copo de nieve
snub _v_ desairar
snub _n_ desaire
soak _v_ empapar, remojar
soak in _v_ penetrar
soak up _v_ absorber
soar _v_ remontarse
sob _v_ sollozar
sob _n_ sollozo
sober _adj_ sobrio
so-called _adj_ llamado
sociable _adj_ sociable
socialism _n_ socialismo

socialist _adj_ socialista
socialize _v_ alternar
society _n_ sociedad
sock _n_ calcetín
sod _n_ césped
soda _n_ refresco
sofa _n_ sofá
soft _adj_ blando
soften _v_ ablandar
softly _adv_ suavemente
softness _n_ suavidad
soggy _adj_ remojado
soil _v_ ensuciar
soil _n_ tierra
soiled _adj_ manchado
solace _n_ alivio
solar _adj_ solar
solder _v_ soldar
soldier _n_ soldado
sold-out _adj_ agotado
sole _n_ suela
sole _adj_ único
solely _adv_ solamente
solemn _adj_ solemne
solicit _v_ solicitar
solid _adj_ sólido, duro
solidarity _n_ solidaridad
solitary _adj_ solitario
solitude _n_ soledad
soluble _adj_ soluble
solution _n_ solución
solve _v_ solucionar, resolver (resuelva)
solvent _adj_ solvente
somber _adj_ sombrío
some _adj_ algunos
somebody _pro_ alguien
someday _adv_ algún día
somehow _adv_ de algún modo
someone _pro_ alguien

S

something *pro* algo
sometimes *adv* a veces
someway *adv* de algún modo
somewhat *adv* algo
son *n* hijo
song *n* canción
son-in-law *n* yerno
soon *adv* pronto
soothe *v* aliviar
sorcerer *n* hechicero
sorcery *n* hechicería
sore *n* llaga
sore *adj* doloroso
sorrow *n* pena, dolor
sorrowful *adj* triste
sorry *adj* arrepentido
sort *v* clasificar (clasifique), seleccionar
sort *n* especie de, tipo
sort out *v* clasificar
soul *n* alma
sound *n* sonido
sound *v* sonar; parecer
sound out *v* sondear
soup *n* sopa
sour *adj* amargo, agrio
source *n* fuente
south *n* sur
southbound *adv* hacia el sur
southeast *n* sudeste
southern *adj* sureño
southerner *n* del sur
southwest *n* suroeste
souvenir *n* recuerdo
sovereign *adj* soberano
sovereignty *n* soberanía
soviet *adj* soviético
sow *iv* sembrar
spa *n* balneario

space *n* espacio, sitio
space out *v* espaciar
spacious *adj* espacioso, amplio
spade *n* pala
Spain *n* España
span *v* extenderse
span *n* espacio; tramo
Spaniard *n* español
Spanish *adj* español
spank *v* zurrar, azotar
spanking *n* azote
spare *v* librar; perdonar
spare *adj* sobrante
spare part *n* repuesto
sparingly *adv* con moderación
spark *n* chispa
spark off *v* desencadenar
spark plug *n* bujía
sparkle *v* destellar
sparrow *n* gorrión
sparse *adj* escaso, esparcido
spasm *n* espasmo
speak *iv* hablar
speaker *n* altavoz; orador
spear *n* lanza
spearhead *v* encabezar
special *adj* especial
specialize *v* especializarse
specialized *adj* especializado
specialty *n* especialidad
species *n* especies
specific *adj* específico
specimen *n* muestra, ejemplar, espécimen
speck *n* mota, grano
spectacle *n* espectáculo
spectator *n* espectador
speculate *v* especular
speculation *n* especulación

S

speech *n* discurso
speechless *adj* mudo
speed *iv* acelerar
speed *n* rapidez, velocidad
speedily *adv* rápidamente
speedy *adj* veloz
spell *iv* deletrear
spell *n* hechizo
spelling *n* ortografía
spend *iv* gastar
spending *n* gastos
sperm *n* esperma
sphere *n* esfera
spice *n* especia
spicy *adj* picante
spider *n* araña
spider web *n* telaraña
spill *iv* derramar
spill *n* derrame
spin *iv* dar vueltas; hilar
spine *n* espina dorsal
spineless *adj* débil
spinster *n* solterona
spirit *n* espíritu, ánimo
spiritual *adj* espiritual
spit *iv* escupir
spite *n* rencor
spiteful *adj* rencoroso
splash *v* salpicar
splendid *adj* espléndido
splendor *n* esplendor
splint *n* tablilla
splinter *n* astilla
splinter *v* astillarse
split adj dividido, partido
split *n* separación, división
split *iv* partir, repartir, separar
split up *v* separarse
spoil *v* estropear

spoils *n* despojos, botín
sponge *n* esponja
sponsor *n* patrocinador
spontaneity *n* espontaneidad
spontaneous *adj* espontáneo
spooky *adj* horripilante
spool *n* carrete
spoon *n* cuchara
spoonful *n* cucharada
sporadic *adj* esporádico
sport *n* deporte
sportsman *n* deportista
sporty *adj* deportista
spot *v* ver, notar
spot *n* lugar; mancha
spotless *adj* inmaculado
spotlight *n* foco
spouse *n* cónyuge
sprain *v* torcerse
sprawl *v* extenderse
spray *v* rociar
spread *iv* extender; untar
spring *iv* brotar; brincar
spring *n* primavera; muelle
springboard *n* trampolín
sprinkle *v* rociar
sprout *v* brotar
spruce up *v* dejar limpio
spur *v* estimular
spur *n* espuela; incentivo
spy *v* espiar
spy *n* espía
squalid *adj* muy sucio
squander *v* despilfarrar
square *adj* cuadrado
square *n* plaza; cuadrado
squash *v* aplastar
squeak *v* rechinar
squeaky *adj* chirriante

squeamish *adj* miedoso
squeeze *v* apretar; exprimir
squeeze in *v* hacer lugar
squeeze up *v* apretarse
squid *n* calamar
squirrel *n* ardilla
stab *v* apuñalar
stab *n* puñalada
stability *n* estabilidad
stable *adj* estable, permanente
stable *n* estable, cuadra, caballeriza
stack *v* amontonar
stack *n* montón
staff *n* personal
stage *n* escenario; etapa
stage *v* organizar
stagger *v* tambalearse
staggering *adj* asombroso
stagnant *adj* estancado
stagnate *v* estancarse
stagnation *n* estancamiento
stain *v* manchar, teñir
stain *n* mancha, tinte
stair *n* escalón
staircase *n* escalera
stairs *n* escalera
stake *n* riesgo; poste, estaca
stake *v* arriesgar, apostar, estacar
stale *adj* rancio
stalemate *n* empate
stalk *v* acechar, seguir
stalk *n* tallo
stall *n* puesto, casilla
stall *v* ganar tiempo
stammer *v* tartamudear
stamp *v* sellar; patear
stamp *n* estampilla, sello
stamp out *v* eliminar
stampede *n* estampido

stand *iv* estar de pie
stand *n* puesto
stand for *v* defender
stand out *v* destacar
stand up *v* ponerse de pie
standard *n* norma, estandarte
standardize *v* estandarizar
standing adj fijo, permanente
standing *n* reputación; de pie
standpoint *n* punto de vista
standstill *adj* paralizado
staple *v* grapar
staple *n* grapa
stapler *n* grapadora
star *n* estrella
starch *n* almidón
starchy *adj* almidonado
stare *v* mirar fijo
stark *adj* desolador
start *v* empezar
start *n* comienzo
startle *v* sobresaltar
startled *adj* sobrecogido
starvation *n* hambre
starve *v* pasar hambre
state *n* estado; nación
state *v* decir, declarar
statement *n* declaración
station *n* estación
stationary *adj* parado, fijo, estacionario
stationery *n* papelería
statistic *n* estadística
statue *n* estatua
status *n* posición; estado
statute *n* estatuto
staunch *adj* fiel, leal
stay *v* quedarse
stay *n* estancia

S

steady *adj* firme; continuo
steak *n* chuleta
steal *iv* robar
stealthy *adj* sigiloso, callado
steam *n* vapor
steel *n* acero
steep *adj* empinado
stem *n* tallo
stem *v* contener
stench *n* hedor
step *n* paso; escalón
step down *v* dimitir
step out *v* salir un rato
step up *v* aumentar
stepbrother *n* hermanastro
step-by-step *adv* paso a paso
stepdaughter *n* hijastra
stepfather *n* padrastro
stepladder *n* escalera
stepmother *n* madrastra
stepsister *n* hermanastra
stepson *n* hijastro
sterile *adj* estéril
sterilize *v* esterilizar
stern *n* popa
stern *adj* severo, firme
sternly *adv* con firmeza
stew *n* guisado
stewardess *n* azafata
stick *n* palo, bastón
stick *iv* pegar, fijar
stick around *v* quedarse
stick out *v* sobresalir
stick to *v* seguir
sticker *n* etiqueta
sticky *adj* pegajoso
stiff *adj* tieso, duro
stiffen *v* endurecerse
stiffness *n* rigidez

stifle *v* reprimir; ahogar
stifling *adj* sofocante
still n alambique, silencio
still *adj* inmóvil
still *adv* todavía
stimulant *n* estimulante
stimulate *v* estimular
stimulus *n* estímulo
sting *iv* picar
sting *n* picadura; aguijón
stinging *adj* punzante
stingy *adj* tacaño
stink *iv* apestar
stink *n* hedor, peste
stinking *adj* hediondo
stipulate *v* estipular
stir *v* menear; mover
stir up *v* agitar
stitch *v* coser, suturar
stitch *n* puntada
stock *v* acumular, surtir
stock *n* existencias, acciones
stocking *n* media
stockpile *n* reservas
stockroom *n* almacén
stoic *adj* estoico
stomach *n* estómago
stone *n* piedra
stone *v* apedrear
stool *n* taburete
stop *v* parar(se), detener
stop *n* parada
stop by *v* visitar
stop over *v* hacer escala
storage *n* almacén
store *v* almacenar
store *n* tienda
stork *n* cigüeña
storm *n* tormenta

S

stormy *adj* tempestuoso
story *n* cuento; planta, piso
stove *n* estufa
straight *adj* recto, derecho
straighten out *v* enderezar
strain *v* colar, escurrir
strain *n* tensión, agobio
strained *adj* tirante, tenso
strainer *n* colador
strait *n* estrecho
stranded *adj* sin recursos
strange *adj* raro
stranger *n* extraño
strangle *v* estrangular
strap *n* correa
strategy *n* estrategia
straw *n* paja
strawberry *n* fresa
stray *adj* extraviado
stray *v* extraviarse
stream *n* arroyo; riada
street *n* calle
streetcar *n* tranvía
streetlight *n* farol
strength *n* fuerza
strengthen *v* reforzar
strenuous *adj* agotador
stress *n* estrés, énfasis
stressful *adj* estresante
stretch *n* tramo
stretch *v* estirar
stretcher *n* camilla
strict *adj* estricto
stride *iv* dar zancadas
strife *n* lucha
strike *n* huelga
strike *iv* pegar
strike back *v* atacar
strike out *v* tachar

strike up *v* entablar
striking *adj* sorprendente
string *n* cuerda; hilera
stringent *adj* riguroso
strip *n* tira, franja
strip *v* desnudar
stripe *n* raya
striped *adj* rayado
strive *iv* esforzarse, luchar por
stroke *n* golpe; embolia
stroll *v* pasear
strong *adj* fuerte
structure *n* estructura
struggle *v* luchar
struggle *n* lucha
stub *n* colilla; resguardo
stubborn *adj* testarudo
student *n* estudiante
study *v* estudiar
stuff *n* cosas; materia
stuff *v* llenar, rellenar
stuffing *n* relleno
stuffy *adj* mal ventilado
stumble *v* tropezar
stun *v* dejar atónito
stunning *adj* imponente
stupendous *adj* estupendo
stupid *adj* estúpido
stupidity *n* estupidez
sturdy *adj* firme, fuerte
stutter *v* tartamudear
style *n* estilo
subdue *v* dominar
subdued *adj* sumiso
subject *v* someter
subject *n* asignatura; tema
sublime *adj* sublime
submerge *v* sumergir
submissive *adj* sumiso

S

139

submit *v* presentar
subpoena *v* citar
subpoena *n* citación
subscribe *v* suscribir
subscription *n* subscripción
subsequent *adj* posterior
subsidiary *adj* filial, subsidiario
subsidize *v* subvencionar
subsidy *n* subvención
subsist *v* subsistir
substance *n* sustancia
substandard *adj* deficiente
substantial *adj* sustancial
substitute *v* sustituir
substitute *n* suplente
subtitle *n* subtítulo
subtle *adj* sutil
subtract *v* restar
subtraction *n* resta, sustracción
suburb *n* suburbio
subway *n* metro, trenes (subterráneos)
succeed *v* tener éxito
success *n* éxito
successful *adj* exitoso
successor *n* sucesor
succulent *adj* suculento
succumb *v* sucumbir
such *adj* tal
suck *v* chupar
sucker *adj* bobo, ingenuo, chupador
sudden *adj* repentino
suddenly *adv* de repente
sue *v* demandar
suffer *v* sufrir
suffer from *v* padecer
suffering *n* sufrimiento
sufficient *adj* suficiente
suffocate *v* sofocar

sugar *n* azúcar
suggest *v* sugerir
suggestion *n* sugerencia
suggestive *adj* sugestivo
suicide *n* suicidio
suit *n* traje
suitable *adj* apropiado
suitcase *n* maleta
sulfur *n* sulfuro
sullen *adj* malhumorado
sum *n* suma
sum up *v* resumir
summarize *v* resumir
summary *n* resumen, sumario
summer *n* verano
summit *n* cumbre
summon *v* convocar
sumptuous *adj* suntuoso
sun *n* sol
sun block *n* crema antisolar
sunburn *n* quemadura
Sunday *n* domingo
sundown *n* atardecer
sunglasses *n* gafas de sol
sunken *adj* hundido
sunny *adj* soleado
sunrise *n* amanecer
sunset *n* crepúsculo
superb *adj* magnífico
superfluous *adj* superfluo
superior *adj* superior
superiority *n* superioridad
supermarket *n* supermercado
superpower *n* superpotencia
supersede *v* suplantar
superstition *n* superstición
supervise *v* supervisar
supervision *n* supervisión
supper *n* cena

S

supple *adj* flexible
supplier *n* distribuidor
supplies *n* suministros
supply *v* suministrar
support *v* apoyar
supporter *n* partidiario
suppose *v* suponer
supposing *c* suponiendo que
supposition *n* suposición
suppress *v* suprimir
supremacy *n* supremacía
supreme *adj* supremo
surcharge *n* recargo
sure *adj* seguro
surely *adv* seguramente
surf *v* navegar
surface *n* superficie
surge *n* aumento
surgeon *n* cirujano
surgery n cirugía
surgical *adv* quirúrgico
surname *n* apellido
surpass *v* superar
surplus *n* superávit, excedente
surprise *v* sorprender
surprise *n* sorpresa
surrender *v* rendirse
surrender *n* rendición
surround *v* rodear
surroundings *n* alrededores
surveillance *n* vigilancia
survey *n* encuesta, estudio
survival *n* supervivencia
survive *v* sobrevivir
survivor *n* superviviente
susceptible *adj* susceptible
suspect *v* sospechar
suspect *n* sospechoso
suspend *v* suspender

suspenders *n* tirantes
suspense *n* duda, suspense
suspension *n* suspensión
suspicion *n* sospecha
suspicious *adj* sospechoso
sustain *v* sostener
sustenance *n* sustento
swallow *v* tragar
swamp *n* pantano, ciénaga
swamped *adj* abrumado
swan *n* cisne
swap *v* cambiar
swap *n* intercambio
swarm *n* enjambre
sway *v* mover, influir
swear *iv* jurar
sweat *n* sudor
sweat *v* sudar
sweater *n* suéter
Sweden *n* Suecia
Swedish *adj* sueco
sweep *iv* barrer
sweet *adj* dulce
sweeten *v* endulzar
sweetheart *n* novio
sweetness *n* dulzura
sweets *n* dulces
swell *iv* hinchar
swelling *n* hinchazón
swift *adj* rápido
swim *iv* nadar
swimmer *n* nadador
swimming *n* natación
swindle *v* estafar
swindle *n* estafa
swindler *n* estafador
swing *iv* balancear, oscilar
swing *n* columpio; vaivén
Swiss *adj* suizo

S

switch _v_ cambiar
switch _n_ interruptor; cambio
switch off _v_ apagar
switch on _v_ encender
Switzerland _n_ Suiza
swivel _v_ girar
swollen _adj_ hinchado
sword _n_ espada
swordfish _n_ pez espada
syllable _n_ sílaba
symbol _n_ símbolo
symbolic _adj_ simbólico
symmetry _n_ simetría
sympathize _v_ simpatizar
sympathy _n_ compasión
symphony _n_ sinfonía
symptom _n_ síntoma
synagogue _n_ sinagoga
synchronize _v_ sincronizar
synod _n_ sínodo
synonym _n_ sinónimo
synthesis _n_ síntesis
syphilis _n_ sífilis
syringe _n_ jeringa
syrup _n_ jarabe
system _n_ sistema
systematic _adj_ sistemático

**S
T**

T

table _n_ mesa, tabla
tablecloth _n_ mantel
tablespoon _n_ cuchara
tablet _n_ pastilla, tableta
tacit adj tácito

tack _n_ tachuela
tackle _v_ abordar
tact _n_ tacto
tactful _adj_ discreto
tactical _adj_ táctico
tactics _n_ táctica
tag _n_ etiqueta
tail _n_ cola, rabo
tail _v_ seguir a alguien
tailor _n_ sastre
taint n mancha
tainted _adj_ manchado
take _iv_ tomar
take apart _v_ desmontar
take away _v_ quitar
take back _v_ devolver
take in _v_ acoger
take off _v_ despegar
take out _v_ sacar
take over _v_ apoderarse
tale _n_ cuento
talent _n_ talento
talented adj dotado
talk _v_ hablar
talkative _adj_ hablador
tall _adj_ alto
tame _v_ domesticar
tan adj bronceado
tangent _n_ tangente
tangerine _n_ mandarina
tangible _adj_ tangible
tangle _n_ lío
tank _n_ tanque
tantamount to _adj_ equivalente a
tantrum _n_ rabieta
tap _n_ grifo, llave
tap into _v_ utilizar
tape _n_ cassette, cinta
tape recorder _n_ grabadora

tapestry *n* tapiz
tar *n* brea, alquitrán
tarantula *n* tarántula
tardy *adv* tardío
target *n* blanco; meta
tariff *n* tarifa
tarnish *v* manchar
tart *n* tarta
tartar *n* sarro
task *n* tarea
taste *v* probar; saber a
taste *n* gusto; sabor
tasteful *adj* de buen gusto
tasteless *adj* soso
tasty *adj* sabroso
tavern *n* taberna
tax *n* impuesto
tea *n* té
teach *iv* enseñar
teacher *n* maestro
team *n* equipo
teapot *n* tetera
tear *iv* rasgar; romper
tear *n* lágrima
tearful *adj* lloroso
tease *v* tomar el pelo
teaspoon *n* cucharita
technical *adj* técnico
technicality *n* formalidad
technician *n* técnico
technique *n* técnica
technology *n* tecnología
tedious *adj* aburrido
tedium *n* aburrimiento
teenager *n* adolescente
teeth *n* dientes
teeth *v* salir los dientes
telegram *n* telegrama
telepathy *n* telepatía

telephone *n* teléfono
telescope *n* telescopio
televise *v* televisar
television *n* televisión
tell *iv* decir
teller *n* cajero
telling *adj* indicador
temper *n* mal humor
temperate adj moderado
temperature *n* temperatura
tempest *n* tempestad
temple *n* templo; sien
temporary *adj* temporal
tempt *v* tentar
temptation *n* tentación
tempting *adj* tentador
ten *adj* diez
tenacious adj tenaz
tenacity *n* tenacidad
tenant *n* inquilino
tend *v* tender; atender
tendency *n* tendencia
tender *adj* tierno; sensible
tender *v* ofrecer
tenderness *n* ternura; blandura
tendon n tendón
tenet n principio
tennis *n* tenis
tenor *n* tenor
tense *adj* tenso
tension *n* tensión
tent *n* tienda de campaña
tentacle *n* tentáculo
tentative *adj* provisional
tenth *n* décimo
tenuous *adj* tenue
tepid *adj* tibio
term *n* mandato, plazo, término
terminate *v* terminar

terminology n terminología
termite n termita
terms n condiciones
terrace n terraza
terrain n terreno
terrestrial adj terrestre
terrible adj terrible
terrific adj fantástico
terrify v aterrorizar
terrifying adj espantoso
territory n territorio
terror n terror
terrorism n terrorismo
terrorist n terrorista
terrorize v aterrorizar
terse adj rígido
test v probar, examinar
test n prueba, examen
testament n testamento
testify v testificar
testimony n testimonio
testing adj duro
text n texto
textbook n libro de texto
textile adj textil
texture n textura
thank v agradecer
thankful adj agradecido
thanks n gracias
that adj ese, aquel
thaw v descongelar
thaw n deshielo
theater n teatro
theft n robo
theme n tema
themselves pro ellos mismos
then adv entonces
theologian n teólogo
theology n teología

theoretical adj teórico
theory n teoría
therapeutic adj terapéutico
therapist n terapeuta
therapy n terapia
there adv allí
thereby c por eso
therefore adv por lo tanto
thermometer n termómetro
thermostat n termostato
these adj estos, estas
thesis n tesis
they pro ellos
thick adj espeso; grueso
thicken v espesar
thickness n grosura, espesor
thief n ladrón
thigh n muslo
thin adj delgado; claro
thin v adelgazar
thing n cosa
think iv pensar
thinly adv ligeramente
third adj tercero
thirst v tener sed
thirsty adj sediento
thirteen adj trece
thirty adj treinta
this adj este, esta
thorax n tórax
thorn n espina
thorny adj espinoso
thorough adj ninucioso, perfecto
those adj esos, aquellos
though c aunque
thought n pensamiento
thoughtful adj atento
thousand adj mil
thread v enhebrar

thread *n* hilo, rosca	**tickle** *n* cosquillas
threat *n* amenaza	**ticklish** *adj* cosquilloso
threaten *v* amenazar	**tidal wave** *n* maremoto
three *adj* tres	**tide** *n* marea, corriente
thresh *v* trillar	**tidy** *adj* arreglado
threshold *n* umbral	**tie** *v* empatar; atar
thrifty *adj* económico	**tie** *n* corbata; empate
thrill *v* emocionar	**tiger** *n* tigre
thrill *n* emoción	**tight** *adj* apretado; estricto
thrilling adj emocionante	**tighten** *v* apretar
thrive *v* prosperar	**tile** *n* teja; azulejo
throat *n* garganta	**till** *adv* hasta
throb *n* latido, punzada	**till** *v* cultivar, labrar
throb *v* latir	**tilt** *v* inclinar
thrombosis *n* trombosis	**timber** *n* madera
throne *n* trono	**time** *n* tiempo
throng *n* muchedumbre	**time** *v* medir el tiempo
through (thru) *pre* a través de	**timeless** *adj* eterno
throughout pre por todo	**timely** *adj* oportuno
throw *iv* tirar, lanzar	**times** *n* veces
throw away *v* derrochar	**timetable** *n* horario
throw up *v* vomitar	**timid** *adj* tímido
throwback n retroceso	**timidity** *n* timidez
thrust n impulso	**tin** *n* estaño
thrust v empujar, clavar	**tinge** n tono, matiz
thug *n* gamberro	**tinker** v jugar con
thumb v hojear	**tiny** *adj* muy pequeño
thumb *n* dedo pulgar	**tip** *n* punta; propina
thumbs-up n aprobación	**tip** v dar propina; inclinar
thumbtack *n* chincheta	**tip off** v advertir, avisar
thunder *n* trueno	**tip over** v volcar
thunderbolt *n* rayo	**tiptoe** *n* andar de puntillas
thunderstorm *n* tormenta eléctrica	**tired** *adj* cansado
Thursday *n* jueves	**tiredness** *n* cansancio
thus *adv* así	**tireless** *adj* incansable
thwart *v* frustrar, impedir	**tiresome** *adj* pesado, cansado
thyroid *n* tiroides	**tiring** adj cansado
ticket n entrada, boleto	**tissue** *n* tejido, kleenex
tickle *v* hacer cosquillas	**title** *n* título

T

to *pre* a
toad *n* sapo
toast *v* tostar; brindar
toast *n* tostada, brindis
toaster *n* tostador
tobacco *n* tabaco
today *adv* hoy
toddler *n* niño pequeño
toe *n* dedo del pie
toenail *n* uña del pie
together *adv* juntos
toil *v* trabajar duro
toilet *n* retrete
token *n* muestra
tolerable *adj* tolerable
tolerance *n* tolerancia
tolerate *v* tolerar
toll *n* peaje; mortandaz
toll *v* tañer
tomato *n* tomate
tomb *n* tumba
tombstone *n* lápida
tomorrow *adv* mañana
ton *n* tonelada
tone *n* tono
tongs *n* tenazas, pinzas
tongue *n* lengua
tonic *n* tónica
tonight *adv* esta noche
tonsil *n* amígdala
too *adv* también
tool *n* herramienta
tooth *n* diente
toothache *n* dolor de muelas
toothpick *n* palillo de dientes
top *n* cumbre, cima
topic *n* tema
topple *v* derrocar
torch *n* antorcha

torment *v* atormentar
torment *n* tormento
torpedo n torpedo
torpedo v torpedear
torrent *n* torrente
torrid *adj* tórrido
torso *n* espalda
tortoise *n* tortuga
tortuous adj tortuoso
torture *v* torturar
torture *n* tortura
toss *v* tirar, echar
total *adj* total
totalitarian *adj* totalitario
totality *n* totalidad
totter v tambalearse
touch *n* tacto; contacto
touch *v* tocar
touch on *v* aludir
touch up *v* retocar
touchdown n aterrizaje
touching *adj* sentimental
touchy adj delicado
tough *adj* duro, fuerte
toughen *v* endurecer
tour *n* viaje
tourism *n* turismo
tourist *n* turista
tournament *n* torneo
tow *v* remolcar
tow truck *n* grúa
towards *pre* hacia
towel *n* toalla
tower *n* torre
towering *adj* imponente
town *n* ciudad
town hall *n* ayuntamiento
toxic *adj* tóxico
toxin *n* toxina

toy *n* juguete
trace *v* calcar; localizar
track *n* rastro, pista
track *v* seguir el rastro
traction *n* tracción
tractor *n* tractor
trade *n* comercio
trade *v* comerciar
trademark *n* marca de fábrica
trader *n* comerciante
tradition *n* tradición
traffic *n* tráfico
traffic *v* tráficar
tragedy *n* tragedia
tragic *adj* trágico
trail *v* rastrear; arrastrar
trail *n* senda, rastro
trailer *n* remolque
train *n* tren
train *v* adiestrar
trainee *n* aprendiz
trainer *n* entrenador
training *n* entrenamiento
trait *n* rasgo, característica
traitor *n* traidor
trajectory *n* trajectoria
tram *n* tranvía
trample *v* pisotear
trance *n* trance
tranquility *n* tranquilidad
transaction *n* transacción
transcend *v* transcender
transcribe *v* transcribir
transcript *n* transcripción
transfer *v* transladar, transferir
transfer *n* traslado, transferencia
transform *v* transformar
transformation *n* transformación
transfusion *n* transfusión

transient *adj* transitorio
transient n viajero
transit *n* tránsito
transition *n* transición
transitive adj transitivo
translate *v* traducir
translation n traducción
translator *n* traductor
transmit *v* transmitir
transparency n transpariencia
transparent *adj* transparente
transpire v indicar
transplant *v* trasplantar
transport *v* transportar
trap *n* trampa
trap v atrapar
trash *n* basura
trash can *n* cubo de basura
traumatic *adj* traumático
traumatize *v* traumatizar
travel *v* viajar
traveler *n* viajero
tray *n* bandeja
treacherous *adj* traicionero
treachery *n* traición
tread *iv* pisar
treason *n* traición
treasure *n* tesoro
treasurer *n* tesorero
treat *v* tratar
treat *n* regalo
treatment n tratamiento
treatment *n* trato; tratamiento
treaty *n* tratado
tree *n* árbol
tremble *v* temblar
tremendous *adj* tremendo
tremor *n* temblor
trench *n* zanja, trinchera

T

trend *n* tendencia
trendy *adj* de moda
trespass *v* entrar sin permiso
trial *n* juicio; ensaya, prueba
triangle *n* triángulo
tribe *n* tribu
tribulation *n* tribulación
tribunal *n* tribunal
tribute *n* tributo, homenaje
trick *v* engañar
trick *n* engaño; truco
trickle *v* gotear
tricky *adj* difícil
trifle n tontería
trigger *v* desencadenar
trigger *n* gatillo, disparador
trim *v* recortar
trimester *n* trimestre
trimmings *n* guarnición
trip *n* viaje, tropezón
trip *v* tropezar, caerse
triple *adj* triple
triplicate v triplicar
tripod *n* trípodo
triumph *n* triunfo
triumphant *adj* triunfante
trivial *adj* insignificante
trivialize *v* trivializar
trolley *n* tranvía
troop *n* tropa
trophy *n* trofeo
tropic *n* trópico
tropical *adj* tropical
trouble *n* problema, molestia
trouble *v* inquietar, molestar
troublesome *adj* problemático
trousers *n* pantalones
trout *n* trucha
truce *n* tregua

truck *n* camión
trucker *n* camionero
true adj verdadero
truly adv sinceramente
trumped-up *adj* falso
trumpet *n* trompeta
trunk *n* tronco; baúl
trust *v* confiar
trust *n* confianza
truth *n* verdad
truthful *adj* veraz
try *v* tratar, probar
trying adj difícil, duro
tub *n* bañera
tube n tubo, conducto
tuberculosis *n* tuberculosis
Tuesday *n* martes
tug v remolcar
tuition *n* matrícula
tulip *n* tulipán
tumble *v* caer en picado
tummy *n* barriga
tumor *n* tumor
tumult *n* tumulto
tumultuous *adj* tumultuoso
tuna *n* atún
tune *n* melodía, aire
tune *v* sintonizar
tune up *v* afinar
tunic *n* túnica
tunnel *n* túnel
turbine *n* turbina
turbulence *n* turbulencia
turbulent n turbulento
turf *n* césped
Turk *adj* turco
Turkey *n* Turquía
turmoil *n* alboroto
turn *n* vuelta; turno

turn *v* girar; volver
turn back *v* volverse atrás
turn down *v* rechazar
turn in *v* entregar
turn off *v* apagar
turn on *v* encender
turn out *v* resultar
turn over *v* volcar
turn up *v* aparecer
turnout n asistencia total
turret *n* torreón
turtle *n* tortuga
tusk *n* colmillo
tutor *n* tutor
tweezers *n* pinzas
twelfth *adj* duodécimo
twelve *adj* doce
twentieth *adj* vigésimo
twenty *adj* veinte
twice *adv* dos veces
twilight *n* crepúsculo
twin *n* gemelo
twinkle *v* brillar
twist *v* torcer
twist *n* torcedura; giro
twisted *adj* torcido
twister *n* tornado
two *adj* dos
tycoon *n* magnate
type *n* clase; tipo
type *v* escribir a máquina
typhoon n tifón
typical *adj* típico
tyranny *n* tiranía
tyrant *n* tirano

ugliness *n* fealdad
ugly *adj* feo
ulcer *n* úlcera
ultimate *adj* último
ultimatum *n* ultimatum
ultrasound *n* ultrasonido
umbrella *n* paraguas
umpire *n* árbitro
unable *adj* incapaz
unanimity *n* unanimidad
unarmed *adj* desarmado
unassuming *adj* sin pretensiones
unattached *adj* soltero
unavoidable *adj* inevitable
unaware *adj* inconsciente
unbearable *adj* insoportable
unbeatable *adj* invencible
unbelievable *adj* increíble
unbiased *adj* imparcial
unbroken *adj* intacto
unbutton *v* desabrochar
uncertain *adj* incierto
uncle *n* tío
uncomfortable *adj* incómodo
uncommon *adj* raro
unconscious *adj* sin sentido
uncover *v* descubrir
undecided *adj* indeciso
undeniable *adj* innegable
under *pre* debajo, bajo
undercover *adj* secreto
underdog *n* el más débil
undergo *v* sufrir
underground *adj* subterráneo
underlie *v* sostentar
underline *v* subrayar

T
U

underlying *adj* subyacente
undermine *v* socavar
underneath *pre* debajo
underpass *n* paso subterráneo
understand *v* comprender
understandable *adj* comprensible
understanding *adj* comprensivo
undertake *v* emprender
underwear *n* ropa interior
underwrite *v* asegurar
undeserved *adj* inmerecido
undesirable *adj* indeseable
undisputed *adj* indiscutible
undo *v* deshacer
undoubtedly *adv* indudablemente
undress *v* desnudarse
undue *adj* excesivo
unearth *v* desenterrar
uneasiness *n* inseguridad
uneasy *adj* inseguro
uneducated *adj* inculto
unemployed *adj* sin empleo
unemployment *n* desempleo
unending *adj* interminable
unequal *adj* desigual
unequivocal *adj* claro
uneven *adj* desigual
uneventful *adj* sin incidentes
unexpected *adj* inesperado
unfailing *adj* exitoso
unfair *adj* injusto
unfairly *adv* injustamente
unfairness *n* injusticia
unfaithful *adj* infiel
unfamiliar *adj* desconocido
unfasten *v* desatar
unfavorable *adj* desfavorable
unfit *adj* no apto
unfold *v* desdoblar

unforeseen *adj* imprevisto
unforgettable *adj* inolvidable
unfounded *adj* sin fundamento
unfriendly *adj* antipático
unfurnished *adj* sin amueblar
ungrateful *adj* desagradecido
unhappiness *n* tristeza
unhappy *adj* descontento
unharmed *adj* ileso
unhealthy *adj* malsano
unheard-of *adj* inaudito
unhurt *adj* ileso
unification *n* unificación
uniform *n* uniforme
uniformity *n* uniformidad
unify *v* unificar
unilateral *adj* unilateral
union *n* unión
unique *adj* único
unit *n* unidad
unite *v* unir
unity *n* unidad
universal *adj* universal
universe *n* universo
university *n* universidad
unjust *adj* injusto
unjustified *adj* injustificado
unknown *adj* desconocido
unlawful *adj* ilegal
unleaded *adj* sin plomo
unleash *v* desatar
unless *c* a no ser que
unlike *adj* distinto
unlikely *adj* improbable
unlimited *adj* ilimitado
unload *v* descargar
unlock *v* abrir
unlucky *adj* desafortunado
unmarried *adj* soltero

U

unmask *v* desenmascarar
unmistakable *adj* inconfundible
unnecessary *adj* innecesario
unnoticed *adj* desapercibido
unoccupied *adj* desocupado
unofficially *adv* sin confirmar
unpack *v* deshacer
unpleasant *adj* desagradable
unplug *v* desenchufar
unpopular *adj* impopular
unpredictable *adj* imprevisible
unprofitable *adj* no rentable
unprotected *adj* desprotegido
unravel *v* desenredar
unreal *adj* irreal
unrealistic *adj* poco realista
unreasonable *adj* irrazonable
unrelated *adj* no relacionado
unreliable *adj* incierto
unrest *n* malestar
unsafe *adj* peligroso
unselfish *adj* generoso
unspeakable *adj* indecible
unstable *adj* inestable
unsteady *adj* inseguro
unsuccessful *adj* sin éxito
unsuitable *adj* inapropiado
unsuspecting *adj* confiado
unthinkable *adj* inconcebible
untie *v* desatar
until *pre* hasta
untimely *adj* inoportuno
untouchable *adj* intocable
untrue *adj* falso
unusual *adj* insólito
unveil *v* desvelar
unwillingly *adv* de mala gana
unwind *v* relajarse
unwise *adj* imprudente

unwrap *v* desenvolver
upbringing *n* educación
upcoming *adj* venidero
update *v* poner al día
upgrade *v* mejorar
upheaval *n* convulsión
uphill *adv* cuesta arriba
uphold *v* defender
upholstery *n* tapicería
upkeep *n* mantenimiento
upon *pre* sobre
upper *adj* superior
upright *adj* derecho, recto; verticalmente
uprising *n* sublevación
uproar *n* escándalo
uproot *v* desarraigar
upset *v* molestar
upside-down *adv* al revés
upstairs *adv* arriba
uptight *adj* tenso
up-to-date *adj* moderno
upturn *n* mejora
upwards *adv* hacia arriba
urban *adj* urbano
urge *n* impulso
urge *v* animar
urgency *n* urgencia
urgent *adj* urgente
urinate *v* orinar
urine *n* orina
urn *n* urna
us *pro* nosotros
usage *n* uso
use *v* usar, utilizar
use *n* uso, utilización
used to *adj* acostumbrado
useful *adj* útil
usefulness *n* utilidad

U

useless *adj* inservible, inútil
user *n* usuario
usher *n* ujier
usual *adj* normal
usurp *v* usurpar
utensil *n* utensilio
uterus *n* útero
utilize *v* utilizar
utmost *adj* sumo, máximo
utter *v* decir, pronunciar

vacancy *n* libre, vacante
vacant *adj* desocupado
vacate *v* desocupar
vacation *n* vacación
vaccinate *v* vacunar
vaccine *n* vacuna
vacillate *v* vacilar, dudar
vagrant *n* vagabundo
vague *adj* impreciso
vain *adj* vano
vainly *adv* en vano
valiant *adj* valiente
valid *adj* válido, vigente
validate *v* validar
validity *n* validez
valley *n* valle
valuable *adj* valioso
value *n* valor
valve *n* válvula
vampire *n* vampiro
van *n* furgoneta
vandal *n* vándalo

vandalism *n* vandalismo
vandalize *v* destruir
vanguard *n* vanguardia
vanish *v* desaparecer
vanity *n* vanidad
vanquish *v* vencer
vapor n vapor
vaporize *v* vaporizar
variable *adj* variable
varied *adj* variado
variety *n* variedad
various *adj* varios
varnish *v* barnizar
varnish *n* barniz
vary *v* variar
vase *n* jarrón
vast *adj* enorme
vault n bóveda
veal *n* ternera
veer *v* torcer, girar
vegetable *v* legumbre, vegetal
vegetarian *v* vegetariano
vegetation *n* vegetación
vehicle *n* vehículo
veil *n* velo
vein *n* vena
velocity *n* velocidad
velvet *n* terciopelo
vendor n vendedor
venerate *v* venerar
venereal adj venéreo
vengeance *n* venganza
venison *n* carne de venado
venom *n* veneno
vent *n* respiradero
ventilate *v* ventilar
ventilation *n* ventilación
venture *v* arriesgarse
venture *n* riesgo; negocio

verb *n* verbo
verbally *adv* de palabra
verbatim *adv* literalmente
verdict *n* veredicto
verge *n* borde
verification *n* verificación
verify *v* verificar
versatile *adj* versátil
verse *n* verso
versed *adj* versado
version *n* versión
versus *pre* contra
vertebra *n* vértebra
very *adv* muy
vessel *n* barco, vaso, buque
vest *n* chaleco
vestige *n* vestigio
veteran *n* veterano
veterinarian *n* veterinario
veto *v* vetar
viable adj viable
viaduct *n* viaducto
vibrant *adj* vibrante
vibrate *v* vibrar
vibration *n* vibración
vicar n párroco, vicario
vice *n* vicio
vice versa adv al revés
vicinity *n* cercanías
vicious *adj* feroz
victim *n* víctima
victimize *v* tratar mal
victor *n* vencedor
victorious *adj* victorioso
victory *n* victoria
view *n* vista, opinion
view *v* ver, mirar
viewpoint *n* punto de vista
vigil *n* vigilia

vigorous adj vigoroso
vile adj vil
village *n* pueblo, aldea
villager *n* aldeano
villain *n* villano
vindicate *v* justificar
vindictive *adj* vengativo
vine *n* vid, parra
vinegar *n* vinagre
vineyard *n* viña, viñedo
violate *v* violar
violence *n* violencia
violent *adj* violento
violet *n* violeta
violin *n* violín
violinist *n* violinista
viper *n* víbora
virgin *n* virgen
virginity *n* virginidad
virile *adj* viril
virility *n* virilidad
virtually *adv* prácticamente
virtue *n* virtud
virtuous *adj* virtuoso
virulent *adj* virulento
virus *n* virus
visa n visado
visibility *n* visibilidad
visible *adj* visible
vision *n* visión, sentido
visit *n* visita
visit *v* visitar
visitor *n* visitante
visual *adj* visual
visualize *v* visualizar
vital *adj* vital, decisivo
vitality *n* vitalidad
vitamin *n* vitamina
vivacious *adj* vivaz

V

vivid *adj* gráfico
vocabulary *n* vocabulario
vocation *n* vocación
vogue *n* moda
voice *n* voz
void *adj* vacío; nulo
volatile *adj* inestable, volátil
volcano *n* volcán
volleyball *n* vólibol
volt n voltio
voltage *n* voltaje
volume *n* volumen; capacidad
volunteer *n* voluntario
vomit *v* vomitar
vomit *n* vómito
vote *v* votar
vote *n* voto
voting *n* votación
vouch for *v* responder por
voucher *n* vale
vow *v* jurar
vow n voto, promesa
vowel *n* vocal
voyage *n* viaje por mar
voyager *n* pasajero
vulgar *adj* vulgar
vulgarity *n* vulgaridad
vulnerable *adj* vulnerable
vulture *n* buitre

wafer *n* barquillo
wag *v* menear
wage *n* sueldo, salario
wagon *n* vagón
wail *v* llorar
wail *n* lloriqueo, llanto
waist *n* cintura
wait *v* esperar
waiter *n* camarero
waiting *n* espera
waitress *n* camarera
waive *v* renunciar, suspender
wake up *iv* despertarse
walk *v* caminar
walk *n* paseo
walkout *n* huelga
wall *n* pared, muro
wallet *n* cartera
walnut *n* nuez de nogal
walrus *n* morsa
waltz *n* vals
wander *v* vagar, divagar
wanderer *n* vagabundo
wane *v* menguar
want *v* querer
war *n* guerra
ward *n* sala
ward off v parar, rechazar
warden *n* guardián
wardrobe *n* armario, ropero
warehouse *n* almacén
warfare *n* guerra
warm *adj* tibio, caliente
warm up *v* calentarse
warmth *n* calor
warn *v* avisar, advertir

warning *n* aviso
warp *v* doblarse
warped *adj* retorcido
warrant *v* justificar
warrant *n* orden judicial
warranty *n* garantía
warrior *n* guerrero
warship *n* barco de guerra
wart *n* verruga
wary *adj* cauteloso
wash *v* lavar
washable *adj* lavable
washer n lavadora
washing n lavado
wasp *n* avispa
waste *v* desperdiciar
waste *n* desperdicio
waste basket *n* papelera
wasteful *adj* derrochador
watch *n* reloj
watch *v* vigilar
watch out *v* tener cuidado
watchdog n inspector
watchful *adj* vigilante
watchmaker *n* relojero
water *n* agua
water *v* regar
water down *v* diluir
water heater *n* calentador
waterfall *n* cascada
watermelon *n* sandía
waterproof *adj* impermeable
watershed *n* momento crítico
watertight *adj* hermético
watery *adj* aguado
watt *n* vatio
wave *n* onda, ola
waver *v* vacilar
wavy *adj* ondulado

wax *n* cera
way *n* camino; modo
way in *n* entrada
way out *n* salida
we *pro* nosotros
weak *adj* débil
weaken *v* debilitar
weakness *n* debilidad
wealth *n* riqueza
wealthy *adj* rico
weapon *n* arma
wear *n* uso; desgaste
wear *iv* usar; calzar; llevar
wear down *v* agotar
wear out *v* desgastar
weary *adj* cansado, agotado
weather *n* clima, tiempo
weave *iv* tejer
web *n* telaraña; red
web site *n* sitio en la red
wed *iv* casarse
wedding *n* boda
wedge *n* cuña
Wednesday *n* miércoles
weed *n* hierba mala, maleza
weed *v* escardar, eliminar
week *n* semana
weekday *adj* día laborable
weekend *n* fin de semana
weekly *adv* semanalmente
weep *iv* llorar
weigh *v* pesar
weight *n* peso
weighty adj pesado, serio
weird *adj* raro
welcome *v* acoger, recibir
welcome *n* bienvenida
weld *v* soldar
welder *n* soldador

W

welfare n bienestar
well n pozo
well-being n bienestar
well-known adj conocido
well-off adj rico
well-to-do adj acomodado
west n oeste
westbound adv hacia el oeste
western adj occidental
westerner n del occidente
wet adj mojado
whack v golpear, pegar
whale n ballena
wharf n muelle
what adj que
whatever adj lo que
wheat n trigo
wheel n rueda
wheelbarrow n carretilla
wheelchair n silla de ruedas
wheeze v silbar respirando
when adv cuando
whenever adv cada vez que
where adv donde
whereabouts n paradero
whereas c mientras que
whereupon c por lo tanto
wherever c dondequiera que
whether c si, aunque
which adj que
while c mientras que
whim n capricho
whine v quejarse
whip v azotar; batir
whip n látigo
whirl v dar vueltas, girar
whirlpool n remolino
whirlwind n torbellino
whisk away v transladar

whiskers n patillas
whisper v susurrar
whisper n susurro
whistle v silbar
whistle n silbato
white adj blanco
whiten v blanquear
whittle v tallar, rascar
whittle away v reducir
who pro quien
whoever pro cualquiera que
whole adj entero
wholehearted adj sincero
wholesale n al por mayor
wholesaler n mayorista
wholesome adj sano
whom pro quien
whooping adj enorme
why adv por qué
wicked adj malvado
wickedness n maldad
wide adj ancho, amplio
widely adv ampliamente
widen v ampliar
widespread adj extendido
widow n viuda
widower n viudo
width n anchura
wield v ejercer, blandir
wife n esposa
wig n peluca
wiggle v menear
wild adj salvaje
wild boar n jabalí
wilderness n desierto
wildlife n fauna
will n voluntad; testamento
willfully adv a sabiendas
willing adj dispuesto

W

willingly *adv* con gusto
willingness *n* buena voluntad
willow *n* sauce
wily *adj* astuto
wimp *adj* débil
win *iv* ganar
win back *v* recuperar
wind *n* viento
wind *iv* enrollar; serpentear
wind up *v* concluir
winding *adj* tortuoso
windmill *n* molino de viento
window *n* ventana
windpipe *n* tráquea
windshield *n* parabrisas
windy *adj* ventoso
wine *n* vino
winery *n* bodega de vino
wing *n* ala
wink *n* guiño
wink *v* guiñar
winner *n* ganador
winter *n* invierno
wipe *v* limpiar, borrar
wipe out *v* eliminar
wire *n* alambre, cable
wireless *adj* sin cable
wisdom *n* sabiduría
wise *adj* sensato; sabio
wish *v* desear
wish *n* deseo
wit *n* ingenio
witch *n* bruja
witchcraft *n* brujería
with *pre* con
withdraw *v* retirar(se); sacar
withdrawal *n* retirada
withdrawn *adj* retraído
wither *v* marchitarse

withhold *iv* retener
within *pre* dentro
without *pre* sin
withstand *v* resistir, aguantar
witness *n* testigo
witty *adj* ingenioso
wives *n* esposas
wizard *n* mago
wobble *v* temblar; vacilar
woes *n* desgracias
wolf *n* lobo
woman *n* mujer
womb *n* vientre; útero
women *n* mujeres
wonder *v* preguntarse
wonder *n* maravilla
wonderful *adj* maravilloso
wood *n* madera
wooden *adj* de madera
wool *n* lana
woolen *adj* de lana
word *n* palabra
wording *n* redacción
work *n* trabajo
work *v* trabajar; funcionar
work out *v* resolver
workable *adj* viable, factible
workbook *n* cuaderno
worker *n* trabajador
workout *n* ejercicio
workshop *n* taller
world *n* mundo
worldly *adj* mundano
worldwide *adj* mundial
worm *n* gusano, lombriz
worn-out *adj* gastado
worrisome *adj* alarmante
worry *v* preocupar(se)
worry *n* preocupación

W

worrying adj preocupante
worse adj peor
worsen v empeorar
worship n adoración, culto
worst adj el peor
worthless adj sin valor
worthwhile adj valioso
worthy adj digno
would-be adj presunto
wound n herida
wound v herir
woven adj tejido
wrap v envolver
wrap up v resumir
wrapping n envoltura
wrath n ira
wreath n corona de flores
wreck v destrozar
wreckage n escombros
wrench n llave inglesa
wrestle v luchar, forcejear
wrestler n luchador
wrestling n lucha libre
wretched adj desgraciado
wring iv exprimir; sacar
wrinkle v arrugar(se)
wrinkle n arruga
wrist n muñeca de mano
write iv escribir
write down v tomar nota
writer n escritor
writhe v retorcerse
writing n escritura
written adj escrito
wrong adj equivocado
wrongful adj ilegal

x-mas n Navidad
x-ray n radiografía, rayos X

yacht n yate
yam n camote, boniato
yard n yarda
yarn n hilo
yawn n bostezo
yawn v bostezar
year n año
yearly adv anualmente
yearn v anhelar
yeast n levadura
yell v gritar
yellow adj amarillo
yes adv sí
yesterday adv ayer
yet c sin embargo
yield v ceder; producir
yield n réditos
yoke n yugo
yolk n yema
you pro tú, usted
young adj joven
youngster n joven
your adj tu, su
yours pro tuyo
yourself pro tú mismo
youth n juventud
youthful adj juvenil

Z

zap *v* borrar, cambiar
zeal *n* celo
zealous *adj* entusiasta
zebra *n* cebra
zero *n* cero

zest *n* entusiasmo
zinc *n* cinc
zip code *n* código postal
zipper *n* cremallera
zone *n* zona
zoo *n* zoológico
zoology *n* zoología

Z

Spanish-English

Bilingual Dictionaries, Inc.

Abbreviations

English - Spanish

a – article – artículo
adj – adjective - adjetivo
adv – adverb – adverbio
c – conjunction - conjunctión
e – exclamation - exclamación
nf – feminine noun - nombre femenino *
nm – masculine noun - nombre masculino *
pre – preposition - preposición
pro – pronoun - pronombre
v – verb - verbo

*Feminine nouns use the article **la** in the singular form and **las** in the plural form.
*Masculine nouns use the article **el** in the singular form and **los** in the plural form.

A

a *pre* to
abadía *nf* abbey
abajo *adv* down, below
abandonar *v* abandon
abandono *nm* abandonment
abarcar *v* extend
abarrotar *adj* pack, crowd
abastecer *v* supply
abastecimiento *nm* supply
abatido *adj* downcast
abdicar *v* abdicate
abdomen *nm* abdomen
abdominal *adj* abdominal
abeja *nf* bee
aberración *nf* aberration
abertura *nf* opening
abierto *adj* open
abismo *nm* abyss
ablandar *v* soften
abnegación *nf* self-denial
abocado *adj* doomed
abochornar *v* embarrass
abofetear *v* slap, smack
abogado *nm* attorney, lawyer
abogar *v* defend
abolición *v* abolition
abolir *v* abolish
abolladura *nf* dent
abollar *v* dent
abominable *adj* abominable
abonar *v* pay, fertilize
abono *nm* compost; payment
abordar *v* board; tackle
aborrecer *v* detest, loathe
abortar *v* have an abortion
aborto *nm* abortion

abrasar *v* burn
abrazadera *nf* clamp
abrazar *v* embrace, hug
abrazo *nm* embrace, hug
abrelatas *nm* can opener
abreviar *v* shorten
abreviatura *nf* abbreviation
abridor *n* opener
abrigar *v* keep warm
abrigo *mn* overcoat
abril *nm* April
abrir *v* open, unlock
abrirse *v* open up
abrochar *v* fasten
abrogar *v* repeal
abrumar *v* overwhelm
abrupto *adj* steep
absolución *nf* absolution
absoluto *adj* absolute
absolver *v* absolve, acquit
absorber *v* absorb
absorción *nf* absorption
absorto *adj* engrossed in
absorvente *adj* absorbent
abstenerse *v* abstain
abstinencia *nf* abstinence
abstracto *adj* abstract
absurdo *adj* absurd
abuchear *v* boo
abuela *nf* grandmother
abuelo *nm* grandfather
abuelos *nm* grandparents
abultado *adj* bulky
abultar *v* swell, be bulky
abundancia *nf* abundance, glut
abundante *adj* plentiful
abundar *v* abound
aburrido *adj* boring, dull
aburrimiento *nm* boredom, tedium

aburrirse _v_ get bored
abusar _v_ abuse
abusivo _adj_ abusive
abuso _nm_ abuse
acá _adv_ here
acabar _v_ finish
acabar en _v_ end up
academia _nf_ academy
académico _adj_ academic
acaecer _v_ occur
acallar _v_ silence
acalorado _adj_ heated
acampar _v_ camp
acantilado _nm_ cliff
acaparar _v_ hoard
acariciar _v_ caress, pat
acarrear _v_ cause; carry
acaso _adv_ perhaps
acatar _v_ obey, comply
acatarrarse _v_ catch a cold
accesible _adj_ accessible
acceso _nm_ access, entry
accesorio _nm_ accessory
accidental _adj_ accidental
accidente _nm_ accident
acción _nf_ action
accionista _nm_ shareholder
acechar _v_ lurk, stalk
aceite _nm_ oil
aceituna _nf_ olive
acelerador _nf_ accelerator
acelerar _v_ speed up
acento _nm_ accent
acentuar _v_ emphasize
aceptable _adj_ acceptable
aceptación _nf_ acceptance
aceptar _v_ accept
acera _nf_ sidewalk, pavement
acerca de _pre_ about, concerning

acercar _v_ bring closer
acercarse _v_ approach
acero _nm_ steel
acertado _adj_ correct
acertar _v_ get right
acertijo _nm_ riddle
acesible _adj_ accessible
aceso _nm_ access
acesorio _nm_ accessory
achacar _v_ blame
achacoso _adj_ sickly
achaque _nm_ ailment
achatar _v_ flatten
achicharrar _v_ burn
acidez _nf_ acidity, heartburn
ácido _adj_ sour, acid
acierto _nm_ good idea
aclamar _v_ acclaim
aclarar _v_ clarify, rinse
aclimatarse _v_ acclimatize
acogedor _adj_ cozy, homely
acoger _v_ shelter, receive
acogida _nf_ reception
acometer _v_ attack, undertake
acomodado _adj_ affluent
acomodarse _v_ adapt, get used
acompañar _v_ accompany
acongojar _v_ grieve
aconsejable _adj_ advisable
aconsejar _v_ advise, counsel
acontecer _v_ happen, occur
acontecimiento _nm_ event
acorazado _nm_ battleship
acordar _v_ agree
acordarse _v_ remember
acordeón _mn_ accordion
acordonar _v_ seal off, cordon off
acorralar _v_ round up
acortar _v_ shorten

acosar _v_ harass, hound
acoso _nm_ harassment
acostar _v_ put to bed
acostarse _v_ lie, go to bed
acostumbrar _v_ accustom
acostumbrarse _v_ get used
acre _nm_ acre
acrecentar _v_ increase
acreditación _nf_ accreditation
acreedor _n_ creditor
acróbata _nm_ acrobat
actitud _nf_ attitude
activación _nf_ activation
activar _v_ activate
actividad _nf_ activity
activo _adj_ active
actor _nm_ actor
actriz _nf_ actress
actuación _nf_ performance
actual _adj_ actual, current
actuar _v_ act
acuaducto _nm_ aqueduct
acuático _adj_ aquatic
acudir _v_ attend, come
acuerdo _nm_ agreement, accord
acumulación _nf_ accumulation
acumular _v_ accumulate, hoard
acuñar _v_ mint
acurrucarse _v_ huddle
acusación _nf_ accusation
acusado _nm_ defendant
acusador _nm_ accuser
acusar _v_ accuse, charge
acústica _n_ acoustics
acústico _adj_ acoustic
adaptable _adj_ adaptable
adaptación _nf_ adaptation
adaptador _nm_ adapter
adaptar _v_ adapt

adecuado _adj_ appropriate
adelantar _v_ overtake, outrun
adelantarse _v_ get ahead
adelante _adv_ ahead, forward
adelgazar _v_ lose weight
ademán _nm_ gesture
además _adv_ besides, also
adentro _adv_ inland
aderezar _v_ season
adherirse _v_ join
adhesión _nf_ adhesion
adhesivo _adj_ adhesive
adicción _nf_ addiction
adicional _adj_ additional
adictivo _adj_ addictive
adicto _adj_ addicted
adiestrar _v_ train
adinerado _adj_ wealthy
adiós _e_ good-bye
adivinar _v_ guess
adjetivo _nf_ adjective
adjuntar _v_ attach
administrar _v_ administer
administrar mal _v_ mismanage
admirable _adj_ admirable
admiración _fn_ admiration, awe
admirador _nf_ admirer
admirar _v_ admire
admisible _adj_ admissible
admisión _nf_ admission
admitir _v_ admit, accept
adoctrinar _v_ indoctrinate
adolescencia _nf_ adolescence
adolescente _nm_ teenager
adopción _nf_ adoption
adoptar _v_ adopt
adoptivo _adj_ adoptive
adoquín _nm_ cobblestone
adorable _adj_ adorable

adoración *nf* adoration
adorar *v* adore, worship
adornar *v* adorn
adorno *nm* ornament
adquirir *v* acquire
adquisición *nf* acquisition
adrede *adv* on purpose
aduana *nf* customs
adulación *nf* adulation
adular *v* flatter
adulterar *v* adulterate
adulterio *nm* adultery
adúltero *adj* adulterous
adulto *nm* adult, grown up
adverbio *nm* adverb
adversario *nm* adversary
adversidad *nf* adversity
adverso *adj* adverse
advertencia *nf* warning
advertir *v* warn, tip off
Adviento *nm* Advent
aeropuerto *nm* airport
afable *adj* affable
afán *nm* eagerness
afear *v* make ugly
afectar *v* affect
afectivo *adj* affectionate
afecto *nm* affection
afeitarse *v* shave
afeminado *adj* effeminate
aferrarse *v* cling, stick to
affirmar *v* assert
afianzar *v* strengthen
aficion *nf* love
aficionado *adj* fond
aficionado *nm* amateur
afilado *adj* pointed, sharp
afilar *v* sharpen
afiliación *nf* affiliation

afiliarse *v* affiliate
afinidad *nf* affinity
afirmación *nf* assertion
afirmar *v* affirm
afirmativo *adj* affirmative
aflicción *nf* grief, sorrow
afligido *adj* distressed
afligir *v* afflict, distress
aflojar *v* loosen
aflorar *v* surface
afluencia *nf* influx
afortunado *adj* fortunate, lucky
afrenta *nf* insult
africano *adj* African
afrodisiaco *adj* aphrodisiac
afrontar *v* confront
afuera *adv* out, outside
agacharse *v* bend down, crouch
agarradera *nf* handle
agarrado *adj* stingy
agarrar *v* grasp, seize
agarrarse *v* cling, take hold
agasajar *v* treat nicely
agencia *nf* agency
agenda *nf* agenda
agente *nm* officer, agent
ágil *adj* agile
agilidad *nf* agility
agitación *nf* agitation
agitado *adj* hectic
agitador *nm* agitator
agitar *v* shake
aglomeración *nf* agglomeration
agnosticismo *nm* agnosticism
agnóstico *nm* agnostic
agobiado *adj* stressed
agobiar *v* overwhelm
agonía *nf* agony
agonizar *v* agonize

agosto *nm* August
agotamiento *nm* exhaustion
agotar *v* exhaust, deplete
agradable *adj* pleasant, agreeable
agradar *v* please, delight
agradecer *v* thank
agradecido *adj* grateful, obliged
agrandar *v* enlarge
agravamiento *nm* aggravation
agravante *adj* aggravating
agravar *v* get worse
agravio *nm* grievance
agredir *v* attack
agregar *v* add
agresión *nf* aggression
agresivo *adj* aggressive
agresor *nm* aggressor, attacker
agricultor *nm* farmer
agricultura *nf* agriculture
agrietar *v* crack
agrupación *nf* cluster
agrupar *v* cluster, group
agua *nf* water
aguacate *nm* avocado
aguacero *nm* downpour
aguado *adj* watery
aguantar *v* endure, bear
aguar *v* spoil
aguardar *v* wait
agudo *adj* acute, sharp
aguijonear *v* goad
águila *nf* eagle
aguja *nf* needle
agujerear *v* make a hole, drill
agujero *nm* hole
ahí *adv* there
ahogar *v* drown
ahondar *v* go deep
ahora *adv* now

ahorcar *v* hang
ahorrar *v* save
ahorros *nm* savings
ahumado *adj* smoked
ahuyentar *v* chase away
aire *nm* air
airear *v* air
aislamiento *nm* seclusion, isolation
aislar *v* isolate
ajedrez *nm* chess
ajeno *adj* extraneous
ajetreado *adj* busy
ajo *nm* garlic
ajustable *adj* adjustable
ajustado *adj* tight
ajustar *v* adjust, fit
ajuste *nm* adjustment
al aire libre *adv* outdoors
al azar *adv* randomly
al lado de *pre* beside, alongside
al momento *adv* instantly
al otro lado *pre* across
al por mayor *adv* wholesale
al principio *adv* initially
al revés *adv* upside-down
ala *nf* wing
alabanza *nf* praise
alabar *v* praise
alacena *nf* cupboard
alambrada *nf* barbed wire
alambre *nm* wire
alardear *v* boast
alargar *v* lengthen
alarido *nm* shriek
alarma *nf* alarm
alarmante *adj* alarming
alarmista *nm* alarmist
albañil *nm* bricklayer, mason
albaricoque *nm* apricot

albergar *v* shelter
albergue *nm* shelter, hostel
albóndiga *nf* meatball
alborada *nf* dawn, sunrise
albornoz *nm* robe
alboroto *nm* commotion
alcachofa *nf* artichoke
alcalde *nm* mayor
alcance *nm* range
alcantarilla *nf* sewer
alcanzar *v* reach
alcazar *nm* fortress
alcoba *nf* bedroom
alcohólico *adj* alcoholic
alcoholismo *nm* alcoholism
aldea *nf* hamlet, village
aldeano *nm* villager
aleación *nf* alloy
alegar *v* allege
alegoría *n* allegory
alegórico *adj* allegoric
alegrar *v* make happy
alegre *adj* joyful, happy
alegría *nf* joy, happiness
alemán *adj* German
Alemania *nf* Germany
alentar *v* encourage
alergia *nf* allergy
alérgico *adj* allergic
alerta *nf* alert
aleta *nf* fin
aletear *v* flutter
alfabeto *nm* alphabet
alfalfa *nf* alfalfa
alfiler *nm* pin
alfombra *nf* carpet, rug
algas *nf* algae
álgebra *nf* algebra
algo *pro* something

algodón *nm* cotton
alguacil *nm* bailiff
alguien *pro* somebody
algún *adj* some
algunos *adj* some
alhaja *nf* jewel
aliado *adj* allied
aliado *nm* ally
alianza *nf* alliance
aliarse *v* ally
alicates *nm* pliers, cutter
aliento *nm* breath
aligerar *v* lighten, quicken
alimentar *v* feed
alimento *nm* nourishment
alimonia *nf* alimony
alineamiento *nm* alignment
alinear *v* align, line up
alisar *v* smooth
alistarse *v* enlist
aliviar *v* relieve, soothe
aliviarse *v* get well
alivio *nm* relief, solace
allanar *v* flatten, level
allí *adv* there
alma *nf* soul
almacén *nm* warehouse
almacenaje *nm* storage
almacenar *v* store, stock
almanaque *nm* almanac
almeja *nf* clam
almendra *nf* almond
almidón *nm* starch
almirante *nm* admiral
almohada *nf* pillow
almorzar *v* have lunch
almuerzo *nm* lunch, brunch
alojamiento *nm* lodging
alojarse *v* lodge, stay

alondra *nf* lark
alpinismo *nm* mountain climbing
alpinista *nm* mountain climber
alquilar *v* hire, rent
alquiler *nm* renting
alquitrán *nm* tar
alrededor *pro* around
alrededores *nm* outskirts
altamente *adv* highly
altanero *adj* haughty
altar *nm* altar
altavoz *nm* loudspeaker
alteración *nf* alteration
alterar *v* alter
altercado *nm* argument
alternador *n* alternator
alternar *v* alternate, socialize
alternativo *adj* alternative
Alteza *nf* Highness
altibajos *nm* ups and downs
altitud *nf* altitude
altivo *adj* proud
alto *adj* high, tall, loud
altura *nf* height, elevation
alubia *nf* bean
alucinante *adj* amazing
alucinar *v* amaze
aludir *v* refer
alumbrado *nm* lighting
alumbrar *v* brighten
aluminio *nm* aluminum
alumno *nm* pupil
alusión *nf* allusion
alzamiento *nm* uprising
alzar *v* lift, raise
amabilidad *nf* kindness
amable *adj* gracious, kind
amañarse *v* manage
amanecer *nm* dawn, sunrise

amante *nf* lover, mistress
amapola *nf* poppy
amar *v* love
amargado *adj* bitter
amargar *v* embitter
amargo *adj* bitter, sour
amargura *nf* bitterness
amarillo *adj* yellow
amarrar *v* moor, tie
amasar *v* amass
ambición *nf* ambition
ambiente *nm* environment
ambiguedad *nf* ambiguity
ambiguo *adj* ambiguous
ámbito *nm* scope
ambivalencia *nf* ambivalence
ambivalente *adj* ambivalent
ambos *adj* both
ambulancia *nf* ambulance
amedrentar *v* scare
amenaza *nf* threat
amenazador *adj* threatening
amenazar *v* threaten
amenizar *v* entertain
americano *adj* American
ametralladora *nf* machine gun
amígdala *nf* tonsil
amigo *nm* friend
aminorar *v* decrease
amistad *nf* friendship
amistoso *adj* friendly
amnesia *nf* amnesia
amnistía *nf* amnesty
amo *nm* owner
amoldarse *v* adapt
amonestar *v* admonish
amoniaco *nm* ammonia
amontonar *v* pile up, stack
amor *nm* love

amoral *adj* amoral
amoratado *adj* purple, bruised
amordazar *v* muzzle, gag
amorfo *adj* amorphous
amorío *nm* love affair
amoroso *adj* loving
amortajar *v* shroud
amortiguar *v* deaden, muffle
amortizar *v* pay off
amotinarse *v* riot, mutiny
amparar *v* protect
amparo *nm* protection
ampliación *nf* expansion
ampliamente *adv* widely
ampliar *v* broaden, widen
amplificador *nm* amplifier
amplificar *v* amplify
amplio *adj* spacious, ample
ampolla *nf* blister
amputación *nf* amputation
amputar *v* amputate
amueblar *v* furnish
anacronismo *nm* anachronism
añadir *v* add
analfabeto *adj* illiterate
análisis *nm* analysis
analizar *v* analyze
analogía *nf* analogy
anarquía *nf* anarchy
anarquista *nm* anarchist
anatomía *nf* anatomy
ancestral *adj* ancestral
ancho *adj* broad, wide
anchoa *nf* anchovy
anchura *nf* width, breadth
ancla *nf* anchor
andamio *nm* scaffold
andén *nm* platform
andrajo *nm* rag

anécdota *nf* anecdote
añejo *adj* old
anemia *nf* anemia
anémico *adj* anemic
anestesia *nf* anesthesia
anestesiar *v* anesthetize
anestesista *nm* anesthetist
anexión *nf* annexation
anexionar *v* annex
anfibio *adj* amphibious
anfiteatro *nm* amphitheater
anfitrión *nm* host
anfitriona *nf* hostess
ángel *nm* angel
angélico *adj* angelic
angina *nf* angina
anglicano *adj* Anglican
angosto *adj* narrow
angular *adj* angular
ángulo *nm* angle
angustia *nf* anguish
angustiado *adj* distraught
angustiante *adj* distressing
angustiar *v* distress
angustiarse *v* agonize
angustioso *adj* agonizing
anhelar *v* yearn, long for
anidar *v* nest
anillo *nm* ring
animación *nf* animation
animado *adj* lively
animal *nm* animal
animar *v* encourage
animosidad *nf* animosity
aniquilación *nf* annihilation
aniquilar *v* annihilate
aniversario *nm* anniversary
annual *adj* annual
año *nm* year

anoche *adv* last night
anochecer *v* get dark
anochecer *nm* nightfall
anonimato *nm* anonymity
anónimo *adj* anonymous
añoranza *nf* nostalgia
añorar *v* miss
anormal *adj* abnormal
anormalidad *nf* abnormality
anotación *nf* note
anotar *v* take notes
ansia *nf* yearning
ansiar *v* crave, yearn for
ansiedad *nf* anxiety
ansioso *adj* anxious
antagonismo *nm* antagonism
antagonizar *v* antagonize
ante todo *adv* primarily
antecedentes *nm* antecedents
anteceder *v* precede
antecesor *nm* predecessor
antelación *nf* advance
antemano (de) *adv* beforehand
antena *nf* antenna
anteojo *nm* eyeglass
antepasado *nm* ancestor
anterior *adj* previous, former
antes *adv* before
antesala *nf* lobby
anticipación *nf* anticipation
anticipar *v* anticipate
anticipo *nm* preview, advance
anticuado *adj* old-fashioned
antídoto *nm* antidote
antiguamente *adv* formerly
antiguedad *nf* antiquity
antiguo *adj* ancient, old
antipatía *nf* dislike
antipático *adj* unfriendly

antítesis *nf* antithesis
antojo *nm* whim
antorcha *nf* torch
antropología *nf* anthropology
anualmente *adv* yearly
anulación *nf* annulment
anular *v* annul, overrule
anunciar *v* announce
anuncio *nm* announcement
anzuelo *nm* hook
apacentar *v* graze
apacible *adj* gentle, placid
apaciguar *v* pacify
apagar *v* put out, turn off
apagón *nm* blackout
apalear *v* beat
apañarse *v* manage
aparato *nm* gadget, devise
aparcar *v* park
aparecer *v* appear, show up
aparentar *v* pretend
aparente *adj* apparent
aparición *nf* appearance
apariencia *nf* semblance
apartamento *nm* apartment
apartar *v* separate
aparte *adv* apart, besides
apasionado *adj* passionate
apasionar *v* excite
apatía *nf* apathy
apearse *v* get off
apechugar *v* cope with
apegado *adj* attached
apego *nm* attachment
apelación *nf* appeal
apelar *v* appeal
apellido *nm* surname
apenar *v* make sad
apenas *adv* barely, hardly

apéndice *nm* appendix
apendicitis *nf* appendicitis
aperitivo *nm* appetizer
apertura *nf* opening
apestar *v* stink
apestoso *adj* smelly, stinking
apetecer *v* feel like
apetito *nm* appetite
apiadarse *v* feel pity
apiñarse *v* crowd together
apio *nm* celery
aplacar *v* placate
aplastar *v* crush, squash
aplaudir *v* applaud, clap
aplauso *nm* applause
aplausos *nm* cheers
aplazamiento *nm* delay
aplazar *v* postpone, delay
aplicable *adj* applicable
aplicación *nf* application
aplicar *v* apply
apocado *adj* timid
apoderarse *v* take over
apodo *nm* nickname
apogeo *nm* climax
apología *nf* apology
aporrear *v* beat
aportación *nf* input
apostar *v* bet
apóstol *nm* apostle
apostólico *adj* apostolic
apóstrofe *nm* apostrophe
apoyar *v* back up, support
apoyarse *v* lean
apoyo *nm* backing, help
apreciar *v* appreciate
aprecio *nm* appreciation
apremiante *adj* urgent
apremio *nm* urgency

aprender *v* learn
aprendiz *nm* apprentice
aprensivo *adj* apprehensive
apresar *v* capture
apresurado *adj* hasty
apresurarse *v* hurry up
apretado *adj* tight
apretar *v* tighten, squeeze
aprieto *nm* difficulty
aprobación *nf* approval
aprobar *v* approve
apropiado *adj* suitable
aprovechar *v* make use
aprovecharse *v* take advantage
aproximarse *v* approach
aptitud *nf* aptitude
apto *adj* suitable
apuesta *nf* bet
apuñalar *v* stab
apuntar *v* point at, aim
apunte *nm* note
apurarse *v* worry
apuro *nm* worry, trouble
aquario *nm* aquarium
aquellos *adj* those
aquí *adv* here
árabe *adj* Arabic
arable *adj* arable
arado *nm* plough
araña *nf* spider
arañar *v* scratch
arañazo *nm* scratch
arar *v* plow, till
arbitrario *adj* arbitrary
árbitro *nm* umpire, referee
árbol *nm* tree
arbusto *nm* bush, shrub
arcaico *adj* archaic
arcángel *n* archangel

archiduque *n* archduke
archipiélago *nm* archipelago
archivar *v* file, shelve
archivo *nm* archive, file
arcilla *nf* clay
arco *nm* arc, arch
arco iris *nm* rainbow
arder *v* burn
ardiendo *adj* ablaze
ardiente *adj* ardent
arduo *adj* arduous
área *nf* area
arena *nf* sand
argumentar *v* argue
argumento *nm* argument
árido *adj* arid, dry
arisco *adj* surly
aristocracia *nf* aristocracy
aristócrata *adj* aristocrat
aritmética *nf* arithmetic
arma *nm* weapon
arma de fuego *nm* firearm
armada *nf* navy
armadura *nf* armor
armamento *nm* munitions
armar *v* assemble, arm
armario *nm* wardrobe, closet
armisticio *nm* armistice
armonía *nf* harmony
aro *n* hoop
aroma *nm* aroma
aromático *adj* aromatic
arpa *nf* harp
arpón *nm* harpoon
arqueología *nf* archaeology
arquitecto *nm* architect
arquitectura *nf* architecture
arraigado *adj* entrenched
arraigar *v* take root

arrancar *v* pull out
arrasar *v* ravage, raze
arrastrar *v* drag
arrastrarse *v* crawl
arrebatar *v* snatch, seize
arrebato *nm* outburst, fit
arrecife *nm* reef
arreglado *adj* tidy
arreglar *v* arrange, fix
arreglarse *v* groom
arreglárselas *v* cope, manage
arreglo *nm* solution; repair
arremeter *v* attack
arrendar *v* lease
arrendatario *v* tenant
arrepentido *adj* remorseful
arrepentirse *v* repent
arrestar *v* arrest
arresto *nm* arrest
arriba *adv* up, above
arribar *v* arrive
arriendo *nm* lease
arriesgado *adj* risky
arriesgar *v* gamble, risk
arriesgarse *v* venture
arritmia *nf* arrhythmia
arrodillarse *v* kneel down
arrogancia *nf* arrogance
arrogante *adj* arrogant
arrojar *iv* cast, throw
arrollar *v* run over
arroyo *nm* stream
arroz *nm* rice
arruga *nf* wrinkle
arrugar *v* wrinkle
arruinar *v* ruin
arsenal *nm* arsenal
arsénico *nm* arsenic
arte *nm* art

artefacto *nm* artifact
arteria *nf* artery
artesano *nm* craftsman
ártico *nm* arctic
articular *v* articulate
artículo *nm* article, item
artificial *adj* artificial
artillería *nf* artillery
artista *nm* artist
artístico *adj* artistic
artritis *nf* arthritis
arzobispo *nm* archbishop
as *nm* ace
asa *nm* handle
asador *nm* broiler
asaltante *nm* attacker
asaltar *v* assault, raid
asalto *nm* holdup, raid
asamblea *nf* assembly
asar *v* broil, roast
ascender *v* ascend, rise
ascendiente *nm* ancestor
ascenso *nm* promotion
ascensor *nm* elevator
ascético *adj* ascetic
asco *nm* disgust
aseado *adj* neat, clean
asediar *v* siege
asedio *nm* siege
asegurar *v* insure, secure
asegurarse *v* make sure
asentir *v* agree
aseos *nm* restroom
asequible *adj* attainable
asesinar *v* assassinate
asesinato *nm* murder
asesino *nm* assassin, killer
asfalto *nm* asphalt
asfixia *nf* asphyxiation

asfixiar *v* asphyxiate
así *adv* thus
asiento *nm* seat
asignar *v* allocate, assign
asignatura *nf* subject
asilo *nm* asylum
asimilación *nf* assimilation
asimilar *v* assimilate
asimismo *adv* likewise
asir *v* grab
asistencia *nf* attendance, help
asistente *nm* attendant
asistir *v* attend, help
asma *nf* asthma
asmático *adj* asthmatic
asno *nm* donkey
asociación *nf* association
asociar *v* associate
asomarse *v* lean out
asombrar *v* astonish, amaze
asombro *nm* amazement
asombroso *adj* amazing
aspecto *nm* aspect, looks
áspero *adj* rough
aspiración *nf* aspiration
aspiradora *nf* vacuum cleaner
aspirar *v* inhale, aspire
aspirina *nf* aspirin
asqueroso *adj* nasty
asta *nf* flagpole
asterisco *nm* asterisk
asteroide *nm* asteroid
astilla *nf* splinter
astillero *nm* shipyard
astrología *nf* astrology
astrólogo *nm* astrologer
astronauta *nm* astronaut
astronomía *nf* astronomy
astrónomo *nm* astronomer

astuto *adj* shrewd, cunning
asumir *v* assume, accept
asunto *nm* affair, matter
asustar *v* frighten, scare
atacar *v* attack
atadura *nf* tie
atajo *nm* shortcut
atañer *v* concern
ataque *nm* seizure; attack
atar *v* tie
atardecer *nm* sundown
atareado *adj* busy
atascar *v* clog, block
atasco *nm* traffic jam
ataúd *nm* casket, coffin
ateísmo *nm* atheism
atemorizar *v* frighten
atención *nf* attention
atender *v* serve, care for
atenerse a *v* abide by
atentado *nm* attack
atento *adj* attentive
atenuar *v* minimize, lessen
ateo *nm* atheist
aterrador *adj* frightening
aterrar *v* frighten
aterrizaje *nm* landing
aterrizar *v* land
aterrorizar *v* terrorize
atestiguar *v* testify
ático *nm* attic, penthouse
atleta *nm* athlete
atlético *adj* athletic
atmósfera *nf* atmosphere
atmosférico *adj* atmospheric
atolladero *nm* quagmire
atollarse *v* get stuck
atómico *adj* atomic
átomo *nm* atom

atónito *adj* amazed
atontado *v* dazed
atorarse *v* get stuck
atormentar *v* torture
atornillador *nm* screwdriver
atornillar *v* screw
atracador *nm* mugger
atracción *nf* attraction
atraco *nm* mugging
atractivo *adj* attractive
atraer *v* lure, attract
atrapar *v* catch, trap
atrás *adv* at the back
atrasado *adj* backward
atrasar *v* postpone
atravesar *v* cross
atrayente *adj* appealing
atreverse *v* dare
atrevido *adj* daring
atribuir *v* attribute
atrocidad *nf* atrocity
atropellar *v* run over
atroz *adj* atrocious
atún *nm* tuna
aturdido *adj* dazed
aturdir *v* daze, stun
audacia *nf* boldness
audaz *adj* bold
audiencia *nf* audience
auditorio *nm* auditorium
auge *nm* boom, peak
augurar *v* augur
augurio *nm* omen
aula *nf* classroom
aullar *v* howl
aullido *nm* howl
aumentar *v* increase
aumento *nm* increase
aún *adv* still

aún si *c* even if
aunque *c* although
aura *nf* aura
auriculares *nm* earphones
ausencia *nf* absence
ausentarse *v* go away
ausente *adj* absent
auspicios *nm* auspices
austeridad *nf* austerity
austero *adj* austere
australiano *adj* Australian
austriaco *adj* Austrian
autenticidad *nf* authenticity
auténtico *adj* authentic
autentificar *v* authenticate
auto *nm* car
autobús *nm* bus
autocar *nm* coach
autoestima *nf* self-esteem
autógrafo *nm* autograph
automático *adj* automatic
automatizar *v* automate
automóvil *nm* automobile
autonomía *nf* autonomy
autónomo *adj* autonomous
autopista *nf* freeway
autopsia *nf* autopsy
autor *nm* author
autoridad *nf* authority
autoritario *adj* authoritarian
autorización *nf* authorization
autorizar *v* authorize
auxiliar *v* help
auxilio *nm* help
avalancha *nf* avalanche
avance *nm* advance
avanzar *v* advance
avaricia *nf* avarice, greed
avaricioso *adj* greedy

avaro *adj* greedy
avasallar *v* subjugate
ave *nm* bird
avellana *nf* hazelnut
avena *nf* oatmeal
avenida *nf* avenue
aventajar *v* surpass
aventura *nf* adventure
aventurero *nm* adventurer
avergonzado *adj* ashamed
avergonzar *v* embarrass
avería *nf* breakdown
averiarse *v* break down
averiguar *v* find out
aversión *nf* dislike
avestruz *nf* ostrich
aviación *nf* aviation
aviador *nm* aviator, flier
avidez *nf* eagerness
ávido *adj* eager
avión *nm* plane
avisar *v* warn, inform
aviso *nm* warning, notice
avispa *nf* wasp
avispón *nm* hornet
avocado *nm* avocado
ayer *adv* yesterday
ayuda *nf* aid, help
ayudante *nm/f* helper
ayudar *v* assist, help
ayunar *v* fast
ayuntamiento *nm* city
azada *nf* hoe
azafata *nf* stewardess
azar *nm* chance, fate
azotar *v* whip, spank
azote *nm* lash, spanking
azteca *adj* Aztec
azúcar *nm* sugar

azucarado *adj* sweetened
azucena *nf* lily
azufre *nm* sulfur
azul *adj* blue
azulejo *nm* tile

B

bacalao *nm* cod
bache *nm* pothole
bacteria *nf* bacteria
báculo *nm* staff
bahía *nf* bay
bailador *nm* dancer
bailarina *nf* ballerina
baile *nm* dance
bajar *v* go down, lower
bajo *adj* low
bajón *nm* drop
bala *nf* bullet
balada *nf* ballad
balancear *v* swing
balanza *nf* scale
balazo *nm* shot
balbucear *v* stammer
balcón *nm* balcony
balde *nm* pail, bucket
baldosa *nf* floor tile
ballena *nf* whale
ballet *nm* ballet
balneario *nm* spa
balompié *nm* football
balón *nm* ball
balsa *nf* raft
bálsamo *nm* balm

baluarte *nm* bulwark
bambú *nm* bamboo
bañador *nm* swimsuit
bañarse *v* bathe
bancarrota *nf* bankruptcy
banco *nm* bank, bench, pew
banda *nf* band
bandeja *nf* tray
bandera *nf* flag
bandido *nm* bandit
bañera *nf* bathtub
baño *nm* bath, lavatory
banquero *nm* banker
banqueta *nf* sidewalk
banquete *nm* banquet
bar *nm* bar, saloon
barajar *v* shuffle
barandilla *nf* handrail
barato *adj* cheap
barba *nf* beard
barbacoa *nf* barbecue
bárbaro *adj* barbaric
barbero *nm* barber
barbudo *adj* bearded
barca *nf* boat
barcaza *nf* barge
barco *nm* ship, boat
barniz *nm* varnish
barnizar *v* varnish
barómetro *nm* barometer
barón *nm* baron
barquillo *nm* wafer
barra de pan *nf* loaf
barranco *nm* gorge, ravine
barrer *v* sweep
barrera *nf* barrier
barriada *nf* district
barricada *nf* barricade
barriga *nf* belly

B

barril *nm* barrel
barrio *nm* neighborhood
barro *nm* mud
barrote *nm* bar
barullo *nm* uproar
báscula *nf* scales
base *nf* base, basis
básico *adj* basic
básketbol *nm* basketball
basta *e* enough, stop
bastante *adv* enough, quite
bastar *v* be sufficient
bastardo *nm* bastard
bastilla *nf* hem
basto *adj* coarse, rough
bastón *nm* stick
basura *nf* garbage, trash
basurero *nm* trash can
bata *nf* robe, gown
batalla *nf* battle
batallar *v* fight
batallón *nm* battalion
batear *v* bat
batería *nf* battery
batido *nm* shake
batidora *nf* blender
batir *v* beat
batuta *nf* baton
baúl *nm* trunk
bautismo *nm* baptism
bautizar *v* baptize
bautizo *nm* christening
bayoneta *nf* bayonet
bazar *nm* bazaar
beatificar *v* beatify
beato *adj* blessed, pious
bebé *nm* baby
bebedor *nm* drinker
beber *v* drink

bebida *nf* drink
beca *nf* grant
becerro *nm* calf
béisbol *nm* baseball
belga *adj* Belgian
Bélgica *nf* Belgium
belleza *nf* beauty
bellota *nf* acorn
bendecir *v* bless
bendición *nf* blessing
bendito *adj* blessed
beneficiar *v* benefit
beneficiario *nm* beneficiary
beneficio *nm* benefit
beneficioso *adj* beneficial
benévolo *adj* benevolent
bengala *nf* flare
benigno *adj* mild, benign
berrinche *nm* tantrum
berza *nf* cabbage
besar *v* kiss
beso *nm* kiss
bestia *nf* beast
bestialidad *nf* bestiality
betún *nm* shoe polish
biblia *nf* bible
bíblico *adj* biblical
bibliografía *nf* bibliography
biblioteca *nf* library
bibliotecario *nm* librarian
bicho *nm* bug
bicicleta *nf* bicycle
bidón *nm* drum
bien *adv* right, fine, okay
bienestar *nm* well-being
bienhechor *nm* benefactor
bienvenida *nf* welcome
bifurcarse *v* diverge
bigamia *nf* bigamy

bigote *nm* mustache
bikini *nm* bikini
bilateral *adj* bilateral
bilingue *adj* bilingual
bilis *nf* bile
billar *nm* billiards
billete *nm* bill, ticket
billón *adj* billion
billonario *nm* billionaire
bimestral *adj* bimonthly
binoculares *adj* binoculars
biografía *nf* biography
biología *nf* biology
biológico *adj* biological
biopsia *nf* biopsy
biquini *nm* bikini
bisagra *nf* hinge
bisiesto *adj* leap year
bisonte *nm* bison
bisturí *nm* scalpel
bizco *adj* cross-eyed
biznieto *nm* great-grandson
blanco *nm* target
blanco *adj* white
blanco (en) *adj* blank
blancura *nf* whiteness
blandir *v* wield
blando *adj* soft
blanquear *v* bleach, whiten
blasfemar *v* blaspheme, curse
blasfemia *nf* blasphemy
blasfemo *adj* blasphemous
blindado *adj* armored
bloquear *v* block, obstruct
bloqueo *nm* blockade
blusa *nf* blouse
bobada *nf* nonsense
bobo *adj* sucker
boca *nf* mouth

bocadillo *nm* sandwich
bocado *nm* bite, morsel
bocata *nf* sandwich
bochornoso *adj* embarrassing
bocina *nf* horn
boda *nf* wedding
bodega *nf* cellar
bofetada *nf* slap, smack
bofetear *v* slap
boicot *nm* boycott
boina *nf* beret
bola *nf* ball
boletín *nm* bulletin
boleto *nm* ticket
bollo *nm* bun
bolsa *nf* bag
bolsillo *nm* pocket
bolso *nm* handbag
bomba *nf* bomb; pump
bombardero *nm* bomber
bombazo *nf* explosion
bombear *v* pump
bombero *nm* fireman
bombilla *nf* light bulb
bondad *nf* goodness
bonificación *nf* bonus
bonito *adj* pretty
boquete *nm* hole
bordado *adj* embroidered
bordar *v* embroider
borde *nm* brink, curb
borrachera *nf* drunkenness
borracho *adj* drunk
borrador *nm* rough draft
borrar *v* delete, erase
borrasca *nf* storm
borrego *nm* lamb
borrón *nm* stain
borroso *adj* blurred

B

bosque *nm* forest, wood
bosquejar *v* outline, sketch
bosquejo *nm* outline, sketch
bostezar *v* yawn
bostezo *nm* yawn
bota *nf* boot
botar *v* bounce
bote *nm* boat
botella *nf* bottle
botica *nf* pharmacy
botín *nm* booty
botón *nm* button
bóveda *nf* vault
boxeador *nm* boxer
boxeo *nm* boxing
boya *nf* buoy
bozal *nm* muzzle
brasero *nm* brazier
brasileño *adj* Brazilian
bravo *adj* fierce
brazo *nm* arm
brea *nf* tar
brecha *nf* opening
brevaje *nm* concoction, drink
breve *adj* short
brevedad *nf* brevity
brigada *nf* brigade
brillante *adj* bright, shiny
brillar *v* gleam, glow
brillo *nm* brightness
brincar *v* jump
brinco *nm* jump, leap
brisa *nf* breeze
broca *nf* drill
brocha *nf* paintbrush
broche *nm* brooch
brócoli *nm* broccoli
broma *nf* joke
broma (en) *adv* jokingly

bromear *v* joke
bronce *nm* bronze
bronceado *adj* tan
bronco *adj* harsh
bronquitis *nf* bronchitis
brotar *v* germinate
brote *nm* bud, shoot
bruja *nf* witch
brujería *nf* witchcraft
brújula *nf* compass
bruma *nf* mist
brumoso *adj* misty, hazy
brusco *adj* sudden
Bruselas *nf* Brussels
brutal *adj* brutal
brutalidad *nf* brutality
bucear *v* dive
buceo *nm* diving
bueno *adj* fine, good
buey *nm* ox
bueyes *nm* oxen
búfalo *nm* buffalo
bufanda *nf* scarf
bufón *nm* buffoon
buho *nm* owl
buitre *nm* vulture
bujía *nf* spark plug
bulevar *nm* boulevard
bullicio *nm* bustle
bulto *nm* package; lump
buque *nm* ship
burbuja *nf* bubble
burgués *adj* bourgeois
burla *nf* mockery
burlarse *v* mock, make fun
burocracia *nf* bureaucracy
burócrata *nm* bureaucrat
burrada *nf* nonsense
burro *nm* donkey

buscar *v* look for, search
búsqueda *nf* search, quest
busto *nm* bust
butaca *nf* armchair
buzo *nm* diver
buzón *nm* mailbox

C

cabalgar *v* ride
caballería *nf* cavalry
caballero *nm* gentleman
caballo *nm* horse
cabaña *nf* hut, cabin
cabecear *v* nod
cabecilla *nf* ringleader
cabellera *nf* scalp
cabello *nm* hair
cabeza *nf* head
cabezada *nf* doze
cabezonada *nf* stubbornness
cabida *nf* space
cabina *nf* booth, cabin
cabo *nm* cape; corporal
cabra *nf* goat
cabrearse *v* get mad
cabrito *nm* kid
cacahuete *nm* peanut
cacao *nm* cocoa
cacarear *v* crow
cacería *v* hunt
cacharro *nm* piece of junk
cachear *v* search
cachete *nm* cheek; slap
cacho *nm* bit

cachorro *nm* cub, puppy
cacto *nm* cactus
cada *adj* each, every
cada día *adv* everyday
cada hora *adv* hourly
cada uno *adv* apiece
cada uno *pro* everybody
cada vez que *adv* whenever
cadalso *nm* scaffold
cadáver *nm* corpse
cadena *nf* chain
cadera *nf* hip
caducado *adj* out of date
caducar *v* expire
caer *v* fall
caerse *v* fall down
café *nm* coffee
cafeína *nf* caffeine
cafetería *nf* cafeteria
caída *nf* downfall, fall
caimán *nm* alligator
caja *nf* box
cajero *nm* cashier
cajón *nm* drawer
cal *nf* lime
calabacín *nm* zucchini
calabaza *nf* pumpkin
calabozo *nm* dungeon
calamar *nm* squid
calambre *nm* cramp
calamidad *nf* calamity
calamitoso *adj* dire
calar *v* soak
calavera *nm* skull
calcar *v* trace, copy
calcetín *nm* sock
calcinar *v* burn
calcio *nm* calcium
calculadora *nm* calculator

B C

calcular *v* calculate
cálculo *nm* calculation
caldera *nf* boiler
caldo *nm* broth
calendario *nm* calendar
calentador *nm* heater
calentar *v* heat
calentura *nf* fever
calibrar *v* gauge
calibre *nm* caliber
calidad *nf* quality
cálido *adj* warm
caliente *adj* hot
calificar *v* describe
cáliz *nm* chalice
callado *adj* silent
callarse *v* keep silent
calle *nf* street
callejón *nm* alley
callejuela *nf* alley
callo *nm* corn; tripe
calma *nf* calm
calmante *nm* painkiller
calmar *v* calm
calor *nm* heat
caloría *nf* calorie
calumnia *nf* libel, slander
calvo *adj* bald
calzado *nm* footwear
calzar *v* wear
calzoncillos *nm* briefs
cama *nf* bed
cámara *nf* camera
camarada *nm* comrade
camarera *nf* waitress
camarero *nm* waiter
camarón *nm* shrimp
cambiar *v* change, switch
cambio *nm* change

camello *nm* camel
camilla *nf* stretcher
caminar *v* hike, walk
caminata *nf* long walk
camino *nm* journey, way
camión *nm* truck
camionero *nm* trucker
camisa *nf* shirt
camiseta *nf* T-shirt
camisón *nm* nightgown
campamento *nm* camp
campana *nf* bell
campaña *nf* campaign
campanada *nf* chime, stroke
campanario *nm* belfry
campechano *adj* down-to-earth
campeón *nm* champion
campesino *nm* peasant
campo *nm* countryside
camuflage *nm* camouflage
camuflar *v* camouflage
caña *nf* cane; glass of beer
canadiense *adj* Canadian
canal *nm* canal, channel
canalla *nm* scoundrel
canalón *nm* gutter
canario *nm* canary
canasto *nm* basket
cancelación *nf* cancellation
cancelar *v* cancel
cáncer *nm* cancer
canciller *nm* chancellor
canción *nf* song
candado *nm* padlock
candente *adj* red-hot
candidato *nm* candidate
candidatura *nf* candidacy
cándido *adj* naïve
candil *nm* oil lamp

candor *nm* frankness

cañería *nf* pipe

cangrejo *nm* crab

canguro *nm* kangaroo

caníbal *nm* cannibal

canica *nf* marble

canino *adj* canine

canjear *v* exchange

caño *nm* tube, pipe

canoa *nf* canoe

cañon *nm* canyon; cannon

canonizar *v* canonize

canoso *adj* grayish

cansado *adj* tired, tiring

cansancio *nm* tiredness

cansarse *v* get tired

cantante *nm/f* singer

cantar *v* sing

cántaro *nm* pitcher, jug

cantera *nf* quarry

cantidad *nf* amount

cantina *nf* canteen

canto *nm* chant, song

caos *nm* chaos

caótico *adj* chaotic

capa *nf* cape, cloak

capacidad *nf* capacity

capacitar *v* enable; prepare

caparazón *v* shell

capataz *nm* foreman

capaz *adj* able, capable

capellán *nm* chaplain

capilla *nf* chapel

capital *nf* capital

capitalismo *nm* capitalism

capitán *nm* captain

capitular *v* capitulate

capítulo *nm* chapter

capricho *nm* whim

cápsula *nf* capsule

captura *nf* capture

capturar *v* capture

capucha *nf* hood

cara *nf* face

caracol *nm* snail

carácter *nm* character

característica *nf* feature

característico *adj* characteristic

caracterizar *v* characterize

caramelo *nm* candy

caravana *nf* caravan

carbón *nm* charcoal, coal

carbonizado *adj* charred

carbonizar *v* char

carburador *nm* carburetor

carcajada *nf* loud laugh

cárcel *nf* jail

carcelero *nm* jailer

cardenal *nm* cardinal

cardiaco *adj* cardiac

cardiología *nf* cardiology

cardo *nm* thistle

carecer *v* lack

carencia *nf* lack

carestía *nf* shortage

carga *nf* burden, load

cargamento *nm* cargo

cargar *v* burden, load

caricatura *nf* caricature

caricia *nf* caress

caridad *nf* charity

caries *nm* decay

cariñoso *adj* affectionate

carisma *nm* charisma

carismático *adj* charismatic

caritativo *adj* charitable

carne *nf* flesh; meat

carne asada *nf* roast

C

carne de cerdo *nf* pork
carne de vaca *nf* beef
carne picada *nf* mincemeat
carnero *nm* ram
carnicería *nf* butchery
carnicero *nm* butcher
carnívoro *nm* carnivorous
caro *adj* expensive
carpeta *nf* folder
carpintería *nf* carpentry
carpintero *nm* carpenter
carrera *nf* race
carreta *nf* cart
carrete *nm* roll, reel
carretera *nf* road
carretilla *nf* wheelbarrow
carril *nm* lane
carta *nf* letter, epistle
cartel *nm* poster
cartera *nf* wallet
cartero *nm* mailman
cartílago *nm* cartilage
cartón *nm* cardboard
cartucho *nm* cartridge
casa *nf* house, home
casarse *v* marry, wed
cascada *nf* waterfall
cascarón *nm* shell
cascarrabias *nm* grouch
casco *nm* helmet; hull
casero *adj* homemade
caseta *nf* pavilion
casi *adv* almost, nearly
casino *nm* casino
casita *nf* cottage
caso *nm* case
caspa *nf* dandruff
cassette *nm* tape
castaña *nf* chestnut

castellano *adj* Castilian
castidad *nf* chastity
castigable *adj* punishable
castigar *v* punish
castigo *nm* punishment
castillo *nm* castle, chateau
castor *nm* beaver
cataclismo *nm* cataclysm
catalejo *nm* telescope
catalogar *v* rank, classify
catálogo *nm* catalog
catarata *nf* waterfall
catarro *nm* cold
catástrofe *nf* catastrophe
catear *v* fail, flunk
catecismo *nm* catechism
catedral *nf* cathedral
categoría *nf* category, class
categorizar *v* categorize
cateto *nm* peasant
catolicismo *nm* Catholicism
católico *adj* catholic
catorce *adj* fourteen
caudal *nm* flow, volume
caudillo *nm* leader
causa *nf* cause
cautela *nf* caution
cauteloso *adj* wary
cautivar *v* charm
cautiverio *nm* captivity
cautivo *nm* captive
cauto *adj* cautious
cavar *v* dig
caverna *nf* cavern, cave
cavidad *nf* cavity
cavilar *v* ponder
caza *nf* hunting
cazador *nm* hunter
cazar *v* hunt

cesar

cazuela *nf* casserole
cebada *nf* barley
cebar *v* fatten
cebo *nm* bait
cebolla *nf* onion
cebra *nf* zebra
ceder *v* yield; give up
cedro *nm* cedar
cegar *v* blind
ceguedad *nf* blindness
ceguera *nf* blindness
ceja *nf* eyebrow
celda *nf* cell
celebración *nf* celebration
celebrar *v* celebrate
célebre *adj* celebrity
celestial *adj* heavenly
celibato *nm* celibacy
célibe *adj* celibate
celos *nm* jealousy
celoso *adj* jealous
célula *nf* cell
celular *adj* cellular
celulitis *nf* cellulite
cementerio *nm* cemetery
cemento *nm* cement, mortar
cena *nf* supper
cenar *v* dine
cenicero *nm* ashtray
ceñido *adj* tight
ceniza *nf* ash, cinder
censo *nm* census
censor *nm* censor
censura *nf* censorship
censurar *v* censure
centenario *adj* centennial
centeno *nm* rye
centígrado *adj* centigrade
centímetro *nm* centimeter

céntimo *nm* cent
centinela *nm* sentry
central *adj* central
centralizar *v* centralize
centrar *v* centre
centro *nm* center
cepillar *v* brush
cepillo *nm* brush
cera *nf* wax
cerámica *nf* ceramic
cerca *pre* near, close
cerca (de) *adv* closely
cerca de *pre* close to
cercanías *nf* vicinity
cercano *adj* close, nearby
cercar *v* encircle
cerciorarse *v* make sure
cerco *nm* siege
cerdo *nm* pig, hog
cereal *nm* cereal
cerebral *adj* cerebral
cerebro *nm* brain
ceremonia *nf* ceremony
ceremonial *adj* ceremonial
cereza *nf* cherry
cerilla *nf* match
cernerse *v* hang over
cero *nm* zero
cerradura *nf* lock
cerrar *v* close, lock, shut
cerro *nm* hill
cerrojo *nm* bolt
certamen *nm* competition
certeza *nf* certainty
certificado *nm* certificate
certificar *v* certify
cervecería *nf* brewery
cerveza *nf* beer, ale
cesar *v* cease

185

C

cesión *nf* transfer
césped *nm* grass, lawn
cesta *nf* basket, hamper
chabacano *adj* vulgar
chabola *nf* shack
chacal *nm* jackal
chalado *adj* crazy
chaleco *nm* vest
chalet *nm* chalet
chamaca *nf* girl
champán *nm* champagne
champiñón *nm* mushroom
chamuscar *v* scorch
chantaje *nm* blackmail
chantajear *v* blackmail
chaparrón *nm* downpour
chapotear *v* splash
chapuza *nf* shoddy work
chaqueta *nf* coat
charca *nf* pond
charlar *v* chat, chatter
charlatán *nm* charlatan
chasco *nm* disappointment
chasquear *v* click
chasquido *nm* flick
chatarra *nf* scrap
chato *adj* flat
chaval *nm* kid
cheque *nm* check
chequeo *nm* check-up
chequera *nf* checkbook
chica *nf* girl
chícharo *nm* pea
chicle *nm* bubble gum
chiflar *v* hiss, boo
chillar *v* scream, yell
chillido *nm* scream
chimenea *nf* fireplace
chimpancé *nm* chimpanzee

chincheta *nf* thumbtack
chinchón *nm* bump
chipirón *nm* squid
chiquillo *nm* kid
chirriar *v* squeak
chisme *nm* gossip
chispa *nf* spark
chiste *nm* joke
chivo *nm* goat
chocante *adj* odd, startling
chocar *v* crash, collide
chocolate *nm* chocolate
chófer *nm* chauffeur
choque *nm* collision, crash
chorizo *nm* sausage
chorrada *nf* stupidity
chorrear *v* drip
choza *nf* hut
chuleta *nf* steak; chop
chupar *v* suck, soak up
chusma *nf* mob
cianuro *nm* cyanide
cicatriz *nf* scar
ciclista *nm* cyclist
ciclo *nm* cycle
ciclón *nm* cyclone
ciegas (a) *adv* blindly
ciego *adj* blind
cielo *nm* heaven
cien *adj* hundred
ciencia *nf* science
cieno *nm* mud
científico *adj* scientific
científico *nm* scientist
cierre *nm* closing, closure
cierto *adj* certain
ciervo *nm* deer
cifra *nf* number
cigarrillo *nm* cigarette

cigarro *nm* cigar
cigueña *nf* stork
cilindro *nm* cylinder
cima *nf* top, peak
cimiento *nm* foundation
cincel *nm* chisel
cinco *adj* five
cincuenta *adj* fifty
cine *nm* cinema
cínico *adj* cynic
cinismo *nm* cynicism
cinta *nf* ribbon, tape
cintura *nf* waist
cinturón *nm* seat belt
ciprés *nm* cypress
circo *nm* circus
circuito *nm* circuit
circulación *nf* circulation
circular *v* circulate, flow
círculo *nm* circle
circuncidar *v* circumcise
circunspecto *adj* circumspect
circunstancial *adj* circumstantial
circunvalación *nf* bypass
cirio *nm* candle
ciruela *nf* plum, prune
cirujano *nm* surgeon
cisma *nm* schism
cisne *nm* swan
cisterna *nf* cistern
cita *nf* appointment
citar *v* quote
ciudad *nf* city, town
ciudad natal *nf* hometown
ciudadanía *nf* citizenship
ciudadano *nm* citizen
cívico *adj* civic
civilización *nf* civilization
civilizar *v* civilize

clan *nm* clan, group
clandestino *adj* clandestine
clara *nf* egg white
claraboya *nf* skylight
claridad *nf* clarity
clarificación *nf* clarification
clarificar *v* clarify
clarinete *nm* clarinet
clarividente *nm/f* clairvoyant
claro *adj* clear, plainly
clase *nf* class
clásico *adj* classic
clasificado *adj* classified
clasificar *v* classify
claustro *nm* cloister
cláusula *nf* clause
clausura *nf* closing
clausurar *v* close
clavar *v* nail down
clave *nf* code
clavel *nm* carnation
clavícula *nf* collarbone
clavo *nm* nail
clemencia *nf* clemency
clerical *adj* clerical
clérigo *nm* cleric
clero *nm* clergy
cliente *nm* customer
clientela *nf* clientele
clima *nm* climate
climático *adj* climatic
clínica *nf* clinic
cloaca *nf* sewer
clonacion *n* cloning
clonar *v* clone
cloroformo *nm* chloroform
club *nm* club
coacción *nf* coercion
coaccionar *v* coerce

C

coagular v coagulate
coágulo nm clot
coalición nf coalition
cobarde adj coward
cobarde nm coward
cobardía nf cowardice
cobertura nf coverage
cobija nf blanket
cobijarse v take shelter
cobre nm copper
cocaína nf cocaine
cocer v bake
coche nm car, auto
cochino nm hog
cochino adj filthy, dirty
cocido nf stew
cociente nm quotient
cocina nf kitchen
cocinar v cook
cocinero nm cook
coco nm coconut
cocodrilo nm crocodile
cóctel nm cocktail
codearse · rub shoulders
codicia nf greed
codiciar v covet
código nm code
código postal nm zip code
codo nm elbow
codorniz nf quail
coeficiente nm coefficient
coetáneo adj contemporary
coexistir v coexist
cofre nm chest
coger v catch, grab
cohabitar v cohabit
coherente adj coherent
cohesión nf cohesion
cohete nm rocket

cohibido adj shy
cohibir v inhibit
coincidencia nf coincidence
coincidir v coincide
cojear v limp
cojín nm cushion
cojo adj lame, crippled
col nf cabbage
cola nf tail
colaboración n collaboration
colaborador nm collaborator
colaborar v collaborate
colador nm strainer
colapsar v paralyze
colapso nm collapse
colar v strain
colateral adj collateral
colcha nf bedspread
colchón nm mattress
colección nf collection
coleccionista n collector
colectar v collect
colectivo adj collective
colega nm colleague
colegio nm college
cólera nf cholera
colesterol nm cholesterol
colgar v hang
cólico nm colic
coliflor nf cauliflower
colina nf hill
colindante adj adjoining
colisión v collision
collar nm necklace
colmena nf beehive
colmillo nm tooth, fang
colmo nm limit
colocar v put, place
colonia nf cologne; colony

colonial *adj* colonial
colonizar *v* colonize
colono *nm* settler
color *nm* color
colorear *v* color
colorido *adj* colorful
colosal *adj* colossal
columna *nf* column, pillar
columpiar *v* swing
columpio *nm* swing
coma *nf* coma; comma
comadrona *nf* midwife
comandante *nm* commander
comando *nm* commando
comarca *nf* area, region
combate *nm* combat
combatiente *nm* combatant
combatir *v* combat
combinación *nf* combination
combinar *v* combine
combustible *nm* fuel
combustión *nf* combustion
comedia *nf* comedy
comediante *nm* comedian
comedor *nm* dining room
comentar *v* comment
comentario *nm* remark
comer *v* eat
comercial *adj* commercial
comerciante *nm* merchant
comerciar *v* trade
comercio *nm* trade
comestible *adj* edible
comestibles *nm* groceries
cometa *nm* comet; kite
cometer *v* commit
comezón *nm* itching
comicios *nm* elections
cómico *adj* comical

comida *nf* meal, food
comienzo *nm* beginning
comisaría *nf* police station
comisión *nf* commission
comité *nm* committee
como *adv* as, how
como *pre* like
cómoda *n* chest of drawers
comodidades *nf* amenities
cómodo *adj* comfortable
compacto *adj* compact
compadre *nm* buddy
compaginar *v* combine
compañerismo *nm* fellowship
compañero *nm* companion
compañía *nf* company
comparable *adj* comparable
comparación *nf* comparison
comparar *v* compare
comparativo *adj* comparative
comparecer *v* appear
compartir *v* share
compás *nm* compass; rhythm
compasión *nf* compassion
compasivo *adj* merciful
compatible *adj* compatible
compatriota *nm* countryman
compendio *nm* summary
compensar *v* compensate
competencia *nf* competence
competente *adj* competent
competidor *nm* competitor
competir *v* compete
competitivo *adj* competitive
compilar *v* compile
complacer *v* please
complejidad *nf* complexity
complejo *adj* complex
complemento *nm* complement

completar *v* complete
completo *adj* complete
complicación *nf* complication
complicar *v* complicate
cómplice *nm* accomplice
complicidad *nf* complicity
complot *nm* plot
componente *nm* component
componer *v* compose
comportarse *v* behave
composición *nf* composition
compositor *nm* composer
compostura *nf* composure
compra *nf* purchase
comprador *nm* buyer
comprar *v* buy, purchase
comprender *v* understand
comprensión *nf* understanding
compresión *nf* compression
compresor *nm* compressor
comprimir *v* compress
comprobar *v* check, test
compromiso *nm* commitment
compuerta *nf* floodgate
compulsión *nf* compulsion
compulsivo *adj* compulsive
computadora *nf* computer
comulgar *v* take communion
común *adj* common
comunicar *v* communicate
comunidad *nf* community
comunión *nf* communion
comunismo *nm* communism
comunista *adj* communist
comúnmente *adv* commonly
con *pre* with
con cautela *adv* cautiously
con confianza *adv* confidently
con esperanza *adv* hopefully

con fiebre *adv* feverish
con firmeza *adv* sternly
con fluidez *adv* fluently
con gusto *adv* willingly
con razón *adv* justly
con respecto a *adv* regarding
con tal que *c* providing that
coñac *nm* cognac
concebir *v* conceive
conceder *v* accord, grant
concentración *nf* concentration
concentrar *v* concentrate
concepto *nm* concept
concernir *v* concern
concesión *nf* concession
concha *nf* shell
conciencia *nf* conscience
concierto *nm* concert
conciliación *nf* conciliation
conciliar *v* conciliate
conciso *adj* concise
concluir *v* conclude
conclusión *nf* conclusion
concordia *nf* harmony
concreto *adj* concrete
concursante *nm* contestant
concursar *v* compete
concurso *nm* competition
condado *nm* county
conde *nm* count
condenar *v* condemn
condensación *nf* condensation
condensar *v* condense
condesa *nf* countess
condición *nf* condition
condicional *adj* conditional
condiciones *nf* terms
condimentar *v* flavor
condimento *nm* seasoning

C

condonar _v_ condone
cóndor _nm_ condor
conducente _adj_ conducive
conducir _v_ drive, lead
conducta _nf_ behavior
conductor _nm_ driver, conductor
conectar _v_ connect
conejo _nm_ rabbit
conexión _nf_ connection
conferencia _nf_ conference
conferir _v_ confer
confesar _v_ confess
confesión _nf_ confession
confiado _adj_ confident
confianza _nf_ trust
confiar _v_ trust, confide
confidencial _adj_ confidential
configurar _v_ configure
confines _nm_ confines
confirmación _nf_ confirmation
confirmar _v_ confirm
confiscación _nf_ confiscation
confiscar _v_ confiscate
conflicto _nm_ conflict
conformarse _v_ conform
conformidad _nf_ compliance
confortable _adj_ comfortable
confrontar _v_ confront
confundir _v_ confuse
confusión _nf_ confusion
confuso _adj_ confusing
congelación _nf_ freezing
congelador _nm_ freezer
congelar _v_ freeze
congeniar _v_ get along
congestión _nf_ congestion
congestionar _v_ congest
congoja _nf_ anguish
congregar _v_ congregate

congreso _nm_ congress
conjetura _nf_ conjecture
conjugar _v_ conjugate
conjunción _nf_ conjunction
conjunto _nm_ outfit; collection
conjunto (en) _adv_ overall
conmigo _pro_ with me
conmoción _nf_ fuss
conmovedor _adj_ moving
conmutar _v_ commute
cono _nm_ cone
conocer _v_ know
conocido _nm_ acquaintance
conocimiento _nm_ knowledge
conpadecer _v_ pity
conquista _nf_ conquest
conquistador _nm_ conqueror
conquistar _v_ conquer
consagración _nf_ consecration
consagrar _v_ consecrate
consciente _adj_ aware, mindful
consecuencia _nf_ fallout
consecuente _adj_ consistent
consecutivo _adj_ consecutive
conseguir _v_ attain, achieve
consejero _nm_ counselor
consejo _nm_ advice
consenso _nm_ consensus
consentir _v_ consent
conserje _nm_ concierge
conservación _nf_ conservation
conservador _adj_ conservative
conservar _v_ conserve
considerable _adj_ sizable
considerar _v_ consider
consistencia _nf_ consistency
consistir _v_ consist
consolar _v_ console
consolidar _v_ consolidate

consonante *nf* consonant
consorcio *nm* consortium
conspiración *nf* conspiracy
conspirar *v* conspire
constante *adj* constant
constar *v* consist
constatar *v* verify
consternación *nf* dismay
consternar *v* dismay
constiparse *v* get a cold
constitución *nf* constitution
constructor *nm* builder
construir *v* build
consuelo *nm* solace
consulado *nm* consulate
consulta *nf* consultation
consultar *v* consult
consumidor *nm* consumer
consumir *v* consume
consumo *nm* consumption
contabilidad *nf* bookkeeping
contable *nm* bookkeeper
contacto *nm* contact
contados *adj* few
contagioso *adj* contagious
contaminación *nf* contamination
contaminar *v* contaminate
contar *v* count
contar con *v* rely on
contemplar *v* contemplate
contemporáneo *adj* contemporary
contendiente *nm* contender
contenedor *nm* container
contener *v* contain
contenido *nm* contents
contentar *v* please
contento *adj* content, glad
contestar *v* reply
contexto *nm* context

contigo *pro* with you
contiguo *adj* adjoining
continental *adj* continental
continente *nm* continent
contingencia *nf* contingency
continuación *nf* sequel
continuar *v* continue
continuidad *nf* continuity
continuo *adj* ongoing
contorno *nm* outline
contra *pre* against
contrabandista *nm* smuggler
contrabando *nm* contraband
contracción *nf* contraction
contradecir *v* contradict
contrapeso *n* counterweight
contrario *adj* contrary
contrarrestar *v* counteract
contraseña *nf* password
contrastar *v* contrast
contraste *nm* contrast
contratiempo *nm* setback
contratista *n* contractor
contrato *nm* contract
contribuir *v* contribute
contrición *nf* contrition
contrincante *nm* opponent
control *nm* control
controversia *nf* controversy
contundente *adj* compelling
convalecencia *nf* convalescence
convalecer *v* convalesce
convaleciente *adj* convalescent
convencer *v* convince
convención *nf* convention
convencional *adj* conventional
conveniencia *nf* convenience
conveniente *adj* convenient
convenio *nm* agreement

convento *nm* convent
convergir *v* converge
conversación *nf* conversation
conversar *v* converse, talk
conversión *nf* conversion
converso *nm* convert
convertir *v* convert
convidar *v* invite
convincente *adj* convincing
convite *nm* banquet
convivir *v* live together
convocar *v* summon
convoy *nm* convoy
convulsión *nf* convulsion
conyugal *adj* conjugal
cónyuge *nm* spouse
cooperación *n* cooperation
cooperar *v* cooperate
coordinación *nf* coordination
coordinador *nm* coordinator
coordinar *v* coordinate
copa *nf* cup
copia *nf* copy
copiadora *nf* copier
copiar *v* copy
copioso *adj* plentiful
coquetear *v* flirt
coraje *nm* courage
corazón *nm* heart
corbata *nf* necktie
corcho *nm* cork
cordero *nm* lamb
cordial *adj* cordial
cordón *nm* shoelace
cordura *nf* sanity
cornear *v* gore
corneta *nf* cornet
coro *nm* choir
corona *nf* crown, wreath

coronación *nf* coronation
coronel *nm* colonel
corporación *nf* corporation
corporal *adj* corporal
corpulento *adj* corpulent
corral *nm* farmyard
correa *nf* belt, strap
corrección *nf* correction
correctamente *adv* properly
correcto *adj* correct, right
corredor *nm* runner
corregir *v* correct
correo *nm* mail
correos *nm* post office
correr *v* run, race
corresponder *v* correspond
corresponsal *nm* journalist
corrida *nf* bullfight
corriente *adj* ordinary
corroborar *v* corroborate
corroer *v* corrode, eat up
corromper *v* corrupt
corrosión *nf* corrosion
corrupción *nf* corruption
cortada *nf* cut
cortar *v* cut, slice, chop
cortauñas *nf* nail clippers
corte *nf* cut, court
cortejar *v* court
cortés *adj* polite
cortesía *nf* courtesy
corteza *nf* crust, bark
cortina *nf* curtain, drape
corto *adj* short
cosa *nf* thing
cosecha *nf* crop
cosechar *v* reap, harvest
coser *v* sew, stitch
cosmético *adj* cosmetic

C

cósmico *adj* cosmic
cosmonauta *nm* cosmonaut
cosquilloso *adj* ticklish
costa *nf* coast
costado *nm* side
costar *v* cost
costear *v* pay for
costero *adj* coastal
costilla *nf* rib, sparerib
costo *nm* cost
costoso *adj* costly
costra *nf* crust
costumbre *nf* custom, habit
costura *nf* sewing
cotidiano *adj* daily
cotillear *v* gossip
cotorra *nf* parrot
cráneo *nm* skull
cráter *nm* crater
creación *nf* creation
creador *nm* creator
crear *v* create
creatividad *nf* creativity
creativo *adj* creative
crecer *v* grow
crecimiento *nm* growth
credibilidad *nf* credibility
crédito *nm* credit
credo *nm* creed
crédulo *adj* credulous
creencia *nf* belief
creer *v* believe
creíble *adj* believable
crema *nf* cream
cremallera *nf* zipper
crematorio *nm* crematorium
crepúsculo *nm* sunset, twilight
cresta *nf* crest, ridge
creyente *nm* believer

criada *nf* maid
criadero *nm* nursery
criar *iv* breed, rear
criatura *nf* creature
crimen *nm* crime
criminal *adj* criminal
cripta *nf* crypt
crisis *nf* crisis
cristal *nm* glass, crystal
cristalería *nf* glassware
Cristiandad *nf* Christianity
cristianizar *v* Christianize
cristiano *adj* Christian
criterio *nm* criterion
crítica *nf* critique
criticar *v* criticize
crítico *nm* critic
crítico *adj* critical
crónica *nf* chronicle
crónico *adj* chronic
cronología *nf* chronology
cruce *nm* junction
crucero *nm* cruise ship
crucial *adj* crucial
crucificar *v* crucify
crucifijo *nm* crucifix
crucifixión *nf* crucifixion
crucigrama *nm* crossword
crudo *adj* raw
cruel *adj* cruel, harsh
crueldad *nm* cruelty
crujido *nm* creak
crujiente *adj* crispy, crunchy
cruz *nf* cross
cruzada *nf* crusade
cruzado *nm* crusader
cruzar *v* cross
cuaderno *nm* notebook
cuadra *nf* stable; block

cuadrado *adj* square
cuadrilla *nf* group
cuadro *nm* picture
cuajarse *v* curdle
cualquier *adj* whichever
cualquier cosa *pro* everything
cualquiera *pro* anybody
cualquiera que *pro* whoever
cuando *adv* when
cuantioso *adj* substantial
cuarenta *adj* forty
cuaresma *nf* Lent
cuarta parte *nf* quarter
cuartel *nm* barracks
cuarto *adj* fourth
cuarto *nm* room
cuatro *adj* four
cuba *nf* barrel
Cuba *nf* Cuba
cubano *adj* Cuban
cúbico *adj* cubic
cubículo *nm* cubicle
cubierta *nf* cover; deck
cubiertos *nm* silverware
cubo *nm* bucket
cubrir *v* cover
cucaracha *nf* cockroach
cuchara *nf* spoon
cucharada *nf* spoonful
cucharita *nf* teaspoon
cuchichear *v* whisper
cuchilla *nf* blade, razor
cuchillo *nm* knife
cuello *nm* neck; collar
cuenta *nf* account, bill
cuento *nm* tale, story
cuerda *nf* rope, string
cuerdo *adj* sensible, sane
cuerno *nm* horn

cuero *nm* leather
cuerpo *nm* body
cuervo *nm* crow
cuesta *nf* slope
cuesta abajo *adv* downhill
cuesta arriba *adv* uphill
cuestión *nf* issue, matter
cuestionario *nm* questionnaire
cueva *nf* cave
cuidado *nm* care
cuidadoso *adj* careful
cuidar *v* care, look after
culata *nf* butt
culebra *nf* snake
culminante *adj* climatic
culminar *v* culminate
culpa *nf* blame, fault
culpabilidad *nf* guilt
culpable *adj* guilty
culpar *v* blame
cultivar *v* cultivate, grow
culto *nm* worship
culto *adj* literate, learned
cultura *nf* culture
cultural *adj* cultural
cumbre *nf* summit, apex
cumpleaños *nm* birthday
cumplido *nm* compliment
cumplir *v* comply, fulfill
cúmulo *nm* pile
cuna *nf* cradle, crib
cuña *nf* wedge
cuñado *n* brother-in-law
cuneta *nf* gutter
cuota *nf* dues, fee
cupón *nm* coupon
cúpula *nf* dome
cura *nm* priest; cure
curable *adj* curable

C

curación *nf* cure
curandero *nm* healer
curar *v* cure, heal
curiosidad *nf* curiosity
curioso *adj* curious
cursiva *adj* italics
curso *nm* course
curtir *v* harden
curva *nf* curve
cúspide *nf* peak, top
custodia *nf* custody
cutis *nm* complexion
cuyo *pro* whose

D

dadivoso *adj* generous
dado *nm* dice
daga *nf* dagger
dama *nf* lady
dañar *v* harm, damage
danés *adj* Danish
dañino *adj* harmful
daño *nm* damage, harm
danza *nf* dance
danzar *v* dance
dar *v* give
dar cuerda *v* wind
dar forma *v* shape
dar la lata *v* nag
dar la vuelta *v* turn, flip
dar pasos *v* pace
dar patadas *v* kick
dar vueltas *v* spin
dar zancadas *v* stride

dardo *n* dart
darse cuenta *v* realize
darse prisa *v* hasten
datos *nm* data
de *pre* from, of
debajo *adv* below
debajo de *pre* under, beneath
debate *nm* debate
debatir *v* debate
deber *v* owe
deber *nm* duty
debídamente *adv* duly
debido *adj* due
débil *adj* feeble, weak
debilidad *nf* weakness
debilitar *v* weaken
década *nf* decade
decadencia *nf* decadence
decaer *v* decline
decapitar *v* behead
decencia *nf* decency
decente *adj* decent
decepcionante *adj* disappointing
decepcionar *v* disappoint
decidido *adj* determined
decidir *v* decide
decimal *adj* decimal
décimo *adj* tenth
decir *v* say, tell
decisión *nf* decision
decisivo *adj* decisive
declaración *nf* statement
declarar *v* declare
decline *v* decline
declive *nm* slope
decoración *nf* decor
decorar *v* decorate
decorativo *adj* decorative
decoro *n* dignity

decrecer *v* decrease
decrépito *adj* decrepit
decretar *v* decree, order
decreto *nm* decree
dedal *nm* thimble
dedicar *v* dedicate
dedicarse *v* devote
dedo *nm* finger
dedo del pie *nm* toe
deducción *nf* deduction
deducible *adj* deductible
deducir *v* deduce, infer
defección *nf* defection
defecto *nm* fault, flaw
defectuoso *adj* defective
defender *v* defend
defensa *nf* defense
defensor *nm* defender
deficiente *adj* deficient
definición *nf* definition
definir *v* define
definitivo *adj* definitive
deformación *nf* deformity
deformar *v* deform
deforme *adj* deformed
defraudar *v* defraud
defunción *nf* death
degeneracion *nf* degeneration
degenerar *v* degenerate
degollar *v* behead
degradacion *n* degradation
degradante *adj* demeaning
degradar *v* demote, degrade
degradarse *v* demean
degustar *v* taste
deidad *nf* deity
dejadez *nf* neglect
dejar *v* quit, leave
dejar atónito *v* stun

dejar atrás *v* outgrow
dejar caer *v* drop
dejar entrar *v* let in
dejar perplejo *v* mystify
dejar salir *v* let out
dejar sitio *v* move over
dejo *nm* accent
del norte *adj* northern
del occidente *adj* western
del oriente *adj* eastern
del sur *adj* southern
delantal *nm* apron
delante *adv* in front, ahead
delatar *v* betray, snitch
delegar *v* delegate
deleitar *v* delight
deletrear *v* spell
delfín *nm* dolphin
delgado *adj* slim, thin
deliberar *v* deliberate
delicadeza *nf* delicacy
delicado *adj* delicate
delicia *nf* delight
delicioso *adj* delicious
delincuencia *nf* delinquency
delincuente *nm* criminal
delineante *nm* draftsman
delirar *v* be delirious
delito *nm* offense
demacrado *adj* emaciated
demanda *nf* claim, lawsuit
demandante *nm* plaintiff
demandar *v* sue
demasiado *adj* too much
demencia *nf* insanity
demente *adj* insane
democracia *nf* democracy
democrático *adj* democratic
demoler *v* demolish

demolición *nf* demolition
demonio *nm* demon, devil
demonstrativo *adj* demonstrative
demora *nf* delay
demorar *v* delay, be late
demostración *nf* demonstration
demostrar *v* prove
denegar *v* refuse
denigrar *v* denigrate
denominador *nm* denominator
denotar *v* indicate
densidad *nf* density
denso *adj* thick, dense
dental *adj* dental
dentista *nm* dentist
dentro *pre* inside, within
denuncia *nf* accusation
denunciar *v* denounce
deodorante *nm* deodorant
departamento *nm* department
dependencia *nf* dependence
depender *v* depend, hinge
dependiente *nm* sales clerk
deplorable *adj* deplorable
deplorar *v* deplore
deportar *v* deport
deporte *nm* sport
deportista *adj* sporty
deportista *nm* sportsman
depositar *v* put, place
depósito *nm* deposit
depravado *adj* deprave
depreciación *nf* depreciation
depreciar(se) *v* depreciate
depresión *nf* depression
deprimente *adj* depressing
deprimir *v* depress
deprisa *adv* quickly
depurar *v* purify, purge

derecho *adj* straight, honest
derecho *nm* right
derivado *nm* by-product
derivado *adj* derived
derivar *v* derive
derogar *v* repeal
derramar *v* spill, shed
derrame *nm* spilling; stroke
derribar *v* demolish; topple
derritir *v* melt
derrocar *v* overthrow
derrochar *v* squander
derroche *nm* waste
derrota *nf* defeat
derrotar *v* defeat
derrumbar *v* knock down
derrumbarse *v* collapse
desabrido *adj* tasteless
desabrochar *v* unfasten, untie
desacato *nm* disrespect
desacierto *nm* mistake
desacreditar *v* discredit
desactivar *v* defuse
desacuerdo *nm* disagreement
desafiante *adj* defiant
desafiar *v* defy, challenge
desafinado *adj* out of tune
desafío *nm* challenge
desagradable *adj* unpleasant
desagradar *v* dislike
desagradecido *adj* ungrateful
desagrado *nm* displeasure
desahogo *nm* relief
desahuciar *v* give up hope
desairar *v* snub
desaire *nm* rebuff, snub
desalentador *adj* discouraging
desalentar *v* discourage
desalojamiento *nm* ouster

desalojar *v* oust, vacate
desamparado *adj* destitute
desamparar *v* abandon
desangrarse *v* bleed
desanimar *v* discourage
desaparecer *v* disappear
desaparición *nf* disappearance
desapego *nm* indifference
desapercibido *adj* unnoticed
desaprobación *nf* disapproval
desaprobar *v* disapprove
desaprovechar *v* waste
desarmado *adj* unarmed
desarmar *v* disarm
desarme *nm* disarmament
desarraigar *v* uproot
desarrollar *v* develop
desarrollo *nm* development
desarticular *v* break up
desastre *nm* disaster
desastroso *adj* disastrous
desatar *v* unfasten, untie
desatascar *v* clear, unplug
desatender *v* neglect
desatento *adj* inattentive
desatornillar *v* unscrew
desaugarse *v* relieve
desaveniencia *nf* disagreement
desayunar *v* have breakfast
desayuno *nm* breakfast
desbarajuste *nm* mess
desbaratar *v* ruin
desbocado *adj* amok
desbordar *v* overflow
descabellado *adj* crazy
descalabro *nm* disaster
descalificar *v* disqualify
descalzo *adj* barefoot
descansado *adj* restful

descansar *v* relax, rest
descanso *nm* recess, rest
descapotable *adj* convertible
descarado *adj* insolent, rude
descarga *nf* unloading
descargar *v* unload
descaro *nm* nerve
descarrilar *v* derail
descartar *v* discard; rule out
descendencia *nf* offspring
descender *v* descend
descendiente *nm* descendant
descenso *nm* descent, drop
descifrar *v* decipher
descolgar *v* take down
descolorido *adj* faded
descomponerse *v* rot; break down
desconcertado *adj* lost
desconcertante *adj* puzzling
desconcertar *v* baffle
desconcierto *nm* uncertainty
desconectar *v* disconnect
desconfiado *adj* distrustful
desconfianza *nf* mistrust
desconfiar *v* distrust
descongelar *v* defrost, thaw
desconocido *adj* unknown
desconsolado *adj* distressed
descontar *v* deduct
descontento *adj* unhappy
descontinuar *v* discontinue
descortés *adj* impolite
descortesía *n* rudeness
descoser *v* unstitch
descremar *v* skim
describir *v* describe
descripción *nf* description
descuartizar *v* cut up
descubrimiento *nm* discovery

descubrir *v* discover
descuento *nm* discount
descuidado *adj* careless
descuidar *v* neglect
descuido *nm* neglect, mistake
desde *pre* from, since
desdecirse *v* retract, recant
desdén *nm* contempt
desdeñar *v* scorn, despise
desdicha *nf* misfortune
desdichado *adj* unhappy
desdoblar *v* unfold
deseable *adj* desirable
desear *v* wish, desire
desecar *v* dry up
desechable *adj* disposable
desechar *v* throw
desecrar *v* desecrate
desegregar *v* desegregate
desembarcar *v* disembark
desembolsar *v* disburse
desempacar *v* unpack
desempeñar *v* play; exercise
desempleado *adj* unemployed
desempleo *nm* unemployment
desencadenar *v* trigger
desencantado *adj* disenchanted
desenchufar *v* unplug
desengaño *nm* disappointment
desenlace *nm* outcome
desenmascarar *v* unmask
desenredar *v* untangle
desenroscar *v* unscrew
desenterrar *v* exhume
desenvoltura *nf* ease
desenvolver *v* unwrap
desenvuelto *adj* self-confident
deseo *nm* wish, longing
deseoso *adj* eager

desequilibrado *adj* unbalanced
desequilibrio *nm* imbalance
desertar *v* defect
desértico *adj* desert
desertor *nm* deserter
desesperado *adj* desperate
desesperar *v* despair
desfalco *nm* embezzlement
desfavorable *adj* unfavorable
desfigurar *v* disfigure
desfilar *v* parade
desfilaredo *nm* gorge
desfile *nm* parade
desgana *nf* lack of interest
desgarrar *v* tear up
desgastar *v* wear down
desgracia *nf* misfortune
desgraciado *adj* unlucky
desgracias *nf* woes
desgravar *v* deduct
deshacer *v* undo
deshacerse de *v* get rid
deshecho *adj* exhausted
desheredar *v* disinherit
deshidratar *v* dehydrate
deshielo *nm* thaw
deshonestidad *n* dishonesty
deshonesto *adj* dishonest
deshonra *nf* dishonor
deshora *adv* wrong time
desierto *nm* desert
designar *v* designate, name
designio *nm* plan
desigual *adj* unequal; uneven
desigualdad *nf* inequality
desilusión *nf* disillusion
desinfectar *v* disinfect
desinflar *v* deflate
desintegrar *v* disintegrate

desinteresado *adj* disinterested
desistir *v* give up
desleal *adj* disloyal
deslealtad *n* disloyalty
desligar *v* separate
desliz *nm* lapse
deslizar *v* slip, slide
deslumbrante *adj* dazzling
deslumbrar *v* dazzle
desmadre *nm* chaos
desmantelar *v* dismantle
desmayarse *v* faint, pass out
desmembrar *v* dismember
desmenuzar *v* shred
desmontar *v* take apart
desmoralizar *v* demoralize
desmoronado *adj* dilapidated
desmoronarse *v* crumble
desnatar *v* skim
desnudarse *v* undress, strip
desnudez *nf* nudity
desnudo *adj* nude, naked
desnutrición *nf* malnutrition
desobedecer *v* disobey
desobediencia *nf* disobedience
desobediente *adj* disobedient
desocupado *adj* vacant, empty
desocupar *v* vacate
desolación *nf* desolation
desolador *adj* bleak
desorden *nm* disorder, mess
desorientado *adj* disoriented
despabilado *adj* alert
despacho *nm* office
despacio *adv* slowly
desparramar *v* scatter
despavorido *v* terrified
despedazar *v* tear apart
despedida *nf* farewell

despedir *v* dismiss
despegar *v* take off; peel off
despegue *nm* takeoff
despejado *adj* clear
despellejar *v* skin
despensa *nf* pantry
desperdiciar *v* waste
desperdicio *nm* waste
desperdigarse *v* scatter
desperezarse *v* stretch
despertador *nm* alarm clock
despertar *v* wake up
despertar *nm* awakening
despiadado *adj* ruthless
despido *nm* dismissal
despierto *adj* awake
despilfarrar *v* squander
despistado *adj* clueless; lost
despiste *nm* mistake
desplazar *v* displace
desplegar *v* deploy
despliegue *nm* deployment
despojar *v* deprive, rob
despojos *nm* spoils
desposar *v* marry
déspota *nm* despot
despreciable *adj* despicable
despreciar *v* despise
desprecio *nm* contempt
despreocupado *adj* carefree
desprevenido *adj* unprepared
desprovisto *adj* lacking in
después *adv* afterwards
después de *pre* after
desquiciado *adj* deranged
desquite *nm* revenge
destacar *v* stand
destapar *v* open
destartalado *adj* dilapidated

desteñirse *v* fade
desterrar *v* banish
destiempo (a) *adv* out of turn
destierro *nm* exile
destinar *v* assign
destinatario *nm* addressee
destino *nm* fate; destination
destituir *v* dismiss
destornillador *nm* screwdriver
destornillar *v* unscrew
destreza *nf* skill
destrozar *v* wreck
destrucción *nf* destruction
destructor *nm* destroyer
destruir *v* destroy
desuso (en) *adj* not in use
desvalido *adj* destitute
desvalijar *v* rob
desván *nm* attic
desvanecer *v* fade, vanish
desvelar *v* stay awake
desventaja *nf* disadvantage
desviación *nf* detour
desviar *v* divert, re-rout
desvío *nm* diversion
detallar *v* detail, itemize
detalle *nm* detail
detectar *v* detect
detective *nm* detective
detector *nm* detector
detención *nf* detention
detener *v* detain, arrest
detergente *nm* detergent
deteriorar *v* deteriorate
determinar *v* determine
detonar *v* detonate
detrás *adv* behind
detrás de *pre* behind
deuda *nf* debt

deudor *nm* debtor
devaluar *v* devalue
devastador *adj* devastating
devastar *v* devastate
devoción *nf* devotion
devolver *v* refund, repay
devorar *v* devour
devoto *adj* devout
día *nm* day
día de fiesta *nm* holiday
diabético *adj* diabetic
diablo *nm* devil
diácono *nm* deacon
diagnosticar *v* diagnose
diagnóstico *nm* diagnosis
diagonal *adj* diagonal
diagrama *nm* diagram
dialecto *nm* dialect
diálogo *nm* dialogue
diamante *nm* diamond
diámetro *nm* diameter
diariamente *adv* daily
diario *nm* diary
diarrea *nf* diarrhea
dibujar *v* draw
dibujo *nm* drawing
diccionario *nm* dictionary
dicho *nm* saying
diciembre *nm* December
dictador *nm* dictator
dictadura *nf* dictatorship
dictar *v* dictate
diecinueve *adj* nineteen
dieciocho *adj* eighteen
dieciséis *adj* sixteen
diecisiete *adj* seventeen
diente *nm* tooth
dientes *nm* teeth
diestro *adj* skillful

dieta *nf* diet
diez *adj* ten
diezmar *v* decimate
difamar *v* defame
diferencia *nf* difference
diferir *v* defer
difícil *adj* difficult
dificultad *nf* difficulty
dificultades *nf* trials
difundir *v* broadcast
difunto *adj* deceased, late
digerir *v* digest
digestión *nf* digestion
dígito *nm* digit
dignarse *v* deign
dignidad *nf* dignity
digno *adj* worthy
dilación *nf* delay
dilapidar *v* waste
dilatar *v* prolong
dilema *nf* dilemma
diligencia *nf* diligence
diluir *v* dilute
diluvio *nm* deluge, flood
dimensión *nf* dimension
dimitir *v* resign
Dinamarca *nf* Denmark
dinamita *nf* dynamite
dinastía *nf* dynasty
dineral *nm* fortune
dinero *nm* money
diócesis *nf* diocese
Dios *nm* God
diosa *nf* goddess
diploma *n* diploma
diplomacia *nf* diplomacy
diplomático *nm* diplomat
diputado *nm* deputy
dique *nm* dike

dirección *nf* address; direction
directo *adj* direct
director *nm* director
discernir *v* discern
disciplina *nf* discipline
discípulo *nm* disciple
disco *nm* disk, record
discordia *nf* discord
discreción *nf* discretion
discrepancia *nf* discrepancy
discrepar *v* disagree
discreto *adj* discreet
discriminar *v* discriminate
disculpa *nf* apology
disculparse *v* apologize
discurso *nm* speech
discusión *nf* discussion
discutible *adj* debatable
discutir *v* argue, discuss
diseminar *v* spread
diseño *nm* design
disentir *v* disagree
disfigurar *v* deface
disfrazarse *v* disguise
disgustar *v* upset
disimular *v* pretend
disipar *v* dispel
dislocar *v* dislocate
dislocarse *v* sprain
disminuir *v* decrease
disolución *nf* dissolution
disolusionar *v* disappoint
disolver *v* dissolve
disparar *v* shoot, fire
disparate *nm* nonsense
disparo *nm* shot
disparos *nm* gunfire
dispensar *v* dispense
dispersar *v* disperse

D

D

dispersión *nf* dispersal
disponer *v* dispose
disponible *adj* available
disposición *nf* disposal
disputa *nf* dispute
distancia *nf* distance
distante *adj* aloof, distant
distinguir *v* distinguish
distinto *adj* unlike, distinct
distorsión *nf* distortion
distorsionar *v* distort
distracción *nf* distraction
distraer *v* distract
distribución *nf* distribution
distribuidor *nm* supplier
distribuir *v* distribute
distrito *nm* district
disturbio *nm* disturbance
disuadir *v* dissuade
disyuntiva *nf* dilemma
divagar *v* ramble
diván *nm* couch
diversidad *nf* diversity
diversificar *v* diversify
diversión *nf* fun, pastime
diverso *adj* diverse
divertidísimo *adj* hilarious
divertido *adj* amusing
divertir *v* amuse
dividir *v* divide
divino *adj* divine
divisa *nf* currency
división *nf* division
divorciado *nm* divorcee
divorciar *v* divorce
divorcio *nm* divorce
divulgar *v* spread
dobladillo *nm* hem
doblado *adj* pleated

doblar *v* bend, fold
doble *adj* double
doblegar *v* break
doblez *nf* fold, deceit
doce *adj* twelve
docena *nf* dozen
dócil *adj* docile
doctor *nm* doctor
doctrina *nf* doctrine
documental *nm* documentary
documento *nm* document
dólar *nm* dollar
doler *v* hurt
dolor *nm* pain, ache
doloroso *adj* painful
domar *v* tame
domesticado *adj* tamed
domesticar *v* domesticate
doméstico *adj* domestic
dominar *v* dominate
domingo *nm* Sunday
dominio *nm* dominion
don *nm* gift
donante *nm* donor
donar *v* donate
donativo *nm* donation
doncella *nf* maid
donde *adv* where
dondequiera *adv* wherever
dorado *adj* golden
dormido *adj* asleep
dormir *v* sleep
dormitar *v* doze
dormitorio *nm* bedroom
dorso *nm* back
dos *adj* two
dos veces *adv* twice
dosis *nf* dosage
dotado *adj* gifted, talented

dotar _v_ endow
dote _nf_ dowry
dragón _nm_ dragon
dramático _adj_ dramatic
drástico _adj_ drastic
drenaje _nm_ drainage
droga _nf_ drug, dope
drogarse _v_ drug
ducha _nf_ shower
duda _nf_ doubt
dudar _v_ doubt
dudoso _adj_ doubtful
duelo _nm_ duel; mourning
dueño _nm_ owner
dulce _adj_ sweet
dulces _nm_ sweets
dulzura _nf_ sweetness
duodécimo _adj_ twelfth
duplicación _nf_ duplication
duplicar _v_ duplicate
duque _nm_ duke
duquesa _nf_ duchess
duración _nf_ duration
duradero _adj_ lasting
durante _pre_ during
durar _v_ last
durazno _nm_ peach
duro _adj_ hard, tough

ebrio _adj_ drunk
echar _v_ pour, throw
echar a correos _v_ mail
echar abajo _v_ bring down
echar siesta _v_ take a nap
echarse _v_ lie down
echarse atrás _v_ back down
eclipsar _v_ outshine
eclipse _nm_ eclipse
eco _nm_ echo
ecología _nf_ ecology
economía _nf_ economy
económico _adj_ inexpensive
ecuación _nf_ equation
ecuador _nm_ equator
edad _nf_ age
edificar _v_ build
edificio _nm_ building
editar _v_ edit
editor _nm_ publisher
editorial _nf_ editorial
edredón _nm_ comforter
educación _nf_ education
educar _v_ educate
educativo _adj_ educational
efectuar _v_ effect
eficacia _nf_ efficiency
eficaz _adj_ effective
efigie _nf_ effigy
efusión _nf_ outpouring
efusivo _adj_ effusive
egoísmo _nm_ selfishness
egoísta _adj_ selfish
eje _nm_ axis, axle
ejecutar _v_ execute
ejecutivo _nm_ executive

D
E

ejemplar *adj* exemplary
ejemplificar *v* exemplify
ejemplo *nm* example
ejercer *v* exert, practice
ejército *nm* army
ejote *nm* green bean
él *pro* he
él mismo *pro* himself
elaborar *v* brew, make
elástico *adj* elastic
elección *nf* choice, election
electricidad *nf* electricity
electricista *nm* electrician
eléctrico *adj* electric
electrocutar *v* electrocute
electrónico *adj* electronic
elefante *nm* elephant
elegancia *nf* elegance
elegante *adj* elegant
elegible *adj* eligible
elegir *v* elect, pick
elemental *adj* elemental
elemento *nm* element
elevador *nm* elevator
elevar *v* raise, lift
eliminar *v* eliminate
élite *nf* elite
ella *pro* she
ellos *pro* they
ellos mismos *pro* themselves
elocuencia *nf* eloquence
elocuente *adj* eloquent
elogiar *v* praise
elogio *nm* praise
eludir *v* avoid
emanar *v* emanate
emancipar *v* emancipate
embadurnar *v* smear
embajada *nf* embassy

embajador *nm* ambassador
embalar *v* pack
embalsamar *v* embalm
embalse *nm* dam, reservoir
embarazada *adj* pregnant
embarazo *nm* pregnancy
embarcar *v* embark
embargar *v* impound, seize
embargo *nm* seizure
embarrado *adj* muddy
embaucar *v* fool, trick
embelesar *v* captivate
embellecer *v* beautify
embestida *nf* charge
embestir *v* charge
embobar *v* fascinate
embolsarse *v* pocket
emborrachar *v* get drunk
emboscada *nf* ambush
emboscar *v* ambush
embotellar *v* bottle
embrague *nm* clutch
embriagar *v* intoxicate
embriaguez *nf* intoxication
embrión *nm* embryo
embrollar *v* confuse
embrollo *nm* tangle, mess
embrujar *v* bewitch
embrujo *v* spell
embrutecer *v* brutalize
embrutecido *adj* brutalized
embudo *nm* funnel
embustero *nm* liar
emergencia *nf* emergency
emerger *v* emerge
emigrante *nm* emigrant
emigrar *v* emigrate
emisario *nm* emissary
emisión *n* emission

emisora *nf* radio station

emitir *v* emit

emoción *nf* emotion, thrill

emocionante *adj* exciting

emocionar *v* thrill

emotivo *adj* emotional

empalmar *v* join, connect

empalme *nm* connection

empantanado *adj* bogged down

empapar *v* soak

empapelar *v* paper

empaquetar *v* pack

emparejar *v* pair; make even

empastar *v* fill

empaste *nm* filling

empatar *v* tie

empate *nm* draw, tie

empedernido *adj* entrenched

empedrado *adj* paved

empeñado *adj* in debt

empeñar *v* pawn

empeño *nm* determination

empeorar *v* get worse

emperador *nm* emperor

emperatriz *nf* empress

empezar *v* begin, start

empinado *adj* steep

empleado *nm* employee

emplear *v* employ

empleo *nm* employment

empobrecer *v* impoverish

empotrado *adj* built-in

emprender *v* undertake

empresa *nf* enterprise

empresario *nm* entrepreneur

empujar *v* push, shove

empujón *nm* push, shove

empuñadura *nf* hilt

en *at* in, at

en algún lugar *adv* somewhere

en alta voz *adv* aloud

en el futuro *adv* hereafter

en lugar de *adv* instead

en medio de *pre* amid, midst

en ningún lugar *adv* nowhere

en otra parte *adv* elsewhere

en un rato *adv* in a while

enamorado *adj* in love

enamorarse *v* fall in love

enano *nm* dwarf

enarbolar *v* raise

encabezar *v* lead

encadenar *v* chain

encajar *v* fit

encaje *nm* lace

encallar *v* run aground

encaminarse *v* head for

encandilar *v* dazzle

encantador *adj* charming

encantar *v* charm

encanto *nm* charm

encapotado *adj* cloudy

encapuchado *adj* hooded

encaramarse *v* climb

encararse *v* face up

encarcelar *v* imprison, jail

encargado *nm* attendant

encargar *v* order

encargarse *v* take care

encargo *nm* errand

encariñarse *v* grow fond

encarnar *v* embody

encarnizado *adj* fierce

encarrilar *v* guide, direct

encauzar *v* channel

encender *iv* light, turn on

encerar *v* wax

encerrar *adj* lock, shut

encharcado *adj* flooded
enchufar *v* plug, connect
enchufe *nm* plug
encía *nf* gum
enciclopedia *nf* encyclopedia
encima *adv* above, over
encima de *pre* on top of
encina *nf* oak tree
encinta *adj* pregnant
enclave *nm* enclave
encogerse *v* shrink; shrug
encomendar *v* entrust
enconado *adj* heated
enconarse *v* fester
encontrar *v* find
encontrarse *v* meet
encrucijada *nf* crossroads
encuadernar *v* bind
encuadrar *v* center, fit
encubrimiento *nm* cover-up
encubrir *v* hide, conceal
encuentro *nm* encounter
encuerarse *v* get naked
encuesta *nf* poll, survey
ende *adv* therefore
endeble *adj* delicate, weak
endemoniado *adj* possessed
enderezar *v* straighten out
enderezarse *v* straighten up
endeudarse *v* get into debt
endorsar *v* endorse
endrogarse *v* get into debt
endulzar *v* sweeten
endurecer *v* harden
enemigo *nm* enemy, foe
enemistad *nf* feud
energía *nf* energy
enérgico *adj* forceful
enero *nm* January

enfadar *v* annoy
enfado *nm* anger
énfasis *nm* emphasis
enfermar *v* get sick
enfermedad *nf* illness
enfermera *nf* nurse
enfermería *nf* infirmary
enfermo *nm* sick, ill
enflaquecer *v* lose weight
enfocar *v* focus
enfoque *nm* approach
enfrentamiento *nm* confrontation
enfrentarse *v* confront
enfrente *adv* opposite
enfriar *v* chill, cool
enfurecer *v* enrage
engalanar *v* decorate
engañar *v* deceive, fool
enganchar *v* hook, connect
engaño *nm* deceit
engañoso *adj* deceitful
engatusar *v* deceive
engendrar *v* breed; beget
engordar *v* fatten
engorroso *adj* complicated
engrasar *v* lubricate
engrase *nm* lubrication
engreído *adj* conceited
engrudo *nm* paste
engullir *v* swallow
enhebrar *v* thread
enigma *nm* puzzle, mystery
enjabonar *v* soap
enjambre *nm* swarm
enjaular *v* put in a cage
enjuagar *v* rinse
enjugar *v* wipe away
enjuiciar *v* prosecute
enlace *nm* liaison, link

enlatado *adj* canned
enlazar *v* link, connect
enlistarse *v* enlist
enloquecer *v* go crazy
enlutado *adj* in mourning
enmarañado *adj* tangled
enmascarado *adj* masked
enmendar *v* amend, rectify
enmienda *nf* amendment
enmohecerse *v* go moldy
enmudecer *v* fall silent
enojarse *v* get angry
enojo *nm* anger
enorgullecer *v* make proud
enorme *adj* huge
enredarse *v* entangle
enredo *nm* mess, tangle
enrevesado *adj* complicated
enriquecer *v* enrich
enrojecer *v* redden; blush
enrolar *v* enlist
enrollar *v* roll up, wind
enroscar *v* wind
ensalada *nf* salad
ensalzar *v* praise
ensanchar *v* widen
ensayar *v* test, rehearse
ensayo *nm* rehearsal; essay
enseguida *adv* shortly
ensenada *nf* cove
enseñar *v* teach
ensordecer *v* deafen
ensuciar *v* soil, litter
ensuciarse *v* get dirty
ensueño *nm* dream
entablar *v* start
ente *nm* being
entender *v* understand
enterarse *v* find out

entereza *nf* fortitude
enternecer *v* move, touch
entero *adj* entire, whole
enterrar *v* bury
entibiar *v* warm up
entierro *nm* burial
entonar *v* sing
entonces *adv* then
entorno *nm* environment
entorpecer *v* hinder
entrada *nf* entrance; deposit
entrañable *adj* dear
entrañas *nf* bowels
entrante *adj* coming, next
entrar *v* enter, go in
entre *pre* among, between
entreabierto *adj* ajar
entrega *nf* delivery
entregar *v* deliver, hand over
entregarse *v* devote to
entrelazar *v* intertwine
entremezclar *v* mix
entrenador *nm* trainer
entrenamiento *nm* training
entrenar *v* coach, train
entretanto *adv* meanwhile
entretener *v* entertain
entretenido *adj* amused
entrevista *nf* interview
entristecer *v* sadden
entrometerse *v* meddle
entrometido *adj* nosy
entumecerse *v* go numb
entumecido *adj* numb
enturbiar *v* blur
entusiasmar *v* enthuse
entusiasmarse *v* get excited
entusiasmo *nm* enthusiasm
entusiasta *adj* enthusiastic

E

enumerar *v* enumerate, list
envasar *v* can, pack
envase *nm* container
envejecer *v* grow old
envenenar *v* poison
enviado *nm* envoy
enviar *v* send, dispatch
envidia *nf* envy, jealousy
envidioso *adj* envious, jealous
envío *nm* shipment
envoltura *nf* wrapping
envolver *v* wrap; engulf
enyesar *v* plaster
enzarzarse *v* get involved
epidemia *nf* epidemic
epilepsia *nf* epilepsy
episodio *nm* episode
epístola *nf* epistle
epitafio *nm* epitaph
época *nf* epoch, time
equilibrar *v* balance
equilibrio *nm* balance
equipaje *nm* luggage
equipar *v* equip
equiparar *v* equate
equipo *nm* equipment; team
equivalente *adj* equivalent
equivocación *nf* mistake
equivocado *adj* mistaken
equivocarse *v* be wrong
erguido *adj* erect
erigir *v* erect
ermita *nf* chapel
ermitaño *nm* hermit
erosión *nf* erosion
erradicar *v* eradicate
errata *nf* misprint
erróneo *adj* erroneous
error *nm* error, mistake

erudito *adj* learned
erupción *nf* eruption; rash
erutar *v* burp
esbelto *adj* slender
esbozar *v* sketch
esbozo *nm* outline
escabroso *adj* rough, rugged
escabullirse *v* slip away
escala *nf* scale, stop over
escalar *v* climb, scale
escaldar *v* scald
escalera *nf* ladder, stairs
escalofriante *adj* frightening
escalofrío *nm* shiver
escalón *nm* step
escama *nf* flake
escamar *v* make weary
escandalizar *v* scandalize
escándalo *nm* scandal
escandaloso *adj* shocking
escaño *nm* seat
escaparate *nm* store window
escaparse *v* escape
escapatoria *nf* loophole, way out
escape *nm* leakage
escarabajo *nm* beetle
escaramuza *nf* skirmish
escarbar *v* scratch
escarcha *nf* frost
escardar *v* weed
escarmiento *nm* lesson
escarnio *nm* ridicule
escarpado *adj* steep
escasear *v* scarce
escasez *nf* shortage
escaso *adj* scarce
escatimar *v* be stingy, save
escena *nf* scene
escenario *nm* stage

escéntrico *adj* eccentric
escéptico *adj* skeptic
esclarecer *v* clarify
esclavitud *nf* slavery
esclavo *nm* slave
escoba *nf* broom
escocer *v* sting
escoger *v* choose
escollo *nm* obstacle
escolta *nf* escort
escombros *nm* debris, rubble
esconder *v* hide, conceal
escondite *nm* hideout
escopeta *nf* shotgun
escoria *nf* slag, dregs
escorpión *nm* scorpion
escozor *nm* burning
escribir *v* write
escritor *nm* writer
escritorio *nm* desk
escritura *nf* writing
escrúpulos *nm* scruples
escrupuloso *adj* scrupulous
escuchar *v* listen
escudo *nm* shield
escuela *nf* school
esculcar *v* search
escultor *nm* sculptor
escultura *nf* sculpture
escupir *v* spit
escurrir *v* drain, wring out
escusado *nm* bathroom
ese *adj* that
esencia *nf* essence
esfera *nf* sphere; dial
esfinge *nf* sphinx
esforzarse *v* endeavor
esfuerzo *nm* effort
esfumarse *v* disappear

esgrima *nf* fencing
eslabón *nm* link
esmalte *nm* enamel
esmerado *adj* neat
esmeralda *nf* emerald
esmero *nm* care
eso *pro* that
esófago *nm* esophagus
esos *adj* those
espabilado *adj* smart, bright
espacio *nm* space
espacioso *adj* spacious
espada *nf* sword
espalda *nf* back
España *nf* Spain
español *adj* Spanish
español *nm* Spaniard
espantar *v* scare
espantarse *v* get scared
espanto *n* fright
espantoso *adj* frightening
esparcir *v* scatter
espárrago *nm* asparagus
espasmo *nm* spasm
especia *nf* spice
especial *adj* special
especialidad *nf* specialty
especializarse *v* specialize
especie *nf* species; kind
especificar *v* specify
específico *adj* specific
espectáculo *nm* spectacle
espectador *nm* spectator
especular *v* speculate
espejismo *nm* mirage
espejo *nm* mirror
espeluznante *adj* horrific
esperanza *nf* hope
esperar *v* wait, expect

espesar *v* thicken
espeso *adj* thick
espesor *nm* thickness
espía *nm* spy
espiar *v* spy
espiga *nf* ear
espina *nf* thorn
espina dorsal *nm* spine
espinazo *nm* backbone
espinilla *nf* shin; pimple
espinoso *adj* thorny
espionaje *nm* spying
espíritu *nm* spirit
espiritual *adj* spiritual
espléndido *adj* splendid
esplendor *nm* splendor
esponja *nf* sponge
espontaneidad *nf* spontaneity
espontáneo *adj* spontaneous
esporádico *adj* sporadic
esposa *nf* wife
esposas *nf* handcuffs
esposo *nm* husband
esprint *nm* sprint
espuela *nf* spur
espuma *nf* foam; lather
espumoso *adj* sparkling
esqueleto *nm* skeleton
esquema *nf* plan, sketch
esquiar *v* ski
esquilar *v* shear
esquina *nf* corner
esquivar *v* dodge, shun
esta *adj* this
estabilidad *nf* stability
estable *adj* stable
establecer *v* establish
establecerse *v* settle down
establo *nm* stable

estación *nf* season; station
estadio *nm* stadium
estadística *nf* statistic
estado *nm* state; condition
estafa *nf* swindle
estafador *nm* swindler
estafar *v* cheat, swindle
estallar *v* explode
estallido *nm* explosion
estampido *nm* stampede
estampilla *nf* stamp
estancamiento *nm* stagnation
estancarse *v* stagnate
estancia *nf* stay
estandarizar *v* standardize
estandarte *nm* banner
estaño *nm* tin
estanque *nm* pond
estante *nm* shelf
estantería *nf* bookcase
estantes *nm* shelves
estar *v* be
estar de pie *v* stand
estatua *nf* statue
estatuto *nm* statute
este *nm* east
este *adj* this
éste *pro* this one
estela *nf* trail
estera *nf* mat
estéril *adj* barren; sterile
esterilizar *v* sterilize
esternón *nm* breast bone
estética *nf* aesthetics
estético *adj* aesthetic
estiércol *nm* dung, manure
estilo *nm* style
estilográfica *nf* fountain pen
estima *nf* esteem

estimar *v* value, respect
estimulante *adj* stimulating
estimular *v* stimulate
estímulo *nm* incentive
estirar *v* stretch
estirón *nm* pull
estival *adj* summer
esto *pro* this
estofado *nm* stew
estoico *adj* stoic
estómago *nm* stomacı.
estorbar *v* bother, hinder
estornudar *v* sneeze
estos *adj* these
éstos *pro* these ones
estrafalario *adj* eccentric
estragos *nm* havoc
estrañarse *v* be surprised
estrangular *v* strangle
estrategia *nf* strategy
estrato *nm* layer
estrecharse *v* become narrow
estrecheces *nf* difficulties
estrechez *v* tightness
estrecho *adj* narrow
estrecho *nm* strait
estrella *nf* star
estrellarse *v* smash, crash
estremecer *v* shake
estremecerse *v* shake; shudder
estreñido *adj* constipated
estreñimiento *nm* constipation
estrépito *nm* big noise
estrés *nm* stress
estresante *adj* stressful
estribar *v* lie in
estricto *adj* strict
estropear *v* spoil, damage
estructura *nf* structure

estruendo *nm* roar
estrujar *v* squeeze
estuario *nm* estuary
estuche *nm* box
estudiante *nm* student
estudiar *v* study
estudio *nm* study
estufa *nf* stove
estupendo *adj* wonderful
estupidez *nf* stupidity
estúpido *adj* stupid
eternidad *nf* eternity
eterno *adj* eternal
ética *nf* ethics
etiqueta *nf* label, tag
étnico *adj* ethnic
euforia *nf* euphoria
eufórico *adj* elated
Europa *nf* Europe
europeo *adj* European
eutanasia *nf* euthanasia
evacuar *v* evacuate
evadir *v* evade, avoid
evaluación *nf* assessment
evaluar *v* evaluate, assess
evangelio *nm* gospel
evaporar *v* evaporate
evasión *nf* evasion
evasivo *adj* evasive
evento *nm* event
eventual *adj* possible
eventualidad *nf* eventuality
evidencia *nf* evidence
evidente *adj* obvious
evitable *adj* avoidable
evitar *v* avoid
evocar *v* evoke
evolución *nf* evolution
evolucionar *v* evolve

E

exactitud *nf* accuracy
exacto *adj* exact
exagerar *v* exaggerate
exaltar *v* exalt
exámen *nm* examination
examinar *v* examine
excavar *v* excavate
excedente *nm* surplus
exceder *v* exceed
excederse *v* overdo
excelencia *nf* excellence
excelente *adj* excellent
excepción *nf* exception
excepcional *adj* exceptional
excepto *pro* except
excesivo *adj* excessive
exceso *nm* excess
excitación *nf* excitement
excitar *v* excite, arouse
exclamar *v* exclaim
excluir *v* exclude
exclusivo *adj* exclusive
exculpar *v* exonerate
excursión *nf* excursion
excusa *nf* excuse
excusar *v* excuse
exento *adj* exempt
exhaustivo *adj* thorough
exhausto *adj* exhausted
exhibir *v* display, show
exhortar *v* exhort
exigente *adj* demanding
exigir *v* demand
eximir *v* exempt
existencia *nf* existence
existir *v* exist
éxito *nm* success, hit
exitoso *adj* successful
éxodo *nm* exodus

exorbitante *adj* exorbitant
exorcista *nm* exorcist
exótico *adj* exotic
expansión *nf* expansion
expectativa *nf* anticipation
expedición *nf* expedition
expediente *nm* dossier, file
expedir *v* issue
experiencia *nf* experience
experimento *nm* experiment
experto *adj* expert
expiación *nf* atonement
expiar *v* atone
expiración *nf* expiration
expirar *v* expire
explicar *v* explain
explícito *adj* explicit
explorador *nm* explorer
explorar *v* explore
explosión *nf* explosion
explosivo *adj* explosive
explotación *nf* exploitation
explotar *v* exploit
exponer *v* expose; display
exportar *v* export
exposición *nf* exhibition
expresamente *adv* expressly
expresar *v* express
expresión *nf* expression
expreso *adj* express
exprimir *v* wring, squeeze
expropiar *v* expropriate
expulsar *v* expel, eject
expulsión *nf* expulsion
exquisito *adj* exquisite
éxtasis *nm* ecstasy
extático *adj* ecstatic
extender *v* extend, spread
extendido *adj* widespread

E

E
F

extensión *nf* extension
extenso *adj* vast
extenuar *v* weaken
exterior *adj* exterior, outer
exterminar *v* exterminate
externo *adj* external
extinción *nf* extinction
extinguido *adj* extinct
extinguir *v* extinguish
extirpar *v* remove
extorsión *nf* extortion
extracto *nm* excerpt
extradición *nf* extradition
extraer *v* extract, remove
extrañar *v* miss
extranjero *adj* foreign
extranjero *nm* foreigner
extraño *nm* stranger
extraño *adj* odd, strange
extravagante *adj* extravagant
extraviar *v* misplace
extraviarse *v* get lost
extremidades *nf* extremities
extremista *adj* extremist
extremo *adj* extreme
extrovertido *adj* outgoing

fábrica *nf* factory
fabricar *v* manufacture
fábula *nf* fable
fabuloso *adj* fabulous
faceta *nf* facet
facha *nf* look

fachada *nf* front
fácil *adj* easy
facilidad *nf* ease
facilitar *v* facilitate
fácilmente *adv* easily
factible *adj* feasible
factor *nm* factor
factura *nf* invoice
facultad *nf* faculty
facultar *v* authorize
faena *nf* work
faisán *nm* pheasant
faja *nf* sash; stretch
fajo *nm* bundle
falda *nf* skirt
falla *nf* defect; mistake
fallar *v* backfire; falter
fallecer *v* die, pass away
fallo *nm* verdict
falsear *v* falsify
falsedad *nf* falseness, lie
falsificación *nf* forgery
falsificar *v* forge, falsify
falso *adj* fake; untrue
falta *nf* lack; fault
faltar *v* be missing
fama *nf* fame
familia *nf* family
familiar *adj* familiar
familiares *nm* folks
famoso *adj* famous
fanático *adj* fanatic
fanfarronear *v* boast
fango *nm* mud
fantasía *nf* fantasy
fantasma *nm* ghost
fantástico *adj* fantastic
fardo *nm* bundle, bale
faringe *nf* pharynx

farmacéutico *nm* pharmacist
farmacia *nf* pharmacy
fármaco *nm* drug
faro *nm* lighthouse
farol *nm* streetlamp
farsa *nf* farce
fascinante *adj* intriguing
fascinar *v* fascinate
fase *nf* phase
fastidiar *v* bother, annoy
fastidio *nm* annoyance
fastidioso *adj* annoying
fastuoso *adj* lavish
fatal *adj* fatal
fatídico *adj* fateful
fatiga *nf* fatigue
fatigarse *v* get tired
fauna *nf* wildlife
favor *nm* favor
favorable *adj* favorable
favorito *adj* favorite
fe *nf* faith
fealdad *nf* ugliness
febrero *nm* February
fecha *nf* date
fecha tope *nf* deadline
fechado *adj* dated
fechoría *nf* misdeed
fecundo *adj* fertile
federal *adj* federal
felicidad *nf* happiness
felicitar *v* congratulate
feligrés *nm* parishioner
feliz *adj* happy
felonía *nf* felony
femenino *adj* feminine
fenómeno *nm* phenomenon
feo *adj* ugly
féretro *nm* coffin

feria *nf* fair
fermentar *v* ferment
ferocidad *nf* ferocity
feroz *adj* fierce
ferretería *nf* hardware
ferrocarril *nm* railroad
fértil *adj* fertile
fertilidad *nf* fertility
fertilizar *v* fertilize
ferviente *adj* fervent, pious
festejar *v* celebrate
festín *nm* banquet
festividad *nf* festivity
feto *nm* fetus
fiable *adj* reliable
fianza *nf* bail, bond
fiarse *v* trust
fiasco *nm* failure
fibra *nf* fiber
ficción *nf* fiction
ficha *nf* chip, token
fichero *nm* filing draw
ficticio *adj* fictitious
fidelidad *nf* fidelity
fideos *nm* noodles
fiebre *nf* fever
fiel *adj* faithful
fiera *nf* beast
fiero *adj* fierce
fiesta *nf* feast
figura *nf* figure, shape
figurarse *v* imagine
fijar *v* fix
fijarse *v* notice
fila *nf* row
filete *nm* steak, fillet
filo *nm* edge
filosofía *nf* philosophy
filósofo *nm* philosopher

filtro *nm* filter
fin *nm* end, purpose
final *adj* final
final *nm* ending
finalizar *v* finalize
financiar *v* finance, fund
finca *nf* estate, manor
fincar *v* build
fingir *v* feign, pretend
finlandés *adj* Finnish
Finlandia *n* Finland
fino *adj* fine; polite
fiordo *nm* fjord
firma *nf* signature; firm
firmamento *nm* sky
firmar *v* sign
firme *adj* firm, steady
firmeza *nf* firmness, strength
fiscal *nm* prosecutor
física *nf* physics
físico *adj* physical
fisura *nf* crack
flaco *adj* lean, skinny
flagelar *v* whip, scourge
flanquear *v* flank
flaqueza *nf* weakness
flauta *nf* flute
flecha *nf* arrow
flexible *adj* flexible
flirtear *v* flirt
flojedad *v* laziness; weakness
flojo *adj* loose; weak
flor *nf* flower
floreado *adj* floral
florecer *v* bloom, blossom
florero *nm* vase
flota *nf* fleet
flotar *v* float, hover
fluctuar *v* fluctuate

fluidez *nf* fluency; fluidity
fluído *nf* fluid; fluent
fluir *v* flow
flujo *nm* flow
fobia *nf* phobia
foca *nf* seal
foco *nm* focus; bulb
fogata *nf* bonfire
folleto *nm* brochure
follón *v* mess, fuss
fomentar *v* promote
fonda *nf* inn
fondo *nm* bottom; fund
fondo (a) *adv* in depth
fondos *nm* funds
fontanería *nf* plumbing
fontanero *nm* plumber
forastero *nm* outsider
forcejear *v* struggle
forjar *v* forge
forma *nf* form, shape
formación *nf* formation
formal *adj* formal
formalidad *nf* technicality
formalizar *v* formalize
formar *v* form
formato *nm* format
formidable *adj* awesome
fórmula *nf* formula
fornido *adj* very strong
forrar *v* line, cover
forro *nm* lining; cover
fortaleza *nf* fortress; strength
fortificar *v* fortify
fortuna *nf* fortune
forzar *v* force, compel
fosa *nf* grave
fósforo *nm* match
fósil *nm* fossil

F

foso *nm* ditch
fotocopia *nf* photocopy
fotografía *nf* photo
fotógrafo *nm* photographer
fracasar *v* fall through, fail
fracaso *nf* failure, flop
fracción *nf* fraction
fractura *nf* fracture
fracturar *v* fracture, break
fragancia *nf* fragrance
fragata *nf* frigate
frágil *adj* fragile
fragilidad *nf* frailty, weakness
fragmento *nm* fragment
fragua *nf* forge
fraile *nm* friar, monk
francés *adj* French
Francia *nf* France
franco *adj* blunt, frank
francotirador *nm* sniper
franqueza *nf* candor
franquicia *nf* franchise
frasco *nm* flask, jar
frase *nf* phrase, sentence
fraternal *adj* fraternal
fraternidad *nf* fraternity
fraude *nm* fraud
fraudulento *adj* fraudulent
frecuencia *nf* frequency
frecuente *adj* frequent
fregadero *nm* sink
fregar *v* wash, mop
freído *adj* fried
freír *v* fry
frenar *v* rein, curb
frenesí *nm* frenzy
frenético *adj* frenetic
freno *nm* brake
frente *nf* forehead

frente *nm* front
frente (de) *adv* head on
fresa *nf* strawberry
fresco *adj* cool, fresh
frescura *nf* freshness
frialdad *nf* coldness
fríamente *adv* coldly
fricción *nf* friction
frígido *adj* frigid
frijol *nm* bean
frío *nm* cold, chill
frío *adj* chilly, cold
frito *adj* fried
frivolidad *nf* frivolity
frívolo *adj* frivolous
frontera *nf* border, frontier
frotar *v* rub
frugal *adj* frugal
frugalidad *nf* frugality
fruncir *v* frown
frustrar *v* frustrate; foil
fruta *nf* fruit
fruto *nm* result
fuego *nm* fire
fuente *nf* fountain, font
fuera *adv* outside
fuerte *nm* fort
fuerte *adj* loud, strong
fuerza *nf* strength, force
fuga *nf* flight; leak
fugarse *v* escape
fugaz *adj* fleeting
fugitivo *nm* fugitive
fumador *nm* smoker
fumar *v* smoke
fumigar *v* fumigate
función *nf* function
funcionar *v* run, operate
funda *nf* pillowcase

fundación *nf* foundation
fundador *nm* founder
fundamental *adj* fundamental
fundamentos *nm* basics
fundar *v* found
fundir *v* melt; merge
funeral *nm* funeral
funeraria *nf* mortuary
funesto *adj* disastrous
furgoneta *nf* van, pick up
furia *nf* fury
furioso *adj* furious, mad
furor *nm* furor
fusible *nm* fuse
fusil *nm* rifle
fusilar *v* shoot
fusión *nf* fusion
fútbol *nm* football
futuro *adj* future

G

gabardina *nf* raincoat
gabinete *nm* office
gafas *nf* eyeglasses
galacia *nf* galaxy
galardón *nm* award
galería *nf* gallery
galgo *nm* greyhound
gallardía *nf* bravery
gallardo *adj* dashing
galleta *nf* biscuit, cookie
gallina *nf* hen
gallo *nm* rooster
galón *nm* gallon

galopar *v* gallop
gama *nf* range
gamba *nf* prawn
gamberro *nm* hooligan, thug
gana *nf* desire
ganado *nm* livestock, cattle
ganador *nm* winner
ganancia *nf* gain, profit
ganancias *nf* proceeds
ganar *v* earn, gain, win
gancho *nm* hook
ganga *nf* bargain
gangrena *nf* gangrene
gangster *nm* gangster
ganso *nm* goose
garaje *nm* garage
garantía *nf* guaranty
garantizar *v* guarantee
garbanzo *nm* chickpea
garbo *nm* grace
garganta *nf* throat
garra *nf* claw
garrote *nm* club, stick
gas *nm* gas
gasa *nf* gauze
gasolina *nf* gas
gastar *iv* spend
gasto *nm* expense
gastos *nm* expenditure
gástrico *adj* gastric
gatillo *nm* trigger
gatito *nm* kitten
gato *nm* cat
gaviota *nf* seagull
gaznate *nm* throat
géiser *nm* geyser
gelatina *nf* gelatin
gemelo *nm* cuff link; twin
gemido *nm* groan, moan

F
G

gemir *v* whine, moan
gen *nm* gene
genealogía *nf* genealogy
generación *nf* generation
generador *nm* generator
general *nm* general
general *adj* overall, general
general (en) *adv* generally
generalizar *v* generalize
generar *v* generate
genérico *adj* generic
género *nm* gender
generosidad *nf* generosity
generoso *adj* generous
genético *adj* genetic
genial *adj* bright
genio *nm* genius
genocidio *nm* genocide
gente *nf* people
gentil *adj* charming
gentileza *nf* courtesy
gentío *nm* crowd
genuino *adj* genuine, real
geografía *nf* geography
geología *nf* geology
geometría *nf* geometry
geranio *nm* geranium
gerente *nm* manager
germen *nm* germ
gerundio *nm* gerund
gestación *nf* gestation
gestionar *v* take care
gestiones *v* procedure
gesto *nm* gesture
gigante *nm* giant
gimnasia *nf* gymnastics
gimnasio *nm* gymnasium
ginebra *nf* gin
ginecología *nf* gynecology

gira *nf* tour, turn
girafa *nf* giraffe
girar *v* rotate, turn
giro *nm* money order; turn
gitano *nm* gypsy
glaciar *nm* glacier
gladiador *nm* gladiator
glándula *nf* gland
globo *nm* balloon; globe
glóbulo *nm* globule
gloria *nf* glory
glorificar *v* glorify
glorioso *adj* glorious
glotón *nm* glutton
glucosa *nf* glucose
gobernador *n* governor
gobernar *v* govern, rule
gobierno *nm* government
goce *nm* enjoyment
gol *nm* goal
golf *nm* golf
golfista *nm* golfer
golfo *nm* gulf
golosina *nf* candy
golpe *nm* blow; coup
golpeado *adj* beaten
golpear *v* hit, punch, beat
golpecito *nm* tap
goma *nf* eraser; glue
gordo *adj* obese, fat
gorila *nm* gorilla
gorra *nf* cap
gorrión *nm* sparrow
gota *nf* drop; gout
gotear *v* drip, leak
gotera *nf* leak
gozar *v* enjoy
gozo *nm* joy
grabado *nm* engraving

G

G

grabadora *nf* recorder
grabar *v* engrave, record
gracias *nf* thanks
gracioso *adj* cute, funny
grada *nf* step, row
grado *nm* degree
gradual *adj* gradual
graduarse *v* graduate
gráfico *adj* graphic
gramática *nf* grammar
gramo *nm* gram
granada *nf* hand grenade
grande *adj* big, large
grandeza *nf* greatness
grandioso *adj* grandiose
granero *nm* barn, granary
granito *nm* granite
granizar *v* hail
granizo *nm* hail
granja *nf* farm
granjearse *v* earn, win
grano *nm* grain; pimple
granuja *nm* rascal
grapa *nf* staple
grapadora *nf* stapler
grapar *v* staple
grasa *nf* fat, grease
grasiento *adj* greasy, oily
grasoso *adj* fatty, greasy
gratificación *nf* reward
gratificar *v* gratify
gratis *adv* free
gratitud *nf* gratitude
grato *adj* pleasant
gratuito *adj* free
gravar *v* tax
grave *adj* serious
gravedad *nf* seriousness
gravitar *v* gravitate

Grecia *nf* Greece
gremio *nm* guild
griego *adj* Greek
grieta *nf* crack, crevice
grifo *nm* faucet
grillo *nm* cricket
grillos *nm* shackles
gripe *nf* influenza, flu
gris *adj* gray
gritar *v* cry out, shout
griterío *nm* shouting
grosería *nf* rudeness
grosero *adj* crass, gross
grosor *nm* thickness
grotesco *adj* grotesque
grúa *nf* crane
grueso *adj* thick
gruñir *v* growl; grumble
grupo *nm* group
gruta *nf* grotto
guajolote *nm* turkey
guantazo *nm* slap
guante *nm* glove
guapo *adj* handsome
guardameta *nm* goalkeeper
guardar *v* keep
guardería *nf* nursery
guardia *nm* policeman
guardián *nm* guardian
guarida *nf* den
guarnición *nf* garrison
guasa *nf* joke
guerra *nf* war
guerrero *nm* warrior
guerrillero *nm* guerrilla
guía *nm* guide
guiar *v* guide, lead
guijarro *nm* pebble
guillotina *nf* guillotine

guiñar *v* wink at
guinda *nf* cherry
guiño *nm* wink
guión *nm* hyphen; script
guirnalda *nf* garland
guisado *nm* stew
guisante *nm* pea
guisar *v* cook
guitarra *nf* guitar
gusano *nm* worm
gustar *v* taste; like
gusto *nm* flavor, taste

G H

hábil *adj* capable, skilful
habilidad *nf* ability, skill
hábilmente *adv* ably
habitable *adj* habitable
habitación *nf* room
habitante *nm* inhabitant
habitar *v* dwell, inhabit
hábito *nm* habit, custom
hablador *adj* talkative
hablar *v* speak, talk
hacer *v* do, make
hacer añicos *v* shatter
hacer campaña *v* campaign
hacer caso *v* heed
hacer cola *v* line up
hacer cosquillas *v* tickle
hacer cumplir *v* enforce
hacer ejercicios *v* exercise
hacer énfasis *v* emphasize
hacer frente *v* cope

hacer garabatos *v* scribble
hacer gárgaras *v* gargle
hacer gestos *v* gesticulate
hacer reverencia *v* bow
hacer señas *v* beckon
hacer una oferta *iv* bid
hacerse *v* become
hacerse amigo *v* befriend
hacha *nm* ax, hatchet
hacia *pre* towards
hacia adelante *adv* onwards
hacia arriba *adv* upwards
hacia atrás *adv* backwards
hacia dentro *adv* inwards
hacia el este *adv* eastbound
hacia el norte *adv* northbound
hacia el oeste *adv* westbound
hacia el sur *adv* southbound
hacienda *nf* ranch, estate
halagar *v* flatter
halago *nm* flattery
halcón *nm* hawk
halucinar *v* hallucinate
hamaca *nf* hammock
hambre *nm* hunger, famine
hambriento *adj* hungry
hamburguesa *nf* hamburger
harapiento *adj* ragged
harapo *nm* rag
harén *nm* harem
harina *nf* flour
harto *adj* fed up; full
hasta *adv* till, until
hastiado *adj* fed up; full
hastío *nm* weariness
haz *nm* bundle
hazaña *nf* accomplishment
hebilla *nf* buckle
hebra *nf* thread

hechicería *nf* sorcery
hechicero *nm* sorcerer
hechizar *v* bewitch
hechizo *nm* spell
hecho *nm* deed; fact
heder *v* stink
hediondo *adj* stinking
hedor *nm* stench, stink
helada *nf* frost
helado *adj* frozen
helado *nm* ice cream
helar *v* freeze
helecho *nm* fern
helicóptero *nm* helicopter
hembra *nf* female
hemisferio *nm* hemisphere
hemorragia *nf* hemorrhage
hendidura *nf* crack
heno *nm* hay
heraldo *nm* herald
heredar *v* inherit
heredera *nf* heiress
heredero *nm* heir
hereditario *adj* hereditary
herejía *nf* heresy
herencia *nf* inheritance
herético *adj* heretic
herida *nf* injury, wound
herido *adj* wounded
herir *v* injure, wound
hermana *nf* sister
hermanastra *nf* stepsister
hermanastro *nm* stepbrother
hermandad *nf* brotherhood
hermano *nm* brother
hermanos *nm* brethren
hermético *adj* airtight
hermoso *adj* beautiful
hermosura *nf* beauty

hernia *nf* hernia
héroe *nm* hero
heróico *adj* heroic
heroína *nf* heroine; heroin
heroísmo *nm* heroism
herradura *nf* horseshoe
herramienta *nf* tool
herrero *nm* blacksmith
herrumbre *nf* rust
hervir *v* boil, simmer
hevilla *nf* buckle
hez *nf* dregs
hidratar *v* moisturize
hidráulico *adj* hydraulic
hidrógeno *nm* hydrogen
hiedra *nf* ivy
hiel *nf* gall, bile
hielo *nm* ice
hiena *nf* hyena
hierba *nf* grass, herb
hierro *nm* iron
hígado *nm* liver
higiene *nf* hygiene
higiénico *adj* hygienic
higo *nm* fig
hija *nf* daughter
hijastra *nf* stepdaughter
hijastro *nm* stepson
hijo *nm* son
hilar *v* spin
hilera *nf* row; string
hilo *nm* yarn; thread
himno *nm* anthem, hymn
hincar *v* stick into
hincarse *v* kneel down
hinchado *adj* swollen
hinchar *v* swell
hinchazón *nm* swelling
hipertensión *nf* hypertension

H

hipnosis *nf* hypnosis
hipnotizar *v* hypnotize
hipo *nm* hiccups
hipocresía *nf* hypocrisy
hipócrita *nm* hypocrite
hipódromo *nm* racetrack
hipopótamo *nm* hippopotamus
hipoteca *nf* mortgage
hipótesis *nf* hypothesis
hipotético *adj* hypothetical
hiriente *adj* offensive, hurting
hispano *adj* Hispanic
histeria *nf* hysteria
histérico *adj* hysterical
historia *nf* history, story
historiador *nm* historian
historial *nm* record
histórico *adj* historical, historic
hito *nm* milestone
hogar *nm* home
hoguera *nf* bonfire
hoja *nf* leaf; sheet; blade
hojear *v* browse
hola *e* hello
Holanda *nf* Holland
holandés *adj* Dutch
holgado *adj* baggy, rich
holgazán *adj* lazy
holocausto *nm* holocaust
hombre *nm* man
hombres *nm* men
hombro *nm* shoulder
homenaje *nm* homage
homicida *nm* murderer
homicidio *nm* homicide
homogéneo *adj* homogenous
homólogo *nm* counterpart
hondo *adj* deep
honestidad *nf* honesty

honesto *adj* honest
hongo *nm* mushroom
honor *nm* honor
honorarios *nm* fee
honra *nf* honor
honradez *nf* honesty
hora *nf* hour
horario *nm* schedule
horca *nf* gallows
horda *nf* horde
horizontal *adj* horizontal
horizonte *nm* horizon
hormiga *nf* ant
hormigón *nm* concrete
hormona *nf* hormone
horno *nm* furnace, oven
horóscopo *nm* horoscope
horrendo *adj* horrendous
horrible *adj* awful, horrible
horripilante *adj* spooky
horror *nm* horror
horrorizado *adj* appalled
horrorizar *v* appall, horrify
horroroso *adj* dreadful
hosco *adj* sullen
hospedarse *v* stay
hospicio *nm* orphanage
hospital *nm* hospital
hospitalidad *nf* hospitality
hospitalizar *v* hospitalize
hostia *nf* host
hostigar *v* harass
hostil *adj* hostile
hostilidad *nf* hostility
hotel *nm* hotel
hoy *adv* today
hoyo *nm* hole, pit
hoz *nf* sickle
hucha *nf* money box

H

hueco *adj* hollow, empty
hueco *nm* hole, gap
huelga *nf* strike, walk out
huella *nf* fingerprint; track
huérfano *nm* orphan
huero *adj* blond
huerta *nf* garden
huerto *nm* orchard
hueso *nm* bone
huésped *nm* guest
huevo *nm* egg
huida *nf* flight
huir *v* flee, escape
humanidad *nf* mankind
humanidades *nf* humanities
humanizar *v* humanize
humano *adj* human, humane
humedad *nf* humidity
humedecer *v* moisten
húmedo *adj* damp, humid
humildad *nf* humility
humilde *adj* humble, lowly
humillar *v* humiliate
humo *nm* smoke
humor *nm* humor, mood
hundir *v* sink, scuttle
hundirse *v* collapse; sink
húngaro *adj* Hungarian
Hungría *nf* Hungary
huracán *nm* hurricane
huraño *adj* unfriendly
hurgar *v* poke
hurtar *v* steal

iceberg *nm* iceberg
ida *nf* departure
idea *nf* idea
ideal *adj* ideal
idéntico *adj* identical
identidad *nf* identity
identificar *v* identify
ideología *nf* ideology
idílico *adj* idyllic
idilio *nm* romance
idiota *nm* idiot
idiotez *nf* idiocy, nonsense
idolatrar *v* worship
idolatría *nf* idolatry
ídolo *nm* idol
idóneo *adj* suitable
iglesia *nf* church
ignorancia *nf* ignorance
ignorar *v* ignore
igual *adj* equal
igualar *v* match; level off
igualdad *nf* equality
ilegal *adj* illegal
ilegible *adj* illegible
ilegítimo *adj* illegitimate
ileso *adj* unhurt
ilícito *adj* illicit
ilimitado *adj* unlimited
ilógico *adj* illogical
iluminar *v* illuminate
ilusión *nf* illusion
ilusionado *adj* excited
ilusionarse *v* get excited
iluso *nm* dreamer
ilustrar *v* illustrate; teach
ilustre *adj* famous

H
I

imagen *nf* image
imaginación *nf* imagination
imaginar(se) *v* imagine
imán *nm* magnet
imbécil *adj* stupid
imbécil *nm* idiot
imitar *v* imitate, mimic
impaciencia *nf* impatience
impacientarse *v* lose patience
impaciente *adj* impatient
impactar *v* impact; move
impacto *nm* impact
impar *adj* odd
imparcial *adj* impartial
impartir *v* give
impasible *adj* impassive
impecable *adj* impeccable
impedimento *nm* obstacle
impedir *v* prevent
imperante *adj* prevailing
imperar *v* rule
imperativo *adj* imperative
imperdible *nm* safety pin
imperfección *nf* imperfection
imperial *adj* imperial
imperialismo *nm* imperialism
imperio *nm* empire
impermeable *nm* raincoat
impermeable *adj* waterproof
impersonal *adj* impersonal
impertérrito *adj* unperturbed
impertinencia *nf* impertinence
impertinente *adj* impertinent
impetuoso *adj* impetuous
implacable *adj* relentless
implantar *v* implant
implementar *v* implement
implicar *v* imply, involve
implícito *adj* implicit

implorar *v* implore
imponente *adj* stunning
imponer *v* impose
imponerse *v* prevail
impopular *adj* unpopular
importación *nf* importation
importancia *nf* importance
importante *adj* important
importar *v* import; mind
importe *nm* amount
importunar *v* bother
importuno *adj* inopportune
imposibilidad *nf* impossibility
imposible *adj* impossible
imposición *nf* imposition
impotente *adj* powerless
impreciso *adj* vague
impredecible *adj* unpredictable
imprenta *nf* printing
imprescindible *adj* essential
impresión *nf* impression
impresionante *adj* impressive
impresionar *v* impress
impreso *adj* printed
impresor *nm* printer
imprevisto *adj* unforeseen
imprimir *v* print
improbable *adj* unlikely
impropio *adj* inappropriate
improvisar *v* improvise
imprudente *adj* unwise
impuesto *nm* levy, tax
impulsar *v* propel; urge
impulsivo *adj* impulsive
impulso *nm* impulse, urge
impune *adj* unpunished
impunidad *nf* impunity
impureza *nf* impurity
impuro *adj* impure

inacesible *adj* inaccessible
inadaptado *adj* misfit
inadmisible *adj* inadmissible
inaguantable *adj* unbearable
inalámbrico *adj* cordless
inapropiado *adj* inappropriate
inasequible *adj* unattainable
inaudito *adj* unheard-of
inaugurar *v* inaugurate
incalculable *adj* incalculable
incansable *adj* tireless
incapacidad *nf* inability
incapacitado *adj* helpless
incapacitar *v* incapacitate
incapaz *adj* incapable
incautarse *v* seize
incendiar *v* set fire
incendiarse *v* burn
incendio *nm* arson, fire
incentivo *nm* incentive
incertidumbre *nf* suspense
incidente *nm* incident
incienso *nm* incense
incierto *adj* uncertain
incinerar *v* cremate
incisión *nf* incision
incitar *v* incite
inclinación *nf* leaning
inclinar *v* tilt, incline
inclinarse *v* bow, bend
incluír *v* include
incoherente *adj* incoherent
incoloro *adj* colorless
incomodidad *nf* discomfort
incómodo *adj* uncomfortable
incompatible *adj* incompatible
incompetente *adj* incompetent
incompleto *adj* incomplete
inconcebible *adj* unthinkable

inconfundible *adj* unmistakable
incongruente *adj* inconsistent
inconsciente *adj* unconscious
inconstante *adj* fickle
incontable *adj* countless
incontinencia *nf* incontinence
inconveniente *nm* inconvenient
incorporar *v* incorporate
incorrecto *adj* inaccurate
incorregible *adj* incorrigible
incredulidad *nf* disbelief
increíble *adj* incredible
incrementar *v* increase
incremento *nm* increment
incruento *adj* bloodless
incubar *v* incubate
inculcar *v* instill
inculto *adj* uneducated
incumbencia *nf* responsibility
incurable *adj* incurable
incurrir *v* incur
indagar *v* investigate
indecencia *nm* indecency
indecible *adj* unspeakable
indecisión *nf* indecision
indeciso *adj* undecided
indefenso *adj* defenseless
indefinido *adv* indefinite
indemnización *nf* indemnification
indemnizar *v* indemnify
independiente *adj* independent
indeseable *adj* undesirable
indicación *nf* sign
indicar *v* indicate
índice *nm* index
indicio *nm* sign, clue
indiferencia *nf* indifference
indiferente *adj* indifferent
indigente *adj* indigent, poor**

indigestión

indigestión *nf* indigestion
indignación *nf* outrage
indignado *adj* outraged
indignar *v* anger
indigno *adj* unworthy
indirecta *nf* innuendo
indiscreto *adj* indiscreet
indispensable *adj* indispensable
indispuesto *adj* not well
indivisible *adj* indivisible
inducir *v* induce
indulgente *adj* lenient
indulto *nm* pardon
indumentaria *nf* clothing
industria *nf* industry
ineficacia *nf* inefficiency
ineficaz *adj* inefficient
ineludible *adj* unavoidable
inepto *adj* inept
inesperado *adj* unexpected
inestable *adj* unstable
inevitable *adj* unavoidable
inexcusable *adj* inexcusable
inexperto *adj* inexperience
inexplicable *adj* inexplicable
infalible *adj* infallible
infame *adj* infamous
infancia *nf* infancy
infantería *nf* infantry
infantil *adj* childish
infarto *nm* heart attack
infección *nf* infection
infectar *v* infect
infectarse *v* get infected
infeliz *adj* unhappy
inferior *adj* inferior
inferioridad *nf* inferiority
inferir *v* infer
infertilidad *nf* infertility

infestar *v* infest
infidelidad *nf* infidelity
infiel *adj* unfaithful
infierno *nm* hell, inferno
infiltrar *v* infiltrate
infinito *adj* infinite
inflamable *adj* flammable
inflamación *nf* swelling
inflamar *v* inflame
inflar *v* inflate
inflexible *adj* inflexible
infligir *v* inflict
influencia *nf* influence
influir *v* influence
influyente *adj* influential
información *nf* information
informal *adj* informal
informalidad *nf* informality
informar *v* brief, inform
informe *nm* report
infracción *nf* infraction
infrarojo *adj* infrared
infrecuente *adj* infrequent
infundado *adj* unfounded
infundir *v* instill, inspire
ingeniarse *v* manage
ingeniero *nm* engineer
ingenio *nm* wit
ingenioso *adj* witty
ingenuo *adj* naive
ingerir *v* swallow
Inglaterra *nf* England
ingle *nf* groin
inglés *adj* English
ingratitud *nf* ingratitude
ingrato *adj* ungrateful
ingrediente *nm* ingredient
ingresar *v* enter
ingresos *nm* income, revenue

inhalar *v* inhale
inherente *adj* inherent
inhumano *adj* inhuman
inicial *adj* initial
iniciales *nf* initials
iniciar *v* start
iniciativa *nf* initiative
injertar *v* graft
injerto *nm* graft
injuria *nf* offence
injuriar *v* offend, insult
injusticia *nf* injustice
injustificado *adj* unjustified
injusto *adj* unfair, unjust
inmaculado *adj* immaculate
inmadurez *nf* immaturity
inmaduro *adj* immature
inmediato *adj* immediate
inmejorable *adj* excellent
inmensidad *nf* magnitude
inmenso *adj* huge
inmersión *nf* immersion
inmigración *nf* immigration
inmigrante *nm* immigrant
inmigrar *v* immigrate
inminente *adj* imminent
inmiscuirse *v* meddle
inmobilizar *v* immobilize
inmoral *adj* immoral
inmoralidad *nf* immorality
inmortal *adj* immortal
inmortalidad *nf* immortality
inmóvil *adj* still
inmundo *adj* filthy
inmune *adj* immune
inmunidad *nf* immunity
inmunizar *v* immunize
innecesario *adj* unnecessary
innegable *adj* undeniable

innumerable *adj* countless
inocente *adj* innocent
inofensivo *adj* harmless
inolvidable *adj* unforgettable
inoportuno *adj* untimely
inoxidable *adj* stainless
inquietar *v* worry
inquieto *adj* restless
inquilino *nm* tenant
inquisición *nf* inquisition
insaciable *adj* insatiable
insatisfecho *adj* dissatisfied
inscribir *v* enroll
inscripción *nf* inscription
insecto *nm* insect
inseguridad *nf* insecurity
inseguro *adj* uneasy
insensato *adj* foolish
insensible *adj* insensitive
inseparable *adj* inseparable
insertar *v* insert
inservible *adj* useless
insignificante *adj* insignificant
insinceridad *nf* insincerity
insinuación *nf* hint
insinuar *v* insinuate
insípido *adj* insipid, tasteless
insistencia *nf* insistence
insistente *adj* pushy
insistir *v* insist
insolación *nf* sunstroke
insólito *adj* unusual
insolvente *adj* bankrupt
insomnio *nm* insomnia
insoportable *adj* unbearable
inspeccionar *v* inspect
inspiración *nf* inspiration
instalar *v* install
instantáneo *adj* instantaneous

instante *nm* instant
instar *v* urge
instigar *v* instigate
instinto *nm* instinct
institución *nf* institution
instructor *nm* instructor
instruír *v* teach
insuficiente *adj* insufficient
insulso *adj* insipid
insultar *v* insult
insulto *nm* insult
insurgencia *nf* insurgency
insurrección *nf* insurrection
intachable *adj* blameless
intacto *adj* intact
integrar *v* integrate
integridad *nf* integrity
integro *adj* entire
inteligente *adj* intelligent
intemperie *nf* open air
intención *nf* intention
intencionado *adj* deliberate
intensidad *nf* intensity
intensificar *v* intensify
intensivo *adj* intensive
intenso *adj* intense
intentar *v* try
intercalar *v* insert
intercambiar *v* swap
intercambio *nm* exchange
interceder *v* intercede
interceptar *v* intercept
interés *nm* interest
interesado *adj* interested
interesante *adj* interesting
interferir *v* interfere
interior *adj* inner, interior
intermediario *nm* intermediary
interminable *adj* endless

interno *adj* internal
interpretar *v* interpret
intérprete *v* interpreter
interrogar *v* question
interrumpir *v* interrupt
interruptor *nm* switch
intervalo *nm* gap, interval
intervenir *v* intervene
intestino *nm* intestine
intimidad *nf* intimacy
intimidar *v* intimidate
íntimo *adj* intimate
intocable *adj* untouchable
intolerable *adj* intolerable
intolerancia *nf* intolerance
intranquilo *adj* restive, worried
intravenoso *adj* intravenous
intrépido *adj* intrepid
intriga *nf* intrigue, plot
intrincado *adj* complicated
intrínsico *adj* intrinsic
introducir *v* introduce
introvertido *adj* introvert
intruso *nm* intruder
inundación *nf* flooding
inundar *v* flood
inusitado *adj* unusual
inútil *adj* useless
invadir *v* invade
invalidar *v* override
inválido *adj* disable
invasión *nf* invasion
invasor *nm* invader
invencible *adj* invincible
invención *nf* invention
inventar *v* invent, devise
inventario *nm* inventory
invento *nm* invention
invernadero *nm* greenhouse

inverosímil *adj* unlikely
inversión *nf* investment
invertebrado *adj* invertebrate
invertir *v* invest
investigación *nf* inquiry, probe
investigar *v* investigate
invierno *nm* winter
invisible *adj* invisible
invitado *nm* guest
invitar *v* invite
invocar *v* invoke
inyección *nf* injection
inyectar *v* inject
ir *v* go
ira *nf* anger
ironía *nf* irony
irracional *adj* irrational
irrazonable *adj* unreasonable
irreal *adj* unreal
irrefutable *adj* irrefutable
irregular *adj* irregular
irrelevante *adj* irrelevant
irreparable *adj* irreparable
irresistible *adj* irresistible
irreverente *adj* irreverent
irreversible *adj* irreversible
irrevocable *adj* irrevocable
irritación *nf* exasperation
irritar *v* irritate, annoy
irrompible *adj* unbreakable
isla *nf* island, isle
islámico *adj* Islamic
Italia *nf* Italy
italiano *adj* Italian
itinerario *nm* itinerary
izar *v* hoist
izquierdo *adj* left

J

jabalí *nm* boar
jabón *nm* soap
jactarse *v* brag, boast
jadeante *adj* breathless
jadear *v* pant
jaguar *nm* jaguar
jalar *v* pull
jamás *adv* never
jamón *nm* ham
Japón *nm* Japan
japonés *adj* Japanese
jaque *nm* check
jaqueca *nf* migraine
jarabe *nm* syrup
jardín *nm* garden
jardinero *nm* gardener
jarra *nf* jug, pitcher
jarrón *nm* vase
jaula *nf* cage
jazmín *nm* jasmine
jefe *nm* leader, chief
jenjibre *nm* ginger
jerarquía *nf* hierarchy
jerez *nm* sherry
jeringa *nf* syringe
jinete *nm* rider
jirafa *nf* giraffe
jornal *nm* wages
jornalero *nm* day laborer
joroba *nf* hump
jorobado *adj* hunchbacked
jorobar *v* ruin
joven *adj* young
jovial *adj* cheerful
joya *nf* jewel
joyería *nf* jewelry store

I
J

joyero *nm* jeweler
juanete *nm* bunion
jubilación *nf* retirement
jubilarse *v* retire
júbilo *nm* joy
jubiloso *adj* jubilant
Judaísmo *nm* Judaism
judía *nf* bean
judío *nm* Jew
judío *adj* Jewish
juego *nm* set, game
juerga *nf* party
jueves *nm* Thursday
juez *nm* judge
jugada *nf* move
jugador *nm* player
jugar *v* play
jugarse *v* risk, gamble
jugo *nm* juice
jugoso *adj* juicy
juguete *nm* toy
juguetón *adj* playful
juicio *nm* judgment; trial
juicioso *adj* wise
julio *nm* July
junco *nm* reed
jungla *nf* jungle
junio *nm* June
junta *nf* council
juntar *v* join; gather
juntarse *v* get together
junto *adj* adjacent
juntos *adv* together
jurado *nm* jury
juramento *nm* oath
jurar *v* swear, vow
justicia *nf* justice
justificar *v* justify
justo *adj* just, fair

juvenil *adj* youthful
juventud *nf* youth
juzgado *nm* courthouse
juzgar *v* judge

karate *nm* karate
kilogramo *nm* kilogram
kilómetro *nm* kilometer
kilovatio *nm* kilowatt
kiosco *nm* newsstand

L

laberinto *nm* maze, labyrinth
labio *nm* lip
labor *nf* work
laborable *adj* working day
laboratorio *nm* laboratory
labrar *v* carve
labriego *nm* peasant
lacio *adj* straight
lácteo *adj* milky
ladearse *v* tilt, lean
ladera *nf* hillside, slope
ladrar *v* bark
ladrillo *nm* brick
ladrón *nm* burglar, thief
lagarto *nm* lizard
lago *nm* lake
lágrima *nf* tear

laguna *nf* lagoon
laico *nm* lay
lamentable *adj* regrettable
lamentar *v* regret, lament
lamer *v* lick
laminar *v* laminate
lámpara *nf* lamp
lana *nf* wool
lana (de) *adj* woolen
lancha *nf* small boat
langosta *nf* lobster, locust
languidecer *v* languish
lánguido *adj* languid
lanza *nf* spear, lance
lanzar *v* launch; throw
lanzarse *v* plunge
lápida *nf* tombstone
lápiz *nm* pencil
lapso *nm* interval, span
largo *adj* lengthy, long
laringe *nf* larynx
lascivo *adj* lewd
láser *nm* laser
lástima *nf* pity
lastimar *v* hurt
lastimoso *adj* pitiful
lata *nf* can, tin
latente *adj* latent
lateral *adj* lateral
latido *nm* heartbeat
latigazo *nm* lash
látigo *nm* whip
latir *v* throb, beat
latitud *nf* latitude
latón *nm* brash
lavabo *nm* toilet
lavadora *nf* washing machine
lavandería *nf* laundry
lavaplatos *nm* dishwasher

lavar *v* wash
laxante *adj* laxative
laxo *adj* lax
lazo *nm* ribbon; bond
leal *adj* loyal
lealtad *nf* loyalty
lección *nf* lesson
leche *nf* milk
lechería *nf* dairy
lechero *nm* milkman
lecho *nf* bed
lechoso *adj* milky
lechuga *nf* lettuce
lechuza *nf* owl
lector *nm* reader
lectura *nf* reading
leer *v* read
legal *adj* legal
legalizar *v* legalize
legar *v* bequeath
legión *nf* legion
legislación *nf* legislation
legislador *nm* lawmaker
legislar *v* legislate
legislatura *nf* legislature
legitimar *v* legitimate
legítimo *adj* authentic
legua *nf* league
legumbre *nf* vegetables
lejanía *nf* distance
lejano *adj* faraway
lejía *nf* bleach
lejos *adv* far, away
lema *nm* motto, slogan
leña *nf* firewood
leñador *nm* woodcutter
lencería *nf* lingerie
lengua *nf* language; tongue
leño *nm* log

L

lenteja *nf* lentil
lentitud *nf* slowness
lento *adj* slow
león *nm* lion
leona *nf* lioness
leopardo *nm* leopard
lepra *nf* leprosy
leproso *nm* leper
lerdo *adj* clumsy, slow
lesión *nf* injury
lesionar *v* injure
letal *adj* lethal
letanía *nf* litany
letargo *nm* lethargy
letrero *nm* placard, sign
leucemia *nf* leukemia
levadura *nf* leaven, yeast
levantar *v* raise, lift
levantarse *v* get up, rise
leve *adj* light, feint
ley *nf* law
leyenda *nf* legend
liarse *v* get involved
liberación *nf* liberation
liberal *adj* broadminded
liberar *v* free, liberate
libertad *nf* freedom, leeway
libertino *adj* dissolute
libidinoso *adj* lustful
libra *nf* pound
librar *v* spare, save
libre *adj* free; vacant
librería *nf* bookstore
librero *nm* bookseller
librito *nm* booklet
libro *nm* book
licencia *nf* license, permit
licenciado *adj* graduated
licenciarse *v* graduate

lícito *adj* lawful, legal
licor *nm* liqueur
licuado *nm* milkshake
licuadora *nf* blender
líder *nm* leader
liderazgo *nm* leadership
lidiar *v* fight
liebre *nf* hare
lienzo *nm* canvas
liga *nf* league; rubber band
ligamento *nm* ligament
ligero *adj* light; fast
lija *nf* sandpaper
lima *nf* file
limar *v* file
limitación *nf* limitation
limitar *v* limit
límite *nm* boundary, limit
límites *nm* confines, limits
limón *nm* lemon
limonada *nf* lemonade
limosna *nf* alms, handout
limosnero *nm* beggar
limpiar *v* clean, cleanse
limpieza *nf* cleaning
limpio *adj* clean
linaje *nm* descent
lince *nm* lynx
linchar *v* lynch
lindar *v* adjoin
lindo *adj* pretty
línea *nf* line
lino *nm* linen
linterna *nf* flashlight
lío *nm* tangle, mess
liquidación *nf* sellout
liquidar *v* liquidate
líquido *nm* liquid, fluid
lirio *nm* lily

lisiado *adj* crippled, injured
lisiar *v* maim
liso *adj* smooth, even
lisonja *nf* compliment
lista *nf* list
listo *adj* clever, ready
litera *nf* berth
literalmente *adv* literally
literatura *nf* literature
litigar *v* litigate
litigio *nm* lawsuit
litoral *nm* coastline
litro *nm* liter
liturgia *nf* liturgy
liviano *adj* light
lívido *adj* livid
llaga *nf* sore, wound
llama *nf* flame
llamada *nf* call
llamar *v* call
llamarada *nf* flare
llamas (en) *adv* alight
llamativo *adj* loud, striking
llano *adj* even, flat
llanta *nf* rim
llanto *nm* sobbing
llanura *nf* plain
llave *nf* key
llave inglesa *nf* wrench
llavero *nm* key ring
llegada *nf* arrival
llegar *v* arrive
llenar *v* fill
lleno *adj* full
llevadero *adj* bearable
llevar *v* carry; wear
llevar a cabo *v* carry out
llevar consigo *v* entail
llevarse bien *v* get along

llorar *v* cry, weep
llorar la muerte *v* mourn
lloriquear *v* whine
lloro *nm* crying
llover *v* rain
lloviznar *v* drizzle
lluvia *nf* rain
lluvioso *adj* rainy
lo que *adj* whatever
loable *adj* praiseworthy
lobo *nm* wolf
lóbrego *adj* gloomy
lóbulo *nm* lobe
local *nm* premises
localidad *nf* locality
localizar *v* locate
loción *nf* lotion
loco *adj* crazy, insane
locuaz *adj* talkative
locura *nf* madness, folly
locutor *nm* announcer
lodo *nm* mud
lógica *nf* logic
lógico *adj* logical
lograr *v* accomplish
logro *nm* achievement
loma *nf* hill
lombriz *nf* worm
lomo *nm* loin
lona *nf* canvas
longitud *nf* length
loro *nm* parrot
losa *nf* gravestone
lote *nm* batch
lotería *nf* lottery
loza *nf* china set
lubina *nf* sea bass
lucha *nf* struggle, fight
lucha libre *nf* wrestling

L

luchador *nm* wrestler
luchar *v* fight, struggle
lúcido *adj* lucid
lucir *v* shine
lucirse *v* show off
lucrativo *adj* lucrative
lucro *nm* gain, profit
luego *adv* afterwards, then
lugar *nm* spot, place
lugarteniente *nm* deputy
lúgubre *adj* gloomy
lujo *nm* luxury
lujoso *adj* luxurious
lujuria *nf* lust
lumbre *nf* fire
luminoso *adj* bright
luna *nf* moon
luna de miel *nf* honeymoon
lunes *nm* Monday
lupa *nf* magnifying glass
lustrar *v* polish
lustre *nm* burden
luto *nm* mourning
luz *nf* light

maceta *nf* flower pot
machacar *v* mash, crush
machista *adj* chauvinist
macho *nm* male
machucar *v* bruise
macizo *adj* solid
madera *nf* lumber, wood
madera (de) *adj* wooden

maderería *nf* lumberyard
madero *nm* log
madrastra *nf* stepmother
madre *nf* mother, mom
madriguera *nf* burrow
madrugada *nf* dawn
madrugar *v* get up early
madurar *v* ripen, mature
madurez *nf* maturity
maduro *adj* mature, ripe
maestro *nm* teacher
magia *nf* magic
magistrado *nm* magistrate, judge
magistral *adj* masterful
magnate *nm* tycoon
magnético *adj* magnetic
magnetismo *nm* magnetism
magnífico *adj* wonderful
magnitud *nf* magnitude
mago *nm* magician
magullar *v* bruise
mahometano *adj* Islamic
maíz *nm* corn
majadero *adj* silly, stupid
majestad *nf* majesty
majestuoso *adj* majestic
majo *adj* nice
mal *adv* badly
mal *nm* evil
malabarista *nm* juggler
malaria *nf* malaria
malcriar *v* spoil
maldad *nf* wickedness
maldecir *v* damn, curse
maldición *nf* curse
maldito *adj* damned
maleante *adj* criminal
maleante *nm* crook
maleducado *adj* rude

malentendido *nm* misunderstanding
malestar *nm* discomfort
maleta *nf* suitcase
maletero *nm* porter
maletín *nm* briefcase
malévolo *adj* malevolent
maleza *nf* weeds
malgastar *v* waste
malhechor *nm* delinquent
malhumorado *adj* sullen
malicia *nf* malice
malicioso *adj* malicious
maligno *adj* malignant
malla *nf* mesh
malo *adj* bad
malogrado *adj* untimely death
malograr *v* spoil, ruin, waste
maloliente *adj* smelly
malsano *adj* unhealthy
maltratar *v* mistreat
maltrato *nm* mistreatment
malvado *adj* wicked
malversar *v* embezzle
mamar *v* suck
maña *nf* skill
manada *nf* herd, pack
mañana *nf* morning
mañana *adv* tomorrow
mancha *nf* blemish, stain
manchar *v* stain, defile
manco *adj* one-armed
mandado *nm* errand
mandar *v* command
mandarina *nf* tangerine
mandato *nm* precept, order
mandíbula *nf* jaw
mandíl *nm* apron
mando *nm* command
mandón *adj* bossy

manejable *adj* manageable
manejar *v* manage; operate
manejarse *v* get by
manejo *nm* handling
manera *nf* way
maneras *nf* manners
manga *nf* sleeve
mango *nm* handle
mangonear *v* boss around
manguera *nf* hose
manía *nf* habit
maniatar *v* tie
maniático *adj* maniac
manicomio *nm* madhouse
manifestar *v* declare, show
manifiesto *nm* manifesto
manifiesto *adj* evident, clear
maniobra *nf* maneuver
maniobrar *v* maneuver
manipular *v* manipulate
manirroto *adj* extravagant
manivela *nf* crank, handle
mano *nf* hand
mano de obra *nf* manpower
manojo *nm* bunch
manosear *v* touch, fondle
mañoso *adj* skilful
manotazo *nm* slap
mansedumbre *nf* meekness
mansión *nf* mansion
manso *adj* meek, docile
manta *nf* blanket
manteca *nf* lard, fat
mantel *nm* tablecloth
mantener *v* maintain, keep
mantenimiento *nm* upkeep
mantequilla *nf* butter
manto *nm* cloak
manual *mn* handbook

M

manual *adj* manual
manuscrito *nm* manuscript
manzana *nf* apple
manzano *nm* apple tree
mapa *nm* map
maqueta *nf* model
maquillaje *nm* makeup
maquillar *v* make up
máquina *nf* machine
mar *nm* sea
maratón *nm* marathon
maravilla *nf* marvel, wonder
maravillar *v* amaze
maravilloso *adj* wonderful
marca *nf* brand; mark
marcador *nm* marker
marcapasos *nm* pacemaker
marcar *v* mark, dial
marcha *nf* departure; gear
marchar *v* march
marcharse *v* go, leave
marchitarse *v* wither
marco *nm* frame; setting
marea *nf* tide
mareado *adj* dizzy, seasick
maremoto *nm* tidal wave
mareo *nm* dizziness
marfil *nm* ivory
margarita *nf* daisy
márgen *nm* margin
marginal *adj* marginal
marido *nm* husband
marina *nf* navy
marinero *nm* sailor
marino *adj* marine
marioneta *nf* puppet
mariposa *nf* butterfly
mariscal *nm* marshal
marisco *nm* shellfish

mármol *nm* marble
marqués *nm* marquis
marrano *nm* pig
marrano *adj* dirty
marrón *adj* brown
Marruecos *nm* Morocco
marte *nm* Mars
martes *nm* Tuesday
martillar *v* hammer
martillo *nm* hammer
mártir *nm* martyr
martirio *nm* martyrdom
marxista *adj* Marxist
marzo *nm* March
más *adj* more
más (de) *adv* extra
más allá *adv* beyond
más bien *adv* rather
más o menos *adv* so-and-so
masa *nf* dough; mass
masacre *nm* massacre
masaje *nm* massage
masajista *nm* masseur
mascar *v* chew, munch
máscara *nf* mask
masculino *adj* masculine, male
masilla *nf* putty
masivo *adj* massive
masón *nm* mason
masoquismo *nm* masochism
masticar *v* chew
mástil *nm* mast
mata *nf* bush
matanza *nf* slaughter
matar *v* kill, slaughter
matasellos *nm* postmark
matemáticas *nf* math
materia *nf* matter; subject
material *nm* material

materialismo *nm* materialism
maternal *adj* maternal
maternidad *nf* motherhood
matiz *nm* nuance, shade
matón *adj* bully
matorral *nm* bushes
matrícula *nf* registration
matricularse *v* register, enroll
matrimonio *nm* marriage
maullar *v* meow
máxima *nf* maxim
máximo *adj* maximum
mayo *nm* May
mayonesa *nf* mayonnaise
mayor *adj* senior, older
mayordomo *nm* butler
mayoría *nf* majority
mayorista *nm* wholesaler
mayúscula *nf* capital letter
mazapán *nm* marzipan
mecánico *nm* mechanic
mecanismo *nm* mechanism
mecanizar *v* mechanize
mecedora *nf* rocking chair
mecer *v* rock
mecha *nf* wick, fuse
mechero *nm* lighter
medalla *nf* medal
medallón *nm* medallion
media *nf* stocking
mediador *nm* mediator
mediano *adj* medium
medianoche *nf* midnight
mediar *v* mediate
medicina *nf* medicine
médico *nm* doctor
medida *nf* measure
medida (a) *adv* custom-made
medieval *adj* medieval

medio *nm* center
mediocre *adj* mediocre
mediocridad *nf* mediocrity
mediodía *nf* midday, noon
medios *nm* means
medir *v* measure
meditación *nf* meditation
meditar *v* meditate
médula *nf* marrow
medusa *nf* jellyfish
mejilla *nf* cheek
mejor *adj* better
mejora *nf* improvement
mejorar *v* improve
mejunje *nm* concoction
melancolía *nf* melancholy
melena *nf* long hair
mellizo *nm* twin
melocotón *nm* peach
melodía *nf* melody
melódico *adj* melodic
melón *nm* melon
membrana *nf* membrane
membrecía *nf* membership
membrillo *nm* quince
memorable *adj* memorable
memoria *nf* memory
memorias *nf* memoirs
memorizar *v* memorize
mención *nf* mention
mencionar *v* mention
mendigar *v* beg
mendigo *nm* beggar
menear *v* stir, move
menguante *adj* decreasing
menguar *v* decrease, wane
meningitis *nf* meningitis
menisco *nm* cartilage
menopausia *nf* menopause

M

menor *adj* younger

menos *adj* less, minus

menoscabar *v* diminish

menospreciar *v* belittle, despise

menosprecio *nm* scorn

mensaje *nm* message

mensajero *nm* messenger

menstruación *nf* menstruation

mensual *adj* monthly

menta *nf* mint

mentalidad *nf* mentality

mentalmente *adv* mentally

mente *nf* mind

mentecato *nm* fool

mentir *v* lie

mentira *nf* lie

mentirilla *nf* white lie

mentiroso *adj* liar

mentón *nm* chin

menú *nm* menu

menudo (a) *adv* often

meollo *nm* marrow

mercadillo *nm* street market

mercado *nm* market

mercancía *nf* merchandise

mercenario *nm* mercenary

mercurio *nm* mercury

merecer *v* deserve

merienda *nf* snack

mérito *nm* merit

meritorio *adj* deserving

merluza *nf* hake

mermelada *nf* marmalade

mero *adj* mere, simple

merodear *v* prowl

mes *nm* month

mesa *nf* table

mesera *nf* barmaid

mesero *nm* barman

meseta *nf* plateau

Mesías *nm* Messiah

mesón *nm* inn

mestizo *adj* mixed race

mesura *nf* moderation

meta *nf* goal

metáfora *nf* metaphor

metálico *adj* metallic

meteoro *nm* meteor

meter la pata *v* goof

meter miedo *v* intimidate

meterse en líos *v* embroil

meticuloso *adj* meticulous

metido *adj* involved

metódico *adj* methodical

método *nm* method

metralla *nf* shrapnel

métrico *adj* metric

metro *nm* meter; subway

mexicano *adj* Mexican

mezcla *nf* blend, mixture

mezclar *v* blend, mix

mezclarse *v* mingle, mix

mezquindad *nf* pettiness

mezquino *adj* petty, mean

mezquita *nf* mosque

mi *adj* my

microbio *nm* germ

micrófono *nm* microphone

microondas *nm* microwave

microscopio *nm* microscope

miedo *nm* fear

miedo (de) *adj* scary

miedoso *adj* timid

miel *nf* honey

miembro *nm* member

mientras *c* as, while

mientras tanto *adv* meanwhile

miércoles *nm* Wednesday

M

miga *nf* crumb
migraña *nf* migraine
migratorio *adj* migratory
mil *adj* thousand
milagro *nm* miracle
milagroso *adj* miraculous
milenio *nm* millennium
milicia *nf* militia
miligramo *nm* milligram
milímetro *nm* millimeter
militante *adj* militant
militar *nm* soldier
milla *nf* mile
millaje *nm* mileage
millón *nm* million
millonario *adj* millionaire
mimar *v* pamper, spoil
mimo *nm* caress
mina *nf* mine
minar *v* mine, undermine
mineral *nm* mineral, ore
minero *nm* miner
miniatura *nf* miniature
minifalda *nf* miniskirt
mínimo *nm* minimum
ministerio *nm* ministry
ministro *nm* minister
minoría *nf* minority
minucioso *adj* meticulous
minusválido *adj* disabled
minuto *nm* minute
mío *pro* mine
miope *adj* short-sighted
miopía *nf* near-sightedness
mirada *nf* look
mirador *nm* viewpoint
miramiento *nm* consideration
mirar *v* look
mirar fijo *v* stare, gaze

mirilla *nf* peephole
misa *nf* mass
miserable *adj* miserable
miseria *nf* misery
misericordia *nf* mercy
misil *nm* missile
misión *nf* mission
misionero *nm* missionary
mismo *adj* same
misterio *nm* mystery
misterioso *adj* mysterious
místico *adj* mystic
mitad *nf* half
mitigar *v* mitigate
mitin *nm* rally, meeting
mito *nm* myth
mitología *nf* mythology
mixto *adj* mixed
mobiliario *nm* furniture
mobilizar *v* mobilize
mochila *nf* backpack
moción *nf* motion, vote
moco *nm* mucus
mocoso *adj* brat
moda *nf* vogue, fashion
moda (de) *adj* fashionable
modales *nm* manners
modelar *v* model
modelo *nm* model
moderación *nf* restraint
moderado *adj* moderate
moderar *v* moderate
modernizar *v* modernize
moderno *adj* modern
modestia *nf* modesty
modesto *adj* modest
modificar *v* modify
modismo *nm* idiom
modista *nf* dressmaker

M

M

modo *nm* way, manner
modorra *nf* drowsiness
mofarse *v* make fun
moho *nm* mildew, mold
mojado *adj* wet
mojar *v* moisten, dip
mojarse *v* get wet
molde *nm* mold
moldear *v* mold
moldura *v* molding
molécula *nf* molecule
moler *v* grind
molestar *v* bother, annoy
molestarse *v* get upset
molestia *nf* discomfort
molido *adj* exhausted; ground
molino *nm* mill
momento *nm* moment
momia *nf* mummy
momificar *v* mummify
monarca *nm* monarch
monarquía *nf* monarchy
monasterio *nm* monastery
monástico *adj* monastic
moneda *nf* coin, currency
monedero *nm* purse
monigote *nm* idiot
monja *nf* nun
monje *nm* monk
mono *nm* monkey
mono *adj* pretty, cute
monogamia *nf* monogamy
monólogo *nm* monologue
monopolio *nm* monopoly
monopolizar *v* monopolize
monotonía *nf* monotony
monótono *adj* monotonous
monstruo *nm* monster
monstruoso *adj* monstrous

montaña *nf* mountain
montañoso *adj* mountainous
montar *v* mount, ride
monte *nm* mount, mountain
montón *nm* heap, stack, pile
montura *nf* frame
monumento *nm* monument
mora *nf* blackberry
morada *nm* dwelling
morado *adj* purple
moral *adj* moral
moraleja *nf* moral
moralidad *nf* morality
moralizar *v* moralize
morboso *adj* morbid
mordaz *adj* biting
mordaza *nf* gag
mordedura *nf* bite
morder *v* bite
mordisco *nm* bite, nibble
morena *nf* brunette
moreno *adj* brown; tanned
moretón *nm* bruise
morfina *nf* morphine
moribundo *adj* dying
morir *v* die
moro *adj* Moorish
morriña *nf* homesickness
morro *nm* nose
morsa *nf* walrus
mortaja *nf* shroud
mortal *adj* deadly, lethal
mortalidad *nf* mortality
mortífero *adj* deadly
mortificar *v* mortify
mosaico *nm* mosaic
mosca *nf* fly
mosquito *nm* mosquito
mostaza *nf* mustard

mostrador *nm* counter
mostrar *v* show
mota *nf* speck
mote *nm* nickname
motel *nm* motel
motín *nm* mutiny, riot
motivar *v* motivate
motivo *nm* motive
moto *nf* scooter
motocicleta *nf* motorcycle
motor *nm* engine, motor
motora *nf* motorboat
mover *v* move
movible *adj* movable
móvil *adj* mobile
móvil *nm* motive; cell phone
movilizar *v* mobilize
movimiento *nm* movement
mozo *nm* young boy
muchacha *nf* girl
muchacho *nm* boy, lad
muchedumbre *nf* crowd
mucho *adj* much, a lot of
muchos *adj* many
muda *nf* change of clothes
mudanza *nf* moving
mudar *v* change
mudarse *v* relocate; change
mudo *adj* dumb; silent
muebles *nm* furniture
mueca *nf* grimace
muela *nf* molar
muelle *nm* wharf; spring
muerte *nf* death
muerto *adj* dead, deceased
muestra *nf* sample, token
mugre *nf* dirt, filth
mugriento *adj* dirty, filthy
mujer *nf* woman

mujeres *nf* women
mujeriego *adj* womanizer
mula *nf* mule
muleta *nf* crutch
multa *nf* fine, penalty
multar *v* fine
múltiple *adj* multiple, many
multiplicar *v* multiply
multitud *nf* multitude
mundano *adj* worldly
mundial *adj* worldwide
mundo *nm* world
muñeca *nf* wrist; doll
municiones *nf* ammunition
municipio *nm* borough
muralla *nf* wall
murciélago *nm* bat
murmullo *nm* murmur
murmurar *v* murmur
muro *nm* wall
músculo *nm* muscle
museo *nm* museum
musgo *nm* moss
música *nf* music
músico *nm* musician
muslo *nm* thigh
mustio *adj* withered
musulmán *nm* Muslim
mutilar *v* mutilate, maim
mutuo *adj* mutual
muy *adv* very

M

N

nabo *nm* turnip
nacer *v* be born
nacido *adj* born
nacimiento *nm* birth
nación *nf* nation
nacional *adj* national
nacionalidad *nf* nationality
nacionalizar *v* nationalize
nada *nf* nothing
nadador *nm* swimmer
nadar *v* swim
nadie *pro* nobody
naranja *nf* orange
narcótico *nm* narcotic
nardo *nm* lily
nariz *nf* nose
narrar *v* narrate, tell
nata *nf* cream
natillas *nf* custard
nativo *adj* native
natural *adj* natural
naufragar *v* sink
naufragio *nm* shipwreck
náufrago *nm* castaway
náusea *nf* nausea
nauseabundo *adj* sickening
navaja *nf* knife
nave *nf* nave; ship
navegador *nm* browser
navegar *v* navigate, sail
Navidad *nf* Christmas
navío *nm* ship
neblina *nf* haze, mist
necesario *adj* necessary
necesidad *nf* need
necesitado *adj* needy

necesitar *v* need
necio *adj* foolish
nectarina *nf* nectarine
nefasto *adj* disastrous
negación *nf* denial
negar *v* deny
negativa *nf* refusal
negativo *adj* negative
negligencia *nf* negligence
negligente *adj* negligent
negociante *nm* businessman
negociar *v* negotiate
negocio *nm* business
negro *adj* black
nervio *nm* nerve
nervioso *adj* nervous
neto *adj* net
neurótico *adj* neurotic
neutral *adj* neutral
neutralizar *v* neutralize
nevada *nf* snowfall
nevar *v* snow
nevera *nf* icebox
nexo *nm* link
ni *c* nor, neither
nicotina *nf* nicotine
nido *nm* nest
niebla *nf* fog
nieto *nm* grandson
nieve *nf* snow
nilón *nm* nylon
niñera *nf* babysitter
niñez *nf* childhood
ninfa *nf* nymph
ninguno *pro* no one
niño *nm* baby, child
niño pequeño *nm* toddler
niños *nm* children
nitrógeno *n* nitrogen

nivel *nm* level
no *adv* not
no obstante *c* nonetheless
noble *adj* noble
nobleza *nm* nobility
noche *nf* night
noche (de) *adv* nightly
noción *nf* notion
nocivo *adj* harmful
nocturno *adj* nocturnal
nogal *nm* walnut tree
nombrar *v* appoint, name
nombre *nm* noun; name
nómina *nf* payroll
noria *nf* waterwheel
norma *nf* norm, rule
normal *adj* normal
normalizar *v* normalize
normas *nf* guidelines
noroeste *nm* northeast
norte *nm* north
norteño *adj* northerner
Noruega *nf* Norway
noruego *adj* Norwegian
nosotros *pro* we
nostalgia *nf* nostalgia
nostálgico *adj* homesick
nota *nf* footnote; grade
notable *adj* remarkable
notar *v* notice
notario *nm* notary
noticias *nf* news
noticiero *nm* newscast
notificación *nf* notification
notificar *v* notify
notorio *adj* notorious
novato *adj* inexperienced
novedad *nf* novelty
novela *nf* novel

novelista *nm* novelist
noveno *adj* ninth
noventa *adj* ninety
novia *nf* bride
noviazgo *nm* courtship
novicio *nm* novice
noviembre *nm* November
novio *nm* fiancé
nubarrón *nm* storm cloud
nube *nf* cloud
nublado *adj* cloudy
nuclear *adj* nuclear
núcleo *nm* core
nudista *nm* nudist
nudo *nm* knot
nuera *nf* daughter-in-law
nuestro *adj* our
nuestro *pro* ours
nueve *adj* nine
nuevo *adj* new
nuevo (de) *adv* again
nuez *nf* walnut
nulo *adj* null, void
numerar *v* number
número *nm* number
numeroso *adj* numerous
nunca *adv* never
nutria *nf* otter
nutrición *nf* nutrition
nutrir *v* nourish
nutritivo *adj* nutritious

N

o *c* or
obedecer *v* obey
obediencia *nf* obedience
obeso *adj* obese
obispo *nm* bishop
objeción *nf* objection
objetar *v* object
objetivo *nm* objective
objeto *nm* object; aim
oblicuo *adj* oblique
obligación *nf* obligation
obligar *v* bind, compel
obligatorio *adj* compulsory
obra *nf* work; play
obra maestra *nf* masterpiece
obrero *nm* worker
obscenidad *nf* obscenity
obsceno *adj* lewd, obscene
obscuridad *nf* darkness
obsequiar *v* give a present
obsequio *nm* gift, present
observar *v* notice, observe
observatorio *nm* observatory
obsesión *nf* obsession
obsesionar *v* obsess
obstaculizar *v* hinder, obstruct
obstáculo *nm* obstacle
obstáculos *nm* red tape
obstante (no) *adv* however
obstinado *adj* obstinate
obstinarse *v* insist on
obstrucción *nf* obstruction
obstruir *v* obstruct
obtener *v* get, obtain
obturar *v* plug, block
obvio *adj* obvious

ocasión *nf* occasion
ocasionar *v* cause
ocaso *nm* decline; sunset
occidental *adj* western
océano *nm* ocean
ochenta *adj* eighty
ocho *adj* eight
ocio *nm* leisure
ocioso *adj* idle
octavo *adj* eighth
octubre *nm* October
ocultar *v* conceal, hide
oculto *adj* hidden
ocupación *nf* occupation
ocupado *adj* busy
ocupar *v* occupy
ocurrencia *nf* idea
ocurrir *v* occur
odiar *v* hate
odio *nm* hatred
odioso *adj* hateful
odisea *nf* odyssey
odómetro *nm* odometer
oeste *nm* west
ofender *v* offend
ofensa *nf* offense
ofensiva *nf* offensive
ofensivo *adj* offensive
oferta *nf* bid, offer
oficial *adj* official
oficiar *v* officiate, preside
oficina *nf* office, bureau
oficio *nm* craft, job
ofrecer *v* offer
ofrecerse *v* volunteer
ofrenda *nf* offering
ofuscar *v* confuse
oído *nm* hearing
oír *v* hear

ojal *nm* buttonhole
ojeada *nf* glance, peek
ojear *v* glance, have a look
ojo *nm* eye
ola *nf* wave
oleada *nf* big wave
oleoducto *nm* pipeline
oler *v* smell
olfatear *v* sniff
olimpiada *nf* Olympics
oliva *nf* olive
olivo *nm* olive tree
olla *nf* pot
olmo *nm* elm
olor *nm* odor, smell
oloroso *adj* fragrant
olvidar *v* forget
olvido *nm* oblivion
ombligo *nm* navel, belly button
omisión *nf* omission
omitir *v* omit
once *adj* eleven
onceavo *adj* eleventh
onda *nf* wave, ripple
ondulado *adj* wavy
onza *nf* ounce
opaco *adj* opaque
opción *nf* option
opcional *adj* optional
ópera *nf* opera
operación *nf* operation
operar *v* operate
opinar *v* think
opinión *nf* opinion
opio *nm* opium
oponerse *v* oppose, object
oportunidad *nf* opportunity
oportuno *adj* timely
oposición *nf* opposition

opresión *nf* oppression
oprimir *v* oppress
optar *v* opt for, choose
óptico *adj* optical
optimismo *nm* optimism
optimista *adj* optimistic
optometrista *nm* optician
opuesto *adj* opposite
opulencia *nf* opulence
oración *nf* prayer; sentence
oral *adj* oral
orangután *nm* orangutan
órbita *nf* orbit
orden *nm* order
ordenación *nf* ordination
ordenado *adj* neat
ordenador *nm* computer
ordenar *v* ordain
ordeñar *v* milk
ordinario *adj* common
oreja *nf* ear
orfanato *nm* orphanage
organismo *nm* organism
organista *nm* organist
organización *nf* organization
organizar *v* organize
órgano *nm* organ
orgullo *nm* pride
orgulloso *adj* proud
orientación *nf* orientation
oriental *adj* eastern, oriental
oriente *nm* orient, east
orificio *nm* orifice
origen *nm* origin
original *adj* original
originar *v* cause
originarse *v* originate
orilla *nf* shore; edge
orina *nf* urine

Ocurrio

O

orinar *v* urinate
oriundo *adj* native
ornamentar *v* decorate
oro *nm* gold
orquesta *nf* orchestra
ortodoxo *adj* orthodox
ortografía *nf* spelling
oruga *nf* caterpillar
osar *v* dare
oscilar *v* fluctuate, swing
oscurecer *v* darken
oscuridad *nf* darkness
oscuro *adj* dark, obscure
oso *nm* bear
ostentoso *adj* ostentatious
ostra *nf* oyster
otoño *nm* autumn, fall
otorgar *v* bestow, award
otro *adj* another, other
ovación *nf* cheer, ovation
ovalado *adj* oval
ovario *nm* ovary
oveja *nf* sheep
ovular *v* ovulate
óvulo *nm* ovule
oxidado *adj* rusty
oxidar *v* rust
oxígeno *nm* oxygen
oyente *nm* listener

pacer *v* graze
paciencia *nf* patience
paciente *adj* patient
pacificar *v* pacify
pacífico *adj* peaceful
pacotilla (de) *adj* shoddy
pactar *v* agree
pacto *nm* pact, deal
padecer *v* suffer
padrastro *nm* stepfather
padre *nm* father; priest
padres *nm* parents
padrino *nm* godfather
paga *nf* pay, wages
pagadero *adj* payable
pagano *adj* pagan
pagar *v* pay
página *nf* page
pago *nm* payment, fee
país *nm* country
paisaje *nm* landscape
paisano *nm* countryman
paja *nf* straw
pajar *nm* haystack
pájaro *nm* bird
paje *nm* page
pala *nf* shovel, spade
palabra *nf* word
palabra (de) *adv* verbally
palacio *nm* palace
paladar *nm* palate
palanca *nf* lever
palco *nm* box
palidez *nf* paleness
pálido *adj* pale
paliza *nf* beating

palma *nf* palm
palmada *nf* pat
palmera *nf* palm tree
palo *nm* stick
paloma *nf* dove, pigeon
palomitas *nf* popcorn
palpar *v* touch, feel
palpitación *nf* palpitation
palpitar *v* beat, throb
pan *nm* bread
panadería *nf* bakery
panadero *nm* baker
pañal *nm* diaper
pancarta *nf* banner
páncreas *nm* pancreas
pandilla *nf* gang
pánico *nm* panic
paño *nm* cloth
panorama *nm* panorama
pantalla *nf* screen; lampshade
pantalón corto *nm* shorts
pantalones *nm* trousers, pants
pantano *nm* reservoir
pantera *nf* panther
pañuelo *nm* handkerchief
panza *nf* belly
Papa *nm* Pope
papá *nm* dad
Papado *nm* papacy
papas fritas *nf* fries
papel *nm* paper
papeleo *nm* paperwork
papelera *nf* wastebasket
paperas *nf* mumps
paquete *nm* package
par *nm* pair
para *pre* for
parábola *nf* parable
parabrisas *nm* windshield

paracaídas *nm* parachute
parachoque *nm* fender
parada *nf* stop
paradero *nm* whereabouts
parado *adj* idle
paradoja *nf* paradox
paraguas *nf* umbrella
paraíso *nm* paradise
paralelo *adj* parallel
parálisis *nf* paralysis
paralizado *adj* standstill
paralizar *v* paralyze
paranoico *adj* paranoid
parar *v* halt, stop
parásito *nm* parasite
parcial *adj* partial, biased
parecer *v* seem
parecerse *v* resemble
parecido *nm* likeness
parecido *adj* alike, similar
pared *nf* wall
pareja *nf* couple; mate
parejo *adj* even
parentesco *nm* relationship
paréntesis *nm* parenthesis
paridad *nf* parity
pariente *nm* relative
parir *v* give birth
parlamento *nm* parliament
paro *nm* unemployment
parpadear *v* blink
párpado *nm* eyelid
parque *nm* park
parra *nf* grapevine
párrafo *nm* paragraph
parrilla *nf* grill
párroco *nm* pastor, vicar
parroquia *nf* parish
parroquiano *nm* parishioner

P

parte *nf* part
parte (en) *adv* partly
participación *nf* involvement
participar *v* participate
participio *nm* participle
partícula *nf* particle
particular *adj* particular
partida *nf* departure
partidario *nm* follower
partido *nm* party; game
partir *v* leave; break
parto *nm* birth
pasa *nf* raisin
pasado *adj* past, last
pasaje *nm* fare; crossing
pasajero *nm* passenger
pasaporte *nm* passport
pasar *v* elapse, pass
pasatiempo *nm* pastime
Pascua *nf* Easter
pasear *v* stroll
pasillo *nm* aisle, corridor
pasión *nf* passion
pasivo *adj* passive
pasmar *v* astound
pasmoso *adj* astounding
paso *nm* pace, step
pasta *nf* paste
pastar *v* graze
pastel *nm* cake
pasteles *nm* pastry
pastilla *nf* pill, tablet
pastor *nm* shepherd
pata *nf* leg; paw
patata *nf* potato
patear *v* kick
patente *nf* patent
patente *adj* obvious
paternal *adj* paternal

paternidad *nf* paternity
patético *adj* pathetic
patíbulo *nm* gallows
patillas *nf* sideburns
patín *nm* skate
patinar *v* skate
patio *nm* courtyard, patio
pato *nm* duck
patria *nf* homeland
patriarca *nm* patriarch
patrimonio *nm* patrimony
patriota *nm* patriot
patriótico *adj* patriotic
patrocinador *nm* sponsor
patrocinar *v* patronize
patrón *nm* patron
patrono *nm* employer
patrulla *nf* patrol
paulatino *adj* slow
pausa *nf* pause
pausado *adj* slow
pausterizar *v* pasteurize
pavimento *nm* pavement
pavo *nm* turkey
pavo real *nm* peacock
pavor *nm* terror
payaso *nm* clown
paz *nf* peace
peaje *nm* toll
peatón *nm* pedestrian
peca *nf* freckle
pecado *nm* sin
pecador *nm* sinner
pecaminoso *adj* sinful
pecar *v* sin
pecho *nm* chest, breast
peculiaridad *nf* mannerism
peculiar *adj* peculiar
pedagogía *nf* pedagogy

pedal *nm* pedal
pedante *adj* pedantic
pedazo *nm* piece, bit
pediatra *nm* pediatrician
pegajoso *adj* sticky
pegamento *nm* glue
pegar *v* hit; glue, stick
peinado *nm* hairdo
peinar *v* comb
peine *nm* comb
pelar *v* peel
peldaño *nm* step
pelear *v* scuffle, fight
pelele *nm* puppet
peliagudo *adj* difficult
pelícano *nm* pelican
película *nf* film, movie
peligrar *v* be in danger
peligro *nm* danger, peril
peligroso *adj* dangerous
pellejo *nm* skin
pellizcar *v* nip, pinch
pellizco *nm* nip, pinch
pelo *nm* hair
pelota *nf* ball
pelotón *nm* platoon, squad
peluca *nf* hairpiece, wig
peludo *adj* hairy
peluquera *nf* hairdresser
peluquero *nm* barber
pena *nf* grief, regret
peña *nf* rock
penal *adj* penal
penalizar *v* penalize
peñasco *nm* boulder
pendiente *nm* earring
pendiente *adj* pending
penetrar *v* penetrate
penicilina *nf* penicillin

península *nf* peninsula
penique *nm* penny
penitencia *nf* penance
penitente *nm* penitent
penoso *adj* laborious
pensamiento *nm* thought
pensar *v* think
pensión *nf* pension
pentágono *nm* pentagon
penuria *nf* shortage
peón *nm* laborer; pawn
peor *adj* worse
pepino *nm* cucumber
pequeño *adj* petite, small
pera *nf* pear
percance *nm* setback
percatarse *v* realize
percepción *nf* perception
percha *nf* hanger
percibir *v* perceive, receive
perdedor *nm* loser
perder *v* lose
perdición *nf* ruin, disgrace
pérdida *nf* loss
perdido *adj* missing, lost
perdigón *nm* pellet
perdiz *nf* partridge
perdón *nm* forgiveness
perdonable *adj* forgivable
perdonar *v* forgive, pardon
perdurar *v* last
perecedero *adj* perishable
perecer *v* perish
peregrinación *nf* pilgrimage
peregrino *nm* pilgrim
perejil *nm* parsley
perenne *adj* everlasting
pereza *nf* laziness
perezoso *adj* lazy

P

perfección *nf* perfection
perfecto *adj* perfect
perfil *nm* profile
perforación *nf* perforation
perforar *v* perforate, drill
perfume *nm* perfume
pergamino *nm* parchment
pericia *nf* skill
perico *nm* parrot, parakeet
periferia *nf* outskirts
perímetro *nm* perimeter
periódico *nm* newspaper
periódico *adj* periodic
periodista *nm* reporter
periodo *nm* period, term
perjudicar *v* harm, damage
perjudicial *adj* damaging
perjuicio *nm* damage
perjurio *nm* perjury
perla *nf* pearl
permanecer *v* remain
permanente *adj* permanent
permiso *nm* permission
permitir *v* permit, allow
pernicioso *adj* harmful
pero *c* but
perpetrar *v* perpetrate
perpetuo *adj* permanent
perplejo *adj* bewildered
perrera *nf* kennel
perro *nm* dog
persecución *nf* chase, persecution
perseguir *v* chase, persecute
perseverar *v* persevere
persiana *nf* blind
persistencia *nf* persistence
persistente *adj* persistent
persistir *v* persist
persona *nf* person

personal *adj* personal
personal *nm* staff, personnel
personalidad *nf* personality
personificar *v* personify
perspectiva *nf* viewpoint
perspicaz *adj* shrewd
persuadir *v* persuade
persuasión *nf* persuasion
persuasivo *adj* persuasive
pertenecer *v* belong, pertain
pertenencias *nf* belongings
pertinente *adj* relevant
pertrechar *v* supply
perturbar *v* disturb, perturb
peruano *adj* Peruvian
perverso *adj* perverse
pervertido *adj* pervert
pervertir *v* pervert
pesa *nf* scale
pesadez *nf* heaviness
pesadilla *nf* nightmare
pesado *adj* heavy
pésame *nm* condolence
pesar *v* weigh
pescado *nm* seafood, fish
pescador *nm* fisherman
pescuezo *nm* neck
pesebre *nm* manger
pesimismo *nm* pessimism
pesimista *adj* pessimistic
pésimo *adj* awful
peso *nm* weight
pestaña *nf* eyelash
pestañear *v* blink
pestillo *nm* bolt
pez *nm* fish
piadoso *adj* pious, kind
picado *adj* minced
picado (en) *adv* nosedive

P

picadura *nf* bite, sting
picar *v* bite, sting, mince
picazón *nm* itching
pie *nm* foot
pie (de) *adv* standing
pierna *nf* leg
pies *nm* feet
pieza *nf* piece
pigmeo *nm* pygmy
pijamas *nm* pajama
pila *nf* battery
pilar *nm* pillar
píldora *nf* pill
pillar *v* catch
piloto *nm* pilot
pimienta *nf* pepper
pimiento *nm* bell pepper
piña *nf* pineapple
pinchar *v* puncture; prick
pinchazo *nm* puncture; prickle
pinguino *nm* penguin
pino *nm* pine tree
pinta *nf* pint
pintar *v* paint
pintor *nm* painter
pintoresco *adj* picturesque
pintura *nf* paint; painting
pinza *nf* clothes pin
piojo *nm* louse
pionero *nm* pioneer
pipa *nf* pipe
piragua *nf* canoe
pirámide *nf* pyramid
piraña *nf* piranha
pirata *nm* pirate
piratería *nf* piracy
pirómano *nm* arsonist
piropo *nm* flattery
pisada *nf* footprint

pisar *v* tread, step on
piscina *nf* pool
piso *nm* floor, apartment
pisotear *v* trample
pista *nf* clue
pistola *nf* gun, pistol
pistolero *nm* gunman
pistón *nm* piston
pitar *v* honk, referee
pizarra *nf* blackboard
pizca *nf* bit, pinch
placa *nf* badge, plate
placentero *adj* delightful
placer *nm* pleasure
plaga *nf* plague
plagado *adj* infested
plan *nm* plan
planchar *v* iron
planear *v* glide; plan
planeta *nm* planet
planicie *nf* plain
plano *nm* blueprint
plano *adj* flat
planta *nf* plant
plantar *v* plant
plantear *v* pose
plástico *nm* plastic
plastificar *v* laminate
plata *nf* silver
plataforma *nf* platform
plátano *nm* banana
platero *nm* silversmith
platicar *v* chat
platillo *nm* saucer
platino *nm* platinum
plato *nm* dish, plate
playa *nf* beach
plaza *nf* square
plazo *nm* period

P

plegar *v* fold
plegaria *nf* prayer
pleito *nm* lawsuit
pleno *adj* full
pliegue *nm* crease, pleat
plomero *nm* plumber
plomo *nm* lead
pluma *nf* feather; pen
plural *adj* plural
plusvalía *nf* capital gain
población *nf* population
poblar *v* populate
pobre *nm* poor
pobreza *nf* poverty
poco *adj* little
pocos *adj* few
podar *v* prune
poder *v* can, may
poder *nm* power
poderoso *adj* powerful
podredumbre *nf* rot
podrido *adj* rotten
poema *nm* poem
poesía *nf* poetry
poeta *nm* poet
polaco *adj* Polish
polar *adj* polar
polea *nf* pulley
polémica *nf* controversy
polémico *adj* controversial
polen *nm* pollen
policía *nm* policeman, cop
policía *nf* police
poligamia *nf* polygamy
polígamo *adj* polygamist
polilla *nf* moth
polio *nm* polio
política *nf* politics
político *nm* politician

póliza *nf* policy
pollito *nm* chick
pollo *nm* chicken
polo *nm* pole
Polonia *nf* Poland
polución *nf* pollution
polvo *nm* dust, powder
pólvora *nf* gunpowder
polvoriento *adj* dusty
pomada *nf* cream
pomelo *nm* grapefruit
pompa *nf* pomp
pomposidad *nf* pomposity
pómulo *nm* cheekbone
ponderar *v* ponder
poner *v* set, put; lay
pontífice *nm* pontiff
ponzoña *nf* poison
popular *adj* popular
popularizar *v* popularize
por *pre* along, by
por ciento *adv* percent
por eso *c* therefore
por la borda *adv* overboard
por la presente *adv* hereby
por lo tanto *adv* therefore
por lo visto *adv* apparently
por partes *adv* piecemeal
por poderes *adv* proxy
por qué *adv* why
por razón de *pre* because of
porcelana *nf* porcelain
porcentage *nm* percentage
porción *nf* portion
pordiosero *adj* downtrodden
porfiar *v* insist
pormenor *nm* detail
poro *nm* pore
poroso *adj* porous

porque _c_ because
porqué _nm_ reason
porquería _nf_ crap, mess
porra _nf_ stick, club
porrazo _nm_ blow
portada _nf_ cover
portador _nm_ bearer
portátil _adj_ portable
portavoz _nf_ spokesman
portazo _nm_ slam
portero _nm_ doorman
pórtico _nm_ porch
Portugal _nf_ Portugal
portugués _adj_ Portuguese
posada _nf_ inn
posar _v_ pose
poseer _v_ own, possess
posesión _nf_ ownership
posesivo _adj_ possessive
posibilidad _nf_ possibility
posible _adj_ possible
posición _nf_ position
positivo _adj_ positive
posponer _v_ postpone
postal _nf_ postcard
poste _nm_ pole
posteridad _nf_ posterity
posterior _adj_ posterior
postizo _adj_ fake
postre _nm_ dessert
póstumo _adj_ posthumous
postura _nf_ pose, attitude
potable _adj_ drinkable
potaje _nm_ stew, soup
potencial _adj_ potential
potente _adj_ powerful
potestad _nf_ authority
potro _nm_ colt, pony
pozo _nm_ well

práctica _nf_ practice
practicar _v_ practice
práctico _adj_ practical
pradera _nf_ meadow, prairie
pragmático _adj_ pragmatist
preámbulo _nm_ preamble
precario _adj_ precarious
precaución _nf_ precaution
precavido _adj_ wary
precedente _nm_ precedent
preceder _v_ precede
precepto _nm_ commandment
precintar _v_ seal
precio _nm_ price, cost, fare
precioso _adj_ precious
precipicio _nm_ precipice
precipitarse _v_ rash
precisar _v_ specify
precisión _nf_ precision
preciso _adj_ accurate
precoz _adj_ precocious
precursor _nm_ forerunner
predecir _v_ prophesy
predicador _nm_ preacher
predicar _v_ preach
predicción _nf_ prediction
predilección _nf_ predilection
predilecto _adj_ favorite
predisponer _v_ predispose
predispuesto _adj_ predisposed
predominar _v_ predominate
predominio _nm_ prevalence
prefabricar _v_ prefabricate
prefacio _nm_ preface
preferencia _nf_ preference
preferible _adj_ preferable
preferir _v_ prefer
prefijo _nm_ prefix
pregonar _v_ announce

P

pregunta *nf* question
preguntar *v* ask, question
preguntarse *v* wonder
prehistórico *adj* prehistoric
prejuicio *nm* prejudice
preliminar *adj* preliminary
preludio *nm* prelude
prematuro *adj* premature
premeditar *v* premeditate
premiar *v* reward
premio *nm* award, prize
premisa *nf* premise
premonición *nf* premonition
preñada *adj* pregnant
prenda *nf* garment
prender *v* catch fire
prensa *nf* press
prensar *v* press
preocupación *nf* worry, concern
preocupado *adj* uneasy
preocupante *adj* worrying
preocupar(se) *v* worry
preparación *nf* preparation
preparado *adj* ready
preparar *v* prepare
preparativos *nm* arrangements
preparatorio *adj* preparatory
preposición *nf* preposition
prerequisito *nm* prerequisite
prerrogativa *nf* prerogative
presa *nf* prey; dam
presagiar *v* foreshadow
presagio *nm* omen
prescindir *v* disregard
prescribir *v* prescribe
prescripción *nf* prescription
presencia *nf* presence
presenciar *v* be present
presentación *nf* presentation

presentar *v* introduce
presentarse *v* show up
presente *adj* present
presentimiento *nm* feeling
presentir *v* have a feeling
preservar *v* preserve
presidencia *nf* presidency
presidente *nm* president
presidio *nm* penitentiary
presidir *v* preside
presión *nf* pressure
presionar *v* pressure
preso *nm* prisoner
prestado *adj* borrowed
prestamista *nm* pawnbroker
préstamo *nm* loan
prestar *v* lend, loan
presteza *nf* promptness
prestigio *nm* prestige
presumido *adj* conceited
presumir *v* show off
presunción *nm* presumption
presunto *adj* presumed
presuponer *v* presuppose
presuposición *nf* presumption
presupuesto *nm* budget
pretender *v* pretend
pretensión *nf* pretension
pretexto *nm* excuse, pretext
prevalecer *v* prevail
prevalente *adj* prevalent
prevención *nf* prevention
prevenir *v* prevent
preventivo *adj* preventive
prever *v* foresee
previo *adj* previous
previsión *nf* foresight
primacía *nf* primacy
primado *nm* primate

P

primavera *nf* spring
primero *adj* first
primitivo *adj* primitive
primo *nm* cousin
primordial *adj* paramount
princesa *nf* princess
principal *adj* main
príncipe *nm* prince
principiante *nm* beginner
principio *nm* beginning
prioridad *nf* priority
prisa *nf* haste, rash
prisa (de) *adv* hastily
prisión *nf* prison
prisionero *nm* prisoner
prisma *nm* prism
privación *nf* deprivation
privado *adj* private
privar *v* deprive
privilegio *nm* privilege
probabilidad *nf* probability
probabilidades *nf* odds
probable *adj* probable
probar *v* prove; test; taste
problema *nm* problem
problemático *adj* problematic
procedencia *nf* origin
proceder *v* proceed
procedimiento *nm* procedure
procesar *v* prosecute
procesión *nf* procession
proceso *nm* process
proclamar *v* proclaim
procrear *v* procreate
procurar *v* try; get
prodigio *nm* prodigy
prodigioso *adj* prodigious
producción *nf* production
producir *v* produce

producto *nm* product
productor *nm* producer
proeza *nf* feat, deed
profanar *v* desecrate
profano *adj* profane
profecía *nf* prophecy
proferir *v* utter
profesar *v* profess
profesión *nf* profession
profesional *adj* professional
profesor *nm* professor
profeta *nm* prophet
prófugo *adj* fugitive
profundidad *n* depth
profundizar *v* deepen
profundo *adj* deep
programa *nm* program
programador *nm* programmer
programar *v* program
progresar *v* progress
progresista *adj* progressive
progreso *nm* progress
prohibición *nf* prohibition
prohibir *v* prohibit, forbid
projectil *nm* missile
prójimo *nm* fellow man
prole *nf* offspring
proliferar *v* proliferate
prólogo *nm* prologue
prolongado *adj* protracted
prolongar *v* prolong
promedio *nm* average
promesa *nf* pledge, promise
prometedor *adj* promising
prometer *v* pledge, promise
promiscuo *adj* promiscuous
promoción *nf* promotion
promover *v* promote
pronombre *nm* pronoun

P

pronosticar *v* predict
pronóstico *nm* forecast
pronto *adv* soon
pronunciar *v* pronounce
pronunciar mal *v* mispronounce
propaganda *nf* propaganda
propagar *v* propagate
propensión *nf* propensity
propenso *adj* prone
propicio *adj* favorable
propiedad *nf* property
propietario *nm* owner
propina *nf* gratuity, tip
propio *adj* own
proponer *v* propose
proporción *nf* proportion
proposición *nf* proposition
propósito *nm* purpose
propósito (a) *adv* on purpose
propuesta *nf* proposal
propulsar *v* stimulate
prórroga *nf* extension
prorrogar *v* extend
prosa *nf* prose
proscribir *v* outlaw, ban
prosperar *v* thrive
prosperidad *nf* prosperity
próspero *adj* prosperous
próstata *n* prostate
prostitución *nf* prostitution
protección *nf* protection
proteger *v* protect
protesta *nf* protest
protestar *v* protest
provecho *nm* benefit
provechoso *adj* fruitful, useful
proveer *v* provide
provenir *v* come from
proverbio *nm* proverb

providencia *nf* providence
provincia *nf* province
provisional *adj* provisional
provocación *nf* provocation
provocar *v* provoke
proximidad *nf* proximity
próximo *adj* next
proyectar *v* project
proyectil *nm* projectile
proyecto *nm* project
prudencia *nf* prudence
prudente *adj* prudent
prueba *nf* proof, test
psicología *nf* psychology
psiquiatra *nm* psychiatrist
psiquiatría *nf* psychiatry
psíquico *adj* psychic
púa *nf* prickle
pubertad *nf* puberty
publicación *nf* publication
publicar *v* publish
publicidad *nf* publicity
público *adj* public
puchero *nm* cooking pot
pudín *nm* pudding
pudor *nm* modesty
pudrir *v* rot, decay
pueblo *nm* village
puente *nm* bridge
puerco *adj* filthy
pueril *adj* childish
puerta *nf* door, gate
puerto *nm* harbor, port
pues *c* then
puesta *nf* sunset
puesto *nm* post, stall
pulga *nf* flea
pulgada *nf* inch
pulir *v* polish

pulmón *nm* lung
pulmonía *nf* pneumonia
pulpa *nf* pulp
púlpito *nm* pulpit
pulpo *nm* octopus
pulsación *nf* beat
pulsar *v* pulsate
pulsera *nf* bracelet
pulso *nm* pulse
pulverizar *v* pulverize
puñal *nf* dagger
puñalada *nf* stab
puñetazo *nm* punch
puño *nm* cuff; fist
punta *nf* tip
puntada *nf* stitch
puntapié *nm* kick
puntiagudo *adj* pointed
puntillas (de) *adv* tiptoe
punto *nm* dot; point
punto culminante *nm* highlight
punto de vista *nm* viewpoint
puntuación *nf* score; grade
puntual *adj* punctual
punzada *nf* prick, beat
punzante *adj* sharp
pupitre *nm* desk
puré *nm* puree
pureza *nf* purity
purga *nf* purge
purgar *v* purge
purgatorio *nm* purgatory
purificación *nf* purification
purificar *v* purify
puritano *adj* puritan
puro *adj* pure
púrpura *nf* purple
pus *nf* pus
pútrido *adj* rotten

Q

que *adj* what, which
quebrado *adj* broken
quebrantar *v* transgress
quebrar *v* go bankrupt; break
quedarse *v* stay, remain
queja *nf* complaint
quejarse *v* complain
quejón *adj* grumpy
quemadura *nf* burn
quemar *v* burn
quemarropa (a) *adv* point-blank
querella *nf* dispute
querer *v* wish, want
querido *adj* dear, beloved
queso *nm* cheese
quiebra *nf* bankruptcy
quiebra (en) *adj* bankrupt
quien *pro* who
quienquiera *pro* whoever
quieto *adj* quiet
quilate *nm* carat
quimera *nf* dream
química *nf* chemistry
químico *adj* chemical
quince *adj* fifteen
quinientos *adj* five hundred
quinto *adj* fifth
quiosco *nm* kiosk
quirúrjico *adj* surgical
quisquilloso *adj* fuzzy
quiste *nm* cyst
quitamanchas *nm* cleaner
quitar *v* remove
quizá *adv* maybe, perhaps

P
Q

R

rábano *nm* radish
rabia *nf* rabies; anger
rabieta *nf* tantrum
rabioso *adj* furious
rabo *nm* tail
racimo *nm* bunch
ración *nf* allotment, portion
racional *adj* rational
racionalizar *v* rationalize
racionar *v* ration
racismo *nm* racism
racista *adj* racist
racún *nm* raccoon
radiación *nf* radiation
radiador *nm* radiator
radiante *adj* radiant
radiar *v* radiate
radical *adj* radical
radicar *v* originate
radio *nf* radio
radiografía *nf* X-ray
ráfaga *nf* gust, burst
raído *adj* shabby
raíz *nf* root
raja *nf* slice; crack
rajar *v* slit
rajatable (a) *adv* strictly
ralámpago *nm* flash
rallar *v* grate
rama *nf* bough, branch
ramificación *nf* ramification
ramo *nm* bouquet, bunch
rampa *nf* chute, ramp
rana *nf* frog
rancho *nm* ranch
rancio *adj* stale

rango *nm* rank, class
ranura *nf* groove, slot
rapar *v* shave
rápidamente *adv* quickly
rapidez *nf* speed
rápido *adj* quick, fast
raptar *v* kidnap
raqueta *nf* racquet
raramente *adv* seldom
rareza *nf* oddity, quirk
raro *adj* rare, weird, odd
rascacielos *nm* skyscraper
rascar *v* scratch
rasgar *v* tear, slash
rasgo *nm* trait, feature
rasguñar *v* scratch
rasguño *nm* scratch
raso *adj* flat, leveled
raspadura *nf* scratch, scrape
raspar *v* scrape
rastrear *v* trail, track
rastrillo *nm* rake
rastro *nm* trace
rasurarse *v* shave
rata *nf* rat
ratero *nm* pickpocket
ratificar *v* ratify
rato *nm* a while
ratón *nm* mouse
ratones *nm* mice
raudal *nm* torrent
raya *nf* stripe, line
rayado *adj* striped
rayar *v* cross out; verge on
rayo *nm* beam, ray
raza *nf* breed, race
razón *nf* reason
razonable *adj* reasonable
razonar *v* reason

R

razones *nf* grounds
reacción *nf* reaction
reaccionar *v* react
reacio *adj* reluctant
reactivar *v* reactivate
readmitir *v* reinstate
reajustar *v* readjust, reset
reajuste *nm* readjustment
real *adj* real, royal
realeza *nf* royalty
realidad *nf* reality
realidad (en) *adv* actually
realismo *nm* realism
realización *nf* fulfillment
realizar *v* fulfill, achieve
realzar *v* enhance
reanimar *v* revive
reanudación *nf* resumption
reanudar *v* resume
reaparecer *v* reappear
rearme *nm* rearmament
rebaja *nf* reduction
rebajar *v* reduce, lower
rebanada *nf* slice
rebaño *nm* flock, herd
rebasar *v* overtake, exceed
rebatir *v* rebut, refute
rebelarse *v* rebel
rebelde *nm* rebel
rebelión *nf* rebellion
rebosar *v* overflow
rebotar *v* bounce
recado *nm* errand
recaída *nf* relapse
recalcar *v* stress, emphasize
recalcitrante *adj* recalcitrant
recámara *n* bedroom
recambio *nm* spare part
recapacitar *v* reflect

recapitular *v* recap
recargar *v* recharge
recargo *nm* surcharge
recatado *adj* modest
recato *nf* modesty
recaudar *v* collect
recelo *nm* mistrust
recepción *n* reception
recesión *nf* recession
receta *nf* recipe
recetar *v* prescribe
rechazar *v* reject, repulse
rechazo *nm* rejection
rechinar *v* creak, squeak
rechistar *v* protest
rechoncho *adj* plump
recibimiento *nm* welcome
recibir *v* receive
recibo *nm* receipt
reciclar *v* recycle
reciente *adj* recent
recinto *nm* enclosure
recio *adj* strong
recipiente *nm* container
recíproco *adj* reciprocal
recitar *v* recite
reclamación *nf* claim
reclamar *v* claim
reclamo *nm* claim
reclinar *v* recline
recluir *v* confine
recluso *nm* inmate
recluta *nm* recruit
reclutar *v* recruit
recobrar *v* recover
recogedor *nm* dustpan
recoger *v* gather, pick up
recolectar *v* harvest
recomendar *v* recommend

R

recompensa *nf* reward
recompensar *v* reward
reconciliar *v* reconcile
reconocer *v* recognize
reconquistar *v* recapture
reconsiderar *v* reconsider
reconstruir *v* rebuild
recopilación *nf* compilation
recopilar *v* compile
recordar *v* recall, remind
recordatorio *nm* reminder
recorrer *v* travel
recorrido *nm* route
recortar *v* cut out; trim
recorte *nm* clipping
recostar *v* lean
recreación *nf* recreation
recrear *v* recreate
recreo *v* recreation
recriminar *v* reproach
recrudecer *v* worsen
recrutamiento *nm* recruitment
rectangular *adj* oblong
rectángulo *nm* rectangle
rectificar *v* rectify, correct
recto *nm* rectum
recto *adj* straight, honest
rector *nm* director
recuento *nm* recount
recuerdo *nm* memory
recuperación *nf* recovery
recuperar *v* recover
recurrir *v* resort, turn to
recurso *nm* recourse
red *nf* net, network
redada *nf* roundup
redención *nf* redemption
redil *nm* sheepfold
redimir *v* redeem

réditos *nm* yield
redoblar *v* redouble
redondear *v* round
redondel *nm* circle
redondo *adj* round
reducción *nf* reduction
reducir *v* reduce
reelegir *v* reelect
reembolsar *v* reimburse
reembolso *nm* reimbursement
reemplazar *v* replace
referencia *nf* reference
referente *adj* referring to
referirse *v* refer to
refinanciar *v* refinance
refinar *v* refine
refinería *nf* refinery
reflejar *v* reflect, mirror
reflejo *nm* reflex, reflection
reflexión *nf* reflection
reflexionar *v* ponder
reflexivo *adj* reflexive
reforma *nf* reform
reformar *v* reform
reforzar *v* reinforce
refrán *nm* proverb, saying
refrenar *v* curb
refrendar *v* endorse
refrescante *adj* refreshing
refrescar *v* refresh
refresco *nm* refreshment
refriega *nf* skirmish, brawl
refrigerar *v* refrigerate
refuerzo *nm* reinforcement
refugiado *nm* refugee
refugiarse *v* take refuge
refugio *nm* haven, shelter
refunfuñar *v* grumble
refutar *v* refute

R

regalar *v* give away
regalo *nm* gift, present
regañar *v* scold, chide
regaño *nm* scolding
regar *v* irrigate, water
regatear *v* haggle, bargain
regazo *nm* lap
regeneración *nf* regeneration
regente *nm* regent
régimen *nm* regime
regimiento *nm* regiment
regio *adj* regal
región *nf* region
regional *adj* regional
regir *v* govern
registrarse *v* register
regla *nf* ruler
regocijarse *v* rejoice
regocijo *nm* joy
regordete *adj* chubby
regresar *v* return
regreso *nm* return
regularizar *v* regulate
regularmente *adv* regularly
rehabilitar *v* rehabilitate
rehacer *v* redo, remake
rehén *nm* hostage
rehusar *v* refuse
reimprimir *v* reprint
reina *nf* queen
reinar *v* reign, rule
reincidir *v* relapse
reino *nm* kingdom
reinoceronte *nm* rhinoceros
reír *v* laugh
reiterar *v* reiterate
reja *nf* grille
rejuvenecer *v* rejuvenate
relación *nf* relationship

relajación *nf* relaxation
relajarse *v* relax
relámpago *nm* lightning
relatar *v* tell, recount
relativo *adj* relative
relato *nm* tale
relegar *v* relegate
relevante *adj* relevant
relevar *v* replace
relevo *nm* replacement
religión *nf* religion
religioso *adj* religious
reliquia *nf* relic
rellenar *v* refill; stuff
relleno *nm* padding
reloj *nm* watch, clock
relojero *nm* watchmaker
reluciente *adj* bright
relucir *v* glitter, shine
remachar *v* hammer
remar *v* row
remarcar *v* stress
rematar *v* finish off
remedar *v* mimic
remediar *v* remedy
remedio *nm* remedy
remendar *v* repair, mend
remiendo *nm* patch, mend
remisión *nf* remission
remitir *v* remit
remo *nm* oar
remodelar *v* remodel
remojar *v* soak
remolacha *nf* beet
remolcar *v* tow, tug
remolino *nm* whirlpool
remontarse *v* soar; go back
remordimiento *nm* remorse
remoto *adj* remote

R

remunerar v remunerate
renacimiento nm rebirth
rencilla nf quarrel
rencor nm grudge, resentment
rencoroso adj resentful
rendición nf surrender
rendido adj exhausted
rendija nf crack, gap
rendimiento nm output
rendirse v surrender
renglón nm printed line
reñir v quarrel
reno nm reindeer
renovación nf renewal
renovar v renew, revamp
renta nf rent
rentable adj profitable
rentar v rent
renuncia nf resignation
renunciar v renounce, resign
reorganizar v reorganize
reparación nf reparation
reparar v mend, repair
reparo n qualm, problem
repartir v share
repasar v review, revise
repatriar v repatriate
repelente adj repulsive
repente (de) adv suddenly
repentino adj sudden
repetición nf repetition
repetir v repeat
repetirse v recur
repicar v toll
replegarse v withdraw
repleto adj replete, full
repollo nm cabbage
reponer v replenish
reponerse v recover

reportar v report
reporte nm report
reposar v rest
reposo nm repose, rest
repostar v refuel
repostería nf pastry
reprender v rebuke
represalia nf reprisal
representar v represent
represión nf repression
reprimenda nf rebuke
reprimir v repress
reprochar v reproach
reproche nm reproach
reproducción nf replica
reproducir v reproduce
reptil nm reptile
república nf republic
repudiar v repudiate
repuesto nm spare part
repugnancia nf disgust
repugnante adj disgusting
repulsión nf repulsion
reputación nf reputation
requerir v require
requisito nm requirement
resaltar v highlight, stress
resbaladizo adj slippery
resbalar v slide, slip
resbalón nm slip
rescatar v ransom, rescue
rescate nm rescue, ransom
rescindir v cancel, rescind
resentimiento nm resentment
resentirse v resent
reservación nf reservation
reservado adj aloof, reserved
reservar v reserve
resfriado nm cold

R

resfriarse *v* catch a cold
residencia *nm* residence
residente *adj* resident
residir *v* reside
residuo *nm* residue, waste
resignar *v* resign
resignarse *v* resign oneself
resistencia *nf* resistance
resistente *adj* strong
resistir *v* resist, withstand
resolución *nf* resolution
resolver *v* resolve, settle
resonar *v* resound
resorte *nm* spring
respaldar *v* back, support
respaldo *nm* support
respectivo *adj* respective
respetar *v* respect
respeto *nm* respect
respetuoso *adj* respectful
respiración *nf* breathing
respiradero *nm* vent
respirar *v* breathe
respiro *nm* respite, breath
resplandecer *v* shine
resplandor *nm* brilliance
responder *v* answer, reply
responsable *adj* responsible
respuesta *of* answer, reply
resquicio *nm* crack, opening
resta *nf* subtraction
restante *adj* remaining
restar *v* subtract
restaurante *nm* restaurant
restaurar *v* restore
restitución *nf* restitution
restituir *v* return
resto *nm* remainder
restos *nm* remains

restregar *v* scrub
restricción *nf* constraint
restringir *v* restrict, curtail
resucitar *v* revive
resuelto *adj* determined; solved
resultado *nm* outcome, result
resultar *v* result, happen
resumen *nm* summary
resumen (en) *adv* briefly
resumir *v* summarize
resurgir *v* come back
resurrección *nf* resurrection
retaguardia *nf* rearguard
retaliar *v* retaliate
retar *v* challenge
retardar *v* delay, retard
retención *nf* retention
retener *v* retain, withhold
retirada *nf* withdrawal
retirado *adj* secluded
retirar *v* withdraw, remove
retirarse *v* retreat
retiro *nm* retreat
retocar *v* retouch
retornar *v* return
retractarse *v* retract
retraído *adj* loner, shy
retrasado *adj* late; retarded
retrasar *v* postpone, delay
retrasarse *v* be late
retraso *nm* delay
retratar *v* take a picture
retrato *nm* portrait
retrete *nm* toilet, bathroom
retroactivo *adj* retroactive
retroceder *v* recede, go back
retroceso *nm* step backwards
retrógado *adj* retrograde
retrospectiva *nf* hindsight

R

retumbar *v* rumble, resound
retumbe *nm* rumble
reuma *nm* rheumatism
reumatismo *nm* rheumatism
reunión *nf* reunion, meeting
reunir *v* convene, gather
reunirse *v* meet
revancha *nf* revenge
revelación *nf* revelation
revelar *v* reveal, disclose
reventa *nf* resale
reventar *v* burst, pop
reventón *nm* blowout
reverencia *nf* bow
reverenciar *v* revere
reversible *adj* reversible
revés *nm* setback
revisar *v* revise, check
revisión *nf* revision, check
revista *nf* magazine
revivir *v* revive; relive
revocación *nf* repeal
revocar *v* repeal, revoke
revolcarse *v* roll around
revolotear *v* flutter
revoltoso *adj* naughty
revólver *v* revolver, gun
revuelo *nm* commotion
revuelta *nf* revolt
revuelto *adj* mixed
rey *nm* king
reyerta *nf* brawl
rezagarse *v* lag behind
rezar *v* pray
ría *nf* estuary
riachuelo *nm* creek
riada *nf* flood
ribera *nf* bank
rico *adj* wealthy, rich

ridículo *adj* ridiculous
riego *nm* watering
rienda *nf* rein
riesgo *nm* risk
rifa *nf* raffle
rigidez *nf* stiffness
rígido *adj* rigid, terse, stiff
rigor *nm* rigor
riguroso *adj* strict
rima *nf* rhyme
riña *nf* quarrel
rincón *nm* corner
riñón *nm* kidney
río *nm* river
riqueza *nf* wealth
risa *nf* laughter
risible *adj* laughable
risueño *adj* cheerful
ritmo *nm* rhythm
rito *nm* rite
rival *nm* rival
rivalidad *nf* rivalry
rizado *adj* curly
rizar *v* curl
rizo *nm* curl
robar *v* steal, rob
roble *nm* oak
robo *nm* theft, robbery
robustecer *v* strengthen
robusto *adj* robust
roca *nf* boulder, rock
roce *nm* friction
rociar *v* sprinkle, spray
rocío *nm* dew
rocoso *adj* rocky
rodaja *nf* slice
rodear *v* surround
rodilla *nf* knee
rodillo *nm* roller

R

roedor *nm* rodent
roer *v* gnaw
rogar *v* beg, plead
rojo *adj* red
rollo *nm* scroll, reel
romance *nm* romance
romería *nf* pilgrimage
rompecabezas *nm* puzzle
romper *v* break
ron *nm* rum
roña *nf* dirt, grime
roncar *v* snore
ronco *adj* hoarse
ronquido *nm* snore
ropa *nf* clothing
ropa blanca *nf* linen
ropa de cama *nf* bedding
ropa interior *nf* underwear
ropero *nm* wardrobe
rosa *nf* rose
rosado *adj* pink
rosal *nm* rosebush
rosario *nm* rosary
rosca *nf* thread; cake
rostro *nm* face
rotación *nf* rotation
roto *adj* broken, torn
rótula *nf* kneecap
rótulo *nm* title, inscription
rotundo *adj* outright
rotura *nf* fracture
rozar *v* rub
rubí *nm* ruby
rubio *adj* blond
rubor *nm* blush
ruborizarse *v* blush
rudimentario *adj* rudimentary
rudo *adj* rude
rueda *nf* wheel

ruedo *nm* bullring
rugido *nm* roar
rugir *v* roar
ruido *nm* noise
ruidoso *adj* noisy
ruina *nf* ruin
ruiseñor *nm* nightingale
ruleta *nf* roulette
Rumania *nf* Romania
rumano *adj* Romanian
rumiar *v* chew; ponder
rumor *nm* rumor, hearsay
ruptura *nf* break
rural *adj* rural
Rusia *nf* Russia
ruso *adj* Russian
rústico *adj* rustic
ruta *nf* route
rutina *nf* routine

S

sábado *nm* Saturday
sábana *nf* sheet
saber *v* know
saber (a) *adv* namely
sabiduría *nf* wisdom
sabiendas (a) *adv* knowingly
sabio *adj* wise
sabor *nf* taste
saborear *v* relish, savor
sabotaje *nf* sabotage
sabotear *v* sabotage
sabroso *adj* tasty
sacapuntas *nm* sharpener

R
S

sacar *v* take out
sacerdocio *nm* priesthood
sacerdote *nm* priest
sacerdotisa *nf* priestess
saciar *v* satisfy
saco *nm* sack
sacramento *nm* sacrament
sacrificio *nm* sacrifice
sacrilegio *nm* sacrilege
sacudida *nf* jerk, jolt
sacudir *v* jolt, shake
sádico *adj* sadist
saeta *nf* arrow
sagaz *adj* shrewd
sagrado *adj* sacred
sal *nf* salt
sala *nf* room
salado *adj* salty
salario *nm* salary, pay
salchicha *nf* sausage
saldar *v* pay off; settle
saldo *nm* balance
salida *nf* exit, departure
salir *v* depart, go out
saliva *nf* saliva
salmo *nm* psalm
salmón *nm* salmon
salón *nm* lounge, parlor
salpicar *v* splash
salsa *nf* sauce, gravy
saltamontes *nm* grasshopper
saltar *v* jump, leap
saltarse *v* skip
salto *nm* leap, jump
salud *nf* health
saludar *v* greet, nod
saludos *nm* greetings
salvación *nf* salvation
salvado *nm* bran

salvado *adj* saved
salvador *nm* savior
salvaguardar *adj* safeguard
salvaje *adj* savage, wild
salvajismo *nm* savagery
salvar *v* save
salvavidas *nm* lifejacket
salvo *adj* safe
saña *nf* rage
sanar *v* heal
sanción *nf* sanction
sancionar *v* sanction
sandalia *nf* sandal
sandez *nf* stupidity
sandía *nf* watermelon
sangrar *v* bleed
sangre *nf* blood
sangriento *adj* bloody, gory
sanguijuela *nf* leech
sanguinario *adj* bloodthirsty
sanidad *adj* health; sanity
sano *adj* healthy
santidad *nf* holiness
santificar *v* sanctify
santo *nm* saint
santo *adj* holy
santuario *nm* sanctuary
sapo *nm* toad
saque *nm* kickoff
saquear *v* loot, plunder
saqueo *nm* loot, plunder
sarampión *nm* measles
sarcasmo *nm* sarcasm
sarcástico *adj* sarcastic
sardina *nf* sardine
sargento *nm* sergeant
sarro *nm* tartar, plaque
sartén *nf* pan, frying pan
sastre *nm* tailor

S

satánico *adj* satanic
satélite *nm* satellite
sátira *nf* satire
satisfacción *nf* satisfaction
satisfacer *v* satisfy
satisfactorio *adj* satisfactory
saturar *v* saturate
sauce *nm* willow
savia *nf* sap
sazonar *v* flavor, season
sebo *nm* grease
secadora *nf* dryer
secar *v* dry
sección *nf* section
secesión *nf* secession
seco *adj* dried, dry
secretario *nm* secretary
secreto *nm* secret
secreto *adj* secret
secreto (en) *adv* secretly
secta *nf* sect
sector *nm* sector
secuencia *nf* sequence
secuestrador *nm* kidnapper
secuestrar *v* abduct, kidnap
secuestro *nm* abduction
secundario *adj* secondary
sed *nf* thirst
seda *nf* silk
sedación *nf* sedation
sedado *adj* sedated
sede *nf* seat
sediento *adj* thirsty
seducción *nf* seduction
seducir *v* seduce
segar *v* cut, mow
seglar *adj* layman
segmento *nm* segment
segregación *nf* segregation

segregar *v* segregate
seguir *v* follow
según *pre* according to
según dicen *adv* reportedly
segundo *nm* second
segundo *adj* second
seguramente *adv* surely
seguridad *nf* safety
seguro *adj* safe, sure
seguro *nm* insurance
seis *adj* six
selección *nf* selection
seleccionar *v* select
sellar *v* stamp
sello *nm* postage; seal
selva *nf* forest
semáforo *nm* traffic light
semana *nf* week
semblante *nm* countenance, look
sembrar *v* sow
semejante *adj* similar
semejanza *nf* similarity
semestre *nm* semester
semilla *nf* seed
seminario *nm* seminary
seña *nf* gesture
senado *nm* senate
senador *nm* senator
señal *nf* signal
señalar *v* point, indicate
senda *nf* path
sendero *nm* trail
seno *nm* bosom
señor *nm* lord, mister, sir
señora *nf* lady, madam
señorita *nf* miss
sensación *nf* sensation
sensato *adj* sensible
sensual *adj* sensual

S

sentarse *v* sit
sentencia *nf* sentence
sentenciar *v* sentence
sentido *nm* meaning; sense
sentimental *adj* sentimental
sentimiento *nm* feeling
sentir *v* feel
separación *nf* separation
separar *v* separate
separarse *v* part, secede
septiembre *nm* September
séptimo *adj* seventh
sepulcro *v* tomb, grave
sepultar *v* bury
sequedad *nf* dryness
sequía *nf* drought
séquito *nm* entourage
ser *nm* being
ser *v* be
serenarse *v* calm down
serenata *nf* serenade
serenidad *nf* serenity
sereno *adj* serene
serie *nf* series
seriedad *nf* seriousness
serio *adj* serious
serio (en) *adv* seriously
sermón *nm* sermon
serpiente *nf* serpent, snake
serrar *v* saw
servicio *nm* service
servidumbre *nf* servitude
servilleta *nf* napkin
servir *v* serve
sesenta *adj* sixty
sesión *nf* session, sitting
sesos *nm* brain
seta *nf* mushroom
setenta *adj* seventy

severidad *nf* severity
severo *adj* harsh, severe
sexo *nm* sex
sexto *adj* sixth
sexualidad *nf* sexuality
si *c* if, whether
sí *adv* yes
sicario *nm* assassin
sidra *nf* cider
siembra *nf* sowing
siempre *adv* always
sien *nf* temple
sierra *nf* saw; mountain range
sierra eléctrica *n* chainsaw
siervo *nm* servant
siesta *nf* nap
siete *adj* seven
sífilis *nf* syphilis
sifón *nm* siphon
sigiloso *adj* stealthy
siglo *nm* century
significado *nm* meaning
significar *v* mean, signify
significativo *adj* significant
signo *nm* sign
siguiente *adj* next
sílaba *nf* syllable
silbar *v* hiss, whistle
silbato *nm* whistle
silenciador *nm* muffler
silenciar *v* silence
silencio *nm* silence
silla *nf* chair
silla de montar *nf* saddle
silla de ruedas *nf* wheelchair
sillón *nm* armchair
silueta *nf* silhouette
silvestre *adj* wild
sima *adj* chasm

símbolo *nm* symbol
simetría *nf* symmetry
simiente *nf* seed
simio *nm* ape
simpatía *nf* sympathy
simpático *adj* likable, nice
simpatizar *v* sympathize
simple *adj* simple
simplicidad *nf* simplicity
simplificar *v* simplify
simultáneo *adj* simultaneous
sin *pre* without
sin brillo *adv* mate
sin cesar *adv* ceaselessly
sin confirmar *adv* unofficially
sin control *adj* rampant
sin defectos *adj* flawless
sin dolor *adj* painless
sin embargo *c* however, yet
sin empleo *adj* unemployed
sin entrañas *adj* cold-blooded
sin éxito *adj* unsuccessful
sin fondo *adj* bottomless
sin fundamento *adj* groundless
sin hijos *adj* childless
sin hogar *adj* homeless
sin junturas *adj* seamless
sin límites *adj* boundless
sin mangas *adj* sleeveless
sin nubes *adj* cloudless
sin parar *adv* nonstop
sin pepitas *adj* seedless
sin plomo *adj* unleaded
sin recursos *adj* stranded
sin remedio *adj* hopeless
sin reparar *adv* regardless
sin sentido *adj* unconscious
sin un centavo *adj* penniless
sin valor *adj* worthless

sin vida *adj* lifeless
sinagoga *nf* synagogue
sincerarse *v* level with
sinceridad *nf* sincerity
sincero *adj* sincere
sincronizar *v* synchronize
síndrome *nm* syndrome
sinfín *adj* endless
sinfonía *nf* symphony
singular *adj* singular
siniestro *adj* sinister
sínodo *nm* synod
sintasis *nf* syntax
síntesis *nf* synthesis
síntoma *nm* symptom
sintonizar *v* tune
siquiera *adv* at least
sirena *nf* mermaid
sirvienta *nf* housekeeper
sísmico *adj* seismic
sistema *nm* system
sitiar *v* besiege
sitio *nm* place, site
situación *nf* situation
situado *adj* situated
sobaco *nm* armpit
soberanía *nf* sovereignty
soberano *adj* sovereign
soberbia *nf* pride
soberbio *adj* proud
sobornar *v* bribe
soborno *nm* bribery
sobrante *adj* remaining
sobras *nf* leftovers
sobre *nm* envelope
sobre *pre* over, upon, on
sobre todo *adv* above all
sobrecargar *v* overcharge
sobrecogido *adj* startled

S

sobredosis *nf* overdose
sobreestimar *v* overestimate
sobrellevar *v* endure
sobrenombre *nm* nickname
sobrepasarse *v* go too far
sobrepesar *v* outweigh
sobreponerse *v* overcome
sobresaliente *adj* outstanding
sobresalir *v* excel; stick out
sobresaltarse *v* jump, startle
sobrevivir *v* survive
sobriedad *nf* sobriety
sobrina *nf* niece
sobrino *nm* nephew
sobrio *adj* moderate
socarrón *nm* sarcastic
socavar *v* undermine
sociable *adj* sociable
socialismo *nm* socialism
socialista *adj* socialist
sociedad *nf* society
socio *nm* partner
socorrer *v* help
socorrista *nm* lifeguard
soez *adj* vulgar, obscene
sofá *nm* couch, sofa
sofocante *adj* stifling
sofocar *v* suffocate
soga *nf* rope
sol *nm* sun
solamente *adv* only, solely
solapa *nf* lapel
solar *adj* solar
soldado *nm* soldier
soldador *nm* welder
soldar *v* solder, weld
soleado *adj* sunny
soledad *nf* solitude
solemne *adj* solemn

soler *v* use to
solicitante *v* applicant
solicitar *v* request
solidaridad *nf* solidarity
sólido *adj* solid
solitario *adj* solitary; lonely
sollozar *v* sob
sollozo *nm* sob
solo *adv* alone, lonely
solomillo *nm* sirloin
soltar *v* release; loose
soltero *nm* single, bachelor
solterona *nf* spinster
soluble *adj* soluble
solución *nf* solution
solucionar *v* solve
solvente *adj* solvent
sombra *nf* shadow
sombrero *nm* hat
sombrío *adj* grim, somber
someter *v* subject, submit
somnoliento *adj* drowsy
sonar *v* ring, sound
soñar *v* dream
soneto *nm* sonnet
sonido *nm* sound
sonreír *v* smile
sonrisa *nf* smile
sonrojarse *v* blush
sopa *nf* soup
soplar *v* blow
soplo *nm* puff
sopor *nm* drowsiness
soportar *v* bear
soporte *nm* support
sorber *v* sip
sorbito *nm* sip
sordera *nf* deafness
sordo *adj* deaf

S

sorprendente *adj* amazing
sorprender *v* surprise
sorpresa *nf* surprise
sortear *v* dodge, raffle
sorteo *nm* raffle
sortija *nf* ring
sosegar *v* calm
soso *adj* tasteless
sospecha *nf* suspicion
sospechar *v* suspect
sospechoso *adj* suspect
sostener *v* hold, sustain
sotana *nf* cassock
sótano *nm* basement
su *adj* her, his
suave *adj* soft, smooth
suavidad *nf* softness
subasta *nf* auction
subastador *nm* auctioneer
subastar *v* auction
súbdito *nm* subject
subdividir *v* subdivide
subir *v* go up
súbitamente *adj* suddenly
sublevación *nf* uprising
sublevarse *v* revolt
sublime *adj* sublime
subrayar *v* underline
subscripción *nf* subscription
subsidio *nm* allowance
subsistir *v* subsist, survive
substituir *v* substitute
substraer *n* subtract
subterráneo *adj* underground
subtítulo *nm* subtitle
suburbio *nm* suburb
subvención *nf* subsidy
subvencionar *v* subsidize
subyugar *v* subdue

suceder *v* happen, occur
suceso *nm* event
sucesor *nm* successor
suciedad *nf* dirt
sucio *adj* dirty, messy
suculento *adj* succulent
sucumbir *v* succumb
sudar *v* perspire, sweat
sudario *nm* shroud
sudor *nm* sweat
Suecia *nf* Sweden
sueco *adj* Swedish
suegra *nf* mother-in-law
suegro *nm* father-in-law
suegros *nm* in-laws
suela *nf* sole
sueldo *nm* wage
suelo *nm* floor
suelto *adj* loose
sueño *nm* dream
suero *nm* serum
suerte *nf* luck, lot
suéter *nm* sweater
suficiente *adj* sufficient
sufragar *v* pay for
sufrimiento *y* suffering
sufrir *v* suffer
sugerencia *nf* suggestion
sugerir *v* suggest
sugestión *nf* suggestion
sugestivo *adj* suggestive
suicidio *nm* suicide
Suiza *adj* Switzerland
suizo *adj* Swiss
sujetapapeles *nm* paperclip
sujetar *v* fasten
suma *nf* addition, sum
sumar *v* add
sumario *nm* summary

S

sumergir *v* immerse
sumergirse *v* submerge
suministrar *v* supply
suministro *nm* provision
suministros *nm* supplies
sumir *adj* submerge, plunge
sumiso *v* submissive
suntuoso *adj* sumptuous
superar *v* overcome
superficial *adj* shallow
superficie *nf* surface
superfluo *adj* superfluous
superior *adj* superior; upper
superioridad *nf* superiority
supermercado *nm* supermarket
superpoblado *adj* overcrowded
superpotencia *nf* superpower
superstición *nf* superstition
supervisar *v* supervise
supervivencia *nf* survival
superviviente *nm* survivor
suplantar *v* replace
suplente *adj* substitute
súplica *nf* plea
suplicar *v* beg, plead
suplicio *nm* torture
suplir *v* replace
suponer *v* suppose
suponiendo *c* supposing
suposición *nf* assumption
supremo *adj* supreme
supresión *nf* suppression
suprimir *v* abolish
supuestamente *adv* allegedly
supuesto *adj* alleged
sur *nm* south
surco *nm* furrow
sureño *adj* southern
sureste *nm* southeast

surgir *v* emerge, spring
suroeste *nm* southwest
surtido *nm* assortment
surtir *v* provide
susceptible *adj* susceptible
suscitar *v* arouse
suscribir *v* subscribe
suspender *v* suspend, fail
suspensión *nf* suspension
suspicacia *nf* suspicion
suspicaz *adj* suspicious
suspirar *v* sigh, long for
suspiro *nm* sigh
sustancia *nf* substance
sustancial *adj* substantial
sustentar *v* sustain
sustento *nm* livelihood
sustituir *v* substitute
sustituto *nm* substitute
susto *nm* scare, fright
sustracción *nf* subtraction
sustraer *v* take away
susurrar *v* whisper
susurro *nm* whisper
sutil *adj* subtle
sutilmente *adv* subtly
suyo *pro* his, hers

T

tabaco *nm* tobacco
taberna *nf* tavern, bar
tabernáculo *nm* tabernacle
tabique *nm* partition, wall
tablero *nm* board

S
T

tableta *nf* tablet	**taponar** *v* block
taburete *nm* stool	**taquigrafía** *nf* shorthand
tacaño *adj* stingy	**taquilla** *nf* box office
tachar *v* cross out	**tarántula** *nf* tarantula
tachuela *nf* tack	**tararear** *v* hum
taciturno *adj* somber	**tardanza** *nf* delay
tacón *nm* heel	**tardar(se)** *v* be late
táctica *nf* tactics	**tarde** *adv* late, tardy
táctico *adj* tactical	**tarde** *nf* afternoon, evening
tacto *nm* tact, touch	**tardío** *adj* slow; late
tajada *nf* slice	**tarea** *nf* assignment, task
tajo *nm* cut	**tareas** *nf* homework
tal *adj* such	**tarifa** *nf* tariff, price
taladrar *v* drill	**tarima** *nf* platform
talante *nm* mood	**tarjeta** *nf* card
talento *nm* talent	**tarro** *nm* jar
talla *nf* size	**tarta** *nf* tart, pie
tallar *v* carve	**tartamudear** *v* stutter, stammer
taller *nm* workshop	**tartamudo** *adj* stutterer
tallo *nm* stalk, stem	**tasa** *nf* rate, tax
talón *nm* heel	**tasar** *v* value, assess
tamaño *nm* size	**tasca** *nf* cantina, bar
tambalearse *v* stagger, totter	**tatuaje** *nm* tattoo
también *adv* also, too	**taxi** *nm* cab
tambor *nm* drum	**taza** *nf* cup, mug
tampoco *adv* nor, neither	**tazón** *nm* bawl
tanda *nf* shift	**té** *nm* tea
tangente *nf* tangent	**teatro** *nm* theater
tangible *adj* tangible	**techo** *nm* ceiling
tañido *nm* peal	**tecla** *nf* key
tanque *nm* tank	**teclado** *nm* keyboard
tantear *v* test, feel	**técnica** *nf* technique
tanto *adj* so much	**técnico** *adj* technical
tapadera *nf* lid, cover, cap	**técnico** *nm* technician
tapar *v* plug, cover	**tecnología** *nf* technology
tapia *nf* wall, fence	**tedio** *nm* boredom
tapicería *nf* upholstery	**teja** *nf* tile
tapiz *nm* tapestry	**tejado** *nm* roof
tapón *nm* plug	**tejer** *v* knit, weave

T

tejido *nm* fabric; tissue
tela *nf* fabric, material
telaraña *nf* web
teléfono *nm* telephone
telegrama *nm* telegram
telepatía *nf* telepathy
telescopio *nm* telescope
televisar *v* televise
televisión *nf* television
telón *nm* curtain
tema *nm* theme, topic
temblar *v* tremble
temblor *nm* tremor
temer *v* fear, be afraid
temerario *adj* reckless
temeroso *adj* afraid, fearful
temible *adj* terrifying
temor *nm* fear
temperatura *nf* temperature
tempestad *nf* storm
tempestuoso *adj* stormy
templado *adj* warm
templo *nm* temple
temporada *nf* season
temporal *adj* temporary
temprano *adv* early
tenacidad *nf* tenacity
tenaz *adj* tenacious
tenazas *nf* pliers, tongs
tendedero *nm* clothes line
tendencia *nf* tendency
tendón *nm* tendon
tenebroso *adj* gloomy
tenedor *nm* fork
tener *v* have
tener antipatía *v* dislike
tener cuidado *v* beware
tener éxito *v* succeed
tener horror *v* dread

tener intención *v* intend
tener que *v* have to, must
tener sed *v* thirst
teniente *nm* lieutenant
teñir *v* dye
tenis *nm* tennis
tensar *v* tighten, flex
tensión *nf* tension
tenso *adj* uptight, tense
tentación *nf* temptation
tentáculo *nm* tentacle
tentador *adj* tempting
tentar *v* tempt
tenue *adj* tenuous, faint
teología *nf* theology
teólogo *nm* theologian
teoría *nf* theory
teórico *adj* theoretical
terapeutico *adj* therapeutic
terapia *nf* therapy
tercero *adj* third
terciar *v* mediate
terciopelo *nm* velvet
terco *adj* obstinate
tergiversar *v* distort
terminación *nf* completion
terminar *v* finish
terminología *nf* terminology
termita *nf* termite
termómetro *nm* thermometer
termostato *nm* thermostat
ternera *nf* veal
ternero *nm* calf
ternura *nf* tenderness
terquedad *nf* obstinacy
terraza *nf* terrace
terremoto *nm* earthquake
terrenal *adj* earthly
terreno *nm* land

T

terrestre *adj* terrestrial	**tímpano** *nm* eardrum
terrible *adj* terrible	**tinieblas** *nf* darkness
territorio *nm* territory	**tino** *nm* skill, aim
terror *nm* terror, fright	**tinta** *nf* ink
terrorismo *nm* terrorism	**tinte** *nm* dye
terrorista *nm* terrorist	**tinto** *adj* red
tesis *nf* thesis	**tintorería** *nf* dry cleaners
tesón *nm* tenacity	**típico** *adj* typical
tesorero *nm* treasurer	**tipo** *nm* guy, type
tesoro *nm* treasure	**tipográfico** *adj* printed
testamento *nm* testament	**tira** *nf* strip
testarudo *adj* stubborn	**tirada** *nf* run
testificar *v* testify	**tirador** *nm* marksman; knob
testigo *nm* witness	**tiranía** *nf* tyranny
testimonio *nm* testimony	**tirano** *nm* tyrant
tetera *nf* teapot	**tirante** *adj* tight
tétrico *adj* gloomy	**tirar** *v* pull, throw
texto *nm* text	**tiritar** *v* shiver
textura *nf* texture	**tiro** *nm* shot
tez *nf* complexion	**tirón** *nm* pull
tía *nf* aunt	**tiroteo** *nm* shooting, firing
tibio *adj* lukewarm	**títere** *nm* puppet
tiburón *nm* shark	**titubear** *v* hesitate
tiempo *nm* time; weather	**título** *nm* heading, title
tienda *nf* shop, store	**tiza** *nf* chalk, crayon
tierno *adj* tender	**toalla** *nf* towel
tierra *nf* earth, soil	**tobillo** *nm* ankle
tierra (en) *adv* ashore	**tocado** *adj* nutty
tieso *adj* stiff	**tocante** *pre* with regard to
tiesto *nm* flowerpot	**tocar** *v* touch; play
tifón *nm* typhoon	**tocino** *nm* bacon
tigre *nm* tiger	**todavía** *adv* still
tijeras *nf* scissors	**todos** *adj* all
timar *v* swindle, cheat	**toldo** *nm* awning
timbre *nm* bell	**tolerable** *adj* tolerable
timidez *nf* shyness	**tolerancia** *nf* tolerance
tímido *adj* bashful, shy	**tolerar** *v* tolerate
timo *nm* scam	**tomar** *v* take
timón *nm* helm, rudder	**tomar el pelo** *v* tease

T

tomar el sol *v* bask
tomar prestado *v* borrow
tomate *nm* tomato
tomo *nm* volume
tonel *nm* barrel
tonelada *nf* ton
tónica *nf* tonic
tono *nm* tone
tontería *nf* foolishness
tonto *adj* fool, silly
topar con *v* encounter
tope *nm* limit, end
topo *nm* mole
toque *nm* touch
torbellino *nm* whirlwind
torcer *v* twist
torcerse *v* sprain
torcido *adj* crooked, twisted
torear *v* avoid
torero *nm* bullfighter
tormenta *nf* storm
tormento *nm* torment
tornado *nm* twister
tornarse *v* become
torneo *nm* tournament
tornillo *nm* screw
toro *nm* bull
toronja *nf* grapefruit
torpe *adj* clumsy
torpedear *v* torpedo
torpedo *nm* torpedo
torpeza *nf* clumsiness
torre *nf* tower
torrente *nm* avalanche, stream
torreón *nm* turret
tórrido *adj* torrid
torta *nf* cake
tortículis *nf* stiff neck
tortilla *nf* omelet

tortuga *nf* tortoise, turtle
tortuoso *adj* winding
tortura *nf* torture
torturar *v* torture
tos *nf* cough
tosco *adj* rough
toser *v* cough
tostador *nm* toaster
tostar *v* toast
total *adj* total
totalidad *n* totality
totalitario *adj* totalitarian
totalmente *adv* entirely
tóxico *adj* toxic
toxina *nf* toxin
tozudo *adj* stubborn
trabajador *nm* worker
trabajar *v* work
trabajo *nm* job, work
trabajoso *adj* hard
tradición *nf* tradition
traducir *v* translate
traductor *nm* translator
traer *v* bring
traficante *nm* dealer
traficar *v* trade
tráfico *nm* traffic
tragar *v* swallow
tragedia *nf* tragedy
trágico *adj* tragic
trago *nm* drink
traición *nf* betrayal
traicionar *v* betray
traidor *nm* traitor
traje *nm* suit
trajectoria *nf* trajectory
tramar *v* plot
tramitar *v* transact
trámite *nm* formality, step

tramo *nm* section
trampa *nf* trap; scam
trampear *v* cheat
trampolín *nm* springboard
tramposo *adj* crooked
tramposo *nm* cheater
trance *nm* trance
tranquilidad *nf* tranquility
tranquilizar *v* reassure
transacción *nf* transaction
transbordar *v* transfer
transcender *v* transcend
transcribir *v* transcribe
transcurrir *v* lapse
transeunte *nm* passerby
transferir *v* transfer
transformar *v* transform
transformarse *v* become
tránsfuga *nm* defector
transfusión *nf* transfusion
transición *nf* transition
transigir *v* compromise
tránsito *nm* transit
transitorio *adj* transient
transladar *v* transfer
translado *nm* transfer
transmitir *v* transmit
transparente *adj* transparent
transplantar *v* transplant
transportar *v* transport
transtornado *adj* deranged
tranvía *nm* tram, trolley
trapear *v* mop
trapecio *nm* trapeze
trapo *nm* cloth, rag
tráquea *nf* windpipe
traquetear *v* rattle
trascender *v* transcend
trasero *adj* back, rear

traslado *nm* transfer
traslucir *v* reveal, show
trasnochar *v* stay up late
traspasar *v* go through
traspié *nm* stumble, trip
trasplantar *v* transplant
trasquilar *v* shear
trastero *nm* backroom
trastienda *nf* back room
trastornar *v* disrupt
trastorno *nm* disruption
trastos *nm* junk, old dishes
tratado *nm* treaty
tratamiento *nm* treatment
tratar *v* try; treat
tratar de *v* deal
trato *nm* treatment
traumático *adj* traumatic
traumatizar *v* traumatize
travesía *nf* crossing
travesura *nf* mischief, prank
travieso *adj* naughty
trayecto *nm* journey
trayectoria *nf* path, course
trazado *nm* layout
trazar *v* draw, outline
trébol *nm* shamrock
trece *adj* thirteen
trecho *nm* distance, stretch
tregua *nf* truce
treinta *adj* thirty
tremendo *adj* tremendous
tren *nm* train
trenza *nf* braid
trepar *v* climb
trepidar *v* shake, vibrate
tres *adj* three
treta *nf* trick
triángulo *nm* triangle

tribu _nf_ tribe
tribulación _nf_ tribulation
tribuna _nf_ grandstand
tribunal _nm_ tribunal
tributo _nm_ tribute; tax
trigo _nm_ wheat
trillar _v_ thresh
trimestral _adj_ quarterly
trimestre _nm_ trimester
trinchar _v_ carve
trinchera _nf_ trench
trineo _nm_ sleigh
tripa _nf_ belly, gut
triple _adj_ triple
triplicar _v_ triple
tripulación _nf_ crew
tripular _v_ man
triste _adj_ sad
tristeza _nf_ sadness
triturar _v_ grind; shred
triunfante _adj_ triumphant
triunfar _v_ win
triunfo _nm_ triumph
trivial _adj_ trivial
trivializar _v_ trivialize
triza _nf_ shred, fragment
trofeo _nm_ trophy
tromba _nf_ downpour
trombosis _nf_ thrombosis
trompeta _nf_ trumpet
tronco _nm_ log
trono _nm_ throne
tropa _nf_ troop
tropezar _v_ stumble, trip
tropezarse con _v_ bump into
tropezón _nm_ trip, stumble
tropical _adj_ tropical
trópico _nm_ tropic
tropiezo _nm_ setback; slip

trozo _nm_ bit, chunk, slice
trucha _nf_ trout
truco _nm_ gimmick, trick
trueno _nm_ thunder
tu _adj_ your
tú _pro_ you
tú mismo _pro_ yourself
tuberculosis _nf_ tuberculosis
tubería _nf_ pipe
tubo _nm_ pipe
tuerca _nf_ nut
tuerto _adj_ with one-eye
tufo _nm_ stench; vapor
tulipán _nm_ tulip
tullido _adj_ crippled
tumba _nf_ tomb
tumbar _v_ knock down
tumbarse _v_ lie down
tumor _nm_ tumor
tumulto _nm_ commotion, uproar
tumultuoso _adj_ tumultuous
tunante _adj_ rascal
túnel _nm_ tunnel
túnica _nf_ tunic
tupido _adj_ thick, dense
turba _nf_ crowd
turbar _v_ upset
turbio _adj_ murky
turbulencia _nf_ turbulence
turco _adj_ Turk
turismo _nm_ tourism
turista _nm_ tourist
turnarse _v_ take turns
turno _nm_ turn, shift
Turquía _nf_ Turkey
turrón _nm_ nougat
tutela _nf_ protection
tutor _nm_ tutor, guardian
tuyo _pro_ yours

U

uango *adj* baggy
ubicar *v* locate
ufano *adj* proud
ujier *nm* usher
úlcera *nf* ulcer
ulterior *adj* further
últimamente *adv* lately
ultimar *v* finalize
ultimatum *nm* ultimatum
último *adj* last
ultrajar *v* insult
ultraje *nm* outrage, insult
ultratumba *nf* next life
umbral *nm* threshold
un poco *adv* slightly
un(a) *art* a, an
uña *nf* nail, claw
uña del pie *nf* toenail
una vez *adv* once
una vez que *c* once
unánime *adj* unanimous
unanimidad *nf* unanimity
undécimo *adj* eleventh
ungir *v* anoint
unguento *nm* ointment
unicamente *adv* only
único *adj* sole, unique
unidad *nf* unit, unity
unificación *nf* unification
unificar *v* unify
uniformar *v* standardize
uniforme *nm* uniform
uniformidad *nf* uniformity
unilateral *adj* unilateral
unión *nf* union
unir *v* link, join

unirse *v* unite
universal *adj* universal
universidad *nf* university
universo *nm* universe
uno *adj* one
uno mismo *pro* oneself
untar *v* spread
urbano *adj* urban
urdir *v* plot
urgencia *nf* urgency
urgente *adj* urgent
urgir *v* be urgent
urna *nf* ballot box; urn
usar *v* use, wear
uso *nm* use, wear
usted *pro* you
usuario *nm* user
usura *nf* usury
usurpar *v* usurp, seize
utensilio *nm* utensil
útero *nm* uterus, womb
útil *adj* useful
utilidad *nf* usefulness
utilizar *v* use
uva *nf* grape

V

vaca *n* cow
vacación *nf* vacation
vacante *adj* vacant
vaciar *v* empty
vacilante *adj* hesitant
vacilar *v* hesitate
vacío *nm* emptiness

U
V

vacío *adj* empty
vacuna *nf* vaccine
vacunar *v* vaccinate
vagabundo *nm* vagrant
vagamente *adv* vaguely
vagancia *v* laziness
vagar *v* loiter, roam
vago *adj* vague, lazy
vagón *nm* wagon, carriage
vagoneta *nf* van
vaina *nf* green bean
vajilla *nf* dishes
vale *nm* voucher
valedero *adj* valid
valentía *nf* bravery
valer *v* be worth; be valid
valeroso *adj* brave
valerse *v* fend, manage
validar *v* validate
válido *adj* valid
valiente *adj* bold, brave
valija *nf* bag
valioso *adj* worthwhile
valla *nf* fence
valle *nm* valley
valor *nm* value, worth
valoración *nf* appraisal
valorar *v* appraise; appreciate
vals *nm* waltz
válvula *nf* valve
vampiro *nm* vampire
vanagloriarse *v* boast
vandalismo *nm* vandalism
vándalo *nm* vandal
vanguardia *nm* vanguard
vanidad *nf* vanity
vanidoso *adj* conceited
vano *adj* vain, futile
vano (en) *adv* in vain

vapor *nm* steam; vapor
vaporizar *v* vaporize
vaquero *nm* cowboy
vaqueros *nm* jeans
vara *nf* stick, rod
variable *adj* variable
variación *nf* variation
variado *adj* assorted, varied
variar *v* vary
variedad *nf* variety
varios *adj* several
varón *nm* male
varonil *adj* manly
vasallo *nm* vassal
vasija *nf* container
vaso *nm* glass
vasto *adj* huge, vast
vaticinar *v* predict
vaticinio *nm* prediction
vatio *nm* watt
veces *nf* times
veces (a) *adv* sometimes
vecindad *nf* neighborhood
vecino *nm* neighbor
vecino *adj* neighboring
vedar *v* ban
vegetación *nf* vegetation
vegetal *nm* vegetable
vegetales *nm* produce
vegetariano *adj* vegetarian
vehículo *nm* vehicle
veinte *adj* twenty
veintiuno *adj* twenty-one
vejación *nf* humiliation
vejez *nf* old age
vejiga *nf* bladder
vela *nf* candle, sail
velar *v* look after
velero *nm* sailboat

vello *nm* hair
velloso *adj* hairy
velo *nm* veil
velocidad *nf* velocity
veloz *adj* speedy, fast
vena *nf* vein
venado *nm* deer, elk
vencedor *nm* victor, winner
vencer *v* beat, defeat
venda *nf* bandage
vendar *v* dress, bandage
vendaval *nm* gale
vendedor *nm* seller
vender *v* sell
vendimia *nf* grape harvest
veneno *nm* poison, venom
venenoso *adj* poisonous
venerable *adj* venerable
venerar *v* venerate
venganza *nf* revenge
vengar *v* avenge
vengarse *v* take revenge
vengativo *adj* vindictive
venial *adj* venial
venida *nf* coming
venidero *adj* coming
venir *v* come
venta *nf* sale
ventaja *nf* advantage
ventajoso *adj* advantageous
ventana *nf* window
ventilación *nf* ventilation
ventilador *nm* fan
ventilar *v* air
ventisca *nf* blizzard
ventoso *adj* windy
ver *v* see
veraneante *nm* vacationer
verano *nm* summer

veraz *adj* truthful
verbena *nf* festival
verbo *nm* verb
verdad *nf* truth
verdadero *adj* actual, true
verde *adj* green
verdugo *nm* executioner
verdura *nf* vegetable
veredicto *nm* verdict
vergonzoso *adj* shameful; shy
verguenza *nf* shame
verificación *nf* verification
verificar *v* verify
verosímil *adj* plausible
verruga *nf* wart
versátil *adj* versatile
versión *nf* version
verso *nm* verse
vértebra *nf* vertebra
vertedero *nm* landfill
verter *v* spill, dump
vertiente *nf* slope
vértigo *nm* vertigo
vesícula *nf* gallbladder
vestíbulo *nm* lobby
vestido *nm* dress, garment
vestigio *nm* trace, vestige
vestir *v* wear, clothe
vestirse *v* get dressed
vetar *v* veto
veterano *adj* veteran
veterinario *nm* veterinarian
veto *nm* veto
vez *nf* time
vía *nf* rail
viable *adj* feasible
viaducto *nm* viaduct
viajar *v* travel
viaje *nm* tour, trip

V

viaje por mar *n* voyage
viajero *nm* traveler
víbora *nf* viper
vibración *nf* vibration
vibrante *adj* vibrant, exciting
vibrar *v* vibrate
viceversa *adv* vice versa
viciado *adj* corrupt
vicio *nm* vice
vicisitudes *adj* ups and downs
víctima *nf* victim
victoria *nf* victory
victorioso *adj* victorious
vid *nf* grapevine
vida *nf* life
vidrio *nm* glass
viejo *adj* old, outdated
viento *nm* wind
vientre *nm* womb
viernes *nm* Friday
viga *nf* beam
vigente *adj* valid
vigésimo *adj* twentieth
vigilancia *nf* surveillance
vigilar *v* watch
vigilia *nf* vigil
vigor *adv* vigor, energy
vil *adj* vile
villancico *nm* carol
villano *nm* villain
vilo *nm* suspense
viña *nf* vineyard
vinagre *nm* vinegar
vincular *v* link
vínculo *nm* bond
vino *nm* wine
violación *nf* rape
violador *nm* rapist
violar *v* rape

violencia *nf* violence
violento *adj* violent
violeta *nf* violet
violín *nm* violin
violinista *nm* violinist
viraje *nm* turn
virar *v* turn, swerve
virgen *adj* virgin
virginidad *nf* virginity
virilidad *nf* virility
virrey *nm* viceroy
virtual *adj* virtual
virtud *nf* virtue
virtuoso *adj* virtuous
viruela *nf* smallpox
virulento *adj* virulent
virus *nm* virus
visado *nm* visa
visibilidad *nf* visibility
visible *adj* visible
visión *nf* vision
visita *nf* visit
visitante *nm* visitor
visitar *v* visit
vislumbrar *v* glimpse
víspera *nf* eve
vista *nf* sight, view
vista general *n* overview
vistazo *v* glimpse, look
vistoso *adj* colorful
visual *adj* visual
visualizar *v* visualize
vital *adj* vital
vitalidad *nf* vitality
vitamina *nf* vitamin
vitorear *v* cheer
vituperar *v* insult
viuda *nf* widow
viudo *nm* widower

V

vivaz *adj* vivacious
víveres *nm* supplies
vivero *nm* nursery
vivienda *nf* dwelling, house
viviente *adj* living
vivir *v* live
vivo *adj* alive
vocabulario *nm* vocabulary
vocación *nf* vocation
vocal *nf* vowel
volante *nm* steering wheel
volar *v* fly
volátil *adj* volatile
volcán *nm* volcano
volcar *v* overturn
vólibol *nm* volleyball
voltaje *nm* voltage
voltear *v* turn over
voluble *adj* fickle
volumen *nm* volume
voluminoso *adj* bulky
voluntad *nf* will
voluntario *adj* volunteer
volver *v* return, go back
vomitar *v* vomit
vómito *nm* vomit
voraz *adj* voracious
vosotros *pro* you (pl)
votación *nf* ballot
votante *nm* voter
votar *v* vote
voto *nm* vote; vow
voz *nf* voice
vuelo *nm* flight
vuelta *nf* return, turn
vuelta (de) *adv* back
vuestro *adj* your (pl)
vulgar *adj* vulgar
vulgaridad *nf* vulgarity

vulnerable *adj* vulnerable
vulnerar *v* harm, hurt

y *c* and
ya *adv* already
ya que *c* since
yacer *v* lie
yacimiento *nm* deposit
yarda *nf* yard
yate *nm* yacht
yedra *nf* ivy
yegua *nf* mare
yema *nf* yolk; fingertip
yerno *nm* son-in-law
yeso *nm* plaster
yo *pro* I
yo mismo *pro* myself
yodo *nm* iodine
yugo *nm* yoke
yunque *nm* anvil

zafiro *nm* sapphire
zalamero *adj* flattering
zambullida *nf* plunge
zambullirse *v* dive
zanahoria *nf* carrot
zancudo *nm* mosquito
zanja *nf* ditch

V
W
X
Y
Z

zapatería *nf* shoe store
zapatero *nm* shoemaker
zapato *nm* shoe
zar *nm* czar
zarandear *v* shake
zarpa *nf* claw
zarzamora *nf* blackberry
zinc *nm* zinc
zona *nf* zone

zoología *nf* zoology
zoológico *nm* zoo
zorra *nf* fox
zumbar *v* buzz
zumbido *nm* buzz
zumo *nm* juice
zurcir *v* darn
zurdo *adj* left-handed
zurrar *v* spank

Z

Math
Subject Vocabulary
English-Spanish

Bilingual Dictionaries, Inc.

A

a+bi form: fórmula a+bi

AA triangle similarity: triángulos semejantes AA

AAA triangle similarity: triángulos semejantes AAA

AAS triangle congruence: triángulo congruente AAS

Abelian Group: Campo abeliano

about: aproximadamente

above: mayor a

above zero: sobre cero

abscissa: abscisa

absolute deviation: desviación absoluta

absolute maximum: máximo absoluto

absolute minimum: mínimo absoluto

absolute term: término absoluto

absolute value: valor absoluto

absolute value equation: ecuación de valor absoluto

absolute value function: función de valor absoluto

absolute value inequality: desigualdad de valor absoluto

absolute value of a number: valor absoluto de un número

accompanying diagram: diagrama acompañante

accumulation: acumulación

accumulator: acumulador

accurately label work: identificar (identifique) claramente los pasos del trabajo

act it out: hacer (haga) una representación del problema

acute angle: ángulo agudo

acute triangle: triángulo acutángulo o "triángulo agudó"

add: sumar (sume)

addend: sumando

addition: suma, adición

addition as a binary operation: suma como operación binaria

addition fact: operación aditiva con números elementales

addition property of zero: propiedad aditiva de cero

addition sentence: ecuación de suma

addition sign: signo de suma

additive identity: identidad aditiva

additive inverse: inverso aditivo

additive operation: operación aditiva

additive property of equality: propiedad aditiva de la igualdad

adjacency: adyacencia

adjacent angles: ángulos adyacentes

adjacent side of a triangle: lado adyacente de un triángulo

adjacent sides: lados adyacentes

adjoint: adjunto

algebra: álgebra

algebra of logic: álgebra de lógica

algebraic: algebraico

algebraic analysis: análisis algebraico

algebraic application: aplicación algebraica

algebraic curve: curva algebraica

algebraic equation: ecuación algebraica

algebraic expression: expresión algebraica

algebraic form: forma algebraica

algebraic fraction: fracción algebraica

algebraic function: función algebraica

algebraic identity: identidad algebraica

algebraic inequalities: desigualdades algebraicas

algebraic language: lenguaje algebraico

algebraic manipulation: manipulación algebraica

algebraic pattern: patrón algebraico

algebraic problem: problema algebraico

algebraic product: producto algebraico

algebraic relationship: relación algebraica

algebraic representation: representación algebraica

algebraic solution: solución algebraica

algebraic system: sistema algebraico

algebraically: algebraicamente

algebraically equivalent: algebraicamente equivalente

algebraically independent: algebraicamente independiente

algebraically independent basis: base algebraicamente independiente

algorithm: algoritmo

alike: semejante, idéntica

all possible outcomes: todos los posibles resultados

all together: todo(s) junto(s) o toda(s) junta(s)

alternate angle: ángulo alterno

alternate approach: enfoque alternativo (aproximación alternativa)

alternate exterior angles: ángulos alternos externos

alternate form: forma alterna

alternate interior angle: ángulo alterno interno

alternate permutation: permutación alterna

alternate solution: solución alterna

alternating series: series alternas

ambiguous case: caso ambigüo

amplification: amplificación

analog clock: reloj analógico

analytic: analítico

analytical geometry: geometría analítica

analytical proof: prueba analítica

angle (∠): ángulo (∠)

angle addition postulate: postulado de la suma de los ángulos

angle bisector: bisectriz de un ángulo

angle in a circular segment: ángulo en un segmento circular

angle in standard position: ángulo en posición normal

angle measure: medida de ángulos

angle measure preserved: medida de ángulo conservada

angle of a circular segment: ángulo de un segmento circular

angle of circumference: ángulo de la circunferencia

angle of contingence: ángulo de contingencia

angle of depression: ángulo de depresión

angle of elevation: ángulo de elevación

angle of intersection: ángulo de intersección

angle of rotation: ángulo de rotación

angle pairs: pares de ángulos

angular: angular

angular bisector: bisector angular

angular orientation: orientación angular

angular point: punto angular

annexing zeros to: agregando ceros a

answer: respuesta

ante meridian (a.m.): ante merídiem o antemeridiano (a.m.)

antilogarithm: antilogaritmo

apothem: apotema

apply a variety of strategies: aplicar (aplique) diversas estrategias

approach: enfoque, método

appropriate: según corresponda

appropriate mathematical language: lenguaje matemático apropiado

appropriate mathematical terms: términos matemáticos adecuados

appropriate unit: unidad correspondiente

appropriateness: carácter apropiado

approximability: aproximabilidad

approximate calculation: cálculo aproximado

approximate construction: construcción aproximado

approximate number: número aproximado

approximate rational value: valor racional aproximado

approximate solution: solución aproximada

approximate square root: raíz cuadrada aproximada

approximate value: valor aproximado

approximation: aproximación

approximation of 1st degree: aproximación de primer grado

approximation of root: aproximación de raíz

approximation on the average: aproximación al promedio

arbitrary constant: constante arbitraria

arc length: longitud de arco

arc measure: medida de arcos

arc subtended by a chord: arco sujeto por una cuerda

arccosine: arcocoseno

arcsine: arcoseno

arctangent: arcotangente

area of a circle: área de un círculo

area of a parallelogram using SAS: área de un paralelogramo usando los lados y el ángulo SAS

area of a rectangle: área de un rectángulo

area of a triangle using SAS: área de un triángulo usando los lados y el ángulo SAS

argument conjecture: argumentar (argumente) el contraejemplo de una

arithmetic (numeric) expression: expresión aritmética (numérica)

arithmetic expression: expresión aritmética

arithmetic fact: operación aritmética con números elementales o hecho aritmético

arithmetic fraction: fracción aritmética

arithmetic mean: medida aritmética

arithmetic operation: operación aritmética

arithmetic sequence: secuencia aritmética

arithmetic series: serie aritmética

arithmetic statement: frase aritmética

arithmetically: aritméticamente

around in a full rotation: una vuelta completa

array: matriz, ordenación, conjunto

as long as: siempre y cuando

ASA triangle congruence: triángulo congruente ASA

ascending order: orden ascendente

assignment: asignación

associative: asociativa

associative law: ley asociativa

associative property: propiedad asociativa

associative property of addition: propiedad asociativa de la suma

associative property of multiplication: propiedad asociativa de la multiplicación

associativity: asociabilidad

assumed mean: valor medio asumido

assumption average: asunción promedio

asymmetric relation: relación asimétrica

asymmetrical: asimétrica

asymptote: asíntota

at least: valor mínimo

at most: valor máximo

auxiliary line: línea auxiliar

average error: error promedio

axes: ejes

axis of a conic: eje de una sección cónica

axis of a cylinder: eje de un cilindro

A
B

axis of abscissas: eje de las abcisas

axis of imaginaries: eje imaginario

axis of ordinates: eje de ordenadas

axis of quadric: eje cuádrico

axis of reals: eje real

axis of rotation: eje de rotación

axis of symmetry: eje de simetría

axis of symmetry of a parabola: eje de simetría de una parábola

bar graph: gráfico de barras

barycentric coordinates: coordenadas baricéntricas

base angle: ángulo de la base

base numeral: valor numérico base

base of a 2-dimensional shape: base de una figura de 2 dimensiones o bidimensional

base of a 3-dimensional figure: base de una figura de 3 dimensiones o tridimensional

base of a logarithmic function: base de una función logarítmica

base of a parallelogram: base de un paralelogramo

base of a polygon: base de un polígono

base of a polyhedron: base de un poliedro

base of a rectangle: base de un rectángulo

base of a triangle: base de un triángulo

base of an exponential function: base de una función exponencial

base of cylinder: base del cilindro

base of figure: base de una figura

base of logarithm: base de un logaritmo

base of power: base de una potencia

base ten number system: sistema de numeración decimal

basic cosine curve: curva básica del coseno

basic operation: operación básica

be in proportion: estar en proporción

bell-shaped curve: curva en forma de campana

below zero: bajo cero

Bernoulli experiment: experimento de Bernoulli

best approximation: mejor aproximación

betweeness: propiedad de estar entre dos cosas

biased: parcial, prejuiciado

biased estimator: estimador parcial

biased sample: muestra parcial

biased statistic: estadística parcial

bicondition statement: declaración bicondicional

biconditional: bicondicional

biconditional binary operation: operación binaria bicondicional

bigger: mayor que

biggest: mayor

billions (place value): unidad de billón

bimodal: bimodal

binary arithmetic: aritmética binaria

binary digit: dígito binario

binary form: forma binaria

binary number: número binario

binary numeric system: sistema numérico binario

binary operation: operación binaria

binomial: binomio

binomial curve: curva binómica

binomial expansion: expansión binomial

binomial expression: expresión binómica

binomial probability formula: fórmula de probabilidad binomial

binomial theorem: Teorema de Binomio

bisect: bisecar (biseque) o dividir (divida) en dos partes iguales

bisecting each other: dividir una de otra

bisector: bisectriz

bisector of a segment: bisectriz de un segmento

bivariate: bivariado

bivariate data: datos bivariados

body or rotation: elemento de rotación

bound: unir, ligar

box and whisker plot: diagrama de caja y línea

braces: llaves

brackets: corchetes, paréntesis

c

calculate: calcular (calcule)

calculate distance: calcular (calcule) la distancia

calculate unit price: calcular (calcule) el precio por unidad

calculate volume: calcular (calcule) el volumen

calculated probability: probabilidad calculada

cancellation law: ley de cancelación

cancellation law of addition: ley de cancelación de la suma

cancellation law of multiplication: ley de cancelación de la multiplicación

cancellation method: método de cancelación

cardinal numbers (1-10): números cardinales (del 1 al 10)

Cartesian coordinate system: sistema de coordenadas cartesianas

Cartesian plane: plano cartesiano

categorize: clasificar (clasifique)

causation: causalidad

Celsius: grado Celsius

center-radius equation of a circle: ecuación centro-radio de un círculo

center of a circle: centro de un círculo

center of a conic: centro de una sección cónica

center of a dilation: centro de dilatación

center of a regular polygon: centro de un polígono regular

center of a rotation: centro de rotación

center of a sphere: centro de una esfera

center of gravity: centro de gravedad

center of symmetry: centro de simetría

centiliter (cl): centilitro

central angle: ángulo central

central angle of a regular polygon: ángulo central de un polígono regular

central conic: sección cónica central

central symmetry: simetría central

central tendency: tendencia central

centroid: centroide o baricentro

centroid of triangle: centroide de un triángulo

certain case: caso cierto

certain event: evento cierto

Chain Rule: Regla de Concatenación

championship: campeonato

chance: posibilidad

characteristic and mantissa of charge: característica y mantisa de una carga

chart: tabla, gráfico

checked by factoring: comprobado por factorización

chord at contact: cuerda de contacto

chord of curvature: cuerda de curvatura

C

circle circumscribed about a polygon: círculo circunscrito a un polígono

circle graph: gráfico circular o de pastel

circle inscribed in a triangle: círculo inscrito en un polígono

circular arc: arco circular

circular cone: cono circular

circular curve: curva circular

circular cylinder: cilindro circular

circular function: función circular

circular region: región circular

circumcenter: circuncentro

circumcircle: circuncírculo

circumference: circunferencia

circumference of a circle: circunferencia de un círculo

circumscribe: circunscribir

circumscribed about: circunscrito a

circumscribed circle: círculo circunscrito

circumscribed cone: cono circunscrito

circumscribed figure: figura circunscrita

circumscribed polygon: polígono circunscrito

circumscribed polyhedron: poliedro circunscrito

circumscribed sphere: esfera circunscrita

circumscribed triangle: triángulo circunscrito

clarifying questions: preguntas aclaratorias

class interval: intervalo de clase

classification of triangles: clasificación de triángulos

classifying angle by quadrant: clasificando ángulos de acurdo al cuadrante

clock system: sistema de reloj

clockwise: en sentido de las manecillas del reloj

closed arc: arco cerrado

closed curve: curva cerrada

closed figure: figura cerrada

closed sentence: frase cerrada

closed system: sistema cerrado

closure property: propiedad de encierro

coefficient of a product: coeficiente de un producto

coherent whole: conjunto coherente

collection of data: colección de información

collinear: colineal

collinear points: puntos colineales

collinearity preserved: colinealidad preservada

combination with repetion: combinación con repetición

combination without repitition: combinación sin repetición

combine like radicals: combinar los términos semejantes

combine like terms: combinar términos semejantes

combined method: método combinado

common base: base común

common chord: cuerda común

common denominator: denominador común

common difference: diferencia común

common divisor: divisor común

common external tangent: tangente externa común

common factor: factor común

common internal tangent: tangente interna común

common logarithm: logaritmo común

common monomial factor: factor común del monomio

common multiple: múltiplo común

common perpendicular: perpendicular común

common ratio: razón común

common root: raíz común

common side: lado común

common tangent: tangente común

common vertex: vértice común

commutation relation: relación de conmutación

commutative: conmutativo

commutative group: grupo conmutativo

commutative law: ley conmutativa

commutative property: propiedad conmutativa

commutative property of addition: propiedad conmutativa de la suma

commutative property of multiplication: propiedad conmutativa de la multiplicación

commutativity: conmutatividad

compare numbers: comparar números

compare strategies: comparar (compare) estrategias

compare unit prices: comparar (compare) precios por unidad

compatible numbers: números compatibles •

complement of a set: complemento de un conjunto

complement of a subset: complemento de un subconjunto

complementary angles: ángulos complementarios

complementary divisor: divisor complementario

complementary events: eventos complementarios

complementary function: función complementaria

complete carry: transporte total

complete system: sistema completo

completely convex function: función completamente convexa

completely flat surface: superficie totalmente plana

completing the square: completando el cuadrado

complex closed curve: curva compleja cerrada

complex conjugate: conjugado complejo

complex curve: curva compleja

complex fraction: fracción compleja

complex fractional expressions: expresiones fraccionales complejas

complex number: número complejo

complex plane: plano complejo

complex rational expression: expresión racional compleja

complex root: raíz compleja

compose a number: componer (componga) un número

compose shapes: componer (componga) figuras geométricas

composite number: número compuesto

composition of functions: composición de funciones

composition of transformations: composición de las transformaciones

compound: número complejo

compound event: evento compuesto

compound interest: interés compuesto

compound locus: lugar geometrico compuesto

compound sentence: oración compuesta

compound statement: enunciado compuesto

comprehension: comprensión

computation: cálculo

concave: cóncavo

concave angle: ángulo cóncavo

concave curve: curva cóncava

concave polygon: polígono cóncavo

concave polyhedron: poliedro cóncavo

concavity: concavidad

concentric circles: círculos concéntricos

concrete representations: representaciones concretas

concurrence: concurrencia

concurrent altitudes of a triangle: alturas coexistentes de un triángulo

concurrent angle of a triangle: ángulo coexistente de un triángulo

concurrent lines: rectas concurrentes

concurrent planes: planos coexistentes

concyclic: concíclico

concyclic points: puntos concíclicos

conditional equality: igualdad condicional

conditional equation: ecuación condicional

conditional inequality: desigualdad condicional

conditional probability: probabilidad condicional

conditional sentence: oración condicional

conditional statement: enunciado condicional

cone: cono

congruence: congruencia

congruence symbol: símbolo de congruencia

congruent: congruente

congruent angles: ángulos congruentes

congruent arcs: arcos congruentes

congruent circles: círculos congruentes

congruent figures: figuras congruentes

congruent line segments: segmentos congruentes

congruent polygons: polígonos congruentes

congruent sides: lados congruentes

congruent triangles: triángulos congruentes

conic sections: secciones cónicas

conic without center: sección sin centro

conjecture: conjetura (formule una conjetura), conjeturar

conjugacy: conjugación

conjugate axes: ejes conjugados

conjugate complex number: números complejos conjugados

conjugate imaginary lines: líneas imaginarias conjugadas

conjugate pairs: pares conjugados

conjugate roots: raíces conjugadas

conjugate tangents: tangentes conjugadas

consecant ratio: razón cosecante

consecutive angles: ángulos consecutivos

consecutive even integers: enteros pares consecutivos

consecutive integers: números enteros consecutivos

consecutive intervals: intervalos consecutivos

consecutive odd integers: enteros impares consecutivos

consecutive sides: lados consecutivos

consecutive vertices: vértices consecutivos

consistence: coherencia

consistence of equations: consistencia de ecuaciones

consistency of axioms: consistencia de axiomas

consistent equations: ecuaciones consistentes

constant coefficient: coeficiente constante

constant factor: factor constante

constant function: función constante

constant of dilation: constante de dilatación

constant of proportionality: constante de proporcionalidad

constant term: término constante

continued ration: razón continua

contradictory: contradictorio

contradictory propositions: propuestas contradictorias

contrapositive: contrapositivo

contrapositive of a statement: contrapositivo (o contrarrecíproco) de un enunciado

converse of a statement: recíproco de un enunciado, oración conversa

converse theorem: teorema converso

conversion fact: factor de conversión

convert capacity within a given system: convertir medidas de capacidad dentro de un sistema dado

convert mass within a given system: convertir medidas de masa dentro de un sistema dado

convert measures: convertir las medidas

convert money: convertir divisas o dinero

convert volume within a given system: convertir medidas de volumen dentro de un sistema dado

convert within a given system: convertir dentro de un sistema dado

convex: convexo

convex body: elemento convexo

convex polygon: polígono convexo

convexity: convexidad

coordinate axes: ejes de coordenadas

coordinate curve: curva analítica

coordinate geometry: geometría de coordenadas

coordinate grid: ejes o cuadrilla de coordenadas o coordenadas cartesianas

coordinate plane: plano de coordenadas

coordinate transformation: transformación de coordinadas

coplanar: coplanar

coplanar lines: líneas coplanares

coplanar points: puntos coplanares

correct to the nearest interger: corregir hasta el entero más cercana

correct to the nearest tenth: corregir hasta la décima más cercana

correlation: correlación

correlation coefficient: coeficiente de correlación

correspondence: correspondencia

corresponding angle: ángulo correspondiente

corresponding parts: partes correspondientes

corresponding side: lado correspondiente

corresponding value: el valor correspondiente

cosecant: cosecante

cosecant function: función cosecante

cosine: coseno

cosine function: función cosecante

cosine law: ley del coseno

cosine ratio: razón del coseno

cotangent: cotangente

coterminal angles: ángulos coterminales

count backwards: contar en forma regresiva

count by (n's): contar de "n" en "n"

count on: cuenta progresiva

counterclockwise: en sentido contrario a las manecillas del reloj

counterexample: contraejemplo

counting (natural) numbers: contar números (naturales)

counting number: número cardinal

counting principle: principio de conteo

counting techniques: técnicas de conteo

cross product: producto transversal

cross product of 2 vectors: producto transversal de dos vectores

cross section: sección transversal

cube both sides: elevar ambos lados al cubo

cube root : raíz cúbica

cube root of a number: raíz cúbica de un número

cubic centimeter (cm3): centímetro cúbico

cubic equation: ecuación cúbica

cubic foot: pie cúbico

cubic inch: pulgada cúbica

cubic meter: metro cúbico

cubic number: número cúbico

cubic unit: unidad cúbica

cumulative: acumulativo

cumulative frequency distribution table: tabla de distribución de frecuencias

cumulative frequency histogram: histograma de frecuencias acumuladas

cumulative relative frequency: frecuencia relativa acumulativa

currency symbols: símbolos monetarios

curved line: línea curva

customary measurement system: sistema anglosajón de medidas

customary units of capacity: unidades de capacidad anglosajonas

customary units of mass: unidades de masa anglosajonas

customary units of measure: unidades de medida anglosajonas

cyclic: cíclico

cyclic order: orden cíclico

cyclic vertices of quadrilateral: vértices cíclicos de un cuadrilátero

cylinder surface: superficie cilíndrica

D

dartboard: tabla de dardos

dashed line: línea entrecortada

data frequency table: tabla de frecuencia de datos

daylight: luz diurna

De Morgan's law: ley de De Morgan

decagon: decágono

deciliter: decilitro

decimal fraction: fracción decimal

decimal number: número decimal

decimal number system: sistema numérico decimal

decimal part: parte decimal

decimal place: lugar decimal

decimal point: punto o coma decimal

decimeter: decímetro

deck of cards: juego de cartas

decode: decodificar, decodifique

decoding: decodificar (decodifique)

decompose a number: descomponer (descomponga) un número

decompose shapes: descomponer (descomponga) las figuras geométricas

decrease: diferencia, descender, disminuir

decreasing function: función decreciente

decreasing sequence: secuencia decreciente

deduced statement: afirmación deducida

deductive: deductivo

deductive method: método deductivo

deductive proof: prueba deductiva

deductive reasoning: razonamiento deductivo

defined terms: términos definidos

degenerative curve: curva degenerativa

degree measure: medida del grado de ángulos

degree measure of an angle: medida en grados de un ángulo

degree of a angle: grado de un ángulo

degree of a monomial: grado de un monomio

degree of a polynomial: grado de un polinomio

degree of an equation: grado de una ecuación

denoted by: denotado por

dense domain: dominio denso

dependent equation: ecuaciones dependientes

dependent events: eventos dependientes

dependent linear equations: ecuaciones lineales dependientes

derangement: degradación

derivation: derivación

derived equation: ecuación derivada

descending order: orden descendente

designated value: valor designado

designation: designación

detachment law: ley del desprendimiento

develop formulas: desarrollar (desarrolle) fórmulas

diagonal matrix: matriz diagonal

diagonalization of a matrix: diagonalización de una matriz

diagonals: diagonales

diameter of a circle: diámetro de un círculo

diameter of sphere: diagrama

dichotomy: dicotomía

difference of two perfect squares: diferencia de dos cuadrados perfectos

difference of two squares: diferencia de dos cuadrados

differences: diferencias

differentiate: diferenciar (diferencie)

differnce set: conjunto de diferencia

digital: digital

digital clock: reloj digital

digits: dígitos

dihedral angle: ángulo diedro

dilate: dilatar

dilation: dilatación

dimensionality: dimensionalidad

dimensions of a rectangle: dimensiones de un rectángulo

direct isometry: isometría directa

direct measurement: medida directa

direct proof: prueba directa

direct proportion: proporción directa

direct solution: solución directa

direct transformation: transformación directa

direct variation: variación directa

directed measure: medida dirigida

directrix: directriz

directrix of a parabola: directriz de una parábola

discriminant: discriminante

disjoint: desunir

disjoint elements: elementos disyuntivos

disjoint events: eventos desligados

disjoint sets: conjuntos disyuntivos

distance between a point and a line: distancia entre un punto y una recta

distance between two parallel lines: distancia entre dos rectas paralelas

distance between two points: distancia entre dos puntos

distance formula: fórmula de la distancia

distance from a fixed point: distancia desde un punto fijo

distance perserved: distancia preservada

distance postulate: postulado de la distancia

distinct arrangements: ordenamientos

distinct points: puntos diferentes

distinguishable arrangements: ordenamientos diferenciales

distributive property: propiedad distributiva

distributive property of multiplication over addition: propiedad distributiva de la multiplicación respecto a la suma

distributivity: distributividad

distsinct roots: raíces diferentes

divide A by B: dividir A entre B

divide in half: dividir por la mitad

divide into n evenly: dividir en n partes iguales

divisibility: divisibilidad

divisibility test: prueba de divisibilidad

divisible by: divisible por

division algorithm: algoritmo de la división

division of a line segment: división de un segmento de recta

divisor: divisor

dodecahedron: dodecaedro

domain: dominio

domain of function: dominio de una función

domino: dominó

dot product: producto de punto

dotted line: línea de puntos

double and half angle formulas for trigonometric functions: fórmulas de medio ángulo y doble para funciones trigonométricas

double bar graph: gráfico de barras dobles

double integral: integral doble

double line graphs: gráficos de líneas dobles

double roots: raíz dobles

doubles minus one: dobles menos uno

doubles plus one: dobles más uno

doubling: duplicar, doblar o multiplicar por 2

draw a graph: dibujar (dibuje) un gráfico

draw a picture: dibujar (dibuje) una imagen

draw at random: elegir al azar

draw conclusions: sacar (saque) conclusiones

draw the figure: dibujar la figura

draw the graph of: dibujar el gráfico de

drawings: dibujos

dynamic geometry software: programa informático de geometría dinámica

D E

E

e: e (símbolo del número trascendente 2,7182, que es la base de los logaritmos neperianos)

elapsed time: tiempo transcurrido

element: elemento

element in a set: elemento de un conjunto

elicit: obtener (obtenga)

elimination by substitution: eliminación por sustitución

elimination of irrelevant factors: eliminación de factores irrelevantes

elimination of unknowns: eliminación de variables desconocidas

ellipse: elipse

empirical probability: probabilidad empírica

empirical study: estudio empírico

empty set: conjunto vacío

enumeration: enumeración

equal chance: igual suerte

equal to (=): igual a (=)

equality postulates: postulados de la igualdad

equally likely: posiblemente igual

equally spaced points: puntos igualmente espaciados

equation containing parentheses: ecuación que contiene paréntesis

equation of a line: ecuación de la recta

equiangular: equiangular

equiangular polygon: polígono equiangular

equiangular triangle: triángulo equiangular

equidistance: equidistancia

equidistant: equidistante

equidistant lines: líneas equidistantes

equidistant marks: puntos equidistantes

equilateral polygon: polígono equilátero

equilateral triangle: triángulo equilátero

equivalence: equivalencia

equivalence relation: relación de equivalencia

equivalent customary units of capacity: unidades de capacidad y tablas de equivalencia

equivalent decimals: decimales equivalentes

equivalent equation: ecuación equivalente

equivalent expression: expresión equivalente

equivalent forms: formas equivalentes

equivalent fractions: fracciones equivalentes

equivalent inequality: desigualdad equivalente

equivalent numerical expressions: expresiones numéricas equivalentes

equivalent radicals: radicales equivalentes

equivalent ratios: razones equivalentes

equivalent sentence: oración equivalente

equivalent sets: conjuntos equivalentes

estimation: cálculo aproximado o estimacion

estimation strategies: estrategias para calcular aproximadamente

Euclidean geometry: geometría euclidiana

Euclidean Parallel Postulate: quinto postulado de Euclides

evaluate an algebraic expression: evaluar una expresión algebraica

evaluate conjectures: evaluar (evalúe) conjeturas

evaluate efficiency: evaluar (evalúe) la eficiencia

even: par

even integer: entero par

even number: número par

even whole number: número entero par

evenly distributed: uniformemente distribuido

event that is certain: un evento seguro

everywhere dense: denso en todas sus partes

exact answer: respuesta exacta

exact value: valor exacto

exactly: exactamente

excenter: excéntrico

exchange rate table: tabla de tasas de cambio

existential quantifier: cuantificador existencial

expand a binomial: expandir un binomio

expanded form: forma expandida

expanded notation: notación ampliada

expanded numeral expectation: expectativa numérica ampliada

expansion of binomial: expansión de un binomio

expenses: gastos

experimental design: diseño experimental

experimental probability: probabilidad experimental

experimental results: resultados experimentales

explain mathematical relationships: explicar (explique las) relaciones matemáticas

explicit definition: definición explícita

explore mathematical relationships: explorar (explore las) relaciones matemáticas

exponent: exponente

exponential: exponencial

exponential expression: expresión exponencial

exponential form: forma exponencial

exponential function: función exponencial

exponential growth: crecimiento exponencial

exponential growth and decay: crecimiento y decrecimiento exponencial

exponential notation: notación exponencial

express in simplest radical form: expresar en forma radical simple

express in terms of: expresar en términos de

extend a pattern: extender o continuar un patrón

extend indefinitely: extender indefinidamente

extend models: extender o continuar modelos

extend the number line: extender la línea numérica

extended fact: operación extendida de números elementales

exterior angle: ángulo externo

exterior angle of a triangle: ángulo externo de un triángulo

exterior bisector: bisectriz externo

exterior region: región externa

exterior region of a circle: región exterior de un círculo

external point: punto externo

external secant segment: segmento secante externo

external tangent: tangente externa

externally tangent circles: círculos externamente tangentes

extraction of root: extracción de raíz

extraneous root: raíz extraña

extrapolate: extrapolar (extrapole)

extrapolation method: método de extrapolación

extreme and mean ratio: razón extrema y razón media

extremes (of a proportion): extremos (de una proporción)

extremum: extremo

E
F

F

face of a polyhedron: cara de un poliedro

faces and bases: lados y bases

fact family (related facts): operaciones con números elementales relacionados (familias)

factor a number: factorizar un número

factor a polynomial: factorizar un polinomio

factor a trinomial: factorizar un trinomio

factor completely: factorizar completamente

factor tree: ramificaciones de los factores

factorial: factorial

factorial notation: notación factorial

factoring: descomponer en factores

factorization: factorización

factorization method: método de factorización

Fahrenheit: grado Fahrenheit

fair and unbiased object: objeto justo e imparcial

fair share: porción debida

false : falso

favorable event: evento favorable

favorable outcomes: resultados favorables

fewer than: menor que o menor a

Fibonacci sequence: sucesión de Fibonacci

field theorem: teorema del campo

find the circumference of a circle: encontrar la circunferencia de un círculo

find the solution set: encontrar el sistema de solución

find the value of: encontrar el valor de

finite: finito

finite decimal: decimal finito

finite element: elemento finito

finite extension: extensión finita

finite field: campo finito

finite part: parte finita

finite sample space: espacio muestral finito

finite set: conjunto finito

finite solution: solución finita

finiteness: finito

first-degree equation: ecuación de primer grado

first-degree equation in one: ecuación de primer grado con una variable

first-degree inequality: desigualdad de primer grado

first-degree open sentence in one variable: oración abierta de primer grado con una variable

first-quadrant angle: primero-ángulo del cuadrante o ángulo del primer cuadrante

first quartile: primera cuartilla

five statistical summary: resumen estadístico de cinco datos

fixed angle: ángulo fijo

fixed distance: distancia fija

fixed line: línea fija

fixed point: punto fijo

fixed value: valor fijo

flip (reflection): girar sobre su eje

flow chart: organigrama o diagrama de flujo

focus of a parabola: enfoque de una parábola

focus point: punto focal

foot of an altitude: pie de una altitud

forces: fuerzas

formal and informal proofs: Pruebas formales e informales

formal proof: prueba formal

formed by a transversal: formado por una transversal

formulate: formular (formule)

formulate conclusions from graphs: sacar (saque) conclusiones a partir de gráficos

formulate mathematical questions : formular (formule) preguntas matemáticas

formulate predictions from graphs: hacer predicciones a partir de gráficos

four-digit number: número de cuatro dígitos

four-sided figure: figura de cuatro lados

fourth-quadrant angle: ángulo del cuarto cuadrante

fourths: cuartos

fractional equation: ecuación fraccionaria

fractional exponent: exponente fraccional

fractional expression: expresión fraccional

fractional number: número fraccional

fractional part: parte fraccionaria

fractional radicand: radical fraccional

fractionation: fraccionación o fraccionamiento

frequency (of a data set): frecuencia (de un conjunto de datos)

frequency (of a periodic function): frecuencia (de una función periódica)

 razó

frequency curve: curva de la frecuencia

frequency diagram: diagrama de frecuencia

frequency distribution: distribución de frecuencias

frequency distribution table: tabla de distribución de frecuencias

frequency polygon: polígono de la frecuencia

frequency table: tabla de frecuencia

front-end estimation: cálculo aproximado a partir de los primeros dígitos

function notation: notación de función

function notation for transformations: notación funcional de transformaciones

function rule: regla de función

fundamental counting principle: principio de conteo

fundamental formula: fórmula básica

fundamental relationship: relación básica

fundamental theorem: teorema básico

G

general associative property: propiedad general asociativa

general case: caso general

general commutative property: propiedad general conmutativa

general expression: expresión general

generate solutions: generar soluciones

geometric: geométrico

geometric construction: construcción geométrica

geometric fact: hecho geométrico

geometric figure: figura geométrica

geometric mean: media geométrica

geometric pattern: patrón geométrico

geometric relationships: relaciones geométricas

geometric representation of the circular function: representación geométrica de la función circular

geometric sequence: secuencia geométrica

geometric series: serie geométrica

geometric shape: forma geométrica

geometric solid: sólido geométrico

geometric statement: declaración geométrica

geometry of a circle: geometría del círculo

glide reflection: reflexión de deslizamiento

golden ratio: razón áurea o dorada

golden rectangle: rectángulo áureo o dorado

gram (g): gramo (gr)

graph: gráfico

graph a quadratic equation: graficar una ecuación cuadrática

graph an equation: graficar una ecuación

graph an inequality: graficar una desigualdad

graph of a relation: gráfico de una relación

graph of an equation in 2 variables: gráfico de una ecuación en dos variables

graph of linear open sentence in two variables: gráfico de una oración lineal abierta en dos variables

graph the set: graficar en conjunto

graphic calculator: calculadora gráfica

graphic solution: solución gráfico

graphical method: método gráfico

graphical representation: representación gráfica

graphical solution of equations: solución gráfica de ecuaciones

F
G

graphically: gráficamente

graphs: gráficos

great circle: círculo mayor

greater: mayor

greater than (>): mayor a (>)

greatest common divisor (GCD): máximo común denominador

greatest common factor (GCF): máximo común divisor

greatest common monomial factor: factor común mayor del monomio

greatest integer function: función del entero mayor

grid: cuadrilla

group: grupo

group how many: agrupar cuántos

group theorems: teoremas de grupo

grouped frequency distributions: distribuciones de frecuencias grupales

groups with finite sets: grupos de conjuntos finitos

groups with infinite sets: grupos de conjuntos infinitos

growth factor: factor de crecimiento

half-dollar: medio dólar

half-plane: medio plano

half-turn: medio giro

half-turn about origin: media vuelta alrededor del origen

half hour: media hora

halves: medios, mitades

halving: dividir en mitades o dividir por la mitad

head (of a coin): cara (de una moneda)

heavier: más pesado

hectare: hectárea

height of a 3-dimensional figure: altura de una figura de 3 dimensiones o tridimensional

height of a parallelogram: altura de un paralelogramo

height of a rectangle: altura de un rectángulo

height of a triangle: altura de un triángulo

height of cone: altura del cono

height of cylinder: altura del cilindro

heptagon: heptágono

Heron's formula: fórmula de Herón

hexagon: hexágono

hexahedron: hexaedro

hidden conditional: condicional oculta

higher: más alto

higher terms: términos superiores

highest common divisor: máximo común divisor

highest common factor: factor común máximo

histogram: histograma

homogeneous polynomial: polinomio homogéneo

horizontal distance: distancia horizontal

horizontal format: formato horizontal

horizontal line: línea horizontal

horizontal line symmetry: línea horizontal de simetría

horizontal line test: prueba de la línea horizontal

hour hand: manecilla pequeña del reloj que marca las horas

hundred chart: tabla de cien

hundred thousands: centenas de millar

hundred thousands millions: centenas de mil de millón

hundreds (place value): centenas, posición de las centenas

hundredth (place value): centésimos, unidad de centésima

hyperbola: hipérbola

hyperbolic functions: funciones hiperbólicas

hypotenuse: hipotenusa

hypotenuse and leg triangle congruence: hipotenusa y catetos congruentes

hypothesis: hipótesis

hypothetical proposition: proposición hipotética

I

i: i (símbolo del número $\sqrt{-1}$, unidad de los números imaginarios)

icosahedron: icosaedro

ideas: ideas

identical quantities: cantidades idénticas

identical relation: relación idéntica

identical substitution: substitución idéntica

identical transformation: transformación idéntica

identically vanishing: desapareciendo idénticamente

identify the problem: identificar el problema

identity element: elemento de identidad

identity element for addition: elemento de identidad para la adición

identity element for multiplication: identidad multiplicativa

identity property: propiedad de identidad

identity property of addition: elemento neutro de la suma o característica de identidad de la suma

identity property of multiplication: elemento neutro de la multiplicación o característica de identidad de la multiplicación

identity relation: relación de identidad

identity symbol: símbolo de identidad

if and only if: si y sólo si

image point: punto imagen

image set: conjunto imagen o sistema de imagen

imaginary axis: eje imaginario

imaginary circle: círculo imaginario

imaginary component: componente imaginario

imaginary line: línea imaginaria

imaginary number: número imaginario

imaginary plane: plano imaginario

imaginary point: punto imaginario

imaginary root: raíz imaginaria

imaginary unit: unidad imaginaria

impossible event: evento imposible

impossible outcomes: resultados imposibles

improper fraction: fracción impropia

incenter: en el centro

incenter of a polygon: en el centro (punto de intersección de las bisectrices interiores de los ángulos) de un polígono

incircle: en circulo

inclined plane: plano inclinado

included angle: ángulo contenido o ángulo incluido

included side: lado contenido o lado incluido

inclusion: inclusión

inclusive disjunction: disyunción inclusiva

incommensurable: inconmensurable

incommensurable number: número inconmensurable

incomparability: incomparabilidad

incomparable: incomparable

incomplete quadratic equation: ecuación cuadrática incompleta

incompleteness: incompleto

H
I

inconsistency: inconsistencia

inconsistent equations: ecuaciones inconsistentes

increasing function: función creciente

increasing sequence: secuencia creciente

increasing series: series crecientes

indefinite equation: ecuación indefinida

indefinite form: forma indefinida

indefinitely: indefinidamente

independent event: evento independiente

independent trial: prueba independiente

independent variable: variable independiente

indeterminate coefficient: coeficiente indeterminado

indeterminate form: forma indeterminada

index in statistics: índice de estadísticas

index of a radical: índice de un radical

indicated demonstration: demostración indirecta

indicated root: raíz indicada

indirect measurement: medida indirecta

indirect proof: prueba indirecta

induced mapping: barrido inducido

induction by simple enumeration: inducción por enumeración simple

inductive: inductivo

inductive reasoning: razonamiento inductivo

inequality containing one variable: desigualdad con una variable

inequality involving fractions: desigualdades que envuelven fracciones

inequality symbols: símbolos de desigualdad

inference: inferencia, deducción

inference of immediate: inferencia de lo inmediato

infinite decimal: decimal infinito

infinite extension: extensión infinita

infinite set: conjunto infinito

infinitely great: infinitamente grande

infinitely increasing: aumentando infinitamente

infinitely many: infinitamente mucho

informal indirect proof: prueba indirecta informal

informally: informalmente

inhomogeneous: no homogéneo

infinty: infinito

initial column: columna inicial

initial condition: condición inicial

initial data: información inicial

initial ray: rayo inicial

initial row: fila inicial

initial segment: segmento inicial

initial side of an angle: lado inicial de un ángulo

initial solution: solución inicial

initial term: término interno

initial value: valor inicial

inner center: centro interno

inner point: punto interno

inner scale: escala interior

inner term: término interno

input values: valores de ingreso o imagen de una función

inscribe: inscribir

inscribed: inscrito

inscribed angle: ángulo inscrito

inscribed circle: círculo inscrito

inscribed figure: figura inscrita

inscribed polygon: polígono inscrito

inscribed sphere: esfera inscrita

instead of: en lugar de

instruction: instrucción

integer: número entero

integer coefficients: coeficientes enteros

integral: (perteneciente a, relativo a) números enteros

integral coefficient: coeficiente entero

integral exponent: potencia de números enteros

integral factor: factor integral

integral part: parte integral

integral point: punto integral

integral power: potencia integral

integral radicands: radicales integrales

integral root: raíz cuadrada de números enteros

integral value: valor integral

integrated mathematics: matemática integrada

intercept of a plane: intersección de un plano

intercepted arc: arco interceptado

intercepts: intersecciones

interconnect: interconectar (interconecte)

interest compounded annually: interés compuesto anual

interest compounded continuously: interés compuesto continuamente

interest compounded quarterly: interés compuesto trimestral

interest compounded semiannually: interés compuesto semestral

interest rates: tasas de interés

interior angle: ángulo interno

interior angle of a triangle: ángulo interno de un triángulo

interior of an angle: interior de un ángulo

interior point: punto interior

interior region of a circle: región interior de un círculo

intermediate value: valor intermedio

internal bisector: bisectriz interna

internal division: división interna

internal tangent: tangente interna

internally tangent circles: círculos de tangencia interna

interpolate: interpolar (interpole)

interpolation: interpolación

interpret graphs: interpretar gráficos

interpret models: interpretar (interprete los) modelos

interquartile range: rango intercuartil

intersect: interceptar (intercepte)

intersecting: intersectante

intersecting lines: líneas que se interceptan

intersection: intersección

intersection of loci: intersección de punto geométricos

intersection of sets: intersección de conjuntos

intersection of the graphs: intersección de gráficas

intersection point: punto de intersección

interval notation: notación por intervalos

intransitive: intransitivo

invalid approach: aproximación inválida, enfoque inválido

invariance: invariación

inverse: inverso

inverse correlation: correlación inversa

inverse cosine function: función inversa del coseno

inverse curve: curva inversa

inverse element: elemento simétrico

inverse equation: ecuación inversa

inverse form: forma inversa

inverse function: función inversa

inverse function under composition: función inversa en composición

inverse image: imagen inversa

inverse interpolation: interpolación inversa

inverse logarithm: logaritmo inverso

inverse mapping

inverse mapping: barrido inverso
inverse number: número inverso
inverse of a statement: inversa de un enunciado
inverse of a transformation: inversa de una transformación
inverse operation: operación inversa
inverse property: propiedad inversa
inverse proportion: proporción inversa
inverse proposition: proposición inversa
inverse ratio: razón inversa
inverse relation: relación inversa
inverse sine function: función inversa del seno
inverse statement: declaración inversa
inverse tangent function: función inversa de la tangente
inverse theorem: teorema inverso
inverse transformation: transformación inversa
inverse trigonometric functions: funciones trigonométricas inversas
inverse variation: variación inversa
inversely proportional quantities: cantidades inversamente proporcionales
invertibility: invertibilidad o invertido
investigate conjectures: investigar (investigue las) conjeturas
irrational numbers: números irracionales
irrational root: raíz irracional
irreducibility: irreductibilidad
irreducible algebraic equation: ecuación algebraica irreducible
irreflexive: irreflexible
irreflexive relation: relación irreflexible
irregular polygon: polígono irregular
irregular shape: forma irregular
irrelevant information: información irrelevante, información inaplicable, información sin importancia
irreversible process: proceso irreversible

irreversiblility: irreversibilidad
isogonaltiy: isógonabilidad
isogonal: isógono
isogonal line: línea isógonal
isogonal mapping: barrido isógonal
isogonal transformation: transformación isógonal
isolate the radical: aislar el radical
isometric: isométrico
isometric chart: tabla isométrica
isometric circle: círculo isométrico
isometric correspondence: correspondencia isométrica
isometry: isometría
isosceles trapezoid: trapecio isósceles
isosceles triangle: triángulo isósceles

J

justify statement: justificar la afirmación

K

key sequence: secuencia dominante
key to a graph: leyenda de un gráfico
known function: función conocida
known quantity: cantidad conocida

L

label the solution set: etiquetar el conjunto solución

label work: identificar el trabajo

language of logic (and, or, not): lógica del lenguaje (y, o, no)

larger: más grande que

largest: el más grande

last term: último término

lateral area of a prism: área lateral de un prisma

lateral area of cone: área lateral del cono

lateral edge: borde lateral

lateral edge of prism: borde lateral del prisma

lateral face: cara lateral

lateral point: punto lateral

lateral surface: superficie lateral

lateral surface area: área de superficie lateral

lattice points: red de puntos

latus rectum: lado recto

law of chain rule: ley de la regla de cadena

law of conjunction: ley de conjunción

law of contradiction: ley de contradicción

law of contrapositive: ley de contrapositivo

law of cosines: ley de cosenos

law of De Morgan: ley De Morgan

law of detachment: ley del desprendimiento

law of disjunctive inference: ley de inferencia disyuntiva

law of exponents for division: ley de exponentes para la división

law of exponents for multiplication: ley de exponentes para la multiplicación

law of Modus Tollens: ley de Modus Tollens

law of positive integral exponents: ley de exponentes integrales positivos

law of reasoning: ley de razonamiento

law of simplification: ley de simplificación

law of sines: ley de senos

law of substitution: ley de sustitución

law of the disjunctive addition: ley de la adición disyuntiva

law of the double negation: ley de la doble negación

law of the syllogism: ley del silogismo

laws of exponents: leyes de exponentes

laws of logarithms: leyes de logaritmos

lead coefficient: coeficiente principal

leading coefficient: coeficiente conductor

leading diagonal: diagonal anterior

leading element: elemento guía

leading variable: variable principal

least common denominator (LCD): mínimo común denominador

least common factor (LCF): factor común mínimo

least common multiple (LCM): mínimo común múltiplo

least squares regression line: línea mínima de regresión de cuadrados

left-hand cancellation: cancelación del lado izquierdo

left-hand number: miembro del lado izquierdo

left-hand operation: operación del lado izquierdo

left over: sobrante

leg of a right triangle: cateto de un triángulo rectángulo

leg of an isosceles triangle: lado de un triángulo isósceles

legs of an isosceles trapezoid: catetos de un trapecio isósceles

lemma: lema

length of arc: longitud de arco

L

length of semicircle: longitud de semicírculo

less than (<): menor a (<)

lettered: rotulado

levels of precision: niveles de precisión

lie on the graph of: yace sobre el gráfico de

lie on the line: yace sobre la línea

lighter: más liviano

like denominators: denominadores semejantes

like monomials: monomios semejantes

like numbers: números semejantes

like radicals: radicales semejantes

like terms: términos semejantes

line graph: gráfico lineal

line of best fit: línea de ajuste óptimo

line of equidistances: línea de equidistancia

line of reflection: línea de reflexión

line of sight: línea visual

line of symmetry: línea de simetría

line parallel to the x-or y-axis: línea paralela al eje "x" o "y"

line plot: diagrama lineal

line segment: segmento lineal

line symmetry: simetría lineal

linear coordinates: coordenadas lineales

linear dependence: dependencia lineal

linear equation: ecuación lineal

linear equation in one variable: ecuación lineal de una variable (o incógnita)

linear estimation: estimación lineal

linear expression: expresión lineal

linear form: forma lineal

linear function: función lineal

linear growth: crecimiento lineal

linear independence: independencia lineal

linear inequality: desigualdad lineal

linear inequality in two variables: desigualdad lineal con dos variables

linear measure: medida lineal

linear measure of an arc: medida lineal de un arco

linear open sentence: oración lineal abierta

linear pair: par lineal

linear pair of angles: par lineal de ángulos

linear quadratic system: sistema cuadrático lineal

linear regression: regresión lineal

linear relationship: relación lineal

linear system: sistema lineal

linear transformation: transformación lineal

linear unit: unidad lineal

liter (L): litro (L)

literal coefficient: coeficiente literal

literal constant: constante literal

literal equation: ecuación literal

literal notation: notación literal

locus of points: lugar de puntos

logarithm: logaritmo

logarithm form: forma logarítmica

logic proof: prueba lógica

logical argument: argumento lógico

logical conclusion: conclusión lógica

logical equivalence: equivalencia lógica

logical equivalent: equivalente lógico

logical operation: operación lógica

logical order: orden lógico

logical reasoning: razonamiento lógico

logical sequence: secuencia lógica

logical system: sistema lógico

logically equivalent: lógicamente equivalente

long division: división larga

longer: mas largo

longer than: más largo que

longest: el más largo

L

longitudinal axis: eje longitudinal

look for a pattern: buscar un patrón o mira y sigue un patrón

lower: menor

lower base of cylinder: base inferior del cilindro

lower limit: límite inferior

lowest common denominator (LCD): mínimo común denominador

lowest common multiple (LCM): mínimo común múltiple

lowest terms (of fractions): fracción de términos mínimos

lowest terms (simplest form): términos simplificados (forma más simple)

M

main diagonal: diagonal principal

major arc: arco mayor

major segment: segmento mayor

make a chart: hacer un gráfico o una gráfica

make a diagram: hacer una diagrama

make an organized chart: hacer un gráfico organizado

make an organized list: hacer una lista organizada

make conjectures: sacar conjeturas o hacer conjeturas

make observations: hacer observaciones

manipulation: manipulación

manipulative materials: materiales manipulantes

mantissa: mantisa

map into: trace en

map legend: leyenda del mapa

map onto: trace sobre

map scale: escala del mapa

mapping: barrido

mapping (function): trazado de mapas (función)

marbles: canicas

mathematical argument: argumento matemático

mathematical conjecture: conjetura matemática

mathematical ideas: ideas matemáticas

mathematical induction: inducción matemático

mathematical language: lenguaje matemático

mathematical logic: lógica matemática

mathematical operation: operación matemática

mathematical phenomena: fenómeno matemático

mathematical relationships: relaciones matemáticas

mathematical representation: representación matemática

mathematical sentence: frase matemática

mathematical statement: enunciado matemático

mathematical symbol: símbolo matemático

mathematical visual: visual matemático

mathematics: matemática

maximal: máximo

maximum point: punto máximo

maximum value: valor máximo

mean absolute deviation: desviación absoluta media

mean approximation: aproximación media

mean proportional: media proporcional

mean terms: términos medios

mean terms of proportion: términos medios de una proporción

L
M

mean value: valor medio

means (of a proportion): media aritmética (de una proporción)

measurability: mensurabilidad

measurable: mensurable

measure capacity: medir (mida) la capacidad

measure in radians: medida en radianes

measure of an arc: medida de un arco

measure of angle: medida del ángulo

measure of central angle: medida de un ángulo central

measure of central tendency: medida de tendencia central

measure of dispersion: medida de la dispersión

measure of precision: medida de precisión

measurement system: sistema de medición

measures of central tendency: medidas de tendencia central

measures of dispersion: medidas de dispersión

median: mediana

median of a trapezoid: mediana de un trapecio

median of a triangle: mediana de un triángulo

memory capacity: capacidad de memoria

mental math: cálculo mental

meter (m): metro (m)

method of elimination: método de eliminación

method of exhaustion: método del agotamiento

method of interpolation: método de interpolación

method of successive substitution: método de sustitución sucesiva

method of trial and error: método de aproximaciones o método de prueba y error

method of undetermined coefficients: método de los coeficientes indeterminados

methods of proof: métodos de prueba

metric system: sistema métrico

metric system of measurement: sistema métrico de medición o sistema métrico de medidas

metric units of capacity: unidades métricas de capacidad

metric units of mass: unidades métricas de masa

metric units of measure: unidades métricas de medición o unidades métricas de medida

mid-range: alcance medio

middle term: término medio

midpoint: punto intermedio

midpoint preserved: punto medio preservado

midsegment: segmento intermedio

milligram (mg): miligramo (mg)

milliliter (ml): mililitro (ml)

millimeter (mm): milímetro (mm)

millions: unidades de millón (valor de posición) o millones

minimal solution: solución mínima

minimum point: punto mínimo

minimum value: valor mínimo

minor arc: arco menor

minor segment: segmento menor

minuend: minuendo

minus sign: signo menos

minute hand: manecilla de los minutos

miscellaneous problems: problemas misceláneos

mixed decimal: decimal mezclado

mixed fraction: fracción mixta

mixed number: fracción mixta, número mixto

mod system or module system: sistema de módulo

modal interval: intervalo modal

model problem: problema modelo

model situations: situaciones modelo

model using manipulatives: modelos usando materiales prácticos

modular: modular

Modus Ponens: Modus Ponens

Modus Tollens: Modus Tollens

monomial: monomio

monomial square root: raíz cuadrada

months of the year: meses del año

more than (>): mayor a (>)

multi-fold: doblaje múltiple

multinomial coefficient: coeficiente multinómico

multiple representation: representación múltiple

multiple roots: raíces múltiples

multiplicand: multiplicando

multiplication identity: identidad multiplicativa

multiplication property of inequality: propiedad multiplicativa de la desigualdad

multiplication property of zero: propiedad multiplicativa del cero

multiplication table: tabla de multiplicación

multiplicative inverse (reciprocal): inverso multiplicativo (recíproco)

multiplicity: multiplicidad

multiplier: multiplicador

multiply (multiplication): multiplicar, multiplique (multiplicación)

mutually disjoint: recíprocamente desligados

mutually exclusive: mutuamente excluidos

mutually exclusive events: eventos mutuamente excluyentes

mutually exclusive sets: conjuntos que se excluyen mutuamente

mutually perpendicular: perpendiculares recíprocas

mutually separated sets: conjuntos mutuamente separados

N

n-gon: número (n) de lados

natural logarithm: logaritmo natural

natural number: número natural

nature of the roots: naturaleza de las raíces

nearest: más cercano

nearest degree: grado más cercano

nearest tenth: decima más cercana

necessary and sufficient condition: condición necesaria y suficiente

necessary condition: condición necesaria

negation: negación

negative carry: acarreo negativo

negative correlation: correlación negativa

negative exponent: exponente negativo

negative integer: entero negativo

negative number: número negativo

negative rational numbers: números racionales negativos

negative real number: número real negativo

negative reciprocal: recíproco negativo

negative sign: signo negativo

negative slope: pendiente negativa

nickel: moneda de 5 centavos

no-mathematical sentence: oración no matemática

non-adjacent: no-adyacente

non-adjacent angles: ángulos no adyacentes

non-adjacent side of a triangle: lado no adyacente de un triángulo

non-centered conic: sección cónica no centrada

non-collinear: no colineal

non-collinear set of points: conjunto de puntos no colineales

non-coplanar: no coplanar(es)

non-degenerate: no degenerado

non-dense: no denso

non-empty set: conjunto no vacío

non-enumerable set: conjunto no enumerado

non-Euclidean geometry: geometría no euclidiana

non-homogeneous: no homogéneo

non-negative form: forma no negativa

non-negative numbers: números no negativos

non-perfect squares: cuadrados imperfectos

non-periodic function: función no periódica

non-positive form: forma no positiva

non-positive numbers: números no positivos

non-reflexive relation: relación no reflexiva

non-repeating decimal: decimal no periódico

non-symmetric relation: relación no asimétrica

non-terminating continued fraction: fracción continua interminable

non-terminating decimal: decimal infinito

non-transitive relation: relación no transitiva

non-zero: no cero

nonagon: nonágono

nonlinear equation: ecuación no linear

nonlinear relationship: relación no linear

nonstandard measure: medida no estándar

nonstandard representations: representaciones no estándares

nonstandard units: medidas no estándares

normal curve: curva normal

normal distribution: distribución normal

normalized form: forma normalizada

not equal to: distinto de, no igual a, no equivalente a, distinto de ($\neq$)

not mutually exclusive events: eventos mutuamente no excluyentes

not preserved: no preservado

nought: nada, cero

nowhere dense: considerablemente denso

nth root: raíz elevada a un exponente n

nth term: término elevado a un exponente n

null circle: círculo nulo

null divisor: divisor nulo

null set: conjunto nulo

number axis: eje numérico

number in words: número escrito en palabras

number line: recta numérica

number model: modelo numérico

number of strokes: número de golpes

number sense and operations: Sentido numérico y operaciones numéricas

number sentence: ecuación numérica

number system: sistema numérico

number theory: teoría numérica

numeral: numeral

numeration: numeración

numerator: numerador

numeric (arithmetic) expression: expresión numérica (aritmética)

numeric patterns: patrones numéricos

numerical calculation: cálculo numérico

numerical coefficient: coeficiente numérico

numerical constant: constante numérica

numerical expression: expresión numérico

numerical function: función numérica

numerical order: orden numérico

numerical problem: problema numérico

numerical sentence: oración numérica

numerical solution: solución numérica

numerical symbol: símbolo numérico

numerical tables: tablas numéricas

numerically: numéricamente

objects created using technology: objetos creados por medio de la tecnología

observe patterns: observar (observe los) patrones

obtuse angle: ángulo obtuso

obtuse triangle: triángulo obtusángulo o "triángulo obtuso"

occurrence: acontecimiento

octadic: octádico

octagon: octágono

octagon parallel lines: líneas paralelas de un octágono

octahedron: octaedro

octal system: sistema octal

odd: impar

odd function: función impar

odd integer: entero impar

odd number: número impar

odd whole number: número entero impar

of cones: de conos

of cylinders: de cilindros

of prisms: de prismas

of pyramids: de pirámides

one-digit number: número de un dígito

one-dimensional space: espacio unidimensional

one-half method: método de la mitad

one-half the circumference of a circle: la mitad de la circunferencia de un círculo

one-sided: de un lado

one-to-one correspondence: correspondencia uno a uno

one-to-one function: función uno a uno

one-to-one mapping: trazado uno a uno

one cycle of a trigonometric function: un ciclo de una función trigonométrica

ones (place value): posición de las unidades (lugar de)

ono-to-one function: función biunívoco o función uno a uno

onto: en (sobre)

open arc: arco abierto

open circle: círculo abierto

open curve: curva abierta

open downward: abrir hacia abajo

open expression: expresión abierta

open figure: figura abierta

open half-planes: medios planos abiertos

open interval: intervalo abierto

open polygon: polígono abierta

open sentence: oración abierta

open set: conjunto abierto

open upward: abrir hacia arriba

operation with decimals: operación con decimales

operation with fractions: operación con fracciones

operation with monomial: operación con monomio

operation with set: operación de conjunto

operational method: método operativo, operación u operacional

operations with polynomials: operaciones con polinomios

operative symbol: símbolo operativo

operator: operador

opposite angles: ángulos opuestos

N
O

opposite isometry: isometría opuesta

opposite leg: cateto opuesto

opposite number: número opuesto

opposite orientation: orientación opuesta

opposite point: punto opuesto

opposite rays: semirrectas opuestas

opposite sequence: secuencia opuesta

opposite side: lado opuesto

opposite side in a right triangle: lado opuesto de un triángulo recto

opposite side or angle: lado o ángulo opuesto

opposite transformation: transformación opuesta

opposite vertex: vértice opuesto

oppositely directed: dirigidos opuestamente

optimal approximation: aproximación óptima

oral representations: representaciones orales

order-preserving map: mapa del orden preservado

order of operations: orden de las operaciones

order preserved: orden mantenido

order property: propiedad del orden

ordered field: campo ordenado

ordered number pair: número de pares ordenados

ordered pair: par ordenado

ordinal numbers: números ordinales

ordinate: ordenada

organize work: organizar (organice) el trabajo

organized chart: gráfico organizado

organized list: lista organizada

orientational invariance: invariación orientativa

orthocenter: ortocentro

orthogonal: ortogonal

oscillation: oscilación

ounce (oz): onza (oz)

outcome set: conjunto de resultados

outer term: término exterior

outlier: valor atípico

outmost: el más externo

overlapping triangles: triángulos intercalados

P

pair of factors: par de factores

palindrome: Palíndromo

pan balance: balanza de platillos

parabola: parábola

parabolic function: función parabólica

paragraph proof: prueba de párrafo

parallel line segments: segmentos de rectas paralelas

parallel lines: rectas o líneas paralelas

parallel postulate(s) : postulado(s) del paralelo de Euclides

parallel projection: proyección paralela

parallel section: sección paralela

parallel translation: traslado paralelo

parallelepiped: paralelepípedo

parallelism: paralelismo

parallelism preserved: paralelismo mantenido

parallelogram: paralelogramo

parameter: parámetro

part-to-part ratio: relación parte-parte o "cociente parte-parte"

part-to-whole ratio: relación parte-todo o "cociente parte-todo"

partial products: productos parciales

partial summation: sumatoria

particular postulate: postulado de la partición

Pascal's Triangle: Triángulo de Pascal

pass through a given point: pasar por un punto dado

pattern of numbers: patrón de números

penny: moneda de un centavo

pentadecagon: pentadecágono

per-unit rate: tasa por unidad

percent decrease: disminución porcentual

percent increase: incremento porcentual

percent of increase or decrease: por ciento de aumento o disminución

percent of quantity: porcentaje de una cantidad

percentage error: error de porcentaje

percentile: percentil

percentile rank: rango percentil

perfect cubic expression: expresión cúbica perfecta

perfect square: cuadrado perfecto

perfect square trinomial: trinomio cuadrado perfecto

perform operation: ejecutar la operación

performing computation: realizando cálculos

period (of a function): período (de una función)

period of a repeating decimal: período de un decimal periódico

periodic curve: curva periódica

periodic decimals: decimales periódicos

periodic function: función periódica

periodical fraction: fracción periódica

periodicity: periodicidad

permutable: permutable

permutation: permutación

permutation with repitition: permutación con repetición

perpendicular: perpendicular

perpendicular bisector: bisectriz perpendicular

perpendicular bisector concurrence: concurrencia de bisectrices perpendiculares

perpendicular lines: rectas perpendiculares

perpendicular planes: planos perpendiculares

perpendicular segment: segmento perpendicular

perpendicularity: perpendicularidad

personal references: referencias personales

personal references for capacity: referencias personales de medidas de capacidad

personal references for units of mass: referencias personales de unidades de masa

phase shift: desplazamiento de fase

physical object: objeto físico

pi (π): número irracional pi (equivalente a 3.1419...)

pictograph: pictograma

pictorial representations: representaciones pictóricas

picture graph: gráfica de dibujos

pint (pt): pinta (pt)

pivoting: girando, de giro

place holder: en lugar de

place value: valor de posición o valor de lugar

plane: plano

plane figure: figura plana

plane geometric figures: figuras geométricas planas

plot: trazar, trama, representación gráfica, representar (represente) gráficamente

plot points: asentar puntos

point-slope equation of a line : ecuación punto-pendiente de una recta

point at infinity: punto en el infinito

point of concurrency: punto de concurrencia

point of intersection: punto de intersección

point of reflection: punto de reflexión

point of symmetry: punto de simetría

point of tangency: punto de tangencia

point reflection: reflexión de puntos

polygon: polígono

polygon circumscribed about a circle: polígono circunscrito a un círculo

polygon circumscribed in a circle: polígono circunscrito en un círculo

polygonal line: línea poligónica

polyhedron: poliedro

polynomial: polinomio

polynomial equation: ecuación polinómica

polynomial expression: expresión polinómica

polynomial function: función polinómica

positive correlation: correlación positiva

positive integer: entero positivo

positive number: número positivo

positive power of 10: potencia positiva en base 10

positive rational numbers: números racionales positivos

positive real numbers: número positivo real

positive sign: signo positivo

positive slope: pendiente positiva

possible outcomes: posibles resultados

post-office function: función de correo

post meridian (p.m.): pasado meridiano (p.m.)

postulational: postulacional

postulational system: sistema postulacional

power: potencia

power-of-product law: ley de la potencia de un producto

power-of-quotient law: ley de la potencia de un cociente

power of 10: en base 10

powers of i: potencias de i

pre-image: imagen preliminar

precision measurement: medida de precisión

prime factor: factor primo

prime factorization: factorización prima, descomposición en factores primos

prime number: número primo

prime pair: par primo

prime polynomial: polinomio primo

principal angle: ángulo principal

principal cubic root: raíz cúbica principal

principal diagonal: diagonal principal

principal nth root of K: raíz principal enésima de (k)

principal root: raíz principal

principal solution: solución principal

principal square root: raíz cuadrada principal

prismatic: prismático

probability of an event: probabilidad de un evento

probability with replacement: probabilidad con reemplazo

probability without replacement: probabilidad sin reemplazo

problem solving: resolución de problemas

problem solving strategies: estrategias para resolver los problemas

process of elimination: proceso de eliminación

product of binomials: producto de binomios

product property of proportions: propiedad de multiplicación de las proporciones

proof by contradiction: prueba por contradicción

proper fraction: fracción propia

proper set: conjunto propio

proper subset: subconjunto propio

properties of exponents: propiedades de exponentes

properties of real numbers: propiedades de los números reales

properties preserved: propiedades mantenidas

property of an operation: propiedad de una operación

property of density: propiedad de densidad

proportion by addition: proporción por adición

proportion by inversion: proporción por inversión

proportion by subtraction: proporción por resta

proportional: proporcional

proportional line segments: segmentos proporcionales

proportional reasoning: razonamiento proporcional

proportionality: proporcionalidad

proportionality or direct variation: variación proporcional o directa

proprotion by alternation: proporción por alternación

protractor: prolongador

pure imaginary number: número imaginario puro

pure quadratic equation: ecuación cuadrática pura

pyramidal surface: superficie piramidal

Pythagorean identity: identidad Pitagórica

Pythagorean theorem: teorema de Pitágoras

Pythagorean triple: triple Pitagórico

Q

quadrangle: cuadrángulo

quadrant: cuadrante

quadrantal angle: ángulo cuadrantal

quadratic: cuadrático

quadratic curve: curva cuadrática

quadratic equation: ecuación cuadrática

quadratic formula: fórmula cuadrática

quadratic function: función cuadrática

quadratic inequality: desigualdad cuadrático

quadratic linear equation system: sistema de ecuación cuadrático

quadratic trinomial: trinomio cuadrático

quadratics: cuadrática

quadratix: cuadratriz

quadrature of a conic: cuadratura de una sección cónica

quadrilateral: cuadrilátero

quantifier: cuantificador

quantitative model: modelo cuantitativo

quart (qt): cuarto de galón

quarter-circle: cuarto de círculo

quarter-turn: giro de un cuarto

quarter (coin): moneda de 25 centavos

quartiles: cuartiles

quintupling: quintuplicando

quotient identity: identidad de cociente

R

radian: radián

radian measure: medida del radián

radical equation: ecuación radical

radical expression: expresión radical

radical form: forma radical

radical sign: signo radical

radicand: radicando (sustantivo)

radii: radios

radius of a circle: radio de un círculo

radius of a sphere: radio de una esfera

radius of circumscribed circle: radio del círculo circunscrito

radius of inscribed circle: radio del círculo inscrito

random: al azar

random arrangement: ordenamiento al azar

random event: evento al azar

random number: número al azar

random process: proceso al azar

random sample: muestra aleatoria (o al azar)

random selection: selección al azar

range (of a data set): rango (de un conjunto de datos), intervalo de datos

range (of a function): rango (de una función), variación de una función

rate: tasa de

rate (speed): incremento (velocidad)

rate of change: tasa de cambio

rate of depreciation: índice de interés

rate of interest: tasa de interés

ratio of division: razón de la división

ratio of equality: razón de la igualdad

ratio of similitude: razón de la similitud

ratio scale: escala de la razón

rational coefficient: coeficiente racional

rational equation: ecuación racional

rational expression: expresión racional

rational fraction: fracción racional

rational index: índice racional

rational inequality: inecuación racional

rational number: número racional

rational root: raíz racional

rationale: fundamento lógico, base, fundamento

rationality: racionalidad

rationalization: racionalización

rationalize denominators: racionalizar (racionalice) denominadores

rationalizing factor: factor racionalizante

raw data: datos iníciales

ray: semirrecta

real density: densidad real

real domain: dominio real

real exponent: exponente real

real number: número real

real number axis: eje de los números reales

real number line: línea de número verdadero

real part: parte real

real square root: raíz cuadrada real

real world math: matemática del mundo real

real world situation: situación del mundo real

rearrangement: reorganización

reasonable estimates: estimaciones razonables

reasonableness of a solution: racionabilidad de una solución

reasoning and proof: prueba de razonamiento

reciprocal identity: identidad recíproca

reciprocal logarithmic curve: curva logarítmica recíproca

reciprocal ration: razón recíproca

reciprocal relation: relación recíproca

reciprocal trigonometric functions: funciones trigonométricas recíprocas

recognize connections: reconocer conexiones

record data: archivar datos

rectangular coordinate system: sistema rectangular de coordenadas

rectangular coordinates: coordenadas rectangulares

rectangular hyperbola: hipérbola rectangular

rectangular parallelepiped: paralelepípedo rectangular

rectangular prism: prisma rectangular

rectangular solid: sólido rectangular

rectilinear: rectilíneo

rectilinear asymptote: asíntota rectilínea

rectilinear motion: movimiento rectilineal

rectilinearity: rectilinealidad

recurring decimal: decimal recurrente

recurring period: período recurrente

recursive definition: definición recursiva

reduce to lowest term: reducir a los términos mínimos

reduced equation: ecuación reducida

reduced form: forma reducida

reducibility: reducibilidad

reducible: reducible

reducible equation: ecuación reducible

reducible fraction: fracción reducible

reducible polynomial: polinomio reducible

reference angle: ángulo de referencia

reference frame: marco de referencia

reflected image: imagen reflejada

reflection in a line: reflexión en una línea

reflective postulate: postulado reflexivo

reflex angle: ángulo reflejo

reflexive property of congruence: propiedad reflexiva de la congruencia

reflexive property of equality: propiedad reflexiva de la igualdad

reflexivity: reflexibilidad

regression equation: ecuación de regresión

regression model: modelo de regresión

regroup (regrouping): reagrupar (reagrupe), (reagrupación)

regular dodecahedron: dodecaedro regular

regular icosahedron: icosaedro regular

regular polygon: polígono regular

regular polyhedron: poliedro regular

regular prism: prisma regular

reject root: rechazar una raíz

related facts: hechos relacionados˙

related statement: declaración relacionada

relation of equivalence: relación de equivalencia

relation of identity: relación de identidad

relation symbol: símbolo de relación

relative efficiency: eficacia relativa

relative error: error relativo

relevant information: información relevante

remaining line: línea restante

remote interior angles: ángulos internos alejados

remove parentheses: remover los paréntesis

repeated addition: suma repetida

repeated root: raíz repetida

repeated subtraction: resta repetida

repeated trials: pruebas repetidas

repeating decimal: decimal periódico

repetend: factor de repetición

replacement set: conjunto de reemplazo

respectively: respectivamente

restricted domain: dominio restringido

resultant: resultante

resultant force: fuerza resultante

resulting equation: ecuación resultante

reverse factoring: técnica de factorización inversa

reverse order: orden inverso

R

reverse the process: invertir el proceso

reversibility: reversibilidad

reversible process: proceso reversible

reversible relation: relación reversible

reversible transformation: transformación reversible

rhombohedreon: romboedro

rhomboid: romboide

rhombus: rombo

right angle: ángulo recto

right cancellation law: ley de la cancelación derecha

right circular cone: cono circular recto

right circular cylinder: cilindro circular recto

right parallelepiped: paralelepípedo recto

right prism: prisma recto

right pyramid: pirámide recta

right triangle: triángulo recto

right triangle trigonometry: trigonometría de un triángulo recto

rigid motion: movimiento rígido

roman number: número romano

root of a quadratic equation: raíz de una ecuación cuadrática

root of an equation: raíz de una ecuación

root test: prueba de la raíz

roots of a parabolic function: raíces de una función parabólica

roster form: lista de presencia

rotation axis: eje de rotación

rotational: rotacional

rotational symmetry: simetría rotativa

round a number: redondear un número

round backet: corchetes circulares

round off: redondear

rounded number: número redondeado

rounding: redondeo

rounding error: error de redondeo

rounding off to the nearest tenth: redondeado hasta el decimal más cercano

rule of elimination: regla de eliminación

S

sale price: precio de venta

sales: ventas o ofertas

sample data: muestra de datos

sample mean: media modelo

sample point: punto modelo

sample space: espacio de muestra

sampling: muestreo o muestra

SAS similarity theorem: teorema de semejanza SAS

SAS triangle congruence: triángulo congruente SAS

scalar multiplication: multiplicación escalar

scale drawing: dibujar a escala

scale number: número de escala

scale of a graph: escala de un gráfico

scale ratio: razón de la escala

scale to measure mass: escala para medir la masa

scalene triangle: triángulo escaleno

scatter plot: diagrama de puntos, gráficos de dispersión

scattergram: diagrama de dispersión

scientific calculator: calculadora científica

scientific notation: notación científica

seasons in relation to the months: estaciones en relación con los meses

secant (of an angle): secante (de un ángulo)

secant curve: curva secante

secant function: función secante

secant of a circle: secante de un círculo

secant ratio: razón de secante

secant segment: segmento secante

R
S

secant to a circle: secante a un círculo

second-degree equation: ecuación de segundo grado

second-quadrant angle: ángulo del segundo cuadrante

sector of a circle: sector de un círculo

segment bisector: bisectriz de un segmento

segment of a circle: segmento de un círculo

segmental arc: arco segmental

self-conjugate conic: cono autoconjugado

self-corresponding element: elemento autocorrespondiente

semicircle: semicírculo

sense-preserving mapping: proyección de dirección preservada

sense-reversing: sentido de reversión

sense of a line: sentido de una línea

sense of orientation: sentido de orientación

sense of rotation: sentido de rotación

sequence of points: secuencia de puntos

sequences of intervals: secuencia de intervalos

sequencing: secuenciando

series of increasing powers: serie de potencias crecientes

series of natural number: serie de números naturales

set-builder notation: notación de conjuntos

set of data: conjunto de datos

set of irrational numbers: conjunto de números irracionales

set of numbers: conjunto de números

set of objects: conjunto de objetos

set of rational numbers: conjunto de números racionales

set of real numbers: conjunto de números reales

shaded region: región sombreada

shift of origin: traslado del origen

short-out method: método corto

shorter than: más corto que, más bajo que

shortest: el más corto

side opposite an angle: lado opuesto a un ángulo

sigma: sigma

sigma notation: notación de sigma

signed number: número dirigido

significant digit: dígitos significativos

signless integers: enteros sin signos

similar decimals: decimales similares

similar figures: figuras semejantes

similar polygons: polígonos semejantes

similar terms: términos similares

similar triangles: triángulos semejantes

similar triangles square: cuadrado de triángulos semejantes

similarities: semejanzas

similitude: similitud

simple closed curve: curva simple cerrada

simple difference set: conjunto de diferencia simple

simple equation: ecuación simple

simple event: evento simple

simple interest: interés simple

simple probability: probabilidad simple

simple quadrilateral: cuadrilátero sencillo

simplest form: expresión mínima

simplest radical form: forma radical más simple

simplification: simplificación

simplified proportion: proporción simpli-. ficada

simplified solution: solución simplificada

simplify a fraction: simplificar una fracción

simplify a result: simplificar el resultado

simplify an algebraic expression: simplificar una expresión algebraica

simplify fractions: simplificar fracciones

simplify the expression: simplificar la expresión

S

simultaneous displacement: desplazamiento simultáneo

simultaneous inequalities: desigualdades simultáneas

sine: seno

sine function: función del seno

sine ratio: razón del seno

single-event experiment: experimento simple o único

single event evento: evento simple o ocurrencia única

sixths: sextos

skew lines: líneas oblicuas

skew symmetry: simetría oblicua

skip count: contar por múltiplos de un número

slant: oblicuidad

slant height: altura sesgada (inclinada)

slide (translation): deslizamiento (traslación)

slide rule: regla de cálculo

slope-intercept form: forma pendiente-intersección

slope-intercept method: método pendiente intercepto

slope of a line: pendiente de una línea

smaller: más pequeño que

smallest: el más pequeño

smooth curve: curva continua

social contexts: contextos sociales

social phenomena: fenómeno social

solid : sólido

solid figure: figura sólida

solid geometry: geometría sólida

solid sphere: esfera sólida

solution of the sentence: solución de una oración

solution set: conjunto de soluciones

solution set of an equation: conjunto de soluciones de una ecuación

solution set of an inequality: conjunto de soluciones de una inecuación

solution set of system of equations: conjunto solución de un sistema de ecuaciones

solvability: resolver o solubilidad

solvable: resoluble

solve a fractional equation: resolver una ecuación fraccional

solve a problem: resolver un problema

solve a quadratic equation: resolver una ecuación cuadrática

solve a simpler problem: resolver un problema más simple

solve an equation: resolver una ecuación

solve graphically: resolver gráficamente

solve the equations graphically: resolver las ecuaciones gráficamente

spatial reasoning: razonamiento espacial

spatial relationships: relaciones espaciales

special case: caso especial

specific result: resultado específico

spinner: ruleta

square-root algorithm: algoritmo de la raíz cuadrada

square array: matriz cuadrada

square both sides: elevar al cuadrado ambos lados

square bracket: corchetes cuadrados

square centimeter: centímetro cuadrado (cm^2)

square foot: pie cuadrado (ft^2)

square inch: pulgada cuadrada (in^2)

square meter: metro cuadrato (m^2)

square mile: milla cuadrada (mi^2)

square number: número cuadrado o el cuadrado de

square of a number: el cuadrado de un número

square pyramid: pirámide cuadrada

square root: raíz cuadrada

square root method: método de la raíz cuadrada

S

square root of a fraction: raíz cuadrada de una fracción

square root of a number: raíz cuadrada de un número

square root of the denominator: raíz cuadrada del denominador

square root of the numerator: raíz cuadrada del numerador

square unit: unidad cuadrada

square yard: yarda cuadrada

SSS triangle congruence: triángulo congruente SSS

standard (mathematical) notation: notación estándar (matemática)

standard deviation: desviación estándar

standard deviation (population): desviación normal (población)

standard deviation (sample): desviación normal (muestra)

standard form: forma estándar / corriente

standard form of a number: forma estándar de un número

standard form of a quadratic equation: forma regular de una ecuación cuadrática

standard measure: medida estándar

standard notation: notación estándar

standard position: posición normal

standard position (of an angle): posición normal (de un ángulo)

standard representation: representación estándar

standard units: unidades estándar

statistical estimate of error: estimado estadístico del error

statistical frequency: frecuencia estadística

statistician: estadístico

statistics: estadísticas

statistics and probability: estadísticas y probabilidad

stem-and-leaf plot: diagrama de tallo y hoja

step-by-step carry: transporte paso a paso

step-by-step procedure: procedimiento sistemático

step curve: curva escalonadas

step functions: funciones escalonadas

step graph: gráfico escalonado

straight angle: ángulo recto

straight edge: borde recto

straight line: linea recta

strategy selection: selección de una estrategia

subdivision: subdivisión

subgroup: subgrupo

subscripted variables: variables suscritas

subset: subconjunto

substitute in the formula: sustituir en la formula

substitution: substitución

substitution method: método de sustitución

substitution postulate: postulado en la sustitución

substitution principle: principio de sustitución

substitution property: propiedad de sustitución

substitution property of equality: principio de sustitución de las igualdades

subtend: sostenido

subtend an angle: sostener un ángulo

subtraction fact: operación de resta con números elementales

subtraction property of equality: propiedad de resta de la igualdad

subtraction sentence: enunciado de resta

subtraction sign: signo de resta

subtrahend: sustraendo

successive: sucesivo

successive approximation: aproximación sucesiva

successive displacements: desplazamientos sucesivos

S

successive division: división sucesiva

successive elimination: eliminación sucesiva

successive method of elimination: método sucesivo de eliminación

successive reduction: reducción sucesiva

successive repetitions of the curve: repeticiones sucesivas de la curva

successive steps: pasos sucesivos

successive substitution: sustitución sucesiva

successive terms: términos sucesivos

successive trials: pruebas sucesivas

sufficient condition: condición suficiente

suffix: sufijo

sum and product of roots of a quadratic equation: suma y producto de las raíces de una ecuación cuadrática

sum of a geometric series: suma de una serie geométrica

sum of an arithmetic series: suma de una serie aritmética

sum or difference formulas for trigonometric functions: suma de fórmulas de diferencia para funciones trigonométricas

summability: sumabilidad

summation: adición, suma

summation of series: sumatoria de serie

summation sign: signo de suma

super power: súper potencia

superior angle: ángulo superior

superior arc: arco superior

superscript: superscrito o exponente

supplement: suplemento

supplementary angles: ángulos suplementarios

supportive argument: argumento de apoyo

surd root: raíz sorda

surface area: área de superficie

surface area of cylinders: área de superficie de cilindros

surface area of prisms: área de superficie de prismas

syllogism: silogismo

symbol for operation: símbolo para operación

symbolism: simbolismo

symbols in verbal form: símbolos verbales

symbols in written form: símbolos escritos

symmetric: simétrico

symmetric figure: figura simétrica

symmetric property: propiedad simétrica

symmetric property of equality: propiedad simétrica de la igualdad

symmetric relation: relación simétrica

symmetrical curve: curva simétrica

symmetrical equations: ecuaciones simétricas

system of conics: sistema de conos

system of dependent equations: sistema de ecuaciones dependientes

system of equations: sistema de ecuaciones

system of equations in two variables: sistema de ecuaciones con dos variables

system of inequalities: sistema de desigualdades

system of linear inequalities: sistema de desigualdades lineales

system of sentences: sistema de frases

system of simultaneous equations: sistemas de ecuaciones simultáneas

systematic approach: aproximación sistemática

systems of linear equations: sistemas de ecuaciones lineales

S

T

table of values: tabla de valores

tabulation: tabulación

tail (of a coin): escudo (de moneda)

taller: más alto que

tallest: el más alto

tallies: conteo o registro

tally: cuenta

tally mark: contar con palitos

tangent (of an angle): tangente (de un ángulo)

tangent curve: curva tangente

tangent function: función tangente

tangent of a circle: tangente de un círculo

tangent segment: segmento de tangente

tangent surface: superficie tangente

tangent to a circle: tangente a un círculo

tangential: tangencial

tangential approximation method: método de aproximación tangencial

tangential equation: ecuación tangencial

tautology: tautología

technical writing: redacción técnica

techniques of sampling: técnicas de modelaje

ten thousands: decenas de mil

tens place: posición de las decenas

terminal column: columna terminal

terminal line: línea terminal

terminal side of an angle: lado terminal de un ángulo

terminating decimal: decimal finito

tessellation: teselado

tetrahedron: tetraedro

theorem: teorema

theoretical probability: probabilidad teórica

third-quadrant angle: ángulo del tercer cuadrante

third quartile: tercer cuartilla

thirds: tercios

thought process: proceso deductivo

thousands (place value): unidades de millar

thousandth: milésima

thousandths: miles

three-digit number: número de tres dígitos

three-dimensional figure: figura en tres dimensiones o tridimensional

three dimensional space: espacio tridimensional

tiling: hacer un mosaico o teselación

to challenge thinking: desafiar el pensamiento

to clarify thinking: clarificar el pensamiento

to elicit thinking: propiciar el pensamiento

to extend thinking: extender el pensamiento

topology: topología

total number of possibilities: número total de posibilidades

total number outcomes: número total de resultados

tranposition: transposición

transcendental: trascendental

transcendental curve: curva trascendental

transcendental function: función trascendental

transform the formula: transformar la fórmula

transformational geometry: geometría transformacional

transformational proof: prueba de transformación

transformations of functions and relations: transformaciones de funciones y relaciones

transitive postulate: postulado transitivo

transitive property: propiedad transitiva

transitive property of equality: propiedad transitiva de la igualdad

transitive property of inequality: propiedad transitiva de las desigualdades

T

transitive relation: relación transitiva

transitivity: transitividad

translational symmetry: simetría translacional

transversal: transversal

transverse: transverso

transverse axis: eje transverso

trapezoid: trapecio

tree diagram: diagrama ramificado

trend line: línea de rumbo

trial and error: ensayo y error

trial and error method: aproximaciones sucesivas

trial and error procedure: aproximaciones progresivas

trial divisor: divisor de prueba

triangle inequality: desigualdad triangular

triangle number: número triangular

triangular prism: prisma triangular .

triangular pyramid: pirámide triangular

triangulation: triangulación

trichotomy law: ley de tricotomía

trichotomy postulate: postulado de tricotomía

trichotomy property: propiedad de tricotomía

trigonometric: trigonométrico

trigonometric approximation: aproximación trigonométrica

trigonometric cofunctions: confusiones trigonométricas

trigonometric equation: ecuación trigonométrica

trigonometric functions: funciones trigonométricas

trigonometric identity: identidad trigonométricas

trigonometric series: series trigonométricas

trigonometry: trigonometría

trigonometry of the right triangle: trigonometría del triángulo recto

trihedral: triédrico

trihedral angle: ángulo triédrico

trinomial: trinomio

triple root: raíz triple

trisection: trisección

trisection of an angle: trisección de un ángulo

trisection point: punto de trisección

trisectrix: trisectriz

truncated prism: prisma truncado

truth set: conjunto de verdad

truth table: tabla de verdad

truth value: valor de verdad

turn (rotation): giro (rotación)

turn about the origin: girar alrededor del origen

turning point: punto de giro

two-column proof: prueba a dos columnas

two-digit number: número de dos dígitos

two-dimensional figure: figura en dos dimensiones o bidimensional

two-dimensional space: espacio bidimensional

two-to-one correspondence: correspondencia de dos a uno

type of arc: tipo de arco

types of representations: tipos de representaciones

U

unary: unario

unbiased objects: objetos no polarizados

uncertain truth value: valor de verdad incierto

uncertainty: incertidumbre

T
U

unconditional equation: ecuación incondicional

undefined: no definido

undefined term: término indefinido

undetermined: indeterminado

undetermined coefficient: coeficiente indeterminado

uniform probability: probabilidad uniforme

union of sets: unión de conjuntos

union of the graphs: unión de gráficos

unique solution: solución única

uniqueness: singularidad

uniqueness of order: singularidad de orden

uniqueness of solution: singularidad de solución

unit (cubic unit, square unit): unidad (cúbica, cuadrada)

unit circle: círculo de unidad

unit element: elemento de unidad

unit fraction: fracción unitaria

unit measure: unidad de medida

unit normal: unidad normal

unit rate: tarifa unidad

unit segment: segmento unidad

unit vector: vector unidad

univariate: univariante

univariate data: datos univariantes

universal quantifier: cuantificador universal

universal set: conjunto universal

universal validity: validez universal

universally quantified statement: frase universalmente cuantificada

unknown number: número desconocido

unknown term: término desconocido

unlike denominators: denominadores distintos

unlike radicals: radicales diferentes

unlike terms: términos diferentes

unlimited decimal: decimal ilimitado

unlimited extent: extensión ilimitada

unrestricted: sin restricción

unrounded: no redondeado

unsigned number: número sin signo

unsmoothed curve: curva áspera

unsolvability: insolubilidad

unsolvable: insolucionable

unsuitable value: valor inajustable

upper base of cylinder: base superior del cilindro

upper integral: integral superior

upper limit of summation: límite superior de la suma

upper quartile: cuartil superior

use manipulatives: usar materiales prácticos

valid approach: acercamiento válido

valid argument: argumento válido

valid conclusion: conclusión válida

validity of sample methods: validez de los métodos de muestreo

value of a function: valor de una función

value of a variable: valor de una variable

value of an algebraic expression: valor de una expresión algebraica

vanishing point: punto tendiente a cero o punto de desaparición

variance: variación

variance (population): variación (población)

variance (sample): variación (muestra)

variation: variación

vector: vector

Venn diagram: diagrama de Venn

verbal: verbal

verbal explanation: explicación verbal

verbal expression: expresión verbal

verbal form: forma verbal

verbal form of reasoning: forma verbal de razonamiento

verbal language: lenguaje verbal

verbal process: proceso verbal

verbal sentence: oración verbal

verbal symbols: símbolos verbales

verify claims of others: verificar las aseveraciones de los otros

verify results: verificar los resultados

vertex: vértice

vertex angle: ángulo del vértice

vertex of a cone: vértice de un cono

vertical: vertical

vertical angles: ángulos verticales u opuestos por el vértice

vertical asymptote: asíntota vertical

vertical distance: distancia vertical

vertical format: formato vertical

vertical line: recta vertical

vertical line test: prueba de la recta vertical

vertical line test for function: prueba de la línea vertical para una función

vertical symmetry: simetría vertical

vertices: vértices

visualization: visualización

volume change: cambio de volumen

volume of a cone: volumen de un cono

volume of a cylinder: volumen de un cilindro

volume of a prism: volumen de un prisma

volume of a solid: volumen de un sólido

volume of a solid figure: volumen de una figura sólida

whole number: número entero

whole unit: unidad entera

width of an interval: anchura de un intervalo

with repetition: con repetición

with replacement: con reemplazo

without repetition: sin repetición

without replacement: sin reemplazo

work backwards: trabajar de atrás para adelante

write an equation: escribir una ecuación

written explanation: explicación escrita

written form of reasoning: forma gráfica de razonamiento

written language: lenguaje escrito o gráfico

written representations: representaciones escritas

written symbols: símbolos escritos

V
W

X

x-axis: eje x

x-coordinate: coordenada x

x-intercept: Intersección con el eje x

x-intercept of a line: intercepción de x de una línea

Y

y-axis: eje y

y-coordinate: coordenada y

y-intercept: intersección con el eje y

y-intercept of a line: intercepción de y de una línea

Z

z-axis: eje z

zero as the identity element in addition: cero como el elemento neutro en una suma

zero degree: grado cero

zero divisor: divisor cero

zero exponent: exponente cero

zero of a function: cero de una función

zero product property: propiedad del producto cero

zero property of addition: propiedad de adición del cero

zero property of multiplication: propiedad multiplicativa del cero

zero slope: pendiente cero o cuesta cero

X
Y
Z

Science
Subject Vocabulary
English-Spanish

Bilingual Dictionaries, Inc.

A

abiogenesis: abiogénesis
abiotic: abiótico
abrade: raer, gastar
abrasion: abrasión
absolute age: edad absoluta
absolute alcohol: alcohol absoluto
absolute dating: datación absoluta
absolute magnitude: magnitud absoluta
absolute scale: escala de temperatura Kelvin o escala absoluta
absolute temperature scale: escala absoluta de temperatura
absolute zero: cero absoluto
absorbency: absorbencia
absorption: absorción
absorption coefficient: coeficiente de absorción
absorption plant: planta de absorción
absorption spectrum: espectro de absorción
absorption tube: tubo de absorción
absorptivity: absortividad
abyssal plain: planicie abisal
accelerated filtration: filtración acelerada
accelerating agent: agente de aceleración
acceleration: aceleración
acceleration of gravity: aceleración de la gravedad
accelofilter: filtro acelerado
accentuate: acentuar
acceptor: aceptor
accordance: concordancia
acetaldehyde: acetaldehído
acetone: acetona
acetylcholine: acetilcolina
acetylene: acetileno
acetylene series: serie acetilénica

acid: ácido
acid anhydride: anhídrido de ácido
acid precipitation: lluvia ácida
acid radical: radical ácido
acid rain: lluvia ácida
acid salt: sal ácida
acid soil: suelo ácido
acid test: prueba de acidez
acid treating: tratamiento ácido
acid-base indicator: indicador ácido-base
acid-base neutralization: neutralización ácido-base
acid-base titration: titulación (valoración) ácido-base
acidification: acidificación
acidimeter: acidímetro
acne: acné
acoustics: acústica
acquired characteristics: características adquiridas
acquired immunity: inmunidad adquirida
acquired imunodeficiency syndrome (AIDS): síndrome de inmunodeficiencia adquirida (SIDA)
acromegaly: acromegalia
actinide series: serie actínida
actinium: actinio
actinochemistry: química del actinio
activated support: soporte activado
activated water: agua activada
activation energy: energía de activación
activator: activador
active centers: centros activos
active complex: complejo activo
active immunity: inmunidad activa
active site: sitio activo
active transport: transporte activo
activity support: soporte de la actividad
actual evapotranspiration: evapotranspiración real

adaptation: adaptación
adaptive: adaptante
adaptive radiation: radiación adaptativa
adaptive value: valor adaptativo
addition: suma, adición
addition agent: agente de adición
addition polymer: polímero de adición
addition reaction: reacción de adición
adenine: adenina
adenosine diphosphate (ADP): difosfato de adenosina (DFA)
adenosine monophosphate (AMP): monofosfato de adenosina (MFA)
adenosine tri-phosphate (ATP) : tri-fosfato de adenosina (TFA)
adhesion: adhesión
adiabatic calorimeter: calorímetro adi-abático
adiabatic flame temperature: tempera-tura de llama adiabática
adiabatic temperature change: cambio adiabático de temperatura
adipose tissue: tejido adiposo
adrenal cortex: corteza suprarrenal
adrenal gland: glándula suprarrenal
adrenal medulla: médula suprarrenal
adrenaline: adrenalina
adrenocorticotropic hormone (ACTH): hormona adrenocorticotrópica (HACT)
adsorbent: adsorbente
adsorption: adsorción
adsorption isobar: isobara de adsorción
adsorption isotherm: isoterma de adsorción
aeration: ventilación, aireación
aerobe: aerobio
aerobic: aeróbico
aerobic bacteria: bacteria aeróbica
aerobic respiration: respiración aerobia
aerodynamics: aerodinámica
aerosol: aerosol

afterbirth: placenta
agar: alga agar
agarose: agarosa
agglutination: aglutinación
agglutinin: aglutinina
agglutinogen: aglutinógeno
aggression: agresión
aging: envejecer
air mass: masa de aire
air pollution: contaminación del aire
air pressure: presión de aire (presión atmosférica)
air resistance: resistencia del aire
air sac: saco de aire
air space: espacio de aire
air track: ruta del aire
airfoil: superficie de sustentación
albinism: albinismo
albino: albino
albumen: albúmina
alcohol: alcohol
alcoholic fermentation: fermentación alcohólica
aldehyde: aldehído
algae: alga(s)
algal bloom: alga en flor
alicyclic hydrocarbons: hidrocarburo alicíclico
alimentary canal: tubo digestivo
aliphatic hydrocarbons: hidrocarburo alifático
alkalescence: alcalescencia
alkali: álcali
alkali metal: metal alcalino
alkaline: alcalino
alkaline earth metal: metal alcalino-térreo
alkaline soil: suelo alcalino
alkane: alcano
alkane derivative: derivado de alcano

A

alkene: alqueno

alkyl: alquilo

alkyne: alquino

all or none response: toda o ninguna respuesta

allantosis: alantoides

allele: alelo(s)

allene: aleno

allergen: alérgeno

allergic reactions: reacciones alérgicas

allergy: alergia

allotrope: alótropo

allotropy: alotropía

alloy: aleación

alluvian fan: abanico aluvial

alpha emission: emisión alfa

alpha particle: partícula alfa

alpine glacier: glaciar alpino

altered gene: gen modificado (alterado)

alternating current (AC): corriente alterna (CA)

alternating current generator: generador de corriente alterna

alternation of generation: alternación de generaciones

altimeter: altímetro

alto: alto

alum: alumbre

alumina: óxido de aluminio

alveoli: alvéolos

alveolus: alvéolo

amalgam: amalgama

amber: ámbar

ameba: amiba

ameboid movement: movimiento ameboide

amethyst: amatista

amino acid: aminoácido

amino group: grupo amino

ammeter: amperímetro

ammonia: amoniaco

ammonia liquor: licor de amoniaco

ammonification: amonificación

ammonium: amonio

amniocentesis: amniocentesis

amnion: amnios

amniotic egg: huevo amniótico

amniotic fluid: líquido amniótico

amniotic sac: saco amniótico

amorphous: amorfo

ampere: amperio

amperometry: amperimetría

amphibian: anfibio

amphibole: anfíbol

amphiprotic: anfiprótico

amphoteric: anfotérico

amphoterism: anfoterismo

amplitude: amplitud

amylase: amilasa

anabolism: anabolismo

anaerobe: anaerobio

anaerobic: anaeróbico

anaerobic bacteria: bacteria anaeróbica

analgesic: analgésico

analogous structure: estructura análoga

analyst: analista

analytical balance: balanza analítica

analytical chemisty: química analítica

analytical reagent: reactivo analítico

anaphase: anafase

andesite: andesita

androgen: andrógeno

anemometer: anemómetro

aneroid: aneroide

aneroid barometer: barómetro aneroide

angina pectoris: angina de pecho

angiosperms: angiospermas

angle: ángulo; mover en ángulo
angle of insolation: ángulo de insolación
angstrom: ångström (Å)
angular rate: velocidad angular
angular unconformity: discordancia
angular
anhydride: anhídrido
anhydrous: anhidro
Animalia: mundo animal
anion: anión
annular: anular
anode: ánodo
anomaly: anomalía
antacid: antiácido
Antarctic Continent: Continente Antártico
anterior: anterior asociación
anther: antera
anthracite: antracita
antibiotics: antibióticos
antibody: anticuerpo
antichlor: anticloro
anticline: anticlinal
anticodon: anticodón
anticyclone: anticiclón
antienzyme: antienzima
antifebrin: antifiebrina
antifoaming agent: agente antiespumante
antifreeze: anticongelante
antigen: antígeno
antihistamine: antihistamínico
antimatter: antimateria
antimony: antimonio
antinodal line: línea antinodal
antinode: antinodo
antioxidant: antioxidante
antiparticle: antipartícula
antiseptic: antiséptico
antitoxin: antitoxina
anus: ano

aorta: aorta
apatite: apatita
aphelion: afelio
aphotic zone: zona afótica
apogee: apogeo
apparent daily motion: movimiento
apparent magnitude: magnitud aparente
apparent planetary diameter: diámetro
planetario aparente
apparent solar day: día solar
appendage: apéndice
applied force: fuerza aplicada
approach: planteamiento
appropriate: apropiado
approximately: aproximadamente
aqua regia: agua regia
aquaculture: acuacultura
aqueous: acuoso
aquifer: acuífero
arch: arco
archer: arquero
Archimedes' principle: principio de
Arquímedes
arete: arista
argon: argón
Aristotle: Aristóteles
armature: armadura
arsenic trioxide: trióxido de arsénico
arsenical: arsénico
arsenide: arseniuro
arteriole: arteriola
artery: arteria
arthropod: artrópodo
artificial radioactivity: radioactividad
artificial
artificial selection: selección artificial
asbestos: asbesto
ascending colon: colon ascendente
ascending flow: flujo ascendente

A

---

ascorbic acid: ácido ascórbico

asexual: asexual

asexual reproduction: reproducción asexual

asexually: de modo asexual

aspen: álamo temblón

assembled: montado

assistant: asistente

association neuron: neurona de asociación

assuming: suponiendo

aster: rayo astral

asteroid: asteroide

asthenosphere: astenosfera

asthma: asma

astigmatism: astigmatismo

astronomical: astronómico

astronomical unit: unidad astronómica

atherosclerosis: ateroesclerosis

athlete's foot: pie de atleta

atmosphere: atmósfera

atmospheric pressure: presión atmosférica

atmospheric temperature: temperatura atmosférica

atmospheric variable: variable atmosférica

atom: átomo

atomic absorption spectrometry: espectrometría de absorción atómica

atomic bond: enlace atómico

atomic energy: energía atómica

atomic mass: masa atómica

atomic mass unit: unidad de masa atómica

atomic number: número atómico

atomic pile: pila atómica

atomic radius: radio atómico

atomic weight: peso atómico

atria: aurículas

atrium: atrio

auditory: auditorio, auditivo

auditory canal: canal auditivo

auditory nerve: nervio auditivo

augite: augita

auricle: aurícula

aurora: aurora

aurora borealis: aurora boreal

autoclave: autoclave

autonomic nervous system: sistema nervioso autónomo

autosome: autosoma

autotroph: autótrofo

autotrophic: autotrófico

autotrophic nutrition: nutrición autotrófica

auxin: auxina

average atomic mass: masa atómica promedio

average speed: velocidad promedio

average velocity: velocidad promedio

Avogadro's number (6.022 * 10^23): número de Avogadro (6.022*10^23)

axis: eje

axle: eje (mecánico)

axon: axón

azeotropic: azeotrópico

azimuth: azimut (acimut)

azurite: azurita

B

back-EMF: fuerza electromotriz (FEM) contraria

backwash: estela, agitación

bacterial: bacteriano

bacterial infections: infecciones bacterianas

bacterial pneumonia: pulmonía bacteriana

bacteriophage: bacteriófago

bacterium: bacteria

B

baffle: deflector, desviador, pantalla acústica

baking powder: polvo de hornear

baking soda: bicarbonato de sodio

balanced chemical equation: ecuación química equilibrada

balanced diet: dieta balanceada

balanced equation: ecuación balanceada

balanced forces: fuerzas balanceadas

ball and socket joint: articulación de la rótula

banding: agruparse en bandas o franjas

barium: bario

barium carbonate: carbonato de bario

barium chloride: cloruro de bario

barium nitrate: nitrato de bario

barium sulfate: sulfato de bario

barnacle: percebe

barometric pressure: presión barométrica

barrier beach: barrera costera

barrier island: isla de la barrera

barycenter: baricentro

baryon: barión (partícula sub-atómica)

basalt: basalto

basaltic: basáltica

base: base

base level: nivel de base

base-pairing: parejas de base

basic anhydride: anhídrido básico

basic equation: ecuación básica

basidium: basidio

basin: lavabo

bass: bajo

batholith: batolito

bathymetric map: mapa batimétrico

bauxite: bauxita

baymouth bar: barra de boca

beach: playa

beach face: frente de playa

beaker: vaso de beaker

beam balance: barra de equilibrio

beat: golpe rítmico, oscilación

bedding: estratificarse, distribuirse en capas

bedload: lecho de carga

bedrock: roca firme, lecho de roca

behavior: comportamiento

behavioral: del comportamiento

benchmark: punto de referencia fijo

benedict's solution: solución de Benedict

beneficiation: beneficio

bent: curvado

benthos: bentos

benzaldehyde: benzaldehído

benzene ring: anillo bencénico

benzene series: serie bencénica

benzenesulfonic acid: ácido benzeno-sulfónico

benzenoid: benzenoide

benzidine: bencidina

benzoic acid: ácido benzoico

benzyl alcohol: alcohol bencílico

beriberi: beriberi

berkelium: berquelio

berm: berma, arcén

Bernoulli's principle: principio de Bernoulli

beryllium: berilio

beta particle: partícula beta

bias: predisposición

bicarbonate indicator: indicador de bicarbonato

biceps: bíceps

bicuspid valve: válvula bicúspide

big bang theory: teoría de la Gran Explosión

bilateral symmetry: simetría bilateral

bile duct: conducto biliar

bile pigment: pigmento biliar

billiard: carambola; billar

bimetallic: bimetálico

bimetallic strip: cinta bimetálica

B

binary compound: compuesto binario
binary fission: fisión binaria
binary stars: estrellas binarias
bind: atar, unir, ligar
binder: aglutinante, ligante
binding energy: energía de aglutinación, ligazón, energía enlazante
binocular: binocular
binomial nomenclature: nomenclatura binomial
biochemical: bioquímico
biochemistry: bioquímica
biodegradable: biodegradable
biodiversity: biodiversidad
biogenesis: biogénesis
biogeochemical cycle: ciclo biogeoquímico
biological catalysts: catalizadores biológicos
biological control: control biológico
biological magnification: ampliación biológica
biological vector: vector biológico
biology: biología
biomass: biomasa
biomass energy: energía de biomasa
biome: bioma
bioremediation: bioremediación
biosphere: biosfera
biotechnological: biotecnológico
biotechnology: biotecnología
biotic: biótico
biotic factor: factor biótico
biotite: biotita
birch: abedul
birth canal: canal de nacimiento
birth control: control de natalidad
birth rate: índice de natalidad
bismuth: bismuto
bituminous coal: carbón bituminoso
biuret test: prueba de biuret

black hole: agujero negro
bladder: vejiga
blastula: blástula
blending inheritance: herencia mezclada
blind spot: punto ciego
blinking: parpadeando
blood cavity: cavidad de la sangre
blood circulation: circulación de la sangre
blood clotting: coagulación de la sangre
blood group: grupo sanguíneo
blood plasma: plasma sanguíneo
blood platelet: plaquetas sanguíneas
blood pressure: presión arterial
blood smear: frotis sanguíneo
blood sugar: azúcar de la sangre
blood tissue: tejido sanguíneo
blood transfusion: transfusión de sangre
blood vessel: vaso sanguíneo
blowing agent: agente de soplado
body heat: calor corporal
boiler scale: balanza de caldera
boiling: hirviendo
boiling point: punto de ebullición
boiling point elevation: elevación del punto de ebullición
boldface: negrita
Boltzmann constant: constante de Boltzmann
bond: enlace; lazo; ligar
bond angle: ángulo de enlace
bond energy: energía de enlace
bonding: enlace
bone marrow: médula ósea
bone tissue: tejido óseo
borax: bórax
boric acid: ácido bórico
boroflouride: fluoruro de boro
boron: boro
boron carbide: carburo de boro

boron hydride: hidruro de boro

boron nitride: nitruro de boro

borosilicate: borosilicato

bowling ball: bola de boliche

Bowman's capsule: cápsula de Bowman

bowstring: cuerda de arco

Boyle's Law: Ley de Boyle

brain stem: tronco cerebral

brake fluid: fluido (líquido) de frenos

branch-chain: cadena ramificada

brass: bronce, latón

brazing: soldadura

bread mold: pan de molde

breaker: quebrantador o triturador

breccia: brecha

breeder reactor: reactor generador de neutrones, reactor reproductor

breeding: cria, crianza

bright line spectrum: espectro de líneas brillantes

brine: salmuera

bristle: cerda

broadcast: difusión, emisión o transmisión

broccoli: brócoli

bromine: bromo

bromthymol blue: azul de bromotimol

bronchi: bronquios

bronchus: bronquio

bubble chamber: cámara de burbujas

budding: florecimiento, gemación

buffer: solución buffer o amortiguadora

bug: manipulador; intromisión

bugle: corneta

Bunsen burner: quemador de Bunsen

buoyancy: flotación, fuerza flotante

buoyant: boyante

buoyant force: fuerza boyante

burette: bureta

burglar alarm: alarma contra robo

burning: quemando

butane: butano

butanediol: butanodiol

butanol: butanol

butene: buteno

butyl: butilo

butyl alcohol: alcohol butílico

butyl rubber: goma butílica

butyric acid: ácido butírico

by virtue of: en virtud de

C

cadmium: cadmio

cadmium sulfide: sulfuro de cadmio

calcination: calcinación

calcite: calcita

calcium: calcio

calcium carbide: carburo de calcio

calcium carbonate: carbonato de calcio

calcium chloride: cloruro de calcio

calcium hydroxide: hidróxido de calcio

calcium hypochlorite: hipoclorito de calcio

calcium oxide: óxido de calcio

calcium phosphate: fosfato de calcio

calcium sulfate: sulfato de calcio

calculus: cálculo

caldera: caldera

californium: californio

calomel: calomel

caloric: calórico

caloric theory: teoría calórica

calorie: caloría

calorimeter: calorímetro

calorimetry: calorimetría

cambium: cambium

Cambrian: Cambriano
camper: campista
camphor: alcanfor
candela: candela
cannonball: bala de cañón
canopy: pabellón
capacitance: capacitancia
capacitor: condensador
capallarity: capilaridad
capillary: capilar
capillary action: acción capilar
carbene: carbeno
carbide: carburo
carbocyclic: carbocíclico
carbohydrase: carbohidrasa
carbohydrate: carbohidrato
carbolic acid: ácido carbólico
carbon (C): carbono (C)
carbon black: negro de carbono
carbon cycle: ciclo del carbono
carbon dating: datación por carbono
carbon dioxide (CO2): dióxido de carbono (CO2)
carbon disulfide: disulfuro de carbono
carbon film: película de carbono
carbon fixation: fijación del carbono
carbon grain: grano de carbono
carbon monoxide: monóxido de carbono
carbon tetrachloride: tetracloruro de carbono
carbonate: carbonato
carbonation: carbonatación
carbon-containing: que contiene carbono
carbonic acid: ácido carbónico
carbonide: carbonuro
carboniferous: carbonífero
carboxyl: carboxílico
carboxylic acid: ácido carboxílico
carburetion: carburación

carcinogen: carcinógeno
cardiac muscle: músculo cardíaco
cardiovascular disease: enfermedad cardiovascular
cardiovascular system: sistema cardio-vascular
carnivore: carnívoro
carotene: caroteno
carrier: transportador
carrier wave: onda transportadora
carrying capacity: capacidad de carga
carrying power: poder de conducción
cartilage: cartílago
carton: cartón
cast: vaciado
catabolism: catabolismo
catalase: catalasa
catalyst: catalizador
catenate: encadenado
catfish: siluro (bagre)
catheter: catéter
cathode: cátodo
cathode ray: rayo catódico
cathode ray tube: tubo de rayos catódicos
cation: catión
cattail: totora
caudal fin: aleta caudal
caudal vertabra: vértebra caudal
caudatum: caudatum
cause-and-effect: causa y efecto
cave: cueva
celestial object: objeto celeste
celestial sphere: esfera celeste
cell: célula
cell body: cuerpo celular
cell cycle: ciclo celular
cell division: división celular
cell membrane: membrana celular
cell plate: placa celular

cell specialization: especialización celular

cell theory: teoría celular

cell wall: pared celular

cell-mediated immunity: inmunidad transmitida por célula

cellular respiration: respiración celular

cellulose: celulosa

Celsius (C°): grado Celsius (ºC)

Celsius Scale: escala de Celsio

celtium: celtio

cementation: cementación

Cenozoic Era: Era Cenozoica

centi: centi (prefijo)

centigrade: centígrado

central circulation: circulación central

central nervous system: sistema nervioso central

centrifugal force: fuerza centrifuga

centrifugation: centrifugación

centrifuge: centrífugo

centriole: centriolo

centripetal: centrípeto; centrípeta

centripetal acceleration: aceleración centrípeta

centripetal force: fuerza centrípeta

centromere: centrómero

centrosome: centrosoma

ceramics: cerámicas

cereal group: grupo cereal

cerebellum: cerebelo

cerebral cortex: corteza cerebral

cerebrospinal fluid: líquido cefalorraquídeo

cerebrum: cerebro

cerium: cerio

cervix: cérvix

cesium: cesio

chain reaction: reacción en cadena

chalcopyrite: pirita de cobre, calcopirita

change of direction: cambio de dirección

change of motion: cambio de movimiento

change of speed: cambio de velocidad

channel: canal

charge: carga; cargar

charged: cargado

charging by conduction: cargar por conducción

charging by contact: cargar por contacto

charging by induction: cargar por inducción

Charles' Law: Ley de Charles

chelate: quelato

chemical bond: enlace químico

chemical change: cambio químico

chemical digestion: digestión química

chemical energy: energía química

chemical equation: ecuación química

chemical equilibrium: equilibrio químico

chemical formula: fórmula química

chemical potential energy: energía química potencial

chemical property: propiedad química

chemical reaction: reacción química

chemical system: sistema quimico

chemical weathering: erosión química

chemisorption: quemisorción

chemoautotroph: quimioautotrofo

chemosynthesis: quimiosíntesis

chemotherapy: quimioterapia

chemotroph: quimiotrofo

chipmunk: ardilla

chitin: quitina

chlorate: clorato

chloride: cloruro

chlorine: cloro

chlorine dioxide: dióxido de cloro

chlorite: clorito

chlorofluorocarbons (CFCs): clorofluoro-carbonos (CFCs)

chloroform: cloroformo

chlorohydrin: clorhidrina
chlorophyll: clorofila
chloroplast: cloroplasto
chordate: cordado
chorion: corión
chromatic: cromático
chromatic aberration: aberración cromática
chromatid: cromatida
chromatin: cromatina
chromatography: cromatografía
chrome green: verde cromo
chromic acid: ácido crómico
chromium: cromo
chromium sulfate: sulfato de cromo
chromosomal alteration: alteración cromosómica
chromosomal recombinations: recombinaciones cromosómicas
chromosome: cromosoma
chromosphere: cromosfera
chronological: cronológico
chronometer: cronómetro
chyme: quimo
cilia: cilio(s)
ciliary motion: movimiento ciliar
cinder cone: cono de toba (ceniza)
cinder cone volcano: volcán de cono de ceniza
cinnabar: cinabrio
circuit: circuito
circuit breaker: cortacircuito
circulatory: circulatorio
circulatory system: aparato circulatorio, sistema circulatorio
circumpolar stars: estrellas circumpolares
cirque: circo glaciar
cirro: cirro
cirrus cloud: nube cirrus
citric acid: ácido cítrico

classical mechanics: mecánica clásica
clastic rock: roca clástica
clawed: desgarrado
claws: garras
climate: clima
climax community: comunidad clímax
climax fauna: fauna clímax
climax flora: flora clímax
closed circulatory system: sistema circulatorio cerrado
closed energy system: sistema cerrado de energía
cloud chamber: cámara de vapor
coacervate: coacervado
coal: carbón mineral
coarse adjustment: ajuste grueso
coastal ocean: costa oceánica
cobalt: cobalto
cocci: cocos
coccus: coco
cochlea: cóclea
cocoon: capullo
codominance: codominancia
codon: codón
coefficient: coeficiente
coefficient of friction: coeficiente de fricción
coefficient of linear expansion: coeficiente de expansión lineal
coefficient of volume expansion: coeficiente de expansión de volumen
coefficients: coeficientes
coenzyme: coenzima
coevolution: coevolución
coherent light: luz coherente
cohesive: cohesivo
cohesive force: fuerza cohesiva
coil: rollo, bobina; enrollar
cold front: frente frío

collecting duct: conducto colectivo

colligative properties: propiedades coligativas

collision boundary: limite de colisión

colloid: coloide

colloid chemistry: química coloidal

colloidal dispersion: dispersión coloidal

colloids: coloides

color blindness: daltonismo

colorant: colorante

coloration: coloración

colorimetry: colorimetría

columbium: columbio

combined gas laws: leyes de los gases combinadas

combustion reaction: reacción de combustión

comet: cometa

commensalism: comensalismo

common ancestor: antepasado común

common cold: resfriado común

common ion effect: efecto del ión común

communicable: transmisible

community: comunidad

commutator: conmutador

compaction: compactación

competitive exclusion principle: principio de exclusión competitivo

complementary: complementario

complementary colors: colores complementarios

complementary pigment: pigmento complementario

complete protein: proteína completa

complex carbohydrate: carbohidrato complejo o polisacárido

complex ion: ión complejo

complex multicellular: complejo multicelular

composite: compuesto

composite volcano: volcán compuesto

compost: compuesto de desechos

compost pile: pila de composta

compound: compuesto

compound eye: ojo compuesto

compound light microscope: microscopio óptico compuesto

compound machine: máquina compuesta

compound microscope: microscopio compuesto

compress: compresa; comprimir

compressed gas: gas comprimido

compression wave: onda de compresión

Compton effect: efecto Compton

concave: cóncavo

concave lens: lente cóncavo

concave mirror: espejo cóncavo

concentrated solution: solución concentrada

concentration gradient: gradiente de concentración

conceptual definition: definición conceptual

concurrent forces: fuerzas concurrentes

condensation: condensación

condensation polymer: polímero de condensación

condensation reaction: reacción de condensación

conditioned reflex: reflejo condicionado

conditioning: acondicionamiento

conduction: conducción

conductivity: conductividad

conductor: conductor

configuration: configuración

configurational formula: fórmula configuracional

conformation: conformación

conglomerate: conglomerado

Congo Red: rojo congo

conic projection: proyección cónica
conifer: conífero
coniferous: conífero
coniferous forest: bosque conífero
conjugate pair: par conjugado
conjugation: conjugación
connective tissue: tejido conectivo
consciousness: conocimiento; conciencia
conservation: conservación
conservation factor: factor de conservación
conservation law: ley de conservación
conservation of change: conservación del cambio
conservation of energy: conservación de energía
conservation of environment: conservación del medio ambiente
considered: considerado
consist of: consiste en
consonance: consonancia
constant: constante
constant composition law: ley de las composiciones fijas
constellation: constelación
constituent: constituyente
constructive interference: interferencia constructiva
consumer: consumidor
contact metamorphism: metamorfismo de contacto
contaminant: contaminante
continental climate: clima continental
continental crust: corteza continental
continental drift: deriva continental
continental glacier: glaciar continental
continental plate: placa continental
continental rise: elevación continental
continental shelf: plataforma continental
continental slope: talud continental

continental tropical air mass: masa de aire tropical continental
continuous spectrum: espectro continuo
contour farming: cultivo de contorno
contour feathers: contorno de las plumas
contour interval: distancia entre curvas de nivel
contour line: linea de contorno
contour map: mapa con curvas de nivel (topográfico)
contour plowing: arado de contorno
contraception: anticoncepción
contractile vacuole: vacuola contráctil
control: control
control rod: vara de control
controlled equipment: equipo controlado
controlled experiment: experimento controlado
controlled variable: variable controlada
convalescence: convalecencia
convection: convección
convection cell: convección celular
convection current: corriente de convección
convergence zone: zona de convergencia
convergent boundaries: límites convergentes
convergent cytolysis: citólisis convergentes
convergent evolution: evolución convergente
converging lens: lente convergente
convex: convexo
convex lens: lente convexo
convex mirror: espejo convexo
coordinate covalent bond: enlace covalente coordinado
coordinate system: sistema de coordenadas
coordinating system: sistema de coordinación
copolymer: copolímero
coral: coral

coral reef: arrecife de coral

Coriolis effect: efecto de Coriolis

cornea: córnea

corona: corona

coronary circulation: circulación coronaria

coronay artery: arteria coronaria

corpus luteum: cuerpo lúteo

corrosion: corrosión

cortex: corteza

cortisone: cortisona

cotyledon: cotiledón

coulomb: culombio

Coulomb's Law: Ley de Culombio

courtship behavior: comportamiento de cortejo

covalence: covalencia

covalent bond: enlace covalente

covalent molecule: molécula covalente

cover crop: cultivos de cobertura

coverslip: cubreobjetos

cowper's gland: glándula de Cowper

cracking: agrietamiento

craft: balsa, transbordador

cranial nerve: par craneal o nervio craneal

crate: caja; embalaje

crater: cráter

crayfish: jaiba de río

creep: reptación

crescent: creciente

cresol: cresol

crest: cresta

Cretaceous: cretáceo

cretinism: cretinismo

crevasse: grieta glaciar

critical angle: ángulo crítico

critical mass: masa crítica

critical point: punto crítico

critical pressure: presión crítica

critical temperature: temperatura crítica

crop: cultivo

crop rotation: rotación de cosecha

cross breeding: apareamiento cruzado

cross fertilization: fertilización cruzada

cross pollination: polinización cruzada

cross-bedding: estratificación cruzada

crossing-over: entrecruzamiento

crown glass: corona de cristal

crucible: crisol

crustacean: crustáceo

cryptic coloration: coloración críptica

crystal: cristal

crystal deformation: deformación cristalina

crystal lattice: entramado de cristal, red cristalina

crystalline: cristalino

crystalline structure: estructura cristalina

crystallization: cristalización

cultivated plant: planta cultivada

cumulonimbus clouds: nubes cumulonimbos

curium: curio (Cm)

curvature: curvatura

cuticle: cutícula

cutting: recorte

cyan: cian, magenta

cyanobacteria: cianobacteria

cyanogen: cianógeno

cyclic behavior: comportamiento cíclico

cyclic change: cambio cíclico

cyclic compoud: compuesto cíclico

cycling: ciclo

cycloalkane: cicloalcano

cycloalkene: cicloalqueno

cyclohexane: ciclohexano

cyclosis: ciclosis

cyclotron: ciclotrón

cymbal: movimiento del protoplasma en la célula

cysteine: cisteína
cytokinesis: citocinesis
cyton: citon
cytoplasm: citoplasma
cytoplasmic division: división citoplásmica
cytosine: citosina
cytoskeleton: citoesqueleto

C
D

D

daily motion: movimiento diario
dark reaction: reacción oscura
darwinism: darwinismo
data table: tabla de datos, tabla de información
daughter cell: célula hija
de Broglie Principle: principio de Broglie
deamination: desaminación
deceleration: deceleración, disminución de la velocidad
deci: deci (prefijo)
decibel: decibel
deciduous: de hoja caduca
deciduous forest: bosque deciduo
deciduous tree: árbol caducifolio de hoja grande (deciduo)
declination: declinación
decomposer: descomponer
decomposition: descomposición
decomposition reaction: reacción de descomposición
decrepitation: decrepitación
defecation: defecación
defective gene: gen defectuoso
deficiency disease: enfermedad de carencia
deflation: deflación

deflect: desviar
defoliation: deshoje
deforestation: deforestación
deformation: deformación
dehydrating agent: agente deshidratante
dehydration: deshidratación
dehydration synthesis: síntesis por deshidratación
dehydrogenase: deshidrogenasa
dehydrogenation: deshidrogenación
deionized water: agua desionizada
deka: deca (prefijo)
dekameter: decámetro
deletion: supresión
deliquescence: delicuescencia
delivery tube: tubo de suministro
demographic transition: transición demográfica
demography: demografía
demonstration: demostración
denaturation: desnaturalización
denatured alcohol: alcohol desnaturalizado
dendrite: dendrita
dendritic pattern: patrón dendrítico
denitrification: desnitrificación
denitrifying bacteria: bacteria de desnitrificación
density: densidad
density current: corriente de densidad
density-dependant limiting factor: factor limitante dependiente de la densidad
density-independent limiting factor: factor limitante independiente de la densidad
deoxyribonucleic acid (DNA): ácido desoxirribonucleico (ADN)
deoxyribose: desoxirribosa
dependent variable: variable dependiente
depletion: agotamiento

depolymerization: despolimerización
deposition: deposición
depressant: depresivo
derived: derivado
derived unit: unidad derivada
dermis: dermis
desalination: desalinización
descending flow: flujo descendente
desert: desierto
destructive distillation: destilación destructiva
destructive interference: interferencia destructiva
detection: descubrimiento, detección
detoxication: desintoxicación
detritus: detrito
deuterium: deuterio
deuteron: deuterón
developing agent: agente revelador
deviate: desviarse
Devonian period: período devoniano
dew point: punto de condensación
dewdrop: gota de rocío
dextrorotatory: dextrógiro
dextrose: dextrosa
dialysis: diálisis
diaphragm: diafragma
diastole: diástole
diastolic pressure: presión diastólica
diastrophism: diastrofismo
diatom: diatomea o tierra de infusorios
diatomic gas: gas diatómico
diatomic molecule: molécula diatómica
diborane: diborano
dicarboxylic acid: ácido dicarboxílico
dichotomous: dicótomo
dichotomous key: clave dicotómica
dicot: dicotiledónea
dicotyledon: dicotiledon

died off: se extinguió
diethylamine: dietilamina
difference in electric potential: diferencia en potencia eléctrica
differentiation: diferenciación
diffract: difractar
diffraction: difracción
diffraction grating: rejilla de difracción
diffuse reflection: reflexión difusa
diffusion: difusión
digestion: digestión
digestive enzyme: enzima digestiva
digestive juice: jugo digestivo
digestive system: aparato digestivo, sistema digestivo
dihybird cross: cruce dihíbrido
dihybrid: dihíbrido
dihydroxy alcohol: alcohol dihidroxílico
dike: dique
dilation of blood vessel: dilatación del vaso sanguíneo
diluent: diluyente
dilute solution: solución diluida
dimethylketone: dimetilcetona
dimmer: reductor de luz
dimorphism: dimorfismo
dinitrobenzene: dinitrobenceno
diolefin: diolefina
diorite: diorita
dioxide: dióxido
dip: inmersión; sumergir
dipeptide: dipéptido
diphtheria: difteria
diploid: diploide
dipole: dipolo
direct combination: combinación directa
direct combustion reaction: reacción de combustión directa
direct current (DC): corriente directa (CD)

direct harvesting: cosecha directa
direct rays: rayos directos
directly: directamente
disaccharide: disacárido
disappearing trait: rasgo en vías de extinción
disconformity: disconformidad
discs: discos
disjunction: disyunción
dislocation: dislocación
dispersion: dispersión
displace: desplazar
displacement: desplazamiento, desalojamiento
displacement sediments: sedimentos de desplazamiento
displacement series: series de desplazamiento
disproportionation: desproporción
dissecting microscope: microscopio de disección
dissection: disección
dissociation: disociación
dissonance: disonancia
distance: distancia
distillate: destilado
distillation: destilación
distorted structure: estructura deformada
distributary: distributario
disturb: molestar, perturbar
diuretic: diurético
diurnal: diurno
diverge: divergir
divergence zone: zona de divergencia
divergent boundaries: límites divergentes
diverging lens: lente divergente
divider: divisor
DNA (deoxyribonucleic acid): ADN (ácido desoxirribonucleico)
DNA fingerprinting: identificación por ADN

DNA polymerase: polimerasa del ADN
dockhand: estibador
dolomite: dolomita
dominance: dominió
dominant: dominante
dominant gene: gen dominante
dominant species: especie dominante
dominant trait: rasgo dominante
doping: dopaje
Doppler effect: efecto Doppler
Doppler shift: corrimiento Doppler
dormancy: letargo
dorsal: dorsal
dot diagram: diagrama de puntos
double displacement reaction: doble reaccion de desplazamiento
double bond: enlace doble
double fertilization: fertilización doble
double helix: hélice doble
double slit diffraction: difracción de doble red
double-pan balance: balanza de doble plato
down feathers: plumón
Down's syndrome: síndrome de Down
drainage basin: cuenca de drenaje
drainage patterns: patrones de drenaje
drilling: taladrar
drone: zángano
droplet: gotita
drosophila: drosófila
drug abuse: abuso de drogas
drug dependence: dependencia de la droga
drug overdose: sobredosis de droga
drum: bobina, carrete
drumlin: estría
dry adiabatic lapse rate: intervalo de cambio adiabático seco
duckweed: lenteja de agua
ductile: dúctil

D
E

ductility: ductilidad
ductless gland: glándula sin conducto
dune: duna
duodenum: duodeno
duration of insolation: duración de la insolación
dust storm: tormenta de polvo
dwarfism: enanismo
dynamic equilibrium: equilibrio dinámico
dysentery: disentería
dysprosium: disprosio

E

ear: oído, oreja
ear canal: canal de la oreja (auditivo)
eardrum: tímpano
earthquake: terremoto
earthworm: lombriz
eccentricity: excentricidad
echinoderm: equinodermo
echolocation: ecolocalización
eclipse of the sun: eclipse solar
ecliptic: eclíptico
ecological: ecológico
ecological niche: nicho ecológico
ecological pyramid: pirámide ecológica
ecological succession: sucesión ecológica
ecologically: de modo ecológico
ecology: ecología
economically: económicamente
ecosphere: ecosfera
ecosystem: ecosistema
ecosystem diversity: diversidad de ecosistema
ectoderm: ectodermo

ectotherm: ectotérmico
edema: edema
effective collision: colisión efectiva
effective resistance: resistencia efectiva
effectively: efectivamente
effector: efector
effervescence: efervescencia
efficiency: eficiencia
efflorescence: eflorescencia
egestion: egestión o excreción
egg: óvulo
Einstein: Einstein
einsteinium: einstenio
El Niño: El Niño
elastic collision: colisión elástica
elastic potential energy: energía elástica potencial
elasticity: elasticidad
electric current: corriente eléctrica
electric field: campo eléctrico
electric field intensity: intensidad de campo eléctrico
electric field line: línea de campo eléctrico
electric force: fuerza eléctrica
electric generator: generador eléctrico
electric motor: motor eléctrico
electric potential: potencial eléctrico
electrical conductivity: conductividad eléctrica
electrical energy: energía eléctrica
electrical power: potencia eléctrica
electrocardiogram (EGG or EKG): electrocardiograma
electrochemical: electroquímico
electrochemical cell: celda electroquímica
electrochemistry: electroquímica
electrode: electrodo
electrodeposition: electrodeposición
electrolysis: electrólisis

electrolyte: electrólito

electrolytic conduction: conducción electrolítica

electrolyze: electrolizar

electromagnet: electroimán

electromagnetic: electromagnético

electromagnetic energy: energía electromagnética

electromagnetic force: fuerza electromagnética

electromagnetic induction: inducción electromagnética

electromagnetic spectrum: espectro electromagnético

electromagnetic wave: onda electromagnética

electromagnetism: electromagnetismo

electromotive force (EMF): fuerza electromotriz (FEM)

electromotive series: series electromotrices

electron: electrón

electron cloud: nube de electrones, nube electrónica

electron configuration: configuración electrónica

electron dot diagram: diagrama de punto de electrones

electron microscope: microscopio electrónico

electronegative: electronegativo

electronegativity: electronegatividad

electronic balance: balanza electrónica

electrophoresis: electroforesis

electroplating: electroplatear

electropositive: electropositivo

electroscope: electroscopio

electrostatic force: fuerza electrostática

electrovalence: electrovalencia

electrovalent bonding: enlace electrovalente

element: elemento

elephantiasis: elefantiasis

ellipse: elipse

elliptical: elíptico

elliptical galaxies: galaxias elípticas

elongation: alargamiento

embed: embutir, incrustar, empotrar

embolism: embolia

embolus: émbolo

embryo: embrión

embryo sac: saco embrionario

embryology: embriología

embryonic: embrionaria

embryonic membrane: membrana embrionaria

emission spectrum: espectro de emisión

emit: emitir

emphysema: enfisema

empirical: empírico

empirical formula: fórmula empírica

emulsification: emulsificación

emulsion: emulsión

En Niño effect: efecto de El Niño

enamel: esmalte

end moraine: morena terminal

end product: producto final

endangered species: especies en peligro de extinción

endemic: endémico

endergonic reaction: reacción endergónica

endocrine gland: glándula endocrina

endocrine system: sistema endocrino

endocrinology: endocrinología

endocytosis: endocitosis

endoderm: endodermo

endoparasite: endoparásito

endoplasmic reticulum (ER): retículo endoplásmico (RE)

endoskeleton: endoesqueleto

endosperm: endospermo

endosperm nucleus: núcleo endospermico

endospore: endospora

endothermic: endotérmico

endothermic reaction: reacción endotérmica

endpoint: punto final

energetic: energético o enérgico

energetic state: estado energético

energy crisis: crisis de energía

energy flow: flujo de energía

energy level: nivel de energía

energy pyramid: pirámide de energía

energy resources: recursos energéticos, fuentes de energía

energy sink: depósito de energía

energy source: fuente de energía

engineering: ingeniería

enrichment: enriquecimiento

enthalpy: entalpía

entropy: entropía

environmental: medio ambiental

environmental changes: cambios en el medio ambiente

environmental impact statement: declaración de impacto al medio ambiente

enzyme: enzima

enzyme-substrate complex: complejo enzimasustrato

eon: eón

epicenter: epicentro

epicotyl: epicótilo

epidermis: epidermis

epididymis: epidídimo

epiglottis: epiglotis

epinephrine (adrenaline): epinefrina (adrenalina)

epithelial: epitelial

epithelium: epitelio

epoch: época

epoxy resin: resina epóxica

equator: ecuador

equatorial plane: plano ecuatorial

equatorial plate: placa ecuatorial

equilibrant force: fuerza equilibrante

equilibrium: equilibrio

equilibrium constant: constante de equilibrio

equilibrium position: posición de equilibrio

equinox: equinoccio

equivalent masses: masas equivalentes

era: era

erbium: erbio

erect posture: postura erguida

Erlenmeyer flask: frasco de Erlenmeyer

erosion: erosión

erosional: erosión, desgaste

erratics: errático

escarpment: escarpadura, barranca

escherichia coli (e.coli): escherichia coli

esker: esker

essential amino acid: amino ácido esencial

essentially: esencialmente

ester: ester

esterification: esterificación

estimation: estimación, cálculo

estivate: estivar

estivation: estivación

estrogen: estrógeno

estuary: estuario

ethanal: etanol

ethane: etano

ethanolamine: etanolamina

ethene: eteno

ether: éter

ethics: ética

ethyl: etílico

ethyl acetate: acetato de etilo

E

ethyl alcohol: alcohol etílico
ethyl ether: éter etílico
ethylamine: etilamina
ethylbenzene: etilbenceno
ethylene bromide: bromuro de etileno
ethylene dichloride: dicloruro de etileno
ethylene glycol: etilen glicol
euglena: euglena
eukaryote: eucariote
eukaryotic: eucariota
eukaryotic cell: célula eucariótica
europium: europio
eustachian tube: trompa de Eustaquio
eutectic: eutéctico
eutrophication: eutrofización
evaporation: evaporación
evaporites: evaporitas
evapotranspiration: evapotranspiración
evenly: igualmente; a la par
evenness: uniformidad
evolution: evolución
evolutionary: evolutivo
excited state: estado excitado
exclusive: exclusivo
excrete: excretar
excretion: excreción
excretory: excretorio
exergonic reaction: reacción exergónica
exfoliation: exfoliación
exhalation: exhalación
exhale: exhalar
exhaust: escape; vaciar, gases de combustión
exocrine gland: glándula exocrina
exocytosis: exocitosis
exon: exón
exoskeleton: exoesqueleto, dermatoesqueleto
exothermic: exotérmico

exothermic reaction: reacción exotérmica
expand: dilatarse, extenderse, expandir
explanation: explicación
exposure: exposición
expressed: expresado
extensive properties: propiedades extensivas
extensor: extensor
external circuit: circuito externo
external fertilization: fertilización externa
external force: fuerza externa
external respiration: respiración externa
extinction: extinción
extinction of fauna: extinción de la fauna
extinguishing agent: agente extinguidor
extracellular digestion: digestión extracelular
extraction: extracción
extrapolation: extrapolación
extremely: extremadamente
extrusion: efusión, erupción, extrusión
extrusive: extrusivo
extrusive igneous: ígneas extrusivas
eyepiece: ocular

F

faceted: enfrentado
facilitated diffusion: difusión facilitada
factice: fáctico
Fahrenheit (oF): grado Fahrenheit (ºF)
Fahrenheit scale: escala Fahrenheit
fallopian tube (oviduct): trompa de Falopio (oviducto)
fallout: lluvia radioactiva
fangs: colmillos

Farad: Faradio

farsightedness: hipermetropía (en física), prudencia

fat: grasa

fatty acid: ácido graso

fatty alcohol: alcohol graso

fault: falla

feces: material fecal

feedback mechanism: mecanismo de retroalimentación

feedstock: materia prima

feldspar: feldespato

felsic: félsico

female gamete: gameto femenino

female reproductive system: sistema reproductivo femenino

femur: fémur

fermentation: fermentación

fermentation tube: tubo de fermentación

fermium: fermio

fern: helecho

ferric: férrico

ferroalloy: aleación férrica

ferrous: ferroso

ferrous sulfate: sulfato ferroso

fertilization: fertilización

fertilizer: fertilizar; abono

fetal: fetal

fetal alcohol syndrome: síndrome alcohólico fetal

fetal stress: estrés fetal

fetus: feto

fiber optics: trasmisión por fibra óptica; fibra óptica y sus usos

fibrin: fibrina

fibrinogen: fibrinógeno

fibrous root system: sistema de raíces fibrosas

field of microscope: campo del microscopio

filament: filamento

filler: relleno

filter out: filtrarse

filtered: filtrado

filtrate: filtrar, filtrado

filtration: filtración

fin: aleta

final velocity: velocidad final

finches: pinzones

fine adjustment: ajuste fino

fingerprinting: toma de huellas dactilares

fins: aletas

fiords: fiordos

first filial generation: primera generación filial

first law of motion: primera ley del movimiento

first law of thermodynamics: primera ley de la termodinámica

first neutron: primer neutrón

first quarter: cuarto creciente

first-level consumer: consumidor de primer nivel

first-order-line: línea de primer orden

fission: fisión

fission reactor: reactor de fisión

fixed: fijo

fixed pulley: polea fija

flagella: flagelos

flagellum: flagelo

flammable material: material inflamable

flatworm: platelminto

flexor: músculo flexor

flick: golpecito; quitar con un golpecito

flint glass: cristal de roca

flipper of whale: aletas de ballena

flood plain: llanura de aluvión

florence flask: frasco de florescencia

flotation: flotación

flourspar: fluorita
flow of energy: flujo de energía
flowdiagram: diagrama de flujo
fluid mosaic: mosaico fluido
fluke: trematodo
fluorescence: fluorescencia
fluorescent: fluorescente
fluorescent lamp: tubo fluorescente
fluorescent light: luz fluorescente
fluoridation: fluorización
fluoride: fluoruro
fluorine: flúor
fluorocarbon: fluorocarbono
flux: flujo; derretir
focal: focal
focal length: distancia focal
focal point: punto focal
Foucault pendulum: péndulo de Foucault
focus: foco
fog: niebla
folded: plegado
folded mountains: montañas plegadas
folded strata: estratos plegados
foliated: foliado
folic acid: ácido fólico
follicle: folículo
follicle stimulating hormone (FSH): hormona foliculo-estimulante (HFE)
food allergen: alimentos alergénicos
food chain: cadena alimenticia
food group: grupo alimenticio
food poisoning: envenenamiento por comida
food pyramid: pirámide alimenticia
food vacuole: vacuola alimenticia
food web: cadena alimenticia
foot wall: labio hundido
force: fuerza
force of friction: fuerza de fricción

forceps: fórceps
forensic chemistry: química forense
forest conservation: conservación del bosque
formaldehyde: formaldehído
formic acid: ácido fórmico
formula mass: fórmula de la masa
fossil fuel: combustible fósil, hidrocarburo
fossil record: registro fósil
fossilization: fosilización
fossils: fósiles
four o'clock flower: flor siciliana
fractional distillation: destilación fraccionada
fracture: fractura
fracture zones: zonas de fractura
frame of reference: esquema o marco de referencia
francium: francio
fraternal twin: gemelo fraterno
living organism: organismo vivo
free energy: energía libre
free radical: radical libre
free-fall: caída libre
freeze drying: liofilización
freezing point: punto de congelación
freezing point depression: disminución del punto de congelación
freon: freón
frequency: frecuencia
freshwater: agua fresca
friction: fricción
frictional: friccionar
frictional drag: resistencia al avance
frictionless: sin fricción
frond: fronda
front: frente
fructose: fructosa
fruit fly: mosca frutera

fulcrum: fulcro
full moon: luna llena
functional group: grupo funcional
fundamental particle: partícula fundamental
Fungi: hongos
fungus: hongo
funnel: embudo
fused salt: sal fundida
fusible alloy: aleación fusible
fusion: fusión
fusion reactor: reactor de fusión

G

gabbro: gabro
gadolinium: gadolinio
galactose: galactosa
galactosemia: galactosemia
galaxy: galaxia
galena: galena
gallium: galio
gallium arsenide: arseniuro de galio (GaAs)
gallstone: cálculo biliar
galvanic: galvánico
galvanic cell: batería o célula galvánica
galvanizing: galvanización
galvanometer: galvanómetro
gamete: gameto
gametogenesis: gametogénesis
gametophyte stage: etapa de gametofito
gamma globulin: gamma globulina
gamma ray: rayo gama
ganglion: ganglio
garnet: granate
gas exchange: intercambio de gas

gas giants: planetas gaseosos gigantes
gas law: ley de los gases
gas phase: fase gaseosa
gaseous: gaseoso
gaseous exchange: intercambio gaseoso
gasification: gasificación
gastric juice: jugo gástrico
gastrovascular cavity: cavidad gastrovascular
gastrula: gástrula
gastrulation: gastrulación
gauge: medida; medir
Geiger counter: contador Geiger
Geiger-Muller tube: tubo de Geiger-Müller
gel: gel
gel electrophoresis: electroforesis de gel
gem: gema
gene: gen
gene expression: expresión genética
gene frequency: frecuencia genética
gene linkage: ligación genética
gene mutation: mutación genética
gene splicing: acoplamiento de genes
general theory of relativity: teoría general de la relatividad
generalization: generalización
generator: generador
genetic counseling: asesoramiento genético
genetic disease: enfermedad genética
genetic diversity: diversidad genética
genetic engineering: ingeniería genética
genetic marker: marcador genético
genetic material: material genético
genetic recombination: recombinación genética
genetic variation: variación genética
genetically: genéticamente
genetics: genética

F
G

genome: genoma

genotype: genotipo

genus: género

geocentric model: modelo geocéntrico

geochemistry: geoquímica

geographic isolation: aislamiento geográfico

geographical poles: polos geográficos

geologic history: historia geológica

geologic time scale: escala de cronología geológica

geologist: geólogo

geometric isomer: isómero geométrico

geosyncline: geosinclinal

geothermal energy: energía geotérmica

geotropism: geotropismo

germ theory of disease: teoría del germen de la enfermedad

German measles: sarampión alemán

germanium: germanio

germinate: germinar

germination: germinación

gestation period: período de gestación

geyser: géiser

giant: gigante

giantism: gigantismo

gibberellin: giberelina

giga: giga (prefijo)

gill: agalla

gizzard: molleja

glacial action: acción del glaciar

glacial lakes: lagos glaciares

glacier: glaciar

glass electrode: electrodo de vidrio

glider: planeador

global: global

global climate: clima global

Global Positioning System (GPS): Sistema de Posicionamiento Global (GPS)

global warming: calentamiento global

glomerulus: glomérulo

glucagon: glucagón

gluon: gluón

glyceride: glicérido

glycerin: glicerina

glycerol: glicerol

glycine: glicina

glycogen: glicógeno

glycol: glicol

glycolysis: glicólisis

gneiss: gneis

goiter: bocio

Golgi bodies: aparato de Golgi

gonad: gónada

gonadotropin: gonadotropina

gonorrhea: gonorrea

graded bedding: estratificación escalonada

gradient: gradiente, pendiente

gradualism: gradualismo

gradually: gradualmente

graduated beaker: vaso graduado

graduated cylinder: probeta

graduated pipette: pipeta graduada

grafting: injerto

gram atomic mass: masa atómica en gramos

gram equivalent mass: masa equivalente en gramos

gram molecular mass: masa molecular en gramos

gram molecular volume: volumen molecular en gramos

granitic: granítica

graph: gráfica; representar gráficamente

graphical: gráfico

graphite: grafito

grasshopper: saltamontes

grassland: pastizal

grating: enrejado, rejilla
gravimetric analysis: análisis gravimétrico
gravitation: gravitación
gravitational: gravitacional
gravitational field: campo gravitatorio
gravitational force: fuerza de gravedad
gravitational mass: masa gravitatoria
gravitational potential energy: energía potencial gravitatoria
graviton: gravitón
gravity: gravedad
gray matter: materia gris
Great Red Spot: La Gran Mancha Roja
green algae: alga verde
green plant: planta verde
greenhouse effect: efecto de invernadero
greenhouse gas: gas de efecto invernadero
ground moraine: morena de fondo
ground state: estado fundamental
ground water: agua subterránea
grounding: conexión a tierra
group: agrupar, grupo
growth hormone (GH): hormona del crecimiento (HC)
guanine: guanina
guard cells: células oclusoras
gullet: garganta
gully: arroyo, quebrada, zanjón
guncotton: mecha de algodón
guyot: guyot
gymnosperm: gimnosperma
gypsum: yeso
gypsy moth: polilla gitana
gyroscope: giroscópico

H

habitat: hábitat
habitat fragmentation: fragmentación del habitat
hafnium: hafnio
hair follicle: folículo capilar
half: media vida
half-life: período de vida media
half-reaction: semi-reacción
halite: halita
halogens: halógenos
hand lens: lupa de mano
hanging valley: valle colgante
hanging wall: pared colgante
haploid (monoploid): haploide (monoploide)
hard water: agua dura
hardness: dureza
hardy-weinberg law: ley de Hardy-Weinberg
harmonic: armónico
harmonious: armonioso
harvesting: el cosechar
hatching: incubación
haversian canal: conducto de Havers
hay fever: fiebre del heno
hazardous wastes: desperdicios peligrosos
head erosion: erosión de cabecera
headlamp: farol delantero
headland: cabecera, promontorio, punta
healthy habit: hábito saludable
heart attack: ataque cardíaco
heart muscle: músculo cardíaco
heart transplant: trasplante de corazón
heartbeat cycle: ciclo de palpitaciones del corazón
heart-lung machine: máquina cardiopulmonar
heat: calor
heat effect: efecto de calor

heat energy: energía térmica

heat engine: motor de calor

heat exchange: intercambio de calor

heat of combustion: calor de combustión

heat of condensation: calor de condensación

heat of crystallization: calor de cristalización

heat of dilution: calor de dilución

heat of formation: calor de formación

heat of fusion: calor de fusión

heat of hydration: calor de hidratación

heat of reaction: calor de reacción

heat of solution: calor de solución

heat of sublimation: calor de sublimación

heat of transition: calor de transición

heat of vaporization: calor de vaporización

heat pump: compresor, bomba de calor

heat transfer: transferencia de calor

heavy hydrogen: hidrógeno pesado

heavy water: agua pesada

hecto: ciento (prefijo)

hectometer: hectómetro

Heisenberg uncertainty principle: principio de indeterminación o incertidumbre de Heisenberg

heliocentric model: modelo heliocéntrico

Helium: helio

helix: hélice

hematite: hematita

hemoglobin: hemoglobina

hemolysis: hemólisis

hemophilia: hemofilia

heparin: heparina

hepatic artery: arteria hepática

hepatic portal circulation: circulación portal hepática

herbivore: herbívoro

heredity: herencia

hermaphrodite: hermafrodita

hertz: hertzio

heterocyclic: heterocíclico

heterogeneous mixture: mezcla heterogénea

heterogeneous reaction: reacción heterogénea

heterotroph: heterótrofo

heterotroph hypothesis: hipótesis heterotrófica

heterotrophic: heterotrófico

heterotrophic nutrition: nutrición heterotrófica

heterozygous: heterocigótico

heterozygous genotype: genotipo heterocigótico

hiatus: hiato

hibernation: hibernación

high blood pressure: alta presión sanguínea

high energy bond: enlace de alta energía

high polymer: alto polímero

high pressure: alta presión

high temperature source: fuente de temperatura alta

hiker: excursionista

hillslope: barranco

hindbrain: rombencéfalo

hip joint: articulación de cadera

histamine: histamina

histidine: histidina

histology: histología

histone: histona

holmium: holmio

homeostasis: homeostasis

homeowner: propietario

hominid: homínido

homo sapiens: homo sapiens

homocyclic: homocíclico

homogeneous mixture: mezcla homogénea

homogeneous reaction: reacción homogénea

homogenization: homogenización

homologous: homólogos

homologous chromosome: cromosoma homólogo

homologous series: serie homóloga

homologous structure: estructura homóloga

homopolymer: homopolímero

homozygous: homocigótico

homozygous genotype: genotipo homocigótico

hoofed animal: animal con pezuña

Hooke's law: ley de Hooke

hookworm: anquilostoma

horizon: horizonte

horizontal sorting: distribución horizontal

horizontally: horizontalmente

hormone: hormona

host cell: célula huésped

hot spot: punto caliente

hot water bath: baño caliente de inmersión

hot-melt: fundido caliente

Hubble's Law: ley de Hubble

humectant: humectante

humerus: húmero

humid climate: clima húmedo

humidity: humedad

hummingbird: colibrí

humoral immunity: inmunidad humoral

humus: humus

hurricane: huracán

hybrid: híbrido

hybrid vigor: vigor híbrido

hybridization: hibridación

hydra: hidra

hydrate: hidrato

hydration: hidratación

hydraulic system: sistema hidráulico

hydride: hidruro

hydrocarbon: hidrocarburo

hydrochloric acid: ácido clorhídrico

hydrocolloid: hidrocoloide

hydrocyanic: hidrociánico

hydrodynamics: hidrodinámica

hydroelectric power: energía hidroeléctrica

hydroelectricity: hidroelectricidad

hydrogen bomb: bomba de hidrógeno

hydrogen chloride: cloruro de hidrógeno

hydrogen cyanide: cianuro de hidrógeno

hydrogen fluoride: fluoruro de hidrógeno

hydrogen iodide: ioduro de hidrógeno

hydrogen peroxide: peróxido de hidrógeno

hydrogen sulfide: sulfuro de hidrógeno

hydrogenation: hidrogenación

hydrogenolysis: hidrogenolisis

hydrologic water cycle: ciclo hidrológico del agua

hydrolysis: hidrólisis

hydrolysis constant: constante de hidrólisis

hydronium ion: ion hidronio

hydrophilic: hidrofílico

hydrophobic: hidrofóbico

hydroponics: hidroponía

hydrosphere: hidrósfera

hydrostatics: hidrostática

hydrotropism: hidrotropismo

hydroxyl group: grupo hidroxilo

hygrometer: higrómetro

hygroscopic: higroscópico

hyperparasitism: hiperparasitismo

hypertension: hipertensión

hyperthyroidism: hipertiroidismo

hypertonic solution: solución hipertónica

hyphae: hifa

H

hypochlorous acid: ácido hipocloroso
hypocotyl: hipocotiledon
hyposecretion: hiposecreción
hypothalamus: hipotálamo
hypothesis: hipótesis
hypothyroidism: hipotiroidismo
hypotonic solution: solución hipotónica

I

H
I

ibuprofen: ibuprofeno
ice sheet: capa de hielo
ice wedging: gelifracción
ideal gas: gas ideal
ideal gas law: ley de los gases ideales
ideal mechanical advantage (IMA): ventaja mecánica ideal
identical twin: gemelo idéntico
identity period: período de identidad
igneous: ígneo
igneous rock: roca ígnea
ignition: ignición
ileum: íleon
illuminance: iluminación
illuminated body: cuerpo iluminado
illumination: iluminación
imaginary: imaginario
immersion heater: calentador de inmersión
immiscible: inmiscible
immune response: reacción inmunológica
immune system: sistema inmunológico
immunization: inmunización
impact basin: cráter de impacto
impart: impartir
impermeable: impermeable
impingement black: negro de impacto

implantation: implantación
impregnation: impregnación
imprint: imprimir
imprinting: impresión
impurity: impureza
in vitro fertilization: fertilización in vitro
inborn immunity: inmunidad innata
inbreeding: endogamia o cruzamiento consanguíneo
incandescent: incandescente
incandescent lamp: lámpara incandescente
incandescent light: luz incandescente
incidence: incidencia
incident insolation: insolación incidente
incident pulse: pulso incidente
incident wave: onda incidente
incisors: incisivos
inclined: inclinado
inclined plane: plano inclinado
incoherent light: luz incoherente
incomplete dominance: dominancia incompleta
incomplete protein: proteína incompleta
incompressible: incompresible
incubation period: período de incubación
Indanthrene Blue: azul de indantreno
independent (manipulated) variable: variable independiente (manipulada)
independent assortment: segregación independiente
independent variable: variable independiente
index fossil: fósil índice
index of refraction: índice de refracción
Indian Red: rojo indio
indicator: indicador
indium: indio
induction: inducción
inductive reactance: reactancia inductiva

industrial alcohol: alcohol industrial
industrial diamonds: diamantes industriales
industrial hazard: peligro industrial
industrial melanism: melanismo industrial
inelastic: inflexible
inelastic collision: choque inelástico
inert: inerte
inertia: inercia
inertial mass: inercia de la masa
infantile paralysis: parálisis infantil
infectious disease: enfermedad infecciosa
inferior vena cava: vena cava inferior
inflammable: inflamable
inflammatory response: reacción inflamatoria
infrared: infrarrojo(a)
infrared spectroscopy: espectroscopia infrarroja
infrared waves: ondas infrarrojas
ingestion: ingestión
inhalation: inhalación
inherited adaptation: adaptación heredada
inherited trait: rasgo hereditario
inhibition center: centro de inhibición
inhibitor: inhibidor
initial momentum: momento inicial
initial velocity: velocidad inicial
initiating explosive: explosivo iniciante
innate behavior: comportamiento natural o innato
inner ear: oído interno
innercore: núcleo interno
inorganic: inorgánico
inorganic analysis: análisis inorgánico
inorganic chemistry: química inorgánica
inorganic compound: compuesto inorgánico
input: entrada, alimentación (en física)
inquiry: indagación
insecticide: insecticida

insectivorous plant: planta insectívora
insight: percepción
insolation: insolación
instantaneous: instantáneo
instantaneous speed: velocidad instantánea
instantaneous velocity: velocidad instantánea
instantaneously: instantáneamente
instinct: instinto
instrument: instrumento
instrumental analysis: análisis instrumental
insulator: aislador
insulin: insulina
integrated circuit: circuito integrado
intensity: intensidad
intensity of insolation: intensidad de la insolación
intensity of radiation: intensidad de la radiación
intensive properties: propiedades intensivas
interact: interactuar
interaction: interacción
interbreed(ing): entrecruzamiento
intercellular fluid (ICF) : fluído intercelular (FIC)
interference: interferencia
interferon: interferón
intergrowth: intercalado, entrecruzamiento
interionic attraction: atracciones interiónicas
interlock: enganche, entrelazarse
intermediate: intermediario
intermetallic compound: compuesto intermetálico
internal: interno
internal circuit: circuito interno
internal combustion engine: motor de combustión interna

internal development: desarrollo interno
internal energy: energía interna
internal fertilization: fertilización interna
internal force: fuerza interna
internally: internamente
International Date Line: Línea Internacional de la Fecha
interneuron: interneuróna
interparticle: interpartícula
interphase: interface
interspecific competition: competencia interespecífica
interstage: entre fases
interstellar: interestelar
interstitial: intersticial
intertidal zone: zona litoral
intestinal juice: jugo intestinal
intestinal laboratory: laboratorio
intracellular digestion: digestión intracelular
intron: intrón
intrusive: intrusivo
intrusive igneous rock: roca ígnea intrusiva
invasive species: especie invasora
inversely: inversamente
inversion: inversión
invert: invertir
invertebrate: invertebrado
involuntary muscle: músculo involuntario
ion: ión
ion-exchange reaction: reacción de intercambio iónico
ionic bond: enlace iónico
ionic conduction: conducción iónica
ionization: ionización
ionization constant: constante de ionización
ionization energy: energía de ionización
ionization potential: potencial de ionización

ionogen: ionogénico
ionosphere: ionósfera
ion-product: producto iónico
ion-product constant of water: constante del producto iónico del agua
iridium: iridio
iron (Fe): Hierro (Fe)
Iron Blue: hierro azul
iron oxide: óxido de hierro
irradiation: irradiación
irregular galaxies: galaxias irregulares
irritability: irritabilidad
islets of Langerhans: islotes de Langerhans
isobar: isobara
isolated: aislado
isolated system: sistema aislado
isoline: línea o curva de nivel
isomer: isómero
isomerization: isomerización
isopropyl alcohol: alcohol isopropílico
isostasy: isostasia
iso-surface: iso superficie
isotactic: isotáctico
isotherm: isoterma
isotonic solution: solución isotónica
isotope: isótopo
isotropic: isotrópico
IUPAC system: sistema de IUPAC
ivory black: negro marfil

J

jade: jade
jellyfish: medusa
jet plane: avión de motores a reacción
jet stream: corriente de chorro
jetty: malecón, espigón, muelle
joint: articulación
Joule: joule (unidad de trabajo)
Jupiter: Júpiter
juvenile hormone: hormona juvenil

K

kame: kame, cerro de detrito glacial
karst topography: topografía karst
karyotype: cariotipo
karyotyping: clasificar por cariotipo
kelp forest: bosque de quelpos
Kelvin Scale: escala absoluta (Kelvin de temperaturas)
Kepler's Law of Motion: ley del movimiento de Kappler
keratin: queratina
kernels: núcleos
kerosene: queroseno
ketone: cetona
kidney: riñón
kilo: kilo (prefijo)
kilogram (kg): kilogramo (kg)
kiloliter (kl): kilolitro (kl)
kilometer (km): kilómetro (km)
kilopascal: kilopascal
kilowatt: kilovatio
kilowatt-hour: kilovatio-hora
kinematics: cinemática

kinetic energy: energía cinética
kinetic molecular theory: teoría cinético-molecular
kinetic theory: teoría cinética
kinetics: cinética
kingdom: reino
Klinefelter's syndrome: síndrome de Klinefelter
knapsack: mochila
knee joint: articulación de rodilla
knee-jerk reflex: reflejo automático
krypton: criptón

L

laboratory: laboratorio
laboratory burner: mechero de laboratorio
laccolith: lacolito
lactase: lactasa
lacteal: lácteo
lactic acid: ácido láctico
lactone: lactona
lactose: lactosa
ladybug: mariquita
Lamarckism: lamarquismo
lamella: lámina
lancet: lanceta
land breeze: brisa terrestre
landscape region: región topográfica
landslide: avalancha de tierra
lanthanide series: serie lantánida
lanthanum: lantano
large intestine: intestino grueso
larva: larva
larynx: laringe
latent heat: calor latente

J
K
L

latent solvent: solvente latente
lateral erosion: erosión lateral
lateral fault: falla lateral
lateral moraine: morena lateral
latitude: latitud
latitudinal climate patterns: patrones climáticos latitudinales
lattice: enlistonado, enrejado, retículo cristalino
lava: lava
lava flow: flujo de lava
lava plateau: meseta de lava
law: ley
law of action and reaction: ley de acción y reacción
law of conservation of charge: ley de la conservación de carga
law of conservation of energy: ley de la conservación de energía
law of conservation of mass: ley de conservación de masa
law of conservation of momentum: ley de la conservación del momento (impulso mecánico)
law of dominance: ley de dominancia
law of independent assortment: ley de segregación independiente
law of segregation: ley de segregación
law of use and disuse: ley de uso y desuso
lawn mower: cortadora de césped, podadora
lawrencium: laurencio
layering: ordenar por capas
leach: filtrar, lixiviar
leaching: lixiviación
lead: plomo; alambre
lead chromate: cromato de plomo
leaf sheath: envoltura de la hoja
learned adaptation: adaptación asimilada
leaves: hojas

ledge: borde, berma
leeward: sotavento
left-hand rule: regla de la mano izquierda
legume: legumbre
leguminous plant: planta leguminosa
Lenz's Law: Ley de Lenz
lepton: leptón
leucine: leucina
leukocyte: leucocito
levee: dique
leveling forces: fuerzas niveladoras
lever: palanca
Leyden Jar: botella de Leyden
lichen: liquen
life cycle: ciclo de vida
lift: levantar, fuerza de sustentación
ligament: ligamento
light metal: metal ligero
light wave: onda luminosa
light year: año luz
light-dependent reaction: reacción dependiente de la luz
lignite: lignita
lily: lirio
limiting factor: factor limitante
limiting nutrient: alimento de limitación
limonite: limonita
linear: lineal, alinear
linear accelerator: acelerador lineal
linear velocity: velocidad lineal
liner: forro
lines of force: líneas de fuerza
linked gene: gen ligado o gen relacionado
lipase: lipasa
lipid: lípido
lipid bilayer: bicapa lípida
lipids: lípidos
liquefaction: licuefacción
liquid crystal: cristal líquido

L

liquid phase: fase líquida
liquify: licuar
litharge: litargirio
lithium: litio
lithosphere: litósfera
litmus paper: papel tornasol
litter: hojarasca
living: viviente
living thing: ser viviente
local noon: mediodía, hora local
lock-and-key-hypothesis: hipótesis de llave y cerradura
lockjaw: tétano
locomotion: locomoción
lodestone: piedra imán
loess: loes
logging: registración o registro
logistic growth: crecimiento logístico
long: plantas de día largo
longitude: longitud
longitudinal: longitudinal
longitudinal muscle: músculo longitudinal
longitudinal wave: onda de longitud o longitudinal
longshore current: corriente costera
longshore drift: desplazamiento del litoral
loop of henle: asa de Henle
loudness: ruidoso, estridente, estrepitoso
low pressure: baja presión
low temperature sink: fosa de baja temperatura
lubricant: sustancia lubricante; lubricante
lubricating oil: aceite lubricante
lumen: lumen
luminescent: luminiscente
luminous flux: flujo luminoso
luminous intensity: intensidad luminosa
lunar: lunar
lunar eclipse: eclipse lunar

lunar module: módulo lunar
luster: lustre, brillo
luteinizing hormone (LH): la hormona luteinizante (LH)
lutetium: lutecio
lye: lejía
lymph: linfa
lymph gland: glándula linfática
lymph node: nódulo linfático
lymph vessel: vaso linfático
lymphatic system: sistema linfático
lymphocyte: linfocito
lyophilic: liofílico
lysosome: lisosoma

M

macroanalysis: macroanálisis
macroevolution: macroevolución
macromolecule: macromolécula
macronucleus: macronúcleo
mafic: máfico
magenta: color magenta
maggot: gusano
magma: magma
magnalium: magnalio
magnesia: magnesia
magnesite: magnesita
magnesium: magnesio
magneson: magneson
magnetic declination: declinación magnética
magnetic domain: dominio magnético
magnetic field: campo magnético
magnetic field line: línea de campo magnético

magnetic flux: flujo magnético
magnetic force: fuerza magnética
magnetic induction: inducción magnética
magnetic pole: polo magnético
magnetism: magnetismo
magnetite: magnetita
magnetochemistry: magnetoquímica
magnification: ampliación
magnifier: magnificador
magnifying glass: lente de aumento
magnitude: magnitud
main sequence: secuencia principal
maintaining: el mantener
malachite: malaquita
malathion: malatión
malleability: maleabilidad
maltase: maltasa
maltose: maltosa
mammals: mamíferos
mammary glands: glándulas mamarias
mandible: mandíbula
manganese: manganeso
manganese dioxide: dióxido de manganeso
manganic oxide: óxido mangánico
mangrove: mangle
mangrove swamp: manglar
manipulated (independent) variable: variable (independiente) manipulada
mannitol: manitol
manometer: manómetro
mantle: capa, manto
map legend: leyenda del mapa
map scale: escala del mapa
maria: mares
marine biome: bioma marítimo
marine climate: clima marino
marine terrace: terraza marina
maritime polar airmass: masa de aire polar marítimo

maritime tropical airmass: masa de aire tropical marítimo
marsupial: marsupial
mass: masa
mass action: acción de masas
mass conservation: conservación de la masa
mass defect: defecto de masa
mass extinction: extinción de la masa
mass movement: movimiento en masa
mass number: número de masa
mass spectograph: espectrógrafo de masa
materials scientist: científico de materiales
maternal immunity: inmunidad materna
mates: parejas, compañeros
mathematical science: ciencia matemática
mathematically: matemáticamente
mathematician: matemático
mating: apareamiento
matter: materia
matter wave: onda de materia
mature soil: suelo maduro
mean solar day: día solar medio
meander: meandro
mechanical: mecánico
mechanical advantage: ventaja mecánica
mechanical digestion: digestión mecánica
mechanical energy: energía mecánica
mechanical force: fuerza mecánica
mechanical wave: onda mecánica
mechanical weathering: erosión mecánica
mechanics: mecánica
medical: médico, medica
medicine dropper: gotero medicinal
medium: medio
medulla oblongata: médula espinal
medusa: medusa
mega: mega (prefijo)
megahertz: megahertzio

megawatt: megavatio
meiosis: meiosis
melanin: melanina
melanocyte cell: célula melanocitica
melting: de fusión
melting point: punto de fusión
meltwater: aguanieve
mendelevium: mendelevio
Mendelism: Mendelismo
meninges: meninges
meniscus: menisco
menstrual cycle: ciclo menstrual
menstruation: menstruación
mercury barometer: barómetro de mercurio
mesentery: mesenteria
mesoderm: mesodermo
meson: mesón
mesopause: mesopausa
mesophyll: mesófilo
mesophyte: mesófito
mesosphere: mesosfera
Mesozoic Era: Era Mesozoica
messenger RNA (mRNA): ARN mensajero
metabolic: metabólico
metabolic rate: índice metabólico básico
metabolic waste: desechos metabólicos
metabolism: metabolismo
metal: metal
metal runner: corredor metálico
metallic bond: enlace metálico
metallic conduction: conducción metálica
metalloid: metaloide
metallurgy: metalurgia
metamorphic: metamórfico
metamorphic rock: roca metamórfica
metamorphism: metamorfismo
metamorphosis: metamorfosis
metaphase: metafase

metastasis: metástasis
meteor: meteoro
meteorite: meteorito
meteorology: meteorología
meter stick: varilla métrica
meteroid: meteorito
methanol: metanol
methyl: metil
methyl alcohol: alcohol metílico
methylamine: metilamina
methylene blue: azul de metileno
meticulously: meticulosamente
metric: métrica
metric ruler: regla métrica
mica: mica
micro: microscópico
microanalysis: microanálisis
microclimate: microclima
microdissetion: microdisección
microfarad: microfaradio
microfilament: microfilamento
micrometer: micrómetro
micronucleus: micronúcleo
microorganism: microorganismo
microprocessor: microprocesador
microscope: microscopio
microtubule: microtúbulo
microwaves: microondas
mid: dorsal oceánica
midbrain: mesencéfalo
middle ear: oído medio
mid-latitude cyclone: ciclón de latitud media
mid-ocean ridge: dorsal oceánica
migration: migración
milk tooth: diente de leche
Milky Way Galaxy: Galaxia Vía Láctea
milli: mili (prefijo)
milliampere: miliamperio

millibar: milibar
mimicry: mímica
mineral: mineral
mineral acid: ácido mineral
mineral resources: recursos minerales
mineral water: agua mineral
mirage: espejismo
miscible: miscible
mitochondria: mitocondria
mitosis: mitosis
mitotic cell division: división celular mitótica
mixed: mezclado
mixture: mezcla
models: modelos
moderator: moderador
modification: modificación
modified: modificado
modified Mercalli scale: escala de Mercalli modificada
Mohorovicic discontinuity: discontinuidad de Mohorovicic
moist adiabatic lapse rate: intervalo de cambio adiabático húmedo
Molal boiling point constant: constante molal del punto de ebullición
Molal freezing point constant: constante molal del punto fusión
molality: molalidad
molar solution: solución molar
molar volume: volumen molar
molarity: molaridad
mold: moldura
mole: molécula gramo, mol
molecular: molecular
molecular formula: fórmula molecular
molecular mass: masa molecular
molecular sieve: tamiz molecular
molecule: molécula
mollusca: moluscos

mollusk: molusco
molting: muda
molybdenum: molibdeno
momentum: momento, impetu
Monera: mónera
monocot: monocotiledóneas
monocotyledon: monocotiledón
monoculture: monocultivo
monocyte: monocito
monohybrid cross: cruce monohíbrido
monomer: monómero
monominerallic: monomineral
monomolecular: monomolecular
monoploid: monoploide
monosaccharide: monosacárido
monotreme: monotrema
monoxide: monóxido
moon phase: fase lunar
moraine: morena
morphology: morfología
morula: mórula
motile: móvil
motility: movilidad
motor nerve: nervio motor
motor neuron: neurona motora
movable pulley: polea móvil
mower: segador
mucous membrane: membrana mucosa
multicellular: multicelular
multiple allele: alelo múltiple
multiple birth: nacimiento múltiple
multiple-gene inheritance: herencia de gene
muon: muón
muscle: músculo
muscle contraction: contracción muscular
muscle fatigue: fatiga muscular
muscle tissue: tejido muscular
muscovite: moscovita

muscular: muscular
muscular system: sistema muscular
mussel: mejillón
mutagen: mutágeno
mutagenic agent: agente mutágenico
mutant: mutante
mutation: mutación
mutual: mutuo
mutualism: mutalismo
mycelium: micelio
mycorrhizae: micorriza
myelin sheath: vaina de mielina
myofibril: miofibrina

N

nano: nano (prefijo)
nanometer: nanómetro
nanosecond: nanosegundo
naphtha: nafta
naphthalene: naftaleno
narcotic drug: droga narcótica
nasal: nasal
nasal cavity: cavidad nasal
natural disaster: desastre natural
natural events: acontecimientos naturales
natural gas: gas natural
natural immunity: inmunidad natural
natural levees: diques naturales
natural resource: recurso natural
natural selection: selección natural
nature and nurture controversy: controversia de naturaleza y crianza
nature of the surface: naturaleza de la superficie
neap tide: marea baja

nearsightedness: miopía
nebula: nebulosa
nectar: néctar
negative charge: carga negativa
negative feedback: retroalimentación negativa
nekton: necton
nematode: nematodo
neodymium: neodimio
neon: neón
nephron: nefrona
Neptune: Neptuno
neptunium: neptunio
Nernst distribution law: ley de distribución de Nernst
Nernst equation: ecuación de Nernst
nerve cell (neuron): célula nerviosa (neurona)
nerve cord: cordón nervioso
nerve fiber: fibra nerviosa
nerve impulse: impulso nervioso
nerve net: red nerviosa
nervous system: sistema nervioso
net force: fuerza resultante, fuerza neta
net potential: potencial de red
neural plate: placa neural
neurohormone (neurotransmitter): neurohormona (neurotransmisor)
neuromuscular junction: juntura neuromuscular
neuron: neurona
neurotransmitter: neurotransmisor
neutral red: rojo neutral
neutral solution: solución neutra
neutralization: neutralización
neutralization equivalent: equivalente de neutralización
neutrino: neutrino
neutron: neutrón
neutron star: estrella de neutrones

M
N

neve (fim): nevé, ventisquero

new moon: luna nueva

Newton's First Law of Motion: Primera Ley del Movimiento de Newton

Newton's Second Law of Motion: Segunda Ley del Movimiento de Newton

Newton's Third Law of Motion: Tercera Ley del Movimiento de Newton

niacin: niacina

niche: nicho

night blindness: ceguera nocturna

nimbus: nimbus

niobium: niobio

nitrate: nitrato

nitration: nitración

nitric acid: ácido nítrico

nitric anhydride: anhídrido nítrico

nitric oxide: óxido nítrico

nitride: nitruro

nitriding: nitruración

nitrification: nitrificación

nitrifying bacteria: bacteria nitrificante

nitrile: nitrilo

nitrogen-fixing bacteria: bacteria fijadora de nitrógeno

nitrogen cycle: ciclo del nitrógeno

nitrogen family: familia del nitrógeno

nitrogen fixation: fijación de nitrógeno

nitrogen fixing bacteria: bacteria fijadora de nitrógeno

nitrogenous: nitrogenado

nitrogenous waste: desechos nitrogenados

nitroglycerin: nitroglicerina

nitrous acid: ácido nitroso

nobelium: nobelio

noble gas: gas noble

nodal: nodal

nodal line: línea de nodos

node: nodo

nodule: nódulo

noise pollution: contaminación por ruido

nomenclature: nomenclatura

noncommunicable: intransmisible

nonconformity: inconformidad

nondisjunction: no-disyunción

nonelectrolyte: no electrólito

nonfoliated: no foliado

noninfectious disease: enfermedad no infecciosa

nonliving thing: ser sin vida

non-metallic: no metálico

nonperpendicular component: componente no perpendicular

nonperpendicular components of vector: componentes no perpendiculares de vector

nonplacental mammal: mamífero sin placenta

nonpoint source pollution: contaminación sin fuente establecida

nonpolar: no polar

nonpolar molecule: molécula no polar

nonrenewable: no renovable

nonrenewable energy resource: recurso energético no renovable, fuente de energía no renovable

nonrenewable resource: recurso no renovable

nonsedimentary rock: roca no sedimentaria

nonvascular plant: planta no vascular

noradrenaline: noradrenalina

normal boiling point: punto de ebullición normal

normal fault: falla normal

normal force: fuerza normal

normal salt: sal normal

normal solution: solución normal

normality: normalidad

North Pole: Polo Norte

North Star (Polaris): Polaris, Estrella del Polo Norte

Northern Hemisphere: Hemisferio Norte

northern light: aurora boreal

notochord: notocordio

nuclear bombardment: bombardeo nuclear

nuclear energy: energía nuclear

nuclear fission: fisión nuclear

nuclear fuel: combustible nuclear

nuclear fusion: fusión nuclear

nuclear membrane (envelope): membrana nuclear

nuclear model: modelo nuclear

nuclear potential energy: energía potencial nuclear

nuclear reaction: reacción nuclear

nuclear reactor: reactor nuclear

nuclear waste: desperdicio nuclear

nuclei: núcleos

nucleic acids: ácido nucleicos

nucleoli: nucléolos

nucleolus: nucléolo

nucleon: nucleón

nucleotide: nucleótido

nucleus: núcleo

nuclide: núclido

nutrients: nutrientes

nutritional: nutricional

nymph: ninfa

O

objective lens: lente objetivo

oblate spheroid: esferoide oblato

oboe: oboe

observable: observable

observed value: valor observado

obsidian: obsidiana

obtained: obtenido

occluded front: frente ocluido

ocean-floor spreading: extensión del fondo del océano

oceanic crust: corteza oceánica

oceanography: oceanografía

octagonal: octagonal

octave: octava; octavo

octet: octeto

Ohm's Law: Ley de Ohm

oil: petróleo

olefin: olefina

olfaction: olfato

olfactory bulb: bulbo olfativo

olfactory cell: célula olfatoria

olivine: olivino, peridoto

omnivore: omnívoro

oncogene: oncógeno

one gene-one polypeptide hypothesis: hipótesis un gen-un polipétido

one-hole stopper: tapón de un orificio

ontogeny: ontogenia

oocyst: ovoquiste

oocyte: ovocito

oogenesis: ovogénesis

ooze: exudar

opaque: opaco

open chain: cadena abierta

open circulatory system: sistema circulatorio abierto

operational definition: definición operacional

operon: operón

opossum: zariguëya

optic nerve: nervio óptico

optical axis: eje óptico

optical density: densidad óptica

optical microscope: microscopio óptico

optical rotation: rotación óptica

optics: óptica

optimum: óptimo

orbit: órbita

orbital pair: par orbital

orbital speed: velocidad (rapidez) orbital

orbital velocity: velocidad orbital

order of reaction: orden de reacción

Ordovician Period: período ordovíco

ore: mena

ore deposit: depósito de mena

organ: órgano

organ system: sistema de órganos

organelle: organulo

organic: orgánico

organic acid: ácido orgánico

organic chemistry: química orgánica

organic compound: compuesto orgánico

organic evolution: evolución orgánica

organism: organismo

organometallic: organometálico

original horizontality: horizontalidad original

orographic effect: efecto orográfico

orthoclase: ortoclasa

oscilation: oscilación

oscillate: oscilar

oscilloscope: osciloscopio

osmium: osmio

osmosis: ósmosis

osmotic potencial: potencial osmótico

osmotic pressure: presión osmótica

ossification: osificación

osteoarthritis: osteoartritis

osteoblast: osteoblasto

osteocyte: osteocito

osteology: osteología

osteoporosis: osteoporosis

outbreeding: exogamia

outcrop: afloramiento, asomo

outer core: núcleo exterior (externo)

outer ear: oído externo

outwash: derrubio

outwash plain: llanura de acarreo

ova: óvulos

ovaries: ovarios

ovary: ovario

overabundance: sobreabundancia, super-abundancia

overfishing: pesca excesiva

overgraze: exceso de pastoreo

overtone: armónico

oviduct: oviducto

oviparity: oviparidad

oviparous: ovíparo

ovulation: ovulación

ovule: óvulo

ovum: óvulo

oxalic acid: ácido oxálico

oxbow lake: lago seco

oxidation: oxidación

oxidation number: número de oxidación

oxidation potential: potencial de oxidación

oxidation state: estado de oxidación

oxide: óxido

oxidizing agent: agente oxidante

oxygen acid: oxiácido

oxygen consumption: consumo de oxígeno

oxygen cycle: ciclo de oxígeno

oxygen debt: deuda de oxígeno

oxygen-carbon dioxide cycle: ciclo de oxígeno-dióxido de carbón

oxyhemoglobin: oxihemoglobina

ozone depletion: agotamiento del ozono

ozone layer: capa de ozono

ozone shield: capa protección de ozono

P

pacemaker: marcapasos
packing: embalaje
painstakingly: cuidadosamente
paired: emparejado
Paleozoic Era: Era Paleozoica
palisade mesophyll: mesófila empalizada
palladium: paladio
palm: brazo o soporte de eje, oreja de ancla
pancreatic duct: ducto pancreático
pancreatic juice: jugo pancreático
Pangaea: Pangea
parabolic: parabólico
paraffin: parafina; parafinar
paraffin series: serie parafínica
parallax: paralaje
parallel circuit: circuito paralelo
parallel connection: conexión paralela
parallel force: fuerza paralela
parallel unconformity: discordancia paralela
paramecium: paramecio
parasitic relationship: relación parasítica
parasitism: parasitismo
parasympathetic nervous system (PNS): sistema nervioso parasimpático
parathyroid hormone: hormona paratiroides
parent cell: célula madre, célula progenitora
parent generation: generación parental
parental care: cuidado parental
parental rock: roca madre
parietal lobe: lóbulo parietal
parthenogenesis: partenogénesis
partial pressure: presión parcial
particle accelerator: acelerador de partículas
particulate matter: material en polvo

partition coefficient: coeficiente de partición
parts per million: partes por millón
Pascal's Principle: Principio de Pascal
passive immunity: inmunidad pasiva
passive transport: transporte pasivo
passivity: pasividad
pasteurization: pasteurización
patella: patella
path: trayectoria, senda, camino, sendero
pathogen: patógeno
pathogenic: patogénico
peacock blue: azul pavo real
pearly luster: brillo nacarado
peat: turba
peculiarity: peculiaridad
pedigree: pedigrí
pedigree chart: diagrama de pedigrí, árbol genealógico
peer review: evaluación por pares
pelagic: pelágico
pellagra: pelagra
pelvis: pelvis
peneplane: penillanura
penis: pene
pentane: pentano
penumbra: penumbra
pepsin: pepsina
peptic ulcer: úlcera péptica
peptidase: peptidasa
peptide: péptido
peptide bond: enlace pepitico
peptization: peptización
percent error: porciento de error
percentage by mass: porcentaje en masa
percentage composition: composición en porcentaje
perchlorate: perclorato
performer: ejecutante

P

pericardium: pericardio
peridotite: peridotita
perigee: perigeo
perihelion: perihelio
period: período
periodic law: ley periódica
periodic table: tabla periódica
periosteum: periostio
peripheral nervous system: sistema nervioso periférico
peristalsis: peristalsis
permafrost: capa subterránea de hielo
permanent magnet: imán permanente
permanently: permanentemente
permeability: permeabilidad
permeable: permeable
Permian Period: período pérmico
permineralized remains: restos permin-eralizados
peroxide: peróxido
perpendicular force: fuerza perpendicular
perpendicularly: perpendicularmente
pesticide: pesticida
petri dish: platillo de petri
petrifaction: petrificación
petroleum: petróleo
pH: pH
pH indicator: indicador de pH
pH meter: medidor de pH
pH scale: escala de pH
phagocyte: fagocito
phagocytosis: fagocitosis
pharyngeal pouches: bolsas faríngeas
pharynx: faringe
phase change: cambio de fase
phase contrast microscope: microscopio de contraste de fase
phase equilibrium: equilibrio de fase
phases (moon): fases (de la luna)

phenol: fenol
phenolic: fenólico
phenolphthalide: fenolftaleína
phenomena: fenómeno
phenotype: fenotipo
phenyl: fenil
phenylalanine: fenilalanina
phenylketonuria (PKU): fenilcetonuria PKU
pheromone: feromona
phloem: floema
phosphate: fosfato
phospholipid: fosfolípido
phosphor: fósforo
phosphorescence: fosforescencia
phosphorylation: fosforilación
photic zone: zona luminosa
photo resistor: fotoresistencia
photochemical oxidant: oxidante foto-químico
photochemical smog: smog fotoquímico
photochemistry: fotoquímica
photoelectric colorimeter: colorímetro fotoeléctrico
photoelectric effect: efecto fotoeléctrico
photoflash: luz relámpago
photolysis: fotólisis
photon: fotón
photoperiodism: fotoperiodicidad
photosphere: fotosfera
photosynthesis: fotosíntesis
phototropism: fototropismo
photovoltaic cell: célula fotovoltaica
phylogeny: filogenia
phylum: filum
physical change: cambio físico
physical chemistry: química física
physical equilibrium: equilibrio físico
physical model: modelo físico
physical phenomena: fenómeno físico

physical property: propiedad física
physical weathering: erosión física
physicist: físico o física
physiographic provinces: provincias fisiográficas
physiology: fisiología
physiosorption: fisisorción
physiotherapy: fisioterapia
phytoplankton: fitoplanctón
pico: pico (prefijo)
picofarad: picofaradio
pie chart: diagrama circular
pie graph: gráfico de pastel
piezoelectricity: piezoelectricidad
pigment: pigmento
pineal: pineal
pineal body: cuerpo pineal
pinna: pina
pinocytic vesicle: vesícula pinocítica
pinocytosis: pinocitosis
pioneer species: especie pionera
pipe still: tubo de alambique
pipet: pipeta
pistil: pistilo
piston: pistón
pitch: brea, declive, paso, tono
pith: médula
pith ball: pelota de médula
pituitary dwarfism: enanismo pituitario
pituitary gland: glándula pituitaria
placenta: placenta
placental: placentario
placental mammal: mamífero placentario
placental membranes: membranas de placenta
plagioclase: plagioclasa
plain: planicie
plane mirror: espejo plano
plane polarized: plano polarizado

planetary winds: vientos planetarios
plankton: plancton
plantae: reino de las plantas
plasma: plasma
plasma membrane: membrana plasmática
plasmid: plásmido
plasmolysis: plasmólisis
plasticizer: plastificante
plastid: plastída
plate: plato, placas
plate tectonic theory: teoría de las placas tectónicas
plate tectonics: tectónica de placas
plateau: meseta
platelet: plaqueta
platyhelminthes: platelmintos
pleura: pleura
pleural cavity: cavidad pleural
plexus: plexos
plucking: gelivación
plumule: hojuela
Pluto: Plutón
poaching: caza furtiva
point mutation: punto de mutación
point source pollution: contaminación de fuente establecida
polar: polar
polar bond: enlace polar
polar molecule: molécula polar
polar zone: zona polar
polarity: polaridad
polarization: polarización
polarization potential: potencial de polarización
polarized: polarizado
polarized light: luz polarizada
polarizer: polarizador
polarographic: polarográfico
polarographic analysis: análisis polarográfico

377

polarographic apparatus: aparato polarográfico

polarographic wave: onda polarográfica

polio: polio

pollen grain: grano de polen

pollen tube: tubo de polen

pollinate: polinizar

pollination: polinización

pollutant: contaminante

pollution: contaminación

polonium: polonio

poly-: poli- (prefijo)

polyatomic ion: ion poliatómico

polybasic acid: ácido polibásico

polycarbonate: policarbonato

polychloroprene: policloropreno

polycondensation: policondensación

polycyclic: policíclico

polyelectrolyte: polielectrólito

polyester: poliéster

polyethylene: polietileno

polyethylene glycols: polietilenglicol

polygenic: poligénico

polygenic inheritance: herencia poligénica

polygenic traits: rasgos poligénicos

polyglycol: poliglicol

polyhydric alcohol: alcohol polihídrico

polyisoprene: poliisopreno

polymer: polímero

polymerase chain reaction (PCR): cadena de reacción de la polimerasa

polymerization: polimerización

polyminerallic: polimineral

polymorphism: polimorfismo

polyp: pólipo

polypetide: polipéptido

polyploidy: poliploide

polypropylene: polipropileno

polysaccharide: polisacárido

polystyrene: poliestireno

polytetraflouro ethylene: politetrafluoroetileno

polyvinyl acetate: acetato de polivinilo

polyvinyl alcohol: alcohol polivinílico

polyvinyl chloride: cloruro de polivinilo

polyvinyl ether: éter polivinílico

population: población

population genetics: genética de la población

porifera: porífera

porometric: porométrico

porosity: porosidad

positive charge: carga positiva

positive feedback: retroalimentación positiva

positron: positrón

postanal tail: cola postnatal

posterior: posterior

postulate: postulado; postular

potash: potasa

potassium: potasio

potassium permanganate: permanganato de potasio

potential energy: energía potencial

potential evapotranspiration: evapotranspiración potencial

potentiometer: potenciómetro

potentiometric titration: valoración potenciométrica

pouched mammal: mamífero con bolsa

powder metallurgy: polvo de metalurgia

power: potencia

practically: prácticamente

praseodymium: praseodimio

Precambrian Era: era precámbrica

precipitant: precipitante

precipitate: precipitado

precipitation: precipitación

precipitation titration: titulación por precipitación

precisely: precisamente
predation: depredación
predator: predador o depredador
predator-prey relationship: relación predador-presa
predatory: depredador
preening: acicalarse
pregnancy: embarazo
premature birth: nacimiento prematuro
prepolymer: prepolímero
present-day: hoy día
preservative: preservativo
pressure: presión
pressure gradient: gradiente de presión
presumably: presuntamente
prevailing winds: vientos prevalecientes
prill: granulado
primarily: principalmente
primary: primario
primary (P) waves: ondas primarias
primary alcohol: alcohol primario
primary coil: bobina primaria
primary color: color primario
primary consumer: consumidor de primer nivel
primary pigment: pigmento primario
primary productivity: productividad principal
primary rock: roca primaria
primary root: raíz principal
primary succession: sucesión primaria
primary wave: onda primaria
primate: primate
Prime Meridian: primer meridiano (principal)
principal axis: eje principal
principal focal point: punto focal principal
principal focus: foco principal
principle of original horizontality: principio de la horizontalidad original

principle of superposition: principio de superposición
principle of uniformitarianism: principio de uniformismo
probability of occurrence: probabilidad de ocurrencia
producer: productor
producer gas: gas producido
product: producto
progesterone: progesterona
programmable: programable
projectile motion: movimiento impelente, movimiento balístico, movimiento de proyectil
prokaryote: procariota
promethium: promecio
promoter: promotor
properties: propiedades
prophase: profase
propionic acid: ácido propiónico
proportionality constant: constante de proporcionalidad
propyl: propilo
propylene: propileno
prostaglandin: prostaglandina
prostate gland: próstata
protactinium: protactinio
protease: proteasa
protect: proteger
protein: proteína
prothallus: prótalo
prothrombin: protrombina
protist: protista
Protista: reino Protista
protolysis reaction: reacción de protólisis
proton: protón
proton acceptor: aceptor de protones
proton donor: donante de protones
protoplasm: protoplasma
protozoa: protozoos

P

protozoan: protozoario
Prussian Blue: azul de Prusia
pseudopod: seudópodo
psychosis: psicosis
psychrometer: psicrómetro
ptyalin: tialina
puck: duende, disco de goma
puddle: charco; enfangar
pulley: polea
pull-tab: lengueta de halar
pulmonary artery: arteria pulmonar
pulmonary circulation: circulación pulmonar
pulmonary vein: vena pulmonar
pulsar: pulsar, estrellas pulsantes
pulse: pulso; modular por impulsos; pulsar
pumice: piedra pómez
punctuated equilibrium: equilibrio puntuado
Punnett square: Cuadrado de Punnett
pupa: crisálida
puppies: cachorros
pure dominant: dominante puro
pure recessive: recesivo puro
purine: purina
putty: masilla; enmasillar
pyloric sphincter: esfínter pilórico
pyramind of biomass: pirámide de biomasa
pyrimidine: pirimidina
pyrite: pirita
pyrolysis: pirólisis
pyroxene: piroxeno
pyrrole: pirrol
pyrucic acid: ácido pirúvico

P
Q
R

Q

quadrangular: cuadrangular
qualitative: cualitativo
qualitative analysis: análisis cualitativo
quality control: control de calidad
quanta: cuantos
quantitative: cuantitativo
quantitative analysis: análisis cuantitativo
quantize: cuantificar
quantum mechanics: mecánica cuántica
quantum number: número cuántico
quantum theory: teoría cuántica
quark: quark
quark model nucleon: nucleón de modelo quark
quartz: cuarzo
quartzite: cuarcita
Quaternary Period: período cuaternario
quinine: quinina
quinone: quinona

R

raceway: superficie de rodamiento, pista de rodamiento
racquet: raqueta
radial: radial
radial pattern: patrón radial
radial symmetry: simetría radial
radially: radialmente
radiant energy: energía radiante
radiating canal: canal radial
radiation: radiación
radiative balance: balance radiativo
radicle: radícula

radio telescope: radiotelescopio

radio wave: onda de radio

radioactive: radioactivo

radioactive dating: datación radioactiva

radioactive decay: descomposición radioactiva

radioactive element: elemento radioactivo

radioactive material: material radioactivo

radioactive series: serie radioactiva

radioactivity: radioactividad

radiocarbon: radiocarbono

radio-carbon method: método radiocarbono

radioisotope: radioisótopo

radiometric dating: fechado radiométrico

radiotelescope: radiotelescopio

radiotherapy: radioterapia

radon: radón

radula: rádula

ragweed: ambrosía

rain shadow: sombra de lluvia

rapidly: rápidamente

rare earth: tierra rara

rare gas: gases raros

rare metal: metales raros

rarefaction: rarefacción

rate: índice, velocidad, a razón de

rate-determining step: etapa determinante de la velocidad

ray optics: óptica de rayo

reabsorption: reabsorción

reactant: reactante, reactivo

reaction mechanism: mecanismo de reacción

reaction rate: velocidad de reacción

reactor: reactor

readily: prontamente, inmediatamente

reagent: reactivo

real image: imagen real

rearrangement: reordenamiento

receptor: receptor

receptor molecule: receptor molecular

recessional moraine: morena recesiva

recessive: recesivo

recessive gene: gen recesivo

reclaiming: recuperar

recombinant DNA: ADN recombinado

recombination: recombinación

recombination gamete: gameto recombinado

recombine: recombinar

recrystallization: recristalización

rectangular pattern: patrón rectangular

rectification: rectificación

red blood cell: glóbulos rojos de la sangre

red corpuscle (red blood cell): corpúsculos rojos (glóbulo rojo de la sangre)

red giant: gigante colorado

redefine: redefinir

redox reaction: reacción redox

red-shift: cambio rojizo

reduced: reducido

reducing agent: agente de reducción

reducing flame: llama reductora

reduction: reducción

reduction division (meiosis): división de reducción (meiosis)

reduction potential: potencial de reducción

reed: lámina, carrizo

reef: arrecife

reestablish: restablecer

refer: referir

reference point: punto de referencia

refining: refinación

reflecting telescope: telescopio reflejante

reflex: reflejo

reflex arc: arco de reflejo

R

reflex center: centro de reflejos
reflux: reflujo
reforestation: reforestación
refract: refractar
refracting telescope: telescopio refractivo
refraction: refracción
refractory period: período refractario
refrigerant: refrigerante
refrigerator: frigorífico, nevera, refrigerador
regolith: regolito
regular: regular
regular reflection: reflexión regular
regulated: regulado
reinforcing agent: agente de refuerzo
relative age: edad relativa
relative dating: datación relativa
relative geologic time: tiempo geológico relativo
relative humidity: humedad relativa
relatively: relativamente
relativity: relatividad
remain the same: permanece sin cambios, permanece igual
renal artery: arteria renal
renal circulation: circulación renal
renal portal vein: vena porta renal
renal vein: vena renal
renewable: renovable
renewable energy resource: recurso energético renovable, fuente de energía renovable
renewable resource: recurso renovable
rennin: renina
repetitious: repetitivo
replication: replicación
reproductive isolation: aislamiento reproductivo
research plan: plan de investigación
researcher: investigador

reserve: reserva
residual sediment: sedimento residual
residual soil: suelo residual
resistance: resistencia
resistant to: resistente a
resistor: resistor, resistencia
resolving power of lens: poder resolutivo del lente
resonance: resonancia
resonator: resonador
resources management: manejo de recursos
respiration: respiración
respiratory chain: cadena respiratoria
respiratory surface: superficie respiratoria
respiratory system: aparato respiratorio
respiratory tract: vías respiratorias o tracto respiratorio
restatement: reformulación
resting potential: potencial de reposo
resting stage (interphase): etapa de descanso (interface)
restoring force: fuerza restitutiva
restriction enzyme: enzima de restricción
reticulum: retículo
retina: retina
retrograde motion: movimiento retrógrado
retrovirus: retrovirus
reuse: reutilizar
reverse fault: falla inversa (invertida)
reversed polarity: polaridad invertida
reversible reaction: reacción reversible
revolution: revolución
Rh negative blood: sangre Rh negativo
Rh positive blood: sangre Rh positivo
rhenium: renio
rheostat: reóstato
Rhesus factor (Rh factor): factor Rhesus (factor Rh)

rheumatic fever: fiebre reumática
rheumatoid arthritis: artritis reumatoide
rhizoid: rizoide
rhizome: rizoma
rhodium: rodio
rhyolite: riolita
rib cage: tórax
riboflavin: riboflavina
ribonucleic acid (RNA): ácido ribonucleico
ribose: ribosa
ribosomal RNA: ARN ribosomal
ribosome: ribosoma
Richter scale: escala Richter
rickets: raquitismo
riding a bicycle: andar en bicicleta
rift valley: valle agrietado ó hendido
ring stand: soporte de anillo
ring structure: estructura de anillo
ringing: resonante
ringworm: tiña
rip: rasgón
rip currents: corriente turbulenta
ripped: desgarrado
ripple tank: tanque de ondas
RNA: ARN
RNA polymerase: ARN polimerasa
robot: robot
robotics: robótica
rock: roca
rock cycle: ciclo de la roca
rock flour: harina de roca
rock formation: formación rocosa
rock forming minerals: formacion de rocas minerales
rock resistance: resistencia de la roca
rock salt: sal de roca
rocket: cohete
rocking: meciendo, balanceando

Rocky Mountain spotted fever: fiebre de las Montañas Rocosas
role: papel, rol; interpretación
root hair: raiz capilar
root nodule: nódulo de raíz
root pressure: presión de raíz
rotation: rotación
roughage: alimentos ricos en fibra
roundworm: lombriz intestinal
rubber ball: pelota de goma
rubbing: fricción, frotación
rubella: rubéola
rubidium: rubidio
rudimentary organ: órgano rudimentario
ruler: regla
ruminant: rumiante
runner: tallo trasero
runoff: escorrentía, residuo líquido
ruthenium: rutenio

S

sabin vaccine: vacuna de Sabin
sac: saco
saccharide: sacárido
saccharin: sacarina
saccharose: sacarosa
sag: curva catenaria o de forma de flecha
sal soda: sal sódica
salamander: salamandra
saline: salino
salinity: salinidad
salivary amylase: amilasa salival
salivary gland: glándula salival
salivate: salivar
salk vaccine: vacuna de Salk

R
S

salmonella: salmonela
salt: sal
salt bridge: puente salino
salt marsh: salina
saltation: saltación
saltwater: agua salada
samarium: samario
sandbar: barra costera arenosa
sandstone: arenisca
sandy soil: suelo arenoso
sanitary: sanitario
sanitary landfills: relleno sanitario
saponification: saponificación
sapphire: zafiro
saprophyte: saprófito
saprophytism: saprofitismo
satellite: satélite
saturated compound: compuesto saturado
saturated fats: grasas saturadas
saturated hydrocarbon: hidrocarburo saturado
saturated solution: solución saturada
saturation: saturación
saturation vapor pressure: presión de saturación
saturation zone: zona de saturación
Saturn: Saturno
saxophone: saxofón
scaffold: andamiaje; proveer de andamiaje
scalar: escalar
scalar field: campo escalar
scalar quantity: cantidad escalar
scales: escalas
scallop: venera
scandium: escandio
scattering: dispersión
schematic: esquemático
schist: esquisto

schizophrenia: esquizofrenia
Schwann's cell: célula de Schwann
science: ciencia
scientific data: datos científicos
scientific inquiry: indagación científica
scientific investigation: investigación científica
scientific law: ley científica
scientific literacy: capacidad científica de leer y escribir
scientific method: método científico
scientific model: modelo científico
scientific name: nombre científico
scientific theory: teoría científica
scientific thinking: pensamiento científico, razonamiento científico
scintillation: centelleo
scion: vástago
sclera: sclera
sclereid: escleroide
sclerosis: esclerosis
screw: tornillo
scrotum: escroto
scrubber: depurador
scuba: escafandra autónoma
scurvy: escorbuto
sea anemone: anémona de mar
sea breeze: brisa marina
sea cliff: acantilado o barranca de mar
sea cucumber: pepino de mar
sea floor spreading: expansión del fondo marino
sea level: nivel del mar
sea urchin: erizo de mar
seafloor spreading: expansión del suelo oceánico
sealant: sellante
seamount: montaña marina
season: temporada o estación

S

seasonally: estacionalmente

sebaceous gland: glándula sebácea

sebum: sebo

second filial generation: segunda generación filial

second law of thermodynamics: segunda ley de la termodinámica

second left-hand rule: segunda regla de la mano izquierda

secondary alcohol: alcohol secundario

secondary coil: rollo secundario, bobina secundaria

secondary color: color secundario

secondary consumer: consumidor secundario

secondary mycelium: micelio secundario

secondary pigment: pigmento secundario

secondary sexual characteristics: características sexuales secundarias

secondary succession: sucesión secundaria

secondary wave: onda secundaria

second-order line: línea de segundo orden

secretin: secretina

secretion: secreción

sediment: sedimento

sedimentary rock: roca sedimentaria

sedimentary strata: estrato sedimentario

sedimentation: sedimentación

sedimentation balance: balanza de sedimentación

sedimentation potential: potencial de sedimentación

seed crystal: cristal semilla

seed dispersal: dispersión de semilla

seedling: cultivo en semillero

seep: filtrar, escurrir

seep out: filtrarse

seismic exploration: exploración

seismic wave: onda sísmica

seismograph: sismógrafo

selective breeding: reproducción selectiva, apareamiento selectivo

selective permeability: permeabilidad selectiva

selectively permeable membrane: membrana selectivamente permeable

selenium: selenio

self-fertilization: autofertilización

self-inductance: autoinductancia

self-pollination: autopolinización

semen: semen

semicircular canal: canal semicircular

semiconductor: semiconductor

semilunar valve: válvula semilunar

semimicroanalysis: semi microanálisis

seminal vesicle: vesícula seminal

seminiferous tubule: túbulo seminífero

semipermeable: semipermeable

semipermeable membrane: membrana semipermeable

semisynthetic: semisintético

sense organ: órgano del sentido

senses: sentidos

sensitivity: sensibilidad

sensitization: sensibilización

sensor: detector

sensory area: área sensorial

sensory nerve fiber: fibra nerviosa sensorial

sensory neuron: neurona sensorial

sensory receptor: receptor sensorial

separated: separado

septum: septo, tabique o pared

sequestering agent: agente secuestrante

series circuit: circuito en serie

series connection: conexión en serie

series-parallel circuit: circuito en serie y paralelo

served as: servido como

sessile: sésil

S

setae: cerdas

sewage: aguas residuales

sewage treatment: tratamiento de aguas residuales

sewing needle: aguja de coser

sex cell: gameto, célula sexual

sex chromosome: cromosoma sexual

sex hormone: hormona sexual

sex organ: órgano sexual

sex-linkage inheritance: herencia ligada al sexo

sex-linked gene: gen ligado al sexo

sex-linked trait: rasgo ligado al sexo

sexual: sexual

sexual generation: generación sexual

sexual maturity: madurez sexual

sexual reproduction: reproducción sexual

sexually transmitted disease (STD): enfermedad de transmisión sexual (ETS)

shale: lutita, arcilla esquistosa

sheet erosion: erosión laminar

shield cone: cono de escudo

shield volcano: volcán en escudo

ship builder: constructor naval

shoreline: litoral, costanera

short day plant: planta de día corto

short circuit: cortocircuito; poner en cortocircuito

shortsightedness: miopía

shot-putter: lanzador de bala

shoulder joint: articulación del hombro

shrub layer: capa de arbustos

siamese twin: gemelos siameses

siblings: hermanos y hermanas

sickle cell: célula falciforme

sickle cell anemia: anemia de células falciformes

side effect: efecto secundario

sideral day: día sideral

sideral month: mes sideral

silica gel: silica gel

silicate: silicato

silicon: silicio

silicon carbide: carburo de silicio

silicone: silicona

silicone oil: aceite de silicona

silicon-oxygen tetrahedron: tetraedro de silicio y oxígeno

sill: filón, plancha, intrusiva, alféizar

silt: limo, fango

siltstone: roca de limo, limolita

silurian: silúrico

simple harmonic motion: movimiento armónico simple

simple machine: máquina simple

simple microscope: microscopio simple

simple reflex action: acción de reflejo simple

simple sugar (monosaccharide): azúcar simple (monosacárido)

single displacement reaction: reacción de desplazamiento simple

single circulation: circulación simple

single replacement: monosustitución

single-gene trait: característica de gene sencillo

single-slit diffraction: unica ranura de difracción

sink (energy): reserva natural de energía

sinkable: sumergible

sino-atrial node (S-A node): nudo sino-atrial

sinter: aglomerado

sintered crucible: crisol aglomerado

sinus: seno

siphon: sifón

skating: patinaje

skeletal muscle: músculo esquelético

skeletal system: sistema esquelético

skydiver: paracaidista
sled: trineo
sleeping sickness: encefalitis letárgica
sleet: aguanieve
sliding friction: fricción deslizante
slow oxidation: oxidación lenta
sludge: sedimento
slump: desprendimiento
small intestine: intestino delgado
smelt: eperlano
smog: niebla con humo, niebla tóxica
smokestack: chimenea
smooth muscle: músculo liso o visceral
snap: separación instantánea
sneezing reflex: reflejo de estornudo
Snell's Law: Ley de Snell
snow line: línea de nieve
snowmobile: motonieve, automotor sobre la nieve
soaps: jabones
social behavior: comportamiento social
society: sociedad
socket: tomacorriente, cuenca
soda ash: ceniza de soda
sodium: sodio
sodium bicarbonate: bicarbonato de sodio
sodium chloride: cloruro de sodio
sodium hydroxide: hidróxido de sodio
sodium ion: ión sódico
soil: suelo
soil association: asociación de suelos
soil conservation: conservación de la tierra (del suelo)
soil depletion: desgaste de la tierra (del suelo)
soil erosion: desgaste de la tierra (del suelo)
soil horizon: horizonte del suelo
soil profile: perfil del suelo
soil solution: solución del suelo

soil storage: reserva del suelo
soil texture: tipo o textura de suelo
solar cell: celda solar
solar collector: recolector solar
solar eclipse: eclipse de sol
solar energy: energía solar
solar noon: mediodía solar
solar system: sistema solar
solar time: tiempo solar
solenoid: solenoide
solid bone: hueso sólido
solid phase: fase sólida
solid solution: solución solida
solid state: estado sólido
solid wastes: desechos sólidos
solidification: solidificación
solidify: solidificar
soliquoid: soliquoide
solstice: solsticio
solubility: solubilidad
solubility curve: curva de solubilidad
solubility product constant: constante del producto de solubilidad
solubility product expression: expresión del producto de solubilidad
solute: soluto
solution: solución
solution equilibrium: equilibrio de solución
solvent: solvente
somatic: somático
somatic cell: célula somática
somatic nervous system: sistema nervioso somático
sonar: sonar
soot: hollín, tizne
soprano: soprano
sori: soros
sound quality: calidad del sonido

sound recorder: grabador de sonido

sound wave: onda sonora

source region: nacimiento, fuente

South Pole: Polo Sur

space probe: sonda espacial

space shuttle: trasbordador espacial

space station: estación espacial

spacecraft: astronave, nave espacial

speciation: especiación (especiamiento)

species: especie

species diversity: diversidad de especies

specific gravity: gravedad específica

specific heat: calor específico

specificity: especificar

spectacular: espectacular

spectra: espectro

spectral lines: líneas espectrales

spectrometer: espectrómetro

spectroscope: espectroscopio

spectroscopy: espectroscopia

spectrum: espectro

speed: velocidad

sperm: espermatozoides

sperm duct: conducto espermático

sperm nuclei: núcleos espermáticos

spermatid: espermátidas

spermatocyte: espermatocito

spermatogenesis: espermatogénesis

spermatophyte: espermatofita

sphalerite: esfalerita

sphere: esfera

spherical: esférico

spherical aberration: aberración esférica

sphincter: esfínter

spike: punta

spinal column: columna vertebral

spinal cord: espina dorsal, columna vertebral

spinal nerve: nervio espinal

spindle: huso

spindle fiber: huso mitótico

spiracles: espiráculos

spiral: espiral

spiral galaxies: galaxias espirales

spit: banco de arena

spleen: bazo

splice: juntar

spoiler: freno aerodinámico

spongy bone: hueso esponjoso

spongy layer: capa esponjosa

spongy mesophyll: mesófilo esponjoso

spongy tissue: tejido esponjoso

spontaneous chemical change: cambio químico espontáneo

spontaneous generation: generación espontánea

spontaneous generation theory: teoría de la generación espontánea

spontaneous ignition: ignición espontánea

spontaneous mutation: mutación espontánea

spontaneously: espontáneamente

sporangium: esporángio

spore: espora

spore reproduction: reproducción por esporas

spores: esporas

sporogenesis: esporogénesis

sporophyte generation: generación esporofita

sporophyte stage: etapa de esporofito

sporulation: esporulación

spot test for fat: prueba de mancha para grasa

spring: manantial

spring tide: marea viva

sputum: esputo

squint: estrabismo, ser bizco, mirar de reojo, mirar entrecerrando los ojos

stability constant: constante de estabilidad

stabilization: estabilización

stabilizer: estabilizador

stable compound: compuesto estable

stack: chimenea, pilar de erosión

stages: etapas

staining: manchar

stalactites: estalactitas

stalagmites: estalagmitas

stamen: estambre

staminate flower: flor estaminífera

standard: estándar

standard atmospheric pressure: presión atmosférica normal

standard calomel electrode: electrodo estándar de calomel

standard condition: condición estándar

standard electrode potential: potencial de electrodo estándar

standard heat of formation: calor de formación estándar

standard oxidation-reduction potential: potencial de oxidación reducción estándar

standard pressure: presión estándar

standard solution: solución estándar

standing wave: onda estacionaria

staphylococcus: estafilococo

starfish: estrella de mar

startling: alarmante

static charge: carga estática

static electricity: electricidad estática

static friction: fricción estática

statics: estática

station model: modelo estacional

stationary front: frente estacionario

steady state: estado constante (estable)

steam distillation: destilación con vapor

stearic acid: ácido esteárico

step-down transformer: transformador reductor

step-up transformer: transformador elevador

stereochemistry: estereoquímica

stereoisomer: estereoisómero

stereomicroscope: estereomicroscopio

stereoscope: estereoscopio

sterility: esterilidad

sterilization: esterilización

sterilizing: esterilizar

sternum: esternón

steroid: esteroide

stethoscope: estetoscopio

stigma: estigma

stimulated emission: emisión estimulada

stimuli: estímulos

stinging cell: onidocitos (célula punzante)

stoichiometry: estequiometría

stolon: estolón

stomata: estomas

stopper: tapón

stopwatch: cronómetro

storage tissue: tejido de almacenaje

storm surge: centro de la tormenta

storms: tormentas

STP: presión y temperatura estándar

straight-chain compound: compuesto de cadena lineal

straighten: enderezar(se)

strain: raza; filtrar(se), presión, tensión, carga, esguince, torcedura

strand: fibra

strata: estratos, capas

stratified: estratificado

strato: estrato

stratopause: estratopausa

stratosphere: estratósfera

stratus cloud: nube estrato

S

streak: veta

stream bed: lecho de la corriente (rio)

stream discharge: descarga de corriente

stream draining pattern: patrón de drenaje de la corriente

streptococcus: estreptococo

streptomycin: estreptomicina

striated muscle: músculo estriado

striations: estriaciones

strip cropping: cultivo en franjas

strobe: estroboscopio

strobe light: luz estroboscópica

strobe photography: fotografía estroboscópica

stroma: estroma

strong acid: ácido fuerte

strong base: base fuerte

strong electrolyte: electrólito fuerte

strong force: fuerza de atracción

strong nuclear force: fuerza nuclear fuerte

strontium: estroncio

structural adaptation: adaptación estructural

structural formula: fórmula estructural

subatomic: subatómico

subatomic particle: partícula subatómica

subduction boundary: límite de subducción

sublevel: subnivel

sublimate: sublimar

sublimation: sublimación

submarine: submarino

submarine canyons: cañones submarinos

submergence: inmersión

subscript: subíndice

subshell: semicapa

subsidence: hundimiento

subsoil: subsuelo

subspecies: subespecies

substance: sustancia

substituted hydrocarbon: hidrocarburo sustituido

substitution reaction: reacción de sustitución

substrate: substrato

succession: sucesión

sucrase: sacarasa

sucrose: sucrosa, sacarosa

suction pressure: presión de succión

sufficiently: suficientemente

sulfa drug: sulfamida

sulfide: sulfuro

sulfur: azufre

sulfur dioxide: dióxido de sulfuro

sulfuric acid: ácido sulfúrico

sundial: reloj de sol

sunspots: manchas solares

supercooled: super enfriado

supergiant: super gigante

superior vena cava: vena cava superior

supernova: supernova

superoxides: superóxidos

superposition: sobreposición

supersaturated solution: solución sobresaturada

supersaturation: sobresaturación

supersonic: onda ultrasonora; supersónico

surface activity: actividad superficial

surface chemistry: química de la superficie

surface concentration excess: exceso de concentración superficial

surface current: corriente de superficie

surface orientation: orientación superficial

surface reaction: reacción superficial

surface tension: tensión superficial

surface wave: onda superficial

surface-active agent: agente tenso-activo

surrogate parent: padres substitutos

survival of the fittest: supervivencia del más apto

S

suspension: suspensión

suspension transport: transporte por suspensión

sustainable use: uso sostenible

suture: sutura

swamp: pantano; hundir, inundar

swash: oleaje, chapoteo

S-wave: onda S (secundaria)

sweat gland: glándula sudorípara

Swedish: sueco

swim-bladder: vejiga de flotación

swing seat: silla de oscilación

swirl: torbellino

symbiosis: simbiosis

symbiotic: simbiótico

symmetrical: simétrico

sympathetic: simpático

sympathetic nervous system: sistema nervioso simpático

synapse: sinapsis

synchrocyclotron: sincrociclotrón

synchroton: sincrotrón

syncline: sinclinal

synodic month: mes sinódico

synoptic weather map: mapa sinóptico del tiempo

synthesis gas: gas de síntesis

synthesis reaction: reacción síntesis

synthesize: sintetizar

synthetic: sintético

synthetic resin: resina sintética

systematic method: método sistemático

systemic circulation: circulación sistémica

systole: sístole

systolic pressure: presión sistólica

T

table salt: sal de mesa

tadpole: renacuajo

taiga: taiga

tail fin: aleta

talc: talco

talus: talud

tanker: buque petrolero

tantalum: tántalo o tantalio

tap root: raíz principal

tape measure: cinta métrica

tapeworm: solitaria

tartaric acid: ácido tartárico

taste bud: papila gustativa

taxonomy: taxonomía

Tay-Sachs disease: enfermedad de Tay-Sachs

technetium: tecnecio

technologist: tecnólogo

technology: tecnología

tectonics: tectónica

tellurium: telurio

telophase: telofase

temperate deciduous forest: bosque caducifolio templado

temperate rain forest: bosque lluvioso templado

temperate zone: zona templada

temperature: temperatura

temperature inversion: inversión de temperatura

temperature scale: escala de temperatura

template: plantilla

temporary magnet: imán temporal o temporario

tend to: tiende a

tendon: tendón

tensile: tensor

S
T

tentacles: tentáculos
tephra: tefra
terbium: terbio
terephthalic acid: ácido tereftálico
terminal bud: brote terminal
terminal moraine: morena terminal
terminal velocity: velocidad terminal
ternary: ternario
ternary acid: ácido ternario
ternary compound: compuesto ternario
terraced: en terrazas
terracing: terraceo
terrestrial biome: bioma terrestre
terrestrial motions: movimientos terrestres
terrestrial planets: planetas terrestres
terrestrial radiation: radiación terrestre
terrigenous: terrígeno
tertiary: terciario
tertiary alcohol: alcohol terciario
Terylene: terileno
tesla: tesla
test cross: prueba cruzada
test tube: tubo de ensayo
test tube holder: soporte de tubo de ensayo
test tube rack: gradilla
testis: testículos
testosterone: testosterona
tetanus: tétano
tetrachloride: tetracloruro
tetrad: tétrada
tetraflouroethylene: tetrafluoroetileno
tetragonal system: sistema tetragonal
tetramer: tetrámero
tetraploid: tetraploide
thalassemia: talasemia
thallium: talio
The first law of Thermodynamics: primera ley de la termodinámica

The Law of Conservation of Energy: Ley de Conservación de la Energía
The Law of Conservation of Momentum: Ley de Conservación del Momento
The Law of Reflection: Ley de la Reflexión
The second law of Thermodynamics: segunda ley de la termodinámica
theoretical physicist: físico teórico
theoretical plate: plato teórico
theory: teoría
theory of relativity: teoría de la relatividad
theory of use and disuse: teoría de uso y desuso
thermal: termal
thermal diffusion: difusión térmica
thermal energy: energía térmica
thermal equilibrium: equilibrio termal
thermal expansion: expansión térmica
thermal pollution: contaminación térmica
thermal polymerization: polimerización térmica
thermite: termita
thermobalance: termobalanza o balance térmico
thermochemistry: termoquímica
thermocouple: termopar
thermodynamics: termodinámica
thermoform: termoforma
thermograph: termógrafo
thermometry: termometría
thermonuclear: termonuclear
thermonuclear device: dispositivo termonuclear
thermonuclear reaction: reacción termonuclear
thermoplastic: termoplástico
thermosetting: termoestables
thermosphere: termósfera
thiamine: tiamina
thicker: más grueso

thin film: película fina

thiol: tiol

third-level consumer: consumidor de tercer nivel

thistle tube: tubo de cardo

thoracic duct: conducto torácico

thorium: torio

thrombin: trombina

thromboplastin: tromboplastina

thrombus: trombo

thulium: tulio

thymine: timina

thymus gland: glándula del timo

thyroid gland: glándula tiroides

thyroid-stimulating hormone (TSH): hormona tirotrópica (HTT)

thyroxine: tiroxina

tibia: tibia

tidal range: rango de la marea

tide: marea

tightly: estrechamente

tilted strata: estratos inclinados

timbre: timbre

tincture: tintura

tire: llanta

tissue: tejido

tissue culture: cultivo de tejidos

tissue fluid: fluído de tejido

titanium: titanio

titrant: titrante

titration: titulación, valoración

toluene: tolueno

tombolo: banco de arena

toner: tóner, matizador

tongue rolling: enrollamiento de la lengua

tonsilitis: amigdalitis

tooth decay: caries dentales

tooth root: raíz dental

topographic map: mapa topográfico

topsoil: suelo, superficie de la tierra (del suelo)

tornado: tornado

torsion: torsión

torsion balance: balanza de torsión

total internal reflection: reflexión interna total

toxin: toxina

trace element: elemento de trazas, elemento de rastreo

tracer: indicador radiactivo, trazador

trachea: tráquea

tracheophyte: traqueófito

trade-off: intercambio

trampoline: trampolín

tranquilizer: tranquilizador

transceiver: radio transmisor

transcription: transcripción

transducer: transductor

transduction: transducción

transfer pipette: pipeta de transferencia

transfer RNA (tRNA): ARN de transferencia (tARN)

transference number: número de transferencia

transform boundaries: limite de transformación

transformer: transformador

transgenic: transgénico

transistor: transistor

transition element: elemento de transición

transition series: series de transición

transition zone: zona de transición

translocation: translocación

translucent: translúcido

transmission: transmisión

transmitted wave: onda transmitida

transmutation: trasmutación

transparent: transparente

T

transpiration: transpiración
transpiration pull: atracción transpiracional
transport system: sistema de transporte
transported sediment: sedimento de acarreo
transported soil: terreno de acarreo
transuranic element: elemento trans-uránico
transverse colon: colón transverso
transverse section: sección transversa
transverse wave: onda transversal
trauma: trauma
trellis pattern: patrón de enrejado
trench: atrincherar
triad: tríada
triceps: tríceps
trichloroethylene: tricloroetileno
trichloroflouromethane: triclorofluoro-metano
tricresyl phosphate: fosfato de tricresilo
tricyclic: tricíclico
triethanolamine: trietanolamina
triethylaluminum: trietil aluminio
triglyceride: triglicérido
trihydroxy alcohol: alcohol trihydroxílico
trillion: trillón
trilobite: trilobita
trioxide: trióxido
triple beam balance: balanza de brazo triple
triple bond: enlace triple
triple point: punto triple
triplet code: código triple
triploid: triploide
tritium: tritio
trombone: trombón
trophic level: nivel trófico
tropical rain forest: bosque húmedo tropical
tropical zone: zona tropical

tropics: trópicos
tropism: tropismo
tropopause: tropopausa
troposphere: troposfera
trough: caída, comedero, depresión, punto bajo, camellón
trough zona: de baja presión
true solution: solución verdadera
trypsin: tripsina
tsunami: maremoto
tuba: tuba
tube feet: pie tubular
tuber: tubérculo
tubing: tubería, entubamiento
tubule: túbulo
tundra: tundra
tungsten: tungsteno
tungsten carbide: carburo de tungsteno
tuning fork: diapasón
turbidites: turbiedades
turbidity: turbidez
turbidity currents: corrientes de turbiedad
turbine: turbina
turbulent flow: flujo turbulento
turgid: túrgido
turgor pressure: presión de turgidez
Turner's syndrome: síndrome de Turner
twirl: rotación; hacer girar
two-hole stopper: tapón de dos orificios
Tyndall effect: efecto Tyndall
typhoid: tifoidea

U

ulna: cúbito
ultimate analysis: análisis final
ultracentrifuge: ultracentrifugadora
ultrafiltration: ultrafiltración
ultrasonic: ultrasónico
ultrasonography: ultrasonografía
ultraviolet light: luz ultravioleta
ultraviolet radiation: radiación ultravioleta
ultraviolet waves: ondas ultravioleta
umbilical cord: cordón umbilical
umbilicus: ombligo
umbra: umbra
unaffected: inafectado
unavailability: indisponibilidad
unbalance: desequilibrio; desbalance
unbalanced force: fuerza desequilibrada
uncertainty principle: principio de incertidumbre
unchanged: invariado
unconformity: inconformidad
undiminished: sin merma
unglazed porcelain plate: placa de porcelana mate
unicellular: unicelular
uniform acceleration: aceleración uniforme
uniform circular motion: movimiento circular uniforme
uniform dispersion: dispersión uniforme
uniformitarianism: uniformismo
uniformly: uniformidad
units of force: unidades de fuerza
universal recipient: recipiente universal
unsaturated compound: compuesto insaturado
unsaturated fats: grasas insaturadas
unsaturated hydrocarbon: hidrocarburo no saturado
unsaturated solution: solución no saturada
unsaturation: insaturación
unsorted: revuelto
unstable compound: compuesto inestable
uplifting forces: fuerzas levantadoras
upward: hacia arriba
upwarped mountains: montañas de levantamiento
upwelling: solevantamiento
uracil: uracilo
uranium: uranio
Uranus: Urano
urban desert: desierto urbano
urea: urea
urease: ureasa
ureter: uréter
urethra: uretra
uric acid: ácido úrico
urinary bladder: vejiga urinaria
urinary system: sistema urinario
urine: orina
U-shaped valley: valle en U
uterine lining: endometrio
uterus: útero

V

vaccinated: vacunado
vaccination: vacunación
vaccine: vacuna
vacuole: vacuola
vacuum: vacío; vacío
vacuum condensing point: punto de condensación al vacío
vacuum crystallization: cristalización al vacío

vacuum crystallizer: cristalizador al vacío
vacuum distillation: destilación al vacío
vagina: vagina
valence: valencia
valence electrons: electrones de valencia
valine: valina
valley glacier: valle glaciar
Van der Waals force: fuerzas de Van der Waals
vanadium: vanadio
vane: veleta
Van't Hoff equation: ecuación de Van't Hoff
Van't Hoff isochore: isocora de Van't Hoff
Van't Hoff isotherm: isoterma de Van't Hoff
vapor pressure: presión de vapor
vapor pressure depression: disminución de la presión de vapor
vapor state: estado de vapor
vaporization: vaporización
variability: variabilidad
variable: variable
variable factor: factor variable
variation: variación
variegated leaf: hoja abigarrada
vas deferens: conducto deferente
vascular bundle: envoltorio vascular
vascular cylinder: cilindro vascular
vascular plant: planta vascular
vascular ray: rayo vascular
vascular system: sistema vascular
vascular tissue: tejido vascular
vasoconstriction: vasoconstricción
vasodilation: vasodilatación
vasopressin: vasopresina
vector field: campo vectorial
vector quantity: magnitud vectorial
vector resolution: resolución vectorial
vector sum: suma vectorial

vegetative propagation: propagación vegetativa
vein: vena
velocity: velocidad direccional
velocity of light: velocidad de la luz
vena cava: vena cava
venereal disease: enfermedad venérea
venous flow: flujo venoso
vent: chimenea
ventral: ventral
ventral blood vessel: vaso sanguíneo ventral
ventral nerve cord: cordón de nervio ventral
ventral root: raíz ventral
ventricle: ventrículo
venule: vénula
Venus: Venus
Venus's-flytrap: atrapador de moscas de Venus
vertebrae: vértebra
vertebral column: columna vertebral
vertebrate: vertebrado
vertical rays: rayos verticales
vertically: verticalmente
vesicle: vesícula
vestiges: vestigios
vestigial: vestigial
vestigial structure: estructura vestigial
vibrational: vibratorio, vibracional
vibrational motion: movimiento vibratorio o vibracional
vicinal: vecinal
vigorously: vigorosamente
villi: vellosidades
villus: vellosidad
vinyl: vinilo
vinyl chlorid: cloruro de vinilo
viral disease: enfermedad viral

virtual: virtual
virtual image: imagen virtual
virus: virus
viscera: vísceras
visceral muscle: músculo visceral
viscosity: viscosidad
viscous: viscoso
viscous liquid: líquido viscoso
visible light: luz visible
visible spectrum: espectro visible
vital capacity: capacidad vital
vitamin: vitamina
vitreous: vítreo
viviparous: vivíparas
vocal: vocal
vocal cord: cuerda vocal
volatile liquid: líquido volátil
volatility: volatilidad
volatilize: volatilizar
volcanic ash: ceniza volcánica
volcanic mountains: montañas volcánicas
volcanic neck: cuello volcánico
volcano: volcán
voltage difference: diferencia de voltaje
voltage divider: reductor de voltaje
voltage drop: caída de tensión o voltaje
voltaic: voltaico
voltaic cell: celda voltaica
voltmeter: voltímetro
volume: volumen
volume bottle: botella de volumen
volumetric analysis: análisis volumétrico
volumetric flask: frasco volumétrico
volumetric pipet: pipeta volumétrica
voluntary action: acción voluntaria
voluntary behavior: comportamiento voluntario
voluntary muscle: músculo voluntario
V-shaped valley: valle en V

vulcanization: vulcanización

walking the outcrop: recorrer el afloramiento
waning: menguante
warm front: frente cálido
warm-blooded: de sangre caliente
warning coloration: coloración de aviso
water vascular system: agua del sistema vascular
water budget: disponibilidad de agua
water cycle: ciclo del agua
water gas: gas de agua
water glass: indicador de nivel de agua
water of crystallization: agua de cristalización
water of hydration: agua de hidratación
water pollution: contaminación del agua
water potential: potencial de agua
water purification: purificación del agua
water shed: cuenca, vertiente
water softening: ablandamiento de agua
water table: nivel freático
water vapor: vapor de agua
water vascular system: sistema vascular de agua
waterspout: caño, canalón
wave: onda
wave length: longitud de onda
wave refraction: refracción de la onda
wave speed: velocidad de la onda
wave velocity: velocidad de onda
wax layer: capa de cera
waxes: ceras
waxing: encerar

weak acid: ácido débil
weak base: base débil
weak electrolyte: electrólito débil
weak force: fuerza débil
weasel: comadreja
weather: clima, el estado del tiempo
weather forecasting: pronóstico del tiempo
weathering: desgaste, erosión
weathering agents: agentes de desgaste
wedge: cuña
weed killer: herbicida
weighing bottle: pesaje de botella
weight: peso
wet-bulb depression: depresión del bulbo húmedo (termómetro húmedo)
wetland: zona húmeda, pantano
wet-mount slide: portaobjetos húmedo
wheel and axle: rueda y eje
white blood cell: glóbulo blanco
white corpuscle: corpúsculo blanco
white dwarf: enana blanca
white matter: materia blanca
whole blood: sangre entera
whooping cough: tosferina
wildlife conservation: conservación de la fauna
wilt: marchitar
wind break: contravientos
wind erosion: erosión eólica
wind farm: granja de energía eólica
wind pollination: polinización eólica
wind vane: veleta
windward: barlovento
wings: alas
wingspan: envergadura
wire gauze: gasa de alambre
wood alcohol: alcohol de madera
woody fiber: fibra leñosa

woody stem: tallo leñoso
woolly mammoth: mamut lanudo
work: trabajo
worker bee: abeja obrera

X rays: rayos X
xanthophyll: xantófila
xanthoproteic test: examen de ácido xantoprotéico
x-chromosome: cromosoma-X
xenon: xenón
Xerox: Xerox; xerocopiar
x-value: valor de la X
xylem: xilema
xylene: xileno

Y

y-chromosome: cromosoma-Y

yeast fermentation: fermentación de la levadura

yolk sac: saco vitelino

young landscape: topografía joven

ytterbium: iterbio

yttrium: itrio

y-value: valor de la Y

Z

zenith: cenit

zeolite: zeolita

zero group: grupo cero

zircon: circón

zirconium: zirconio

zodiac: zodiaco

zonation: división en zonas

zone of aeration: zona de ventilación

zone refining: refinación por zonas

zooplankton: zooplancton

zygote: zigoto, cigoto

Y
Z

Social Studies
Subject Vocabulary
English-Spanish

Bilingual Dictionaries, Inc.

A

abandon: abandonar

abolition: abolición

abolitionist: abolicionista

aboriginal: aborigen

absolutism: absolutismo

abuses: abusos

access: acceso

accommodate: acomodar

accompany: acompañar

acculturation: aculturación

achieve: lograr

acquire: adquirir

adapt: adaptar

adequate: adecuado

administration: administración

advantages: ventajas

affirmative action: acción afirmativa

Africa: Africa

African civilization: Civilización Africana

African slaves: esclavos africanos

African-American: afroamericano

Age of Jackson: Era Jacksoniana

Age of Reason: Edad de la Razón

agrarian: agrario

agricultural areas: áreas agrícolas

aid: ayuda

AIDS: SIDA

Albany Plan of Union: Plan de Unión de Albany

Alger Hiss case: caso Alger Hiss

Algonquians: Algonquinos, de la tribu algonquina

alien: extranjero

Alien and Sedition Acts: Leyes de Extranjería y Sedición

Alliance for Progress: Alianza para el Progreso

alliances: alianzas

Allied powers: Aliados, potencias aliadas en la Segunda Guerra Mundial

allies: aliados

alternative solutions: soluciones alternativas

altiplano: altiplano, meseta

amendment: enmienda

American democracy: democracia de Estados Unidos

American Federation of Labor (AFL): Federación Americana del Trabajo

American Railway Union: Sindicato Americano de Ferrocarriles

American Revolution: Guerra de la Independencia de Estados Unidos

American system (Clay): Sistema Americano (Henry Clay)

Americas: las Américas

amnesty: amnistía

ancestor worship: culto a los ancestros

animism: animismo

anit-Semetic: antisemitismo

Annapolis Convention: Convención de Annapolis

annex: anexar

annexation: anexión

annual: anual

Antarctic Circle: Círculo Polar Antártico

Antarctica: Antártida

ante bellum: ante bellum

anthropology: antropología

Anti Federalist: anti federalista

anticipate: anticiparse

Anti-Defamation League: Liga de Antidifamación

Antifederalists: antifederalistas

Anti-Federalists: Antifederalistas

anti-Semitism: antisemitismo

anti-trust: antimonopolista

apartheid: segregación racial

appeasement: apaciguamiento

appointed leaders: líderes designados

appointed office: cargo designado

apportionment: reparto

apprentice: aprendiz

approach: enfoque

appropriate: apropiado o adecuado

Arab League: Liga Arabe

archaeologists: arqueólogos

archeology: arqueología

architectural drawings: dibujos arquitectónicos

Arctic Circle: Círculo Polar Ártico

area: área

areas: áreas

armed forces: fuerzas armadas

armistice: armisticio

army: armada, ejército

arsenal: arsenal

Arsenal of Democracy: Arsenal de Democracia

article: artículo

Articles of Confederation: Artículos de la Confederación

artifacts: artefactos, objetos de artesanía, manualidades

Asia: Asia

Asian-American: Asiático-americano

aspect: aspecto

assassinations: asesinatos

assemble: reunir

assembly line: línea de ensamble, línea de montaje, cadena de ensamble

assign: asignar

assimilate: asimilar

assist: asistir

assume: asumir

astrolabe: astrolabio

astronauts: astronautas

Atlantic Charter: Carta del Atlántico

atlas: atlas

atomic bomb: bomba atómica

authority: autoridad

autobiographies: autobiografías

autobiography: autobiografía

autocracy: autocracia

automation: automatización

automobiles: automóviles

available: disponible

avenues of participation: métodos de participación

Axis powers: potencias del Eje en la Segunda Guerra Mundial

Aztecs: Aztecas

B

B.C.: antes de Cristo, a. de C.

baby boom: explosión de natalidad

baby boom generation: generación de la abundancia (prosperidad) post guerra

Balance of Power: Balance de Poder

Balkans: Balcanes

bank holiday: asueto (día de fiesta) bancario

banking operaciones: bancarias, banca, comercio, bancario

barrio: barrio

barter: cambiar, hacer trueque

Battle of Quebec: Batalla de Quebec

battles: batallas

Bay of Pigs Invasion: Invasión de la Bahía de Cochinos

belief system: sistema de creencias

beliefs: convicciones, creencias

benefit: beneficio
bereaucracy: burocracia
Berlin airlift: puente aéreo a Berlín
Berlin Blockade: Bloqueo de Berlín
Berlin Wall: Muro de Berlín
Bessemer process: proceso Bessemer
bias: parcialidad
Bible: Biblia
bicameral: bicameral
bicameral legislature: legislatura bicameral
big business: las grandes empresas
Big Stick Policy: Política del Garrote
bill: proyecto de ley
Bill of Rights: Declaración de Derechos
biographies: biografías
bipartisan: bipartidista
Black Codes: Códigos Negros
Black Death: Pest Bubónica
Black Panthers: Panteras Negras
Black Power: Poder Negro
Black Tuesday: Martes Negro
blacklist: lista negra
Bleeding Kansas: Kansas agónica
blitzkrieg: blitzkrieg (guerra relámpago)
blockade: bloqueo
bodies of water: caudales de agua
Bolshevik Revolution: Revolución Bolchevique
bonds: bonos, obligaciones
Bonus Army: Ejército bonificado
boomtown: pueblo en auge
border ruffians: rufianes fronterizos
border states: estados fronterizos
Boston Tea Party: Motín del Té en Boston
boundaries: límites
bounty: gratificación
bourgeoisie: burguesía
Boxer Rebellion: Rebelión de los Bóxers
boycott: boicot, boicoteo

branches of government: departamentos del gobierno
brand: marca
brief: breve
British North America Act: Ley de la Norteamérica británica
Bronze Age: Edad de Bronce
bubonic plague: plaga bubónica
Buddhism: Budismo
buffer zone: zona franca
bull market: mercado alcista
bullion: lingotes
Bureau of Indian Affairs: Agencia de Asuntos Indígenas
bureaucracy: burocracia
burgesses: burgueses
Bushido: Bushido
business cycle: ciclo económico
business organization: organización de negocios
buying on a margin: compra por margen
Byzantine: Bizantino

C

cabinet: gabinete consejo de ministros
Californios: californios
Camp David Accord: Acuerdos de Camp David
Canada: Canadá
Canadian Bill of Rights: Declaración de Derechos de Canadá
canal: canal
capital: capital
capital (state and money): capital (estado y dinero)
capital goods: bienes de capital

capital resources: recursos de capital
capitalism: capitalismo
captains of industry: capitanes de la industria
cardinal directions: puntos cardinales
Caribbean: Caribeño(a)
carpetbaggers: aventureros, politicastros
cartel: cartel
cartoons: dibujos animados
case law: caso de ley
cash crop: cosecha comercial, cultivo
caste system: sistema de castas
casualty: casualidad
categories: categorías
Catholic: Católico
Catholicism: Catolicismo
caucus: junta
cede: ceder
celebrations: celebraciones
census: censo
census reports: informes del censo
Central America: Centroamérica
central government: gobierno central
Central Intelligence Agency (CIA): Agencia Central de Inteligencia
challenge: reto
characteristics: características
charter: carta constitucional
charter colony: colonia a carta
charts: carta, mapa
checks and balances: inspecciones y balances, pesos y contrapesos
chemical warfare: guerra química
Cherokee: Cherokee
Chief Justice: Juez Superior
child labor: trabajo o explotación de menores, explotación infantil
child labor laws: leyes de empleo de menores o explotación de menores
China: China

Chinese: chino
Chinese Exclusion Act: Ley de Exclusión de los Chinos
Chippewa: Chippewa u Ojibwa
choices: opciones
chronological order: orden cronológico
circumnavigate: circunnavegar
citizen: ciudadano
city-state: ciudad-estado
civic life: vida cívica, vida civil
civic values: valores cívicos
civil disobedience: desobediencia civil
civil rights: derechos civiles
Civil Rights Acts: Leyes de Derechos Civiles
Civil Rights Movement: movimiento de derechos civiles
civil service: administración pública
civil society: sociedad civil
civil unrest: descontento civil
Civil War: guerra civil, Guerra de Secesión
Civil War Amendments: Enmiendas de la Guerra Civil
clans: clanes
classical: clásico
classical civilizations: civilizaciones clásicas
closed shop: taller cerrado
coast lines: líneas costeras
coeducation: coeducación
Cold War: Guerra Fría
collapse: derrumbarse
collect taxes: recaudar impuestos
collective: colectivo
collective bargaining: negociación colectiva
collective security: seguridad colectiva
colonial era: era colonial
colonial governments: gobiernos coloniales
colonialism: colonialismo
colonists: colonos

colony: colonia

Columbian Exchange: Cambio Colombiano

Columbus Day: Día de la Raza

command economy: economía de mando

Commander-In-Chief: Comandante en Jefe

Commercial Revolution: Revolución Comercial

commission: comisión

commit: cometer

Committees of Correspondence: Comités de Correspondencia

commodity: producto

common good: el bien común

common goods: mercancías comunes

common law: ley común

common sense: sentido común

common welfare: bienestar general

commonwealth: mancomunidad

Commonwealth of Nations: Mancomunidad de naciones

communicate: comunicar

communist nations: países comunistas

Communist Party: Partido Comunista

community: comunidad

community service: servicio comunitario

company town: pueblo de la compañia

compare and contrast: compare y contraste

compromise: acuerdo, compromiso, avenencia, componenda, concesión

Compromise of 1850: Acuerdo del 1850

compulsory education: educación obligatoria

Computer Revolution: Revolución de las Computadoras

concentrate: concentrarse

concentration camp: campo de concentración

concept: concepto

conclude: concluir

concurrent powers: poderes concurrentes

conduct: conducir

Conestoga wagon: carro de Conestoga

confederacy: confederación

confederation: confederación

conference committees: comités de conferencia

confirm: confirmar

conflict: conflicto

conflict resolution: resolución de conflictos

Confucianism: Confucianismo

congresional district: distrito congresional

Congress of Vienna: Congreso de Viena

congressional committees: comités del congreso

Congressional Industrial Organization: Congreso de Organizaciones Industriales

conquistador: conquistador

conscientious objector: objetor por conciencia

conscription: reclutamiento

consent of the governed: consentimiento de los gobernados

consequences: consecuencias

conservation: conservación

Conservation Day: Día de la Conservación

conservation of resources: conservación de recursos

consist: consistir

consolidation: consolidación

conspicuous consumption: consumo conspicuo

constant: constante

constituents: constituyentes

constitution: constitución

Constitution of the State of New York: Constitución del estado de Nueva York

Constitution of the United States: Constitución de Estados Unidos

Constitutional Amendments: Enmiendas a la Constitución

Constitutional Convention: Convención Constitucional

constitutional democracy: democracia constitucional

constitutional government: gobierno constitucional

constitutional monarchy: monarquía constitucional

Consumer Price Index (CPI): Índice de Precios del Consumidor

consumer society: sociedad de consumo

consumers: consumidores

consumption of goods: consumo de bienes

contemporary issues: asuntos contemporáneos

Continental Congress: Congreso continental

Continental Divide: Divisoria continental, línea divisoria continental

continents: continentes

contract: contrato

contrary: contrario

contras: contras

contrast: contrastar

contribute: contribuir

contributions: contribuciones

controversial events: eventos controversiales

controversy: controversia

convenant: convenio

convert: convertir

convince: convencer

cooperate: cooperar

cooperative: cooperativa

corporation: corporación

correspond: corresponder

corruption: corrupción

costs: costos

cotton belt: región algodonera (del sur de los EE.UU.)

cotton gin: desmotadora de algodón

Counter Reformation: contrarreforma

counterculture: contracultura

coup d'etat: golpe de estado

court cases: casos ante la Corte

court packing: plan de rellenar la corte

court-martial: corte marcial

covenant: convenio

craft union: sindicato de oficio

create: crear

credit: crédito

creditor nation: nación acreedora

Creoles: Criollos

criteria: criterios

Crusades: Cruzadas

Cuban Missile Crisis: Crisis de misiles de Cuba

cultural characteristics: características culturales

cultural contributions: contribuciones culturales

cultural differences: diferencias culturales

cultural diffusion: difusión cultural

cultural diversity: diversidad cultural

cultural groups: grupos culturales

cultural identity: identidad cultural

cultural interdependence: interdependencia cultural

cultural patterns: modelos (patrones) culturales

cultural pluralism: pluralismo cultural

cultural revolution: Revolución Cultural

cultural understanding: comprensión cultural

culture: cultura

currency: divisa, moneda circulante, moneda, moneda corriente, dinero en circulación

D

Dark Ages: Edad Oscura

dark horse: candidato por sorpresa

Dawes Act: Ley Dawes

De Witt Clinton: DeWitt Clinton

debate: debate

debtor: deudor

debtor nation: nación deudora

decision-making: toma de decisiones

decisions: decisiones

Declaration of Independence: Declaración de Independencia

decline: declinar

delta: delta

demilitarize: desmilitarizar

demobilization: desmovilización

Democratic: Democrático

Democratic Party: Partido Demócrata

democratic principles: principios democráticos

democratic society: sociedad democrática

democratic values: valores democráticos

demographic patterns: modelos demográficos

demonstrate: demostrar

deny: negar

depression: depresión

depressions: depresiones

deregulation: desregulación

derive: derivarse

desegregation: desegregación

desertification: desertificación

design: diseño

despite: a pesar de

despotism: despotismo

détente: distensión

developed nations: naciones desarrolladas

developing country: país en desarrollo

developing nations: países en vías de desarrollo

developments: desarrollos

device: dispositivo

devote: dedicar

diagrams: diagramas

diaspora: diáspora

differences: diferencias

different: diferente

diminish: disminuir

direct democracy: democracia directa

direct election of Senators: elección directa de los senadores

direct primary: primaria directa

direct versus indirect election: elección directa contra la indirecta

disabled citizens: ciudadanos inhabilitados

disadvantages: desventajas, inconvenientes

disarmament: desarme

discrimination: discriminación

diseases: enfermedades

disenfranchise: privación de derecho

displaced persons: personas desplazadas, expatriados

disputes: conflictos

dissent: disensión

distinct: bien diferenciados

distribute: distribuir

diversity: diversidad

dividend: dividendo

divine right: derecho divino

document: documento

dollar diplomacy: diplomacia del dólar

domestic policy: política interior

dominate: dominar

domino theory: teoría del dominó

double jeopardy: doble riesgo

Dr. Martin Luther King Jr. Day: Día del Dr. Martin Luther King Jr.

draft: reclutamiento

draft evaders: evasores al reclutamiento

draft riots: motines en protesta del reclutamiento

drug cartel: cartel de drogas

drug trafficking: narcotráfico

dry farming: cultivo seco

due process: proceso establecido, con las garantías procesales debidas

Dust Bowl: ventarrones de polvo

Dutch colonies: colonias holandesas

Dutch West India Company: Compañía Holandesa de las Indias Occidentales

dynamic: dinámico

E

Earth's surface: superficie de la Tierra

Eastern Hemisphere: hemisferio oriental

economic: económico(a)

economic capital: capital económico

economic concepts: conceptos económicos

economic decision making: toma de decisiones económicas

economic decisions: decisiones económicas

economic development: desarrollo económico

economic factors: factores económicos

economic growth: crecimiento económico

economic interdependence: interdependencia económica

economic systems: sistemas económicos

economics: economía, ciencia económica

economy: economía

education: educación

effects: efectos

Egypt: Egipto

elastic clause: cláusula flexible

elect: electo, elegido, elegir

elected leaders: líderes elegidos

elected office cargo: cargo público ocupado por un funcionario electo

Election Day: Día de las Elecciones

electoral: electoral

electoral college: colegio electoral

electors: electores

eliminate: eliminar

Ellis Island: Ellis Island o Isla Ellis

emancipate: emancipar

emancipation: emancipación

Emancipation Proclamation: Proclamación de Emancipación

embargo: embargo

Embargo Act: Ley de Embargo

emergence: emergencia

emigrant: emigrante

emigrate: emigrar

emigration: emigración

empathy: empatía

empresario: empresario

enable: permitir

encomienda: encomienda

encomienda system: sistema de encomienda

encounter: encuentro

enforce: hacer cumplir

enforce laws: hacer cumplir las leyes

English Bill of Rights: Carta Inglesa de Derechos

English colonies: colonias inglesas

Enlightenment: Siglo de las Luces

enormous: enorme

ensure: asegurar

entrenched: atrincherado

entrepreneur: empresario

enumerated powers: poderes enumerados

environment: medio ambiente o entorno

environmental factors: factores medio-ambientales

equal rights: igualdad de derechos

equal rights amendment: Enmienda por la Igualdad de Derechos

equality of opportunity: igualdad de oportunidad

equip: equipar

Era of Good Feelings: Era de los Buenos Sentimientos

eras: eras

escalation: escalada

escapism: escapismo, evasión

Espionage Act of 1917: Ley de Espionaje de 1917

establish: establecer

establishment: institución, establecimiento

Estates General: Estados Generales

ethnic: étnico

ethnic backgrounds: orígenes étnicos

ethnic cleansing: limpieza étnica

ethnic conflict: conflicto étnico

ethnic group: grupo étnico

ethnic neighborhoods: vecindarios étnicos

ethnic tension: tensión étnica

ethnicity: origen étnico

ethnocentrism: etnocentrismo

Eurasia: Eurasia

Eurodollar: Dólar Europeo

European Union (E.U.): Unión Europea (U.E.)

evaluate: evaluar

events: eventos

eventual: mucho después

exceed: exceder

excise tax: impuesto indirecto

excommunication: excomulgación

executive branch: rama ejecutiva

executive branch of government: rama ejecutiva del gobierno

executive privilege: privilegio ejecutivo

expand: expandir

expansionism: expansionismo

exploit: explotar

exploitation: explotación

exploration: exploración

explorers: exploradores

export: exportar

extract: extraer

extraterritoriality: extraterritorialidad

F

facilities: instalaciones, dependencias, comodidades

fact: hecho

faction: facción

factors: factores

factors of production: factores de producción

factory system: sistema de fábrica

famine: hambre

Far West: lejano oeste

farmers: granjeros

Fascism: Fascismo

Fascist Party: Partido Fascista

fauna: fauna

favorite son: hijo favorito

federal: federal

federal deficit: déficit federal

federal government: gobierno federal

Federal Reserve Act: Ley de la Reserva Federal

Federal Reserve System: Sistema de Reserva Federal

federal system: sistema federal

Federal System of government

Federal System of government: Sistema de Gobierno Federal

federal union: unión federal

Federalism: Federalismo

Federalist Papers: ensayos federalistas

Federalists: Federalistas

federation: federación

feminist movement: movimiento feminista

Fertile Crescent: Creciente Fértil

festival: festival

feudalism: feudalismo

fiefdom: feudo

Filipinos: Filipinos

finance: financiar

financial institutions: instituciones financieras

First Continental Congress: Primer Congreso Continental

fixed costs: costos fijos

Flag Day: Día de la Bandera

flora: flora

focus: enfocarse

folklore: folklore

folktale: leyenda folklórica popular

forced relocation: reubicación forzada

foreclosure: embargo de bienes muebles o inmuebles (hipotecario)

foreign affairs: asuntos exteriores

foreign aid: ayuda extranjera

foreign markets: mercados extranjeros

foreign policy: política exterior

foreign relations: relaciones exteriores

foreign trade: comercio exterior

Fort Orange: Fuerte Orange o Fuerte Naranja

Fort Sumter: Fuerte Sumter

forty-niners: forty-niners o los cuarenta y nueve

founded: fundamentado

Four Freedoms: Cuatro Libertades

Fourteen Points: Catorce Principios

franchise: franquicia, derecho al voto

free enterprise: libre empresa

free enterprise system: sistema de libre empresa

free silver: plata libre

free trade: libre comercio

freedman: liberto

freedom of expression: libertad de expresión

freedom of religion: libertad de religión

freedom of the press: libertad de imprenta (prensa)

freedom riders: pasajeros (jinetes) de la libertad

freedom to assemble: libertad de asamblea (para reunirse)

freedom trail: camino de la libertad

French and Indian War: Guerra francoindia

French Canadians: francocanadiense

French Colonies: colonias francesas

French Revolution: Revolución Francesa

frigate: fragata

fugitive: fugitivo

Fugitive Slave Law: Ley de Esclavos Fugitivos

function: funcionar

functions of government: funciones del gobierno

fund: fondo

fundamental economic questions: preguntas económicas fundamentales

Fundamental Orders of Connecticut: Órdenes Fundamentales de Connecticut

fundamental values: valores fundamentales

fundamentalism: fundamentalismo

G

G.I. Bill: Carta de Derechos de los Veteranos

Gay Rights Movement: Movimiento por derechos de homosexuales

gender bias: prejuicio de género sexual

gender roles: funciones del género sexual

generation: generación

geographic characteristics: características geográficas

geographic factors: factores geográficos

geographic features or areas: características o áreas geográficas

geographic information: información geográfica

geography: geografía

geological processes: procesos geológicos

Gettysburg: Gettysburg

ghetto: gueto

Gilded Age: Edad Dorada

glasnost: transparencia o apertura

global containment: contención global

global economy: economía mundial

global history: historia global

global market: mercado global

global migration: migración global

global trade: comercio global

global village: villa global

globalization: globalización

globes: globos terrestres

Glorious Revolution: Revolución Gloriosa

goal: meta

gold standard: patrón oro

Good Neighbor Policy: política del buen vecino

goods and services: bienes y servicios

gothic: gótico

governance: administración gubernamental

graduated income tax: impuesto escalonado sobre los ingresos

grandfather clauses: cláusulas de protección

Grange Movement: movimiento granjero

grant: conceder

grass roots campaign: campaña fundamental

Great Britain: Gran Bretaña

Great Compromise: Gran Compromiso

Great Depression: Gran Depresión

Great Migration: Gran Migración

Great Plains: Grandes Llanuras

Great Society: Gran Sociedad

Green Revolution: Revolución Verde

greenbacks: billetes (verdes)-billetes de banco

Gross Domestic Product (GDP): Producto Interno Bruto

Gross National Product (GNP): Producto Nacional Bruto

groups: grupos

guarantee: garantía

guerrilla tactics: tácticas de guerrilla

guerrilla warfare: guerra de guerrillas

Gulf Stream: Corriente del Golfo

H

habeas corpus: hábeas corpus

habitat: hábitat

Hamurabi Code: Código de Hammurabi

Harlem Renaissance: Renacimiento de Harlem

hate crimes: crímenes motivados por el odio

Haymarket Riot: Revuelta de Haymarket

health care: seguro de salud

Hellenistic: helenístico

heroes: héroes

heroines: heroínas

G
H

high crimes: delitos graves
Hinduism: Hinduismo
historic events: eventos históricos
historical: histórico
historical analysis: análisis histórico
historical developments: eventos históricos
historical evidence: evidencia histórica
historical figures: figuras históricas
historical narratives: narraciones históricas
history: historia
HIV: VIH
holding company: compañía de valores
Holidays: días feriados
Holy Land: Tierra Santa
homestead: casa o granja
Homestead Act: Ley de la Heredad
Hoovervilles: Villas de Hoover
hopes: esperanzas
horizontal integration: integración horizontal
House of Burgesses: Casa de Burgueses
House of Representatives: Cámara de Representantes
human capital: capital humano
human dignity: dignidad humana
human migration: migración humana
human needs: necesidades humanas
human resources: recursos humanos
human rights: derechos humanos
human rights violations: violaciones de derechos humanos
human settlements: colonias o instalaciones humanas
human systems: sistemas humanos
Humanism: humanismo
hunters and gatherers: cazadores y recogederos

I

ideals: ideales
ideals of American democracy: ideales de la democracia estadounidense
illegal alien: extranjero ilegal
illegal immigration: inmigración ilegal
Immigration Acts: Leyes de Inmigración
Immigration and Naturalization Service: Negociado de Inmigración y Naturalización
Immigration Quota Acts: Leyes de Cuotas de Inmigración
impacts: impactos
impeach: acusar
impeachment: enjuiciamiento político
imperialist: imperialista
implied powers: poderes implícitos
import: importar
important: importante
imports: importaciones
impressment: requisición
imprisonment: encarcelamiento
inalienable rights: derechos inalienables
inaugurated confederation: confederación inaugurada
incarceration: encarcelamiento
Incas: Incas
income tax: impuesto sobre la renta
inconstitutional: inconstitucional
incumbent: titular
indentured servant: sirvientes por contrato
India: India
Indian Empires: Imperios de la India
Indian Wars: Guerras Indígenas
indigenous development: desarrollo indígena
indigenous peoples: pueblos indígenas
individual: individuo, individual

individual rights: derechos individuales

individual rights to life, liberty, pursuit of happiness: derechos individuales a la vida, la libertad, la búsqueda de la felicidad

indulgences: indulgencias

Indus Valley: Valle del Indo

industrial: industrial

industrial expansion: expansión industrial

industrial growth: crecimiento industrial

industrial power: potencia industrial

Industrial Revolution: Revolución Industrial

Industrial Workers of the World: trabajadores industriales del mundo

industrialism: industrialismo

industrialization: industrialización

inevitable: inevitable

inflation: inflación

infrastructure: infraestructura

initiative: iniciativa

injunction: mandato

Inquisition: inquisición

inspect: inspeccionar

installment buying: comprar a plazos

integrate: integrar

interchangeable parts: partes intercambiables

interdependence: interdependencia

interdependent: interdependiente

Internal Revenue Service (IRS): Servicio de Impuestos Internos

international: internacional

international organizations: organizaciones internacionales

internet: internet

internment: internación

internment camps: campos de internación

interpret: interpretar

interpret law: interpretar la ley

interrelationships: interrelaciones

interstate: interestatal

interstate commerce: comercio interestatal

Interstate Commerce Commission: Comisión de Comercio Interestatal

interstate highway system: red de autopistas interestatales de Estados Unidos

intervene: intervenir

Inuits: Esquimales

inventions: invenciones, inventos

invest: invertir

involve: envolver

Iranian hostage crisis: crisis de rehenes en Irán

Iron Curtain: Cortina de Hierro

ironclad: acorazado

Iroquois: Iroqués (miembro de un grupo de tribus indígenas que viven en EE.UU. y Canadá)

Iroquois Confederacy: Confederación Iroquesa

Islam: Islam

isolate: aislar

isolationism: aislacionismo

issue: emitir, problema

issues: temas; asuntos, asunto

isthmus: istmo

item: artículo

J

Jacksonian democracy: Democracia Jacksoniana

Japanese-American Internment: Entierro de los Japoneses-Americanos

Japanese-Americans: Japoneses-Americanos

Jeffersonian democracy: Democracia Jeffersoniana

jihad: Yihad

Jim Crow laws

Jim Crow laws: leyes de Jim Crow
jingoism: jingoísmo
job: trabajo
joint occupation: ocupación en común
joint-stock company: compañía por acciones
judgments: juicios
judicial: judicial, jurídico
judicial branch: rama judicial, poder judicial
judicial branch of government: rama judicial del gobierno
judicial review: revisión judicial
judiciary: judicial
junta: junta
jury service: servicio de jurado
justify: justificar

K

Kansas-Nebraska Act: Acta Kansas-Nebraska
Kellogg-Briand Pact: Pacto Kellogg-Briand
kindergarten: jardín de niños
Knights of Labor: Caballeros del Trabajo
Know-Nothing Party: Partido de los "No Sabe Nada"
Koran: Corán
Korean War: Guerra de Corea
Ku Klux Klan: Ku Klux Klan

L

labor: laborar
labor force: fuerza laboral
labor markets: mercados laborales
labor movement: movimiento laboral
Labor Standards Act: Ley de Relaciones Del Trabajo
labor union: sindicato laboral, sindicato, gremio
laissez-faire: liberalismo
land bridge: puente de tierra
land formations: formaciones de tierra, formas terrestres, accidentes geográficos
land grants: concesión de tierra
land masses: masa terrestre, gran área de tierra
Land Ordinance of 1785: ordenanza sobre el urbanismo Land Ordinance de 1785
land reform: reforma agraria
land-grant college: colegio de tierras donadas
Land-Lease Act: Ley de Arrendamiento de Tierras (Ayuda de Guerra)
landslide: derrumbe; victoria grande
languages: idiomas, lenguas
Last Frontier: Última Frontera
Latin America: Latinoamérica
League of Nations: Liga de Naciones
legislative branch: poder legislativo
legislative branch of government: poder legislativo del gobierno
legislative process: proceso legislativo
leisure activities: pasatiempos
levy: gravamen
liberal: liberal
library resources: recursos bibliotecarios
life expectancy: expectativa de vida
limited: limitado
limited government: gobierno limitado

limited resources: recursos limitados

Lincoln-Douglas debate: debate Lincoln-Douglas

line item veto: veto selectivo

literacy: alfabetismo

literacy test: prueba de lectura, examen de alfabetismo

lobbyist: cabildero

local community: comunidad local

local government: gobierno local

local region: región local

lock: esclusa

lockout: cierre patronal

locomotive: locomotora

lode: filón

long ago: hace mucho

longhouse: vivienda comunal de los indios iroqueses, agrupación indígena

loose constructionist: interpretación liberal

Louisiana Purchase: Compra de Luisiana

loyalists: colono leal a Gran Bretaña

loyalty: lealtad, devoción, fidelidad

lynching: linchamiento

M

MacArthur Constitution: Constitución MacArthur

machine politics: política de maquinarias

Magna Carta: Carta Magna

maintain: mantener

maize: maíz

major: mayor

majority rule: gobierno de la mayoría

make laws: promulgar o hacer leyes

maldistribution: mala distribución

Mandate of Heaven: Mandato del Cielo

Manhattan Project: Proyecto Manhattan

Manifest Destiny: Doctrina del Destino Manifiesto

manual: manual

manufactured goods: bienes industriales

manufacturing: fabricación, industria manufacturera, manufactura, fabricación o elaboración

manumission: manumisión

market economy: economía del mercado

markets: mercados

Marshall Plan: Plan Marshall

martial law: ley marcial

martyr: mártir

Marxism: Marxismo

Mason-Dixon Line: Línea Mason-Dixon

mass production: fabricación en serie

mass starvation: hambruna

Mayas: Mayas

Mayflower Compact: Pacto de Mayflower

Mecca: Meca

Medicaid: Ayuda Medica

Medicare: seguro médico

megalopolis: megalópolis

Meiji Restoration: Restauración Meiji

melting pot: amalgama de culturas

Memorial Day: Día Conmemorativo

memorials: monumentos conmemorativos

mercantilism: mercantilismo

merchandising: mercadería comercial

merger: fusión

meridian: meridiano

Mesoamerica: Mesoamérica

Mesopotamia: Mesopotamia

mestizos: mestizos

metro area: área metropolitana

Mexican Cession: Cesión Mexicana

Mexican Revolution: Revolución Mexicana

Mexican War: Guerra Mexicana-Americana
Mexicans: Mexicanos
Middle Ages: Edad Media
Middle Atlantic: Atlántico Medio
middle class: clase media
Middle East: Oriente Medio
Midwest : Medio Oeste de Estados Unidos
migrate: migrar
migration: migración
militarism: militarismo
military: ejército, militar, las Fuerzas Armadas
militia: milicia
millennia: milenios
mining: minería, explotación minera, industria minera
ministry: ministerio
minorities: minorías
minority rights: derechos de las minorías
minutemen: hombres de la milicia
mission: misión
Mississippi River: Río Mississippi
Missouri Compromise: Compromiso de Missouri
mobile society: sociedad móvil
mobilization: movilización
modernization: modernización
modify: modificar
Mongol: Mongol
monitor: observar
monopoly: monopolio
monotheism: monoteísmo
Monroe Doctrine: Doctrina de Monroe
monsoon: monzón
Montgomery Bus Boycott: Boicot de los Autobuses en Montgomery
months: meses
monuments: monumentos
Mormon Church: Iglesia Mormona
Mothers of the Plaza De Mayo: Madres de la Plaza de Mayo

motives: motivos
mountain man: hombre montañés
mountains: montañas
movement of people and goods: movimiento de personas y mercancías
muckraker: periodista de investigación
mudslinging: detractar
multicultural(ism): multicultural(ismo)
multinational corporations: corporaciones multinacionales
municipal: municipal
myths: mitos

N

Napoleonic Code: Código de Napoleón
narratives: narrativas
nation state: estado nación
National Association for the Advancement of Colored People (NAACP): Asociación Nacional para el Progreso de la Gente de Color (NAACP)
national debt: deuda nacional
National Grange: Granja Nacional
national level of governments: niveles nacionales de gobiernos
National Organization of Women (NOW): Organización Nacional de la Mujer
national origins: orígenes nacionales
National Socialist Party: Partido Socialista Nacional
nationalism: nacionalismo
Native American Indian: Nativo Americano
nativist: nativista
natural boundaries: fronteras naturales
natural rights: derechos naturales
naturalization: naturalización

naval forces: fuerzas navales

Nazi Germany: Alemania nazi

Nazi Holocaust: Holocausto nazi

Nazism: Nazismo

necessary and proper clause: cláusula necesaria y apropiada

needs: necesidades

Neolithic: neolítico

Neolithic Revolution: Revolución neolítica

network: red sistema

neutral: neutral

neutral rights: derechos de los neutrales

neutrality: neutralidad

nevertheless: no obstante

New Amsterdam: Nueva Ámsterdam (el nombre antiguo de Nueva York)

New Deal: Nuevo Trato

New Federalism: Nuevo Federalismo

New Frontier: Nueva Frontera

New Imperialism: Imperialismo Nuevo

New Netherlands: Nueva Holanda

New Years Day: Año Nuevo

New York State Constitution: Constitución del Estado de Nueva York

newspapers: periódicos

Ninety Five theses: Las Noventa y Cinco Tesis

Nobel Peace Prize: Premio Nobel de la Paz

nomadic: nómada que se mueve de un lugar a otro sin hogar permanente (p. 686)

nonalignment: no alineación

noninterference ("laissez-faire"): no intervencionismo ("laissez-faire")

nonpartisan: no-partidario

non-violence: no-violento; pacifico

normal school: escuela normal

normalcy: normalidad

North America: América del Norte o Norteamerica

North American Free Trade Agreement (NAFTA): Tratado Norteamericano de Libre Comercio

North Atlantic Treaty Organization (NATO): Organización Tratado del Atlántico Norte

northwest: noroeste

Northwest Ordinance: Ordenanza Noroeste

Northwest Passage: Paso Noroeste

notion: noción

now: ahora

nuclear age: edad nuclear

nuclear families: familias nucleares

nuclear family: familia nuclear

nullification: anulación

nullify: anular

Nuremberg Trials: Juicios de Núremberg

O

obtain: obtener

obvious: obvio

occupy: ocupar

occur: ocurrir

oceans: océanos

offensive: ofensiva

old crisis: crisis petrolera

Old Imperialism: Imperialismo Antiguo

oligarchy: oligarquía

oligopoly: oligopolio

Olmec civilization: civilización Olmeca

Open Door Policy: Política de Puertas Abiertas

open range: terreno abierto

open shop: taller no sindicalizado

opinion: opinión

Opium War: Guerra del Opio

opportunity cost: costo de oportunidad

oral history: historia oral

oral tradition: tradición oral

ordinance: ordenanza

ore: mena

Oregon Territory: Territorio de Oregón

Organization of American States (OAS): Organización de Estados Americanos (OEA)

Organization of Petroleum Exporting Countries (OPEC): Organización de Países Exportadores de Petróleo (OPEP)

organizations: organizaciones

Orthodox Christian Church: Iglesia Ortodoxa Cristiana

Ottoman: Otomano

outcome: resultado

overexpansion: expansión exagerada

overpopulation: sobrepoblación

overproduction: exceso de producción

override: vencer

overseer: capataz

P

Pacific Northwest: Noroeste del Pacifico

pacifism: pacifismo

Paleolithic: paleolítico

Palestinian Liberation Organization (PLO): Organización de Liberación Palestina (OLP)

Panama Canal: Canal de Panamá

parallels: paralelos

parent: uno de los padres (padre o madre)

Paris Peace Accords: Acuerdos de Paz de París

parliamentary democracy: democracia parlamentaria

parliamentary system: sistema parlamentario

participate: participar

participatory skills: habilidades para la participación

partisan: partidario

partitioned: subdividido

patent: patente

patriotism: patriotismo

patriots: patriotas

patroon: propietario de tierras, terratenientes holandeses en la época colonial, encomendero holandés

patroonship system: sistema de patrones, regalía de contrato de locación de las tierras

Pax Romana: Paz Romana

peace movement: movimiento de paz

peace treaty: tratado de paz

peacekeeping: mantenimiento de la paz

Pearl Harbor: Pearl Harbor

peasants: campesinos

per capita income: ingreso per cápita

percent: por ciento

perceptions: percepciones

perestroika: perestroika

period: período

periodizations: periodizaciones

persecute: perseguir

Persian Gulf Crisis: Crisis del Golfo Pérsico

Persian Gulf War: Guerra del Golfo Pérsico

perspectives: perspectivas

Peter Stuyvesant: Peter Stuyvesant

petition: petición

pharaoh: faraón

philanthropy: filantropía

philosophy: filosofía

physical: físico

physical characteristics: características físicas

physical environment: condiciones ambientales y materiales

physical feature: aspecto físico

physical map: mapa físico

physical setting: escenario físico

physical systems: sistemas físicos

pioneers: pioneros

places: lugares

Plains States: Estados de la Llanura

plantation: plantación

plantation system: sistema de plantación

planter: plantador

plebian: plebeyo

plebiscite: plebiscito

Pledge of Allegiance: juramento de lealtad (a los EE.UU. y a su bandera)

pluralism: pluralismo

pocket veto: veto de bolsillo

pogroms: pogromos

point of view: punto de vista

policy: política

political: político(a)

political affairs: asuntos políticos

political boundaries: límites políticos, fronteras políticas

political cartoons: caricaturas políticas

political corruption: corrupción política

political institutions: instituciones políticas

political machine: maquinaria política

political map: mapa político

political organization: organización política

political party: partido político

political platform: plataforma política

political power: poder político

political radicals: radicales políticos

political science: ciencia política

political systems: sistemas políticos

poll tax: impuesto de urna

politics: político

polytheism: politeísmo

pool: consorcio

popular sovereignty: soberanía popular

popular vote: voto popular

population density: densidad de población

population distribution: distribución de población

populist movement: movimiento populista

Populist Party: Partido Populista

pork-barrel legislation: legislación del "barril de tocino"

pose: plantear

post Cold War: post Guerra Fría

post-industrial society: sociedad postindustrial

post-modern era: época postmoderna

postwar: posguerra

Poughkeepsie Convention: Convención de Poughkeepsie

preamble: preámbulo

Preamble to the Constitution: Preámbulo de la Constitución

precedent: precedente

Pre-Columbian civilizations: Civilizaciones Pre-Colombinas

predominant: predominante

pre-history: prehistoria

Preindustrial Age: Edad Preindustrial

prejudice: prejuicio

President of the United States: Presidente de los Estados Unidos

President Pro-tempore of the Senate: Presidente provisional del Senado

President's cabinet: gabinete del Presidente

Presidents Day: Día de los Presidentes

presidio: presidio

primary: elección preliminar

primary elections: elecciones primarias

primary source: fuente primaria

Prime Minister: Primer Ministro

principles: principios

principles of democracy: principios democráticos

P

privateer: corsario
privatization: privatización
privileges: privilegios
process: proceso
producers: productores
productivity: productividad
products: productos
professional: profesional
progressive leaders: líderes progresivos
Progressive Movement: Movimiento Progresista
progressive tax: impuesto progresivo
prohibit: prohibir
projects: proyectos
proletariat: proletariado
promote: promover
proportional: proporcional
proportional representation: representación proporcional
proprietary colony: colonia propietaria
proprietorship: propietario
prospect: perspectiva
protect: proteger
protectionalism: proteccionismo
protectionist: proteccionista
protective tariff: tarifa protectora
protectorate: protectorado
Protestantism: protestantismo
psychology: psicología
public benefit: beneficio público
public education: educación pública
public land: tierra pública
public opinion: opinión publica
public policy: política pública
publication: publicación
publish: publicar
pueblo: pueblo
pump priming: inundar la bomba
purchase: comprar

P
Q
R

Puritan Revolution: Revolución Puritana
Puritan work ethic: ética de trabajo puritana
Puritans: Puritanos
purpose of government: función del gobierno
pursue: afanarse
pursuit of happiness: búsqueda de la felicidad
pyramids: pirámides

Q

Quakers: cuáqueros
quantities: cantidades
Quebec Act: Ley de Quebec
quorum: quórum
quota: cuota
Quota Act: Ley de cuotas

R

racial: racial
racial discrimination: discriminación racial
racial group: grupo racial
racial segregation: segregación racial
radical: radical
radios: radios
ragtime: tiempo sincopado
rain forest: selva tropical
ranchero: ranchero
rancho: rancho
range: pradera
ratify: ratificar
rationing: racionamiento

raw material: materias primas
real politik: política real
real wages: salario real
realism: realismo
rebate: rebaja
Rebel: rebelde
recall: elección
recall election: elección de revocación (destitución)
reciprocity: reciprocidad
reconciliation: reconciliación
reconstruction: reconstrucción
Red Guards: Guardias Rojos
Red Scare: Alarmas Rojas
redistribution of wealth: redistribución de riquezas
reductions: reducciones
reference books: libros de referencia
referendum: referéndum
reform movement: movimiento de reforma
reformation: reformación
region: región
regionalism: regionalismo
regions: regiones
register: registro
regulate: regular
Reign of Terror: Época de Terror
reincarnation: reencarnación
reinforce: reforzar
reject: rechazar
relationships: relaciones
relegion: religión
religious belief: creencia religiosa
religious group: grupo religioso
relocate: reubicar
reluctance: renuencia
remove: quitar
Renaissance: Renacimiento
rendezvous: cita

reparations: reparaciones
repeal: revocar
representative: representante
representative democracy: democracia representativa
representatives: representantes
Republican: republicano
Republican government: gobierno Republicano
Republican Party: Partido Republicano
republicanism: republicanismo
require: requerir
reservation: reservación indígena, territorio reservado por el Estado
reserved powers: poderes reservados
resolution: resolución
resolve: resolver
resource: recurso
responsibilities: responsabilidades
restrict: restringir
return to normalcy: regreso a la normalidad
reveal: revelar
revenue: ingresos
revenue tariff: tarifa de ingresos
revival: renacimiento
Revolutionary War: Guerra Revolucionaria
rider: cláusula
right of deposit: derecho de depositar
rights: derechos
rights of the accused: derechos de los acusados
rights of the minority: derechos de la minoría
Right-Wing groups: grupos derechistas
river civilizations (Mesopotamia, Egypt, China, Indus Valley): civilizaciones fluviales (Mesopotamia, Egipto, China, Valle del Indo)
river systems: sistemas fluviales
river valley civilizations: civilizaciones de los valles fluviales

role: papel

roles of citizens: funciones de los ciudadanos

Roman Empire: Imperio Romano

Rome: Roma

Roosevelt Corollary: corolario de Roosevelt

Roosevelt's Executive Order 8802: ley ejecutiva 8802 firmada por Roosevelt

Roosevelt's Treaty of Portsmouth: Tratado de Portsmouth firmado por Roosevelt

roots of American culture: raíces de la cultura estadounidense

Rosenburg trials: Ensayos de Rosenberg

route: ruta

royal colony: colonia real

Rugged Individualism: Individualismo tosco

rule of law: Estado de Derecho

rules: reglas, normas

rural to urban to suburban migration: migración rural a urbana a suburbana

Russian Revolution: Revolución Rusa

Russification: rusificación

S

Sacco and Vanzetti case: caso Sacco y Vanzetti

sachem: cacique

safeguarding individual liberties: proteger las libertades individuales

salutary neglect: indiferencia saludable

same: igual

Samurai: Samurái

Sandinistas: Sandinistas

satellite nations: naciones satélite

satellite-produced images: imágenes producidas por satélite

scabs: costras

scalawags: granujas, bribones

scandals: escándalos

scarce resources: recursos escasos

scholars: eruditos, personas instruidas, escolares

science and technology: ciencia y tecnología

scientific method: método científico

scientific-technological exchanges and connections: intercambios y conexiones científicas y tecnológicas

Scopes trial: juicio Scopes

seaways: rutas marítimas

secede: secesionarse

secession: secesión

Second Continental Congress: Segundo Congreso Continental

secondary source: recurso secundario

sectional: seccional

sectionalism: seccionalismo, faccionalismo, regionalismo

secular: secular

secure: salvaguardar

securities: valores bursátiles

Securities and Exchange Commission (SEC): Comisión de Valores y Divisas

sedition: sedición

Sedition Act of 1918: Ley de Sedición de 1918

segregation: segregación

self: propio, uno mismo

self-determination: autodeterminación

self-government: gobierno autónomo

selling: de venta, relativo a la venta

Senate of the United States: Senado de los Estados Unidos

separate but equal: separado pero igual

separation of church and state: separación de iglesia y estado

separation of powers: separación o división de poderes

separatism: separatismo
separatists: separatistas
Sepoy Mutiny: Motín de los Cipayos
serf: siervo
services: servicios
settle: asentarse, establecerse en una colonia
settlement house: casa de beneficencia
settlement houses: centros comunitarios
settlements: asentamientos, colonias, acuerdos
settler: colono, colonizador
sharecropping: aparcería
shareholder: accionista
Shay's Rebellion: Motín de Shay
Sherman Anti-Trust Act: Ley Sherman Contra Prácticas Monopolísticas
shift: mover
Shintoism: sintoísmo
shogun: shogun
significant: significativo
Silk Road: Ruta de la Seda
similar: similar
similarities: semejanzas
sit-in: protesta sentada
skilled workers: trabajadores manuales (especializados)
slash and burn farming: agricultura de tala y quema
slave code: código de esclavos
slave trade: tráfico de esclavos
slave uprisings: levantamientos de esclavos
slum: tugurio
slums: arrabales
smuggling: contrabandear
social: social
social behavior: conducta social
social class: clase social
social commentary: comentario social
social contract: contrato social

Social Darwinism: Darwinismo social
social gospel: evangelio social
social sciences: ciencias sociales
social scientific method: método científico social
social security: seguro social
social services: servicios sociales
social tensions: tensiones sociales
social-cultural changes and connections: cambios y conexiones socioculturales
Socialist Party: Partido Socialista
Socialist Republics: Repúblicas Socialistas
sociology: sociología
sodbuster: rompedor
sole: único
solving problems: resolución de problemas
Sons of Liberty: Hijos de la Libertad
soup kitchens: comedores para pobres
South America: Sudamérica
sovereignty: soberanía
Soviet Union: Unión Soviética
space race: carrera espacial
Spanish Civil War: Guerra Civil Española
Spanish colonies: colonias españolas
spatial organization: organización espacial
spatial patterns: patrones espaciales
Speaker of the House: El Presidente de la Cámara
Special Olympics: Olimpiadas Especiales
speculator: especulador
sphere of influence: esfera de influencia
spiritual: espiritual
spiritual beliefs: creencias espirituales
spoils system: clientelismo político
Square Deal: Trato Justo
Stamp Act: Ley del Timbre
standard gauge: medida normal
standard of living: nivel de vida
Star Wars Defense: Defensa "Star Wars"

stars and stripes: franjas y estrellas
state action: acción estatal
state government: gobierno estatal
state legislature: legislatura estatal
statehood: estado
state's rights: derechos del estado
Statue of Liberty: Estatua de la Libertad
status: status
status quo: status quo
steamboat: barco de vapor
steerage: entrepuente
stereotype: estereotipo
stewardship theory: teoría de custodia
stock: acciones
stock market: bolsa de valores
stock market crash: quiebra de la bolsa de valores
stories: historias
strategy: estrategia
stratification: estratificación
strengths: fortalezas, puntos fuertes
strict construction: interpretación estricta
strike: huelga
strikebreaker: rompehuelgas
structure: estructura
student rights: derechos estudiantiles
subcontinent: subcontinente
submission: sumisión
sub-Saharan Africa: África subsahariana
subsidy: subsidio
subsistence farming: agricultura de subsistencia
substitute: sustituto
suburban: suburbano
suburbanization: suburbanización
suburbs: afueras, suburbios
sufficient: suficiente
suffrage: sufragio
sum: resumir

super majortiy: gran mayoría
supply and demand: oferta y demanda
supply-side economics: economía de oferta
supremacy clause: cláusula de supremacía
Supreme Court: Suprema Corte
Supreme Court decision: decisión de la Suprema Corte
survive: sobrevivir
sweatshop: fábrica-opresora
symbol: símbolo
symbolize: simbolizar
systems: sistemas

T

tables: tablas o cuadros de números, mesas
Taiping Rebellion: Rebelión Taiping
Tammany Hall: Tammany Hall
Taoism: taoísmo
tariffs: tarifas, aranceles aduaneros
taxation: fijación de impuestos
taxes: impuestos
Teapot Dome Scandal: Escándalo del Teapot Dome
technique: técnica
technological: tecnológico
technological unemployment: desempleo tecnológico
technologies-exchanges of: tecnologías-intercambio de
technology: tecnología
Tejano: tejano
telegraph: telégrafo
temperance: templanza
temperance movement: movimiento de la templanza
tenant farmer: granjero arrendatario

tenement: vivienda

termination: terminación

territorial expansion: expansión territorial

Tet offensive: ofensiva de Tet

Thanksgiving: Acción de Gracias

The Federalist Papers: Los Papeles Federalistas

The Zenger Case: El Caso Zenger

themes: temas o asuntos

then: entonces

theology: teología

theory: teoría

third party: tercer partido

Third World: Tercer Mundo

Three-Fifths Compromise: Compromiso de los Tres Quintos

Tiananmen Square: Plaza Tiananmen

time zones: zonas horarias

timeframes: períodos de tiempo

timeline: cronología, calendario

toleration: tolerancia

topic: tema

Torah: Tora

total war: guerra total la Guerra

totalitarian societies: sociedades totalitarias

totalitarianism: totalitarismo

town meeting: reunión del pueblo

Townsend Plan: Plan de Townsend

towpath: camino de sirga

trade deficit: déficit de comercio

trade imbalance: déficit comercial

trade markets: mercados comerciales

trade union: unión o sindicato de comerciantes

traffic lights: semáforos

transcendentalist: trascendentalista

transcontinental: transcontinental

transmit: transmitir

transport: transportar

transportation: transporte

transportation revolution: revolución del transporte

treaties: tratados

Treaty of Versailles: Tratado de Versalles

trends: tendencias

triangular trade: comercio triangular

tribal groups: grupos tribales

tribalism: tribalismo

tributaries: tributarios

tribute: tributo

trickle down economics: economía de goteo

Triple Alliance: Triple Alianza

Triple Entente: Triple Entente

Tropic of Cancer: Trópico de Cáncer

Tropic of Capricorn: Trópico de Capricornio

Truman Doctrine: Doctrina de Truman

trusts: fideicomisos

turning points: puntos críticos, momentos decisivos

turnpike: autopista de peaje, autopista de pago

Tweed Ring: organización ilegal Tweed Ring

Twelve Tables: Doce Tablas

U

U.S. Constitution: Constitución de los Estados Unidos

ultimate: último o máximo

Uncle Tom's Cabin: La Cabaña del Tío Tom

unconstitutional: inconstitucional

underconsumption: subconsumo

underground railroad: ferrocarril subterráneo

underlie: subyacer

undertake: emprender

Underwood Tariff: Tarifa Underwood

undocumented worker: trabajador indocumentado

unicameral: unicameral

unify: unificar

unionize: sindicar

unions: sindicatos, gremios

unique: único

United Nations: Organización de las Naciones Unidas (ONU)

United Nations Universal Declaration of Human Rights: Declaración Universal de Derechos Humanos de las Naciones Unidas

United States of America: Estados Unidos de América

unlimited needs and wants: necesidades y deseos ilimitados

upward mobility: movilidad ascendente

urban development: desarrollo urbano

urbanization: urbanización

uses of geography: usos de la geografía

utopia: utopía

utopian reform: reforma utópica

V

values: valores

vaquero: vaquero

vassal: vasallo

vaudeville: vodevil

Vedas: vedas

Versailles Treaty: Tratado de Versalles

vertical integration: integración vertical

Veterans Day: Día de los Veteranos

veto: vetar

veto override: anular veto

Vice President: Vice-Presidente

viceroy: virrey

Vietnam: Vietnam

Vietnam War: Guerra de Vietnam

vigilantes: vigilantes

violate: violar

vision: visión

Volstead Act: Ley de Volstead

Voting Rights Act (1965): Ley del Derecho al Voto (1965)

W

wages: salarios

Wagner Act: Ley Wagner

wampum: cuentas cilíndricas hechas de conchas, usadas por los indios norteamericanos como monedas

wants: deseos, necesidades

war against poverty: guerra contra la pobreza

war bonds: bonos de guerra

War Hawks: halcones de Guerra

War of 1812: Guerra de 1812

war strategy: estrategia de guerra

ward: pupilo

Warsaw Pact: Pacto de Varsovia

water masses: masas de agua

Watergate scandal: escándalo Watergate

waterway: canal o desague

weaknesses: debilidades, flaquezas

weapons: armas

Weimer Republic: República de Weimar

welfare capitalism: capitalismo de bienestar

welfare reform: reforma de bienestar

U
V
W

Western Hemisphere: Hemisferio Occidental

Westernization: Occidentalización

westward expansion: expansión hacia el oeste

westward migration: migración hacia el oeste

Whiskey Rebellion: Rebelión del Whisky

white collar: empleado de oficina

White House: Casa Blanca

white supremacy: supremacía blanca

wigwam: choza

wildcat strike: huelga salvaje

women's rights: derechos de la mujer

women's suffrage: sufragio femenino

work ethic: ética laboral

workforce: mano de obra, potencial de mano de obra

working class: clase obrera

working conditions: condiciones laborales

Works Progress Administration: Agencia para la Mejora del Trabajo

Works Project Administration: Administración de Proyectos de Trabajo

world bank: banco mundial

World Court: Corte Mundial

World Court Tribunal: Tribunal de la Corte Mundial

world in spatial terms: mundo en términos espaciales

world power: potencia mundial

world war: guerra mundial

World War I: Primera Guerra Mundial

World War II: Segunda Guerra Mundial

worldview: punto de vista mundial

Wounded Knee: Wounded knee o Rodilla herida

writ of habeus corpus: mandamiento de hábeas corpus

writ of mandamus: mandamiento judicial

writing system: sistema de escritura

writings: obras escritas

Y

Yalta Conference: Conferencia de Yalta

Yankee: yanqui

yellow journalism: periodismo amarillista

Yellow Peril: periodismo amarillo (sensacionalista)

yellow press: prensa amarilla

yeoman: terrateniente

Z

Zionism: Sionismo

zoning: división de zonas

Word to Word® Bilingual Dictionary Series

Albanian - 500X - 345 pgs
ISBN - 978-0-933146-49-5

Amharic - 820X - 362 pgs
ISBN - 978-0-933146-59-4

Arabic - 650X - 378 pgs
ISBN - 978-0-933146-41-9

Bengali - 700X - 372 pgs
ISBN - 978-0-933146-30-3

Burmese - 705X - 378 pgs
ISBN - 978-0-933146-50-1

Cambodian - 710X - 376 pgs
ISBN - 978-0-933146-40-2

Chinese - 715X - 374 pgs
ISBN - 978-0-933146-22-8

Farsi - 660X - 372 pgs
ISBN - 978-0-933146-33-4

French - 530X - 358 pgs
ISBN - 978-0-933146-36-5

German - 535X - 352 pgs
ISBN - 978-0-933146-93-8

Gujarati - 720X - 334 pgs
ISBN - 978-0-933146-98-3

Haitian-Creole - 545X - 362 pgs
ISBN - 978-0-933146-23-5

Hebrew - 665X - 362 pgs
ISBN - 978-0-933146-58-7

Hindi - 725X - 362 pgs
ISBN - 978-0-933146-31-0

Hmong - 728X - 294 pgs
ISBN - 978-0-933146-31-0

Italian - 555X - 362 pgs
ISBN - 978-0-933146-51-8

Japanese - 730X - 372 pgs
ISBN - 978-0-933146-42-6

Korean - 735X - 374 pgs
ISBN - 978-0-933146-97-6

Lao - 740X - 314 pgs
ISBN - 978-0-933146-54-9

Pashto - 760X - 348 pgs
ISBN - 978-0-933146-34-1

Polish - 575X - 358 pgs
ISBN - 978-0-933146-64-8

Portuguese - 580X - 362 pgs
ISBN - 978-0-933146-94-5

Punjabi - 765X - 358 pgs
ISBN - 978-0-933146-32-7

Romanian - 585X - 354 pgs
ISBN - 978-0-933146-91-4

Russian - 590X - 334 pgs
ISBN - 978-0-933146-92-1

Somali - 830X - 320 pgs
ISBN- 978-0-933146-52-5

Spanish - 600X - 400 pgs
ISBN - 978-0-933146-99-0

Swahili - 835X - 308 pgs
ISBN - 978-0-933146-55-6

Tagalog - 770X - 332 pgs
ISBN - 978-0-933146-37-2

Thai - 780X - 354 pgs
ISBN - 978-0-933146-35-8

Turkish - 615X - 348 pgs
ISBN - 978-0-933146-95-2

Ukrainian - 620X - 337 pgs
ISBN - 978-0-933146-25-9

Urdu - 790X - 360 pgs
ISBN - 978-0-933146-39-6

Vietnamese - 795X - 366 pgs
ISBN - 978-0-933146-96-9

All languages are two-way: English-Language /
Language-English. More languages in planning
and production.

Language - Item - Pages
ISBN #

Word to Word® with Subject Vocabulary

Arabic - 653X - 438 pgs
ISBN - 978-0-933146-56-3

Chinese - 718X - 412 pgs
ISBN - 978-0-933146-57-0

Spanish - 603X - 430 pgs
ISBN - 978-0-933146-72-3

Subjects Include: Math, Science and Social Studies.
More languages in planning and production.

Order Information

To order our Word to Word® Bilingual Dictionaries or any other products from Bilingual Dictionaries, Inc., please contact us at (951) 461-6893 or visit us at **www.BilingualDictionaries.com**. Visit our website to download our current Catalog/Order Form, view our products, and find information regarding Bilingual Dictionaries, Inc.

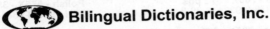 **Bilingual Dictionaries, Inc.**

PO Box 1154 • Murrieta, CA 92564 • Tel: (951) 461-6893 • Fax: (951) 461-3092
www.BilingualDictionaries.com

Special Dedication & Thanks

Bilingual Dicitonaries, Inc. would like to thank all the teachers from various districts accross the country for their useful input and great suggestions in creating a Word to Word® standard. We encourage all students and teachers using our bilingual learning materials to give us feedback. Please send your questions or comments via email to support@bilingualdictionaries.com.